# REAL WORLD BANKING AND FINANCE: PROGRESSIVE PERSPECTIVES FROM *DOLLARS & SENSE*

## Fifth Edition

EDITED BY DANIEL FIRESIDE, AMY GLUCKMAN
AND THE *DOLLARS & SENSE* COLLECTIVE

# REAL WORLD BANKING AND FINANCE
Fifth Edition



ISBN: 978-1-878585-64-6
Published by:
Economic Affairs Bureau, Inc.
*Dollars & Sense*
29 Winter Street
Boston, MA 02108
617-447-2177
dollars@dollarsandsense.org
www.dollarsandsense.org

*Real World Banking and Finance* is edited by the *Dollars & Sense* collective, which also publishes *Dollars & Sense* magazine and the classroom books *Real World Macro, Real World Micro, Real World Globalization, Current Economic Issues, The Wealth Inequality Reader, The Environment in Crisis, Introduction to Political Economy, Unlevel Playing Fields: Understanding Wage Inequality and Discrimination, Striking a Balance: Work, Family, Life*, and *Grassroots Journalism.*

The 2008 Collective:
Faisal Chaudhry, Amee Chew, Daniel Fireside, Amy Gluckman, Amanda Harrow, Toussaint Losier, James McBride, John Miller, Larry Peterson, Linda Pinkow, Paul Piwko, Smriti Rao, Alejandro Reuss, Bryan Snyder, Chris Sturr, Ramaa Vasudevan, Jeanne Winner, and James Woolman.

Cover Art and Design: Nick Thorkelson
Production: Noel Cunningham

Manufactured by Vision Lithographics
Printed in U.S.A.

# CONTENTS


## CHAPTER 1 • MONEY, THE FEDERAL RESERVE, AND THE ECONOMY

What Is Money? *Doug Orr* 1
Focus on the Fed: the Bond Market versus the Rest of Us
*Doug Orr and Ellen Frank* 4
Transforming the Fed *Robert Pollin* 10
Outing Allen Greenspan *John Miller* 15
The Discount Rate *Ellen Frank* 18
Big Lies About Central Banking *Joseph Stiglitz* 20
Bernanke's Dilemma *William Greider* 22
The Fight for Transparency at the Federal Reserve
*Stephen Zarlenga* 23
Money Supply *Ellen Frank* 24
Is the Fed a Conspiracy? *Arthur MacEwan* 26

## CHAPTER 2 • THE BANKING AND FINANCE INDUSTRY

The U.S. Banking Industry in Transition *William K. Black* 29
Hard Times for Bankers: Innovation, Poor Judgment, and Deregulation Bring Down Banks *John Miller* 45
Return from the Dead: The Banking Industry Flies High *Jim Campen* 52
It's a Bank-Eat-Bank World *Jim Campen* 59
Credit Card Pushers Pump Up Profits – And Risk *Abby Scher* 64
U.S. Banks and the Dirty Money Empires *James Petras* 70
The New Old Wall Street Settlement *Nomi Prins* 75
Chase: A Bank for the New Century *Joseph Pluta* 78
No Expense Too Great: A History of the Savings & Loan Bailout
*Dorene Isenburg and Vince Valvano* 84

## CHAPTER 3 • THE STOCK MARKET

Recession Time! The Housing Bubble Bursts the Economy *Dean Baker* 91
Too Much of the Bubbly on Wall Street? *Dean Baker* 93
The Great Stock Illusion *Ellen Frank* 97
Stock Volatility *Ellen Frank* 102
Teaching About Stocks For Fun and Propaganda *Mark Maier* 104
Labor's Capital *Adria Scharf* 108
Dow's All-Time High Inconsequential for Most Americans
*Sylvia Allegretto* 113
Bad News on Main Street is Good News on Wall Street *John Miller* 115
Socially Responsible Investing Comes of Age *Steve Fahrer* 116

## CHAPTER 4 • RETIREMENT FINANCE


Social Security Isn't Broken *Doug Orr* 123
Social Security Q & A *Doug Orr* 128
African Americans and Social Security *William E. Spriggs* 139
Taking One from the Bush Team *Dean Baker* 144
Hijacking the Future *James Ridgeway* 147
When Bad Things Happen to Good Pensions *Teresa Ghilarducci* 148
The Social Security Administration's Cracked Crystal Ball *John Miller* 156
The Myth of the Social Security Trust Fund *Ellen Frank* 159
Social Security's Bet on Stocks *Richard Du Boff* 163


## CHAPTER 5 • FAIR LENDING/PREDATORY LENDING


Lending Insights: Hard Proof That Banks Discriminate *Jim Campen* 167
The Community Reinvestment Act: A Law That Works *Jim Campen* 173
A Matter of Life and Debt *Jabulani Leffall* 179
Flame Broiled Shark *David Swanson* 189
America's Fringe Economy *Howard Karger* 193
Build Homes, Not Jails *Charis E. Kubrin and Gregory D. Squires* 201
The Homeownership Myth *Howard Karger* 205
Three Million Americans Are Debt Poor *Steven Pressman and Robert Scott* 214


## CHAPTER 6 • THE INTERNATIONAL FINANCIAL SYSTEM


Learning from the Southeast Asian Crisis *John Miller* 219
Unfettered Capital Wreaks Havoc *Ellen Frank* 224
Bye Bye IMF? A New Blueprint for the Global Economy *Ellen Frank* 226
The IMF versus the World Bank *Arthur MacEwan* 229
Export Credit Agencies: International Corporate Welfare *Danielle Knight* 231
CAFTA's Debt Trap *Aldo Caliari* 237
The Decline of the Dollar System *James K. Galbraith* 241
Dollar Anxiety *John Miller* 243
George Bush's Favorite Vultures *Greg Palast* 249
Wolfowitz and the World Bank *Larry Peterson* 251
Microcredit and Women's Poverty *Susan F. Feiner & Drucilla K. Barker* 254

Chapter 1

# MONEY, THE FEDERAL RESERVE, AND THE ECONOMY

## WHAT IS MONEY?

**BY DOUG ORR**

*November/December 1993**

We all use money everyday. Yet many people do not know what money actually is. There are many myths about money, including the idea that the government "prints" all of it and that it has some intrinsic value. But actually, money is less a matter of value, and more a matter of faith.

Money is sometimes called the universal commodity, because it can be traded for all other commodities. But for this to happen, everyone in society must believe that money will be accepted. If people stop believing that it will be accepted, the existing money ceases to be money.

In addition to facilitating exchanges, money allows us to "store" value from one point in time to another. If you sell your car today for $4,000, you probably won't buy that amount of other products today. Rather, you store the value as money, probably in a bank, until you want to use it.

The "things" that get used as money have changed over time, and "modern" people often chuckle when they hear about some of them. The Romans used salt (from which we get the word "salary"), South Sea Islanders used shark's teeth, and several societies actually used cows. The "Three Wise Men" brought gold, frankincense and myrrh, each of which was money in different regions at the time.

If money does not exist, or is in short supply, it will be created. In POW camps, where guards specifically outlaw its existence, prisoners use cigarettes instead. In the American colonies, the British attempted to limit the supply of British pounds, because they knew that by limiting the supply of money, they could hamper the development of independent markets in the colonies. Today, the United States uses a similar policy, through the International Monetary Fund, in dealing with Latin America.

To overcome this problem, the colonists began to use tobacco leaves as money. This helped the colonies to develop, but it also allowed the holders of large plots of land to grow their own money! When the colonies gained independence, the new

---

*Dates denote when the article appeared in *Dollars & Sense* magazine.

government decreed gold to be money, rather than tobacco, much to the dismay of Southern plantation owners. Now, rather than growing money, farmers had to find or buy it.

To aid the use of gold as money, banks would test its purity, put it in storage, and give the depositor paper certificates of ownership. These certificates, "paper money," could then be used in place of the gold itself. Since any bank could store gold and issue certificates, by the beginning of the Civil War, over 7,000 different types of "paper money" were in circulation in the United States, none of it printed by the government.

While paper money is easier to use than gold, it is still risky to carry around large amounts of cash. It is safer to store the paper in a bank and simply sign over its ownership to make a purchase. We sign-over the ownership of our money by writing a check. Checking account money became popular when the government outlawed the printing of paper money by private banks in 1864.

## How Banks Create Money

Banks are central to understanding money, because in addition to storing it, they help to create it. Bankers realize that not everyone will withdraw their money at the same time, so they loan out much of the money that has been deposited. It is from the interest on these loans that banks get their profits, and through these loans the banking system creates new money.

If you deposit $100 cash in your checking account at Chase Manhattan Bank, you still have $100 in money to use, because checks are also accepted as money. Chase must set aside some of this cash as "reserves," in case you or other depositors decide to withdraw money as cash. Current regulations issued by the Federal Reserve Bank (the Fed) require banks to set aside three cents out of each dollar. So Chase can make a loan of $97, based on your deposit. Chase does not make loans by handing out cash but instead by putting $97 in the checking account of the person, say Emily, taking out the loan. So from your initial deposit of $100 in cash, the economy now has $197 in checking account money.

The borrower, Emily, pays $97 for some product or service by check, and the seller, say Ace Computers, deposits the money in its checking account. The total amount of checking account money is still $197, but its location and ownership have changed. If Ace Computer's account is at Citibank, $97 in cash is transferred from Chase to Citibank. This leaves just $3 in cash reserves at Chase to cover your original deposit. However, Citibank now has $97 in "new" cash on hand, so it sets aside three cents on the dollar ($2.91) and loans out the rest, $94.09, as new checking account money. Through this process, every dollar of "reserves" yields many dollars in total money.

If you think this is just a shell game and there is only $100 in "real" money, you still don't understand money. Anything that is accepted as payment for a transaction is "real" money. Cash is no more real than checking account money. In fact, most car rental companies will not accept cash as payment for a car, so for them, cash is not money!

Today, there is $292 billion of U.S. currency, i.e. "paper money," in existence.

However, somewhere between 50% to 70% of it is held outside the United States by foreign banks and individuals. The vast majority of all money actually in use in the United States is not cash, but rather checking account money. This type of money, $726 billion, was created by private banks, and was not "printed" by anyone. In fact, this money exists only as electronic "bits" in banks' computers. (The less "modern" South Sea Islanders could have quite a chuckle about that!)

The amount of money that banks can create is limited by the total amount of reserves, and by the fraction of each deposit that must be held as reserves. Prior to 1914, bankers themselves decided what fraction of deposits to hold as reserves. Since then, this fraction has been set by the main banking regulator, the Fed.

Until 1934, gold was held as reserves, but the supply of gold was unstable, growing rapidly during the California and Alaska "gold rushes," and very slowly at other times. As a result, at times more money was created than the economy needed, and at other times not enough money could be created. Starting in 1934, the U.S. government decided that gold would no longer be used as reserves. Cash, now printed by the Fed, could no longer be redeemed for gold, and cash itself became the reserve asset.

Banks, fearing robberies, do not hold all of their cash reserves in their own vaults. Rather, they store it in an account at a regional Fed bank. These accounts count as reserves. What banks do hold in their vaults is their other assets, such as Treasury bonds and corporate bonds.

## The Fed and Bank Reserves

The only role of the government in creating money is through the Fed. If the Fed wants to expand the money supply, it must increase bank reserves. To do this, the Fed buys Treasury bonds from a bank, and pays with a check drawn on the Fed itself. By depositing the check in its reserve account at the Fed, the bank now has more reserves, so the bank can now make more loans and create new checking account money.

By controlling the amount of reserves, the Fed attempts to control the size of the money supply. But as recent history has shown, this control is limited. During the recent recession, the Fed created reserves, but many banks were afraid to make loans, so little new money was created. During the late 1970s, the Fed tried to limit the amount of money banks could create by reducing reserves, but banks simply created new forms of money, just like the POW camp prisoners. In 1979, there was only one form of checking account money. Today, there are many, with odd names such as NOW's, ATS's, repos, and money market deposit accounts.

These amorphous forms of money function only because we believe they will function, which is why the continued stability of the banking system is so critical. Banks do not have cash reserves to cover all checking account money. If, through a replay of the savings & loan debacle, we lose faith in the commercial banking system and all try to take out our "money" as cash, the banks will become insolvent (fail), and the money they have created will simply disappear. This would create a real crisis, since no market economy can function without its money.

# FOCUS ON THE FED: THE BOND MARKET VERSUS THE REST OF US

**BY DOUG ORR AND ELLEN FRANK**
*October 1999*

Why should anyone involved in environmental issues, or education reform efforts, or efforts to house the homeless, or anyone else, care about monetary policy? After all, it only affects the financial markets, right? Wrong. Monetary policy is holding all other social policy hostage, and is part of the cause of the rapid increase in income inequality in the United States. Whenever any policy change is proposed, be it in health care, housing or transportation, the first question politicians ask is "What will the bond market think about this?"

"The bond market" is a euphemism for the financial sector of the U.S. economy and the Federal Reserve Bank (the Fed), which regulates that sector. The Fed is the central bank of the United States government. It controls monetary policy, and has been using its power to help the banking industry and the holders of financial assets, while thwarting government attempts to deal with pressing social problems.

Since 1979, the Fed has had an unprecedented degree of independence from government control. This independence had put it in a position to veto any progressive fiscal policy that the Congress might propose. To understand how this situation developed, we must understand the function of banks, the structure of the Fed, and the role of monetary policy.

## Banks and Instability

Government regulates the banking industry because private sector, profit-driven banking is inherently unstable. Banks do more than just store money — they help create it. If you deposit a dollar in the bank, you still have that dollar. Commercial banks will set aside three cents as "reserves" to "cover" your deposit, and the remaining 97 cents is loaned out to someone else who now has "new money." By making loans, banks create new money and generate profit. The drive to maximize profits often leads banks to become overextended: making too many loans and holding too few reserves. This drive for profits can undermine a bank's stability.

If depositors think the bank is holding too few reserves, or is making overly speculative loans, they might try to withdraw their money as cash. Large numbers of depositors withdrawing cash from a bank at the same time is called a "run on the bank." Since banks only hold 3% of their deposit liabilities as cash, even a moderate-sized "run" would be enough to drain the bank of its cash reserves. If a bank has no reserves, it is insolvent and is forced to close. At that point, all remaining deposits in the bank cease to exist, and depositors lose their money.

The failure of a bank affects more than just that bank's depositors. One bank's excesses tend to shake people's faith in other banks. If the run spreads, "bank panics" can occur. During the 1800s, such panics erupted every 10 to 15 years, bankrupting between 10% and 25% of the banks in the U.S. and creating a recession each time.

## The Creation of the Fed

The panic of 1907 bankrupted some of the largest banks and led to demands for bank reforms that would stabilize the system. Reform proposals ranged from doing almost nothing to nationalizing the entire banking industry. As a compromise, the Federal Reserve was created in 1913. The U.S. Government saw the Fed as a way for bankers to regulate themselves, and structured the Federal Reserve System so that it could be responsive to its main constituents: banks and other financial-sector businesses that are now called, euphemistically, "the bond market." While ideally it should serve the interests of the general public when it conducts monetary policy, in reality the Fed balances two, occasionally conflicting goals: maintaining the stability of "the bond market" and maximizing financial-sector profits. Over time, Congress and the President have varied the degree of independence that they have given to the Fed to choose between these goals.

Initially, the Fed enjoyed a high degree of independence. Unfortunately, it was more successful in aiding bank profits than in stabilizing the system. During the 1920s, the Fed allowed member banks to engage in highly speculative activities, including using depositor's money to play the stock market. While many banks were very profitable, speculative excesses caused almost 20 percent of the banks in existence in 1920 to fail during the following decade. With the onset of the Great Depression, between 1929 and 1933, more than 9000 banks, 38% of the total, failed. Since the Fed had not achieved its first goal, in 1935 Congress responded with laws that put many new regulations on banks, and reduced the Fed's independence.

## Fed Independence Lost

Under the new regulations, commercial banks were restricted to taking deposits and making commercial loans. Thus, the only opportunity for making a profit was to maintain a "spread" between the interest rate paid on deposits and that charged on loans. Loans are made for relatively long terms, and deposits are not. If the short-term interest rate on deposits varies widely, the spread will grow and shrink, which makes bank profits unstable. In order to stabilize bank profits, during the 30 years after 1935, the Treasury mandated that the Fed keep this rate approximately constant.

Under this arrangement, Congress indirectly controlled monetary policy. If Congress wanted to stimulate the economy it could increased government spending or cut taxes. Both led to an increase in spending and an increase in the demand for money. To keep interest rates, which are the price of money, from rising, the Fed must increase the supply of money. Thus, the Fed "accommodated" fiscal policy decisions made by Congress and the President.

During most of this period, growth was moderate and prices were stable. The Fed went along because this arrangement did not threaten bank profits. Starting in the mid-1960s, however, stimulative fiscal policy started to push up the inflation rate, which did threaten bank profits. A confrontation over Fed independence ensued and grew in intensity throughout the 1970s.

## Inflation's Impact

Contrary to the view commonly propagated by the media, inflation does not affect everyone equally. In fact, there are very clear winners and losers. Inflation is an increase in the average level of prices, but some prices rise faster than average and some rise slower. If the price of something you are selling is rising faster than average, you win. Otherwise, you lose. Inflation redistributes income, but in an arbitrary manner. This uncertainty makes inflation unpopular, even to the winners. However, one industry always loses from unexpected inflation, and that industry is finance.

Banks make loans today that will be repaid, with interest, in the future. If inflation reduces the value of those future payments, the banks' profits will be reduced. So bankers are interested in the "real interest rate," that is, the actual (nominal) interest rate on the loan minus the rate of inflation. If the interest rate on commercial bank loans is 7% and the rate of inflation is 3%, the real rate of interest is 4%. In the early post-war period, real interest rates were relatively stable at about 2%.

From 1965 on, unexpected increases in inflation reduced the real interest rate. This cheap credit was a boon to home buyers, farmers, and manufacturers, but it greatly reduced bank profits. Banks wanted inflation cut. The Keynesian view of monetary policy offered a simple but unpopular solution: raise interest rates enough to cause a recession. High unemployment and falling incomes would take the steam out of inflation.

Putting people out of work to help bankers would be a hard sell. The Fed needed a different story to justify shifting its policy from stabilizing interest rates to fighting inflation. That story was monetarism, a theory that claims that changes in the money supply affect prices, but nothing else in the economy.

## The Monetarist Experiment

On October 6, 1979, Fed Chairman Paul Volcker, using monetarist theory as a justification, announced that the Fed would no longer try to keep interest rates at targeted levels. He argued that the Fed policy should concentrate on controlling inflation, and to do so he would now focus on limiting the money supply growth rate. Since neither Congress nor the President attempted to overrule Volcker, this change ushered in an era of unprecedented independence for Fed monetary policy.

During the next three years, the Fed reduced the rate of growth in the money supply, but this experiment did not yield the results predicted by the monetarists. Instead of a swift reduction in the rate of inflation, the most immediate outcome was a rapid rise in the real interest rate and the start of the worst recession since the Great Depression.

As the Keynesian view predicted, the recession occurred because high interest rates slowed economic growth and increased unemployment. In 1979, the unemployment rate was 5.8%. By 1982 it had reached 10.7%, the first double-digit rate since the Depression. With fewer people working and buying products, the inflation rate, which had been 8.7% in 1979, finally started to slow in 1981 and was approaching 4% by the end of 1982. Tight money policies by the Fed kept nominal interest rates from falling as fast as inflation. This raised real interest rates (nominal rates minus inflation) on commercial loans from 0.5% in 1979 to 10% in 1982.

The Fed's fight against inflation had a severe impact on the entire economy. All businesses, especially farming and manufacturing, run on credit. The rise in interest rates, combined with lower prices, squeezed the profits of farmers and manufacturers.

Both of these industries rely heavily on exports, and so were also hurt by the negative effect of high interest rates on the competitiveness of U.S. exports. Real interest rates in the United States were the highest in the world, thereby attracting financial investment from abroad. In order for foreigners to buy financial assets in the U.S., they first had to buy dollars. This demand for dollars drove up their value in international markets. While a "strong" dollar means imports are relatively cheap, it also means that U.S. exports are expensive. Foreign countries could not afford to buy our "costly" agricultural and manufactured exports. As a result, during this period, bankruptcy rates in these two industries were massive, higher than during the 1930s.

Despite its high cost to the rest of the economy, the monetarist experiment did not benefit many banks. Initially, the high real interest rates appeared to help bank profits. Regulations capped the interest rates banks could pay on deposits, but rates charged on loans were not regulated. This increased the profit on loans. Many investors, however, started moving their deposits to less regulated financial intermediaries, such as mutual funds, that could pay higher rates on deposits. In addition, the recession forced many borrowers to declare bankruptcy and default on their loans. Both of these factors pushed banks toward insolvency.

## Reversing Course

It was bank losses, rather than the pain in the rest of the economy, that led Volcker to announce in September 1982 that he was abandoning monetarism. His new policy aimed to provide enough reserves to keep most banks solvent and to allow a slow recovery from the recession. Unemployment remained high for the next five years, so inflation continued to slow. Real interest rates stayed near 8% through 1986, so interest sensitive industries, such as farming and manufacturing, did not take part in the recovery.

Volcker made his allegiance to the banking industry very clear during a meeting, in February 1985, with a delegation of state legislators, laborers, and farmers who were demanding easier money and lower interest rates. He told them, "Look, your constituents are unhappy, mine aren't."

Yet by 1985, the crisis in the savings and loan industry was spreading into commercial banking. To provide cash ("liquidity") to the banks, Volcker allowed the money supply to grow by 12% during 1985 and by 17% in 1986. Monetarists raised the specter of a return to double-digit inflation. Instead, the rate of inflation continued to slow, demonstrating that a simple link between the money supply and inflation does not exist.

## The Veto

Despite the failure and subsequent abandonment of monetarist policies, the Fed still uses monetarist theory to justify its continued focus on "fighting inflation." The myth that monetary policy only affects inflation provides a convenient "cover" that allows the Fed to serve its narrow constituency: "the bond market." During 1998, nominal interest rates appeared low, but because inflation is so low, real interest rates on commercial loans were 6.8% — 3.2 times the post-World War II average. Real interest rates remain high because the " bond market" worries about any possible increase in future inflation.

Fighting inflation benefits the bond market. However, despite the near-depression that monetarism caused in the 1980s and the extremely slow rate of economic growth that has occurred in the 1990s, the Fed continues to claim that fighting inflation serves the interests of the entire country. The public's widespread belief in this myth denies progressives in Congress the support they need to force the Fed back into accommodating fiscal policy. It also provides support for those in Congress that want to block any expansion of social programs.

If Congress decides to spend more for environmental clean-up, housing the homeless, or education, the "bond market" will raise the specter of renewed inflation. The Fed will then raise interest rates, as it did in June of 1999, as a "pre-emptive strike" to prevent inflation. The increase in interest rates, if large enough, will slow the economy, increase unemployment, reduce government revenues, and return the federal budget to a deficit. Since Congress is aware of this probable outcome, and knows it will be incorrectly blamed for it, Congress won't pass any legislation the "bond market" doesn't like. This is how the bond market holds Congress hostage. As long as Congress and the President allow the Fed to follow an inflation-fighting policy, the Fed can maintain a veto threat over the elected government.

The Fed has also played a large role in the rapid increase in income and wealth inequality that started in the 1980s and has accelerated in the 1990s. The two decades following World War II are often called the "golden age" of the U.S. economy. On average, Gross Domestic Product (GDP) grew 4.2% each year, unemployment averaged 4.6%, and real commercial interest rates averaged 2.1%. Average real wages, that is, wages adjusted for inflation, grew at an annual rate of 2.1%, rising from $8.34 an hour in 1950 to $12.75 in 1970 (both measured in 1998 dollars). This period saw the creation of a true middle class in the U.S.

In the two decades since 1980, GDP growth has averaged 2.6% each year, unemployment has averaged 6.6%, and real interest rates averaged 5.9%. Average real wages declined every year from 1980 to 1996. In fact, the real wage in 1996 was exactly the same as in 1968. If wages had continued to grow at 2.1%, the average wage today would be almost twice what it is. Without the slow growth policies of the Fed and the anti-labor policies started under Reagan, the average income of the majority of the people in the U.S. would be twice as large. Instead, we've seen a hollowing out of the middle class, and a rapid transfer of wealth and income to those already wealthy.

By focusing on inflation rather than interest rates, the media deflect attention from a critical social issue — how high interest rates transfer income from the indebted middle class to the very rich. The social consequences of high interest rates can be gauged by looking at the share of interest income in total U.S. personal income. Between 1980 and 1989, real interest rates rose from 1.8% to 6.1%. The share of income received as interest rose from 11% to 15.2%. As rates came back down slightly in the mid-1990s, so did the share of income going to interest.

## Where Do Interest Payments Go?

If ownership of financial assets was evenly distributed among households, the growth in interest income would not be of much importance. When increases in interest rates outstripped wage and salary gains, the typical household would simply gain on the asset side what they were losing on the liability side. An increase in the size of their mortgage payment would be matched by an increase in their interest income.

But ownership of financial assets is heavily concentrated. A mere 7% of families with incomes of $100,000 or more control nearly half of total household net worth. Yet this number understates the concentration of financial wealth. Almost 80% of families in the U.S. have almost no assets, outside the equity in their homes and vehicles. As a result, despite the massive increase in financial asset values during the 1990s, median net worth was no higher in 1995 than it was in 1989. Almost all of the growth in net worth accrued to the few owners of financial assets.

Detailed studies of wealth data collected by the Fed report that in 1995 the wealthiest 10% of households owned 89.8% of all bonds, 88.4% of all stocks, 88.5% of financial trusts, and 91% of other business equity. Despite the media hype about the "democratization" of the stock market, between 1989 and 1995 the concentration of stock ownership increased. In 1995 only 15.3 % of households held stocks directly and only 12% owned shares in mutual funds outside of their retirement accounts.

The "poorest" nine-tenths of the U.S. population — that is most of us — have virtually no financial assets. Such families gain little from rising interest rates. But the higher mortgage, credit card, and auto payments that result take a real toll on living standards. Each uptick in the real interest rate entail a transfer of income from the lowest 90% of the population to the highest 10%. And most of that income goes to the very, very wealthy who are yet another part of the "bond market" served by the Fed.

Economist James Galbraith has called today's high interest rates a form of taxation without representation. The term is apt. Tax increases are passed by Congress which has at least some public oversight. Interest rate hikes are decided by the Fed, an institution over which the President, Congress and the public have virtually no control.

Like taxes, rising interest rates are a drain on the resources and income of the vast majority of U.S. households. But unlike tax revenues that can be used to provide education, environmental clean-up, homeless shelters, roads, airports, and other infrastructure, interest payments flow into the pockets of the very rich, who become ever so much richer.

*Resources:* "Family Finances in the U.S.: Recent Evidence from the Survey of Consumer Finances," Arthur B. Kennickell, Martha Starr-McCluer, and Annika E. Sunden, *Federal Reserve Bulletin* (Jan. 1997); *The State of Working America* 1998-99, Lawrence Mishel, Jared Bernstein, John Schmitt, 1999.

# TRANSFORMING THE FED

**BY ROBERT POLLIN**

*November/December 1992*

The U.S. financial system faces deep structural problems. Households, businesses, and the federal government are burdened by excessive debts. The economy favors short-term speculation over long-term investment. An unrepresentative and unresponsive elite has extensive control over the financial system. Moreover, the federal government is incapable of reversing these patterns through its existing tools, including fiscal, monetary, and financial regulatory policies.

I propose a dramatically different approach: transforming the Federal Reserve System (the "Fed") into a public investment bank. Such a bank would have substantial power to channel credit in ways that counter financial instability and support productive investment by private businesses. The Fed would use its powers to influence how and for what purposes banks, insurance companies, brokers, and other lenders loan money.

The U.S. government has used credit allocation policies, such as low-cost loans, loan guarantees, and home mortgage interest deductions, extensively and with success. Its primary accomplishment has been to create a home mortgage market that, for much of the period since World War II, provided non-wealthy households with unprecedented access to home ownership.

I propose increasing democratic control over the Federal Reserve's activities by decentralizing power to the 12 district Fed banks and instituting popular election of their boards of directors. This would create a mechanism for extending democracy throughout the financial system.

My proposal also offers a vehicle for progressives to address two separate but equally serious questions facing the U.S. economy:

- how to convert our industrial base out of military production and toward the development and adoption of environmentally benign production techniques; and

- how to increase opportunities for high wage, high productivity jobs in the United States. The U.S. needs such jobs to counteract the squeeze on wages from increasingly globalized labor and financial markets.

Transforming the Federal Reserve system into a public investment bank will help define an economic path toward democratic socialism in the United States.

My proposal has several strengths as a transitional program. It offers a mechanism for establishing democratic control over finance and investment — the area where capital's near-dictatorial power is most decisive. The program will also work within the United States' existing legal and institutional framework. We could implement parts of it immediately using existing federal agencies and with minimal demands on the federal budget.

At the same time, if an ascendant progressive movement put most of the program in place, this would represent a dramatic step toward creating a new economic system. Such a system would still give space to market interactions and the pursuit of greed, but would nevertheless strongly promote general well-being over business profits.

## How the Fed Fails

At present the Federal Reserve focuses its efforts on managing short-term fluctuations of the economy, primarily by influencing interest rates. When it reduces rates, it seeks to increase borrowing and spending, and thereby stimulate economic growth and job opportunities. When the Fed perceives that wages and prices are rising too fast (a view not necessarily shared by working people), it tries to slow down borrowing and spending by raising interest rates.

This approach has clearly failed to address the structural problems plaguing the financial system. The Fed did nothing, for example, to prevent the collapse of the savings and loan industry. It stood by while highly speculative mergers, buyouts, and takeovers overwhelmed financial markets in the 1980s. It has failed to address the unprecedented levels of indebtedness and credit defaults of private corporations and households.

## New Roles for the Fed

Under my proposal, the Federal Reserve would shift its focus from the short to the long term. It would provide more and cheaper credit to banks and other financiers who loan money to create productive assets and infrastructure — which promote high wage, high productivity jobs. The Fed would make credit more expensive for lenders that finance speculative activities such as the mergers, buyouts, and takeovers that dominated the 1980s.

The Fed would also give favorable credit terms to banks that finance decent affordable housing rather than luxury housing and speculative office buildings. It would make low-cost credit available for environmental research and development so the economy can begin the overdue transition to environmentally benign production. Cuts in military spending have idled many workers and productive resources, both of which could be put to work in such transformed industries.

Finally, the Fed would give preferential treatment to loans that finance investment in the United States rather than in foreign countries. This would help counter the trend of U.S. corporations to abandon the domestic economy in search of lower wages and taxes.

The first step in developing the Fed's new role would be for the public to determine which sectors of the economy should get preferential access to credit. One example, suggested above, is industrial conversion from military production to investment in renewable energy and conservation.

Once the public establishes its investment goals, the Fed will have to develop new policy tools and use its existing tools in new ways to accomplish them. I propose that a transformed Federal Reserve use two major methods:

- set variable cash ("asset reserve") requirements for all lenders, based on the social value of the activities the lenders are financing; and

- increase discretionary lending activity by the 12 district Federal Reserve banks.

## Varying Banks' Cash Requirements

The Fed currently requires that banks and other financial institutions keep a certain amount of their assets available in cash reserves. Banks, for example, must carry three cents in cash for every dollar they hold in checking accounts. A bank cannot make interest-bearing loans on such "reserves." I propose that the Fed make this percent significantly lower for loans that finance preferred activities than for less desirable investment areas. Let's say the public decides that banks should allocate 10% of all credit to research and development of new environmental technologies, such as non-polluting autos and organic farming. Then financial institutions that have made 10% of their loans in environmental technologies would not have to hold any cash reserves against these loans. But if a bank made no loans in the environmental area, then it would have to hold 10% of its total assets in reserve. The profit motive would force banks to support environmental technologies without any direct expenditure from the federal budget.

All profit-driven firms will naturally want to avoid this reserve requirement. The Fed must therefore apply it uniformly to all businesses that profit through accepting deposits and making loans. These include banks, savings and loans, insurance companies, and investment brokerage houses. If the rules applied only to banks, for example, then banks could circumvent the rules by redefining themselves as another type of lending institution.

## Loans to Banks That Do the Right Thing

The Federal Reserve has the authority now to favor some banks over others by making loans to them when they are short on cash. For the most part, however, the Fed has chosen not to exercise such discretionary power. Instead it aids all banks equally, through a complex mechanism known as open market operations, which increases total cash reserves in the banking system. The Fed could increase its discretionary lending to favored banks by changing its operating procedures without the federal government creating any new laws or institutions. Such discretionary lending would have several benefits.

First, to a much greater extent than at present, financial institutions would obtain reserves when they are lending for specific purposes. If a bank's priorities should move away from the established social priorities, the Fed could then either refuse to make more cash available to it, or charge a penalty interest rate, thereby discouraging the bank from making additional loans. The Fed, for example, could impose such obstacles on lenders that are financing mergers, takeovers, and buyouts.

In addition, the Fed could use this procedure to more effectively monitor and regulate financial institutions. Banks, in applying for loans, would have to submit to the Fed's scrutiny on a regular basis. The Fed could more closely link its regulation to banks' choices of which investments to finance.

Implementing this procedure will also increase the authority of the 12 district banks within the Federal Reserve system, since these banks approve the Fed's loans. Each district bank will have more authority to set lending rates and monitor bank compliance with regulations.

The district banks could then more effectively enforce measures such as the Community Reinvestment Act, which currently mandates that banks lend in their home communities. Banks that are committed to their communities and regions, such as the South Shore Bank in Chicago, could gain substantial support under this proposed procedure.

## Other Credit Allocation Tools

The Fed can use other tools to shift credit to preferred industries, such as loan guarantees, interest rate subsidies, and government loans. In the past the U.S. government has used these techniques with substantial success. They now primarily support credit for housing, agriculture, and education. Indeed, as of 1991, these programs subsidized roughly one-third of all loans in the United States.

Jesse Jackson's 1988 Presidential platform suggested an innovative way of extending such policies. He proposed that public pension funds channel a portion of their money into a loan guarantee program, with the funds used to finance investments in low cost housing, education, and infrastructure.

There are disadvantages, however, to the government using loan guarantee programs and similar approaches rather than the Fed's employing asset reserve requirements and discretionary lending. Most important is that the former are more expensive and more difficult to administer. Both loan guarantees and direct government loans require the government to pay off the loans when borrowers default. Direct loans also mean substantial administrative costs. Interest subsidies on loans are direct costs to government even when the loans are paid back.

In contrast, with variable asset reserve requirements and discretionary lending policies, the Fed lowers the cost of favored activities, and raises the cost of unfavored ones, without imposing any burden on the government's budget.

## Increasing Public Control

The Federal Reserve acts in relative isolation from the political process at present. The U.S. president appoints seven members of the Fed's Board of Governors for 14 year terms, and they are almost always closely tied to banking and big business. The boards of directors of the 12 district banks appoint their presidents, and these boards are also composed of influential bankers and business people within each of the districts.

The changes I propose will mean a major increase in the central bank's role as an economic planning agency for the nation. Unless we dramatically improve democratic control by the public over the Fed, voters will correctly interpret such efforts as an illegitimate grasp for more power by business interests.

Democratization should proceed through redistributing power downward to the 12 district banks. When the Federal Reserve System was formed in 1913, the principle behind creating district banks along with the headquarters in Washington was to disperse the central bank's authority. This remains a valuable idea, but the U.S. government has never seriously attempted it. Right now the district banks are highly undemocratic and have virtually no power.

One way to increase the district banks' power is to create additional seats for them on the Open Market Committee, which influences short-term interest rates by expanding or contracting the money supply.

A second method is to shift authority from the Washington headquarters to the districts. The Board of Governors would then be responsible for setting general guidelines, while the district banks would implement discretionary lending and enforcement of laws such as the Community Reinvestment Act.

The most direct way of democratizing the district banks would be to choose their boards in regular elections along with other local, regional, and state-wide officials. The boards would then choose the top levels of the banks' professional staffs and oversee the banks' activities.

## Historical Precedents

Since World War II other capitalist countries have extensively employed the types of credit allocation policies proposed here. Japan, France, and South Korea are the outstanding success stories, though since the early 1980s globalization and deregulation of financial markets have weakened each of their credit policies. When operating at full strength, the Japanese and South Korean programs primarily supported large-scale export industries, such as steel, automobiles, and consumer electronics. France targeted its policies more broadly to coordinate Marshall Plan aid for the development of modern industrial corporations.

We can learn useful lessons from these experiences, not least that credit allocation policies do work when they are implemented well. But substantial differences exist between experiences elsewhere and the need for a public investment bank in the United States.

In these countries a range of other institutions besides the central bank were involved in credit allocation policies. These included their treasury departments and explicit planning agencies, such as the powerful Ministry of International Trade and Industry (MITI) in Japan. In contrast, I propose to centralize the planning effort at the Federal Reserve.

We could create a new planning institution to complement the work of the central bank. But transforming the existing central banking system rather than creating a new institution minimizes both start-up problems and the growth of bureaucracies.

A second and more fundamental difference between my proposal and the experiences in Japan, France, and South Korea is that their public investment institutions were accountable only to a business-oriented elite. This essentially dictatorial approach is antithetical to the goal of increasing democratic control of the financial system.

The challenge, then, is for the United States to implement effective credit allocation policies while broadening, not narrowing, democracy. Our success ultimately will depend on a vigorous political movement that can fuse two equally urgent, but potentially conflicting goals: economic democracy, and equitable and sustainable growth. If we can meet this challenge, it will represent a historic victory toward the construction of a democratic socialist future.

*Resources:* Robert Pollin, "Transforming the Federal Reserve into a Public Investment Bank: Why it is Necessary; How it Should Be Done," in G. Epstein, G. Dymski and R. Pollin, eds., *Transforming the U.S. Financial System*, M.E. Sharpe, 1993.

# OUTING ALLEN GREENSPAN

**BY JOHN MILLER**

*July/August 2005*

> I'm not a big Alan Greenspan fan. ...I think he's one of the biggest political hacks we have in Washington.
>
> —*Senate Minority Leader Harry M. Reid (D-Nev.) on CNN's "Inside Politics," March 2005*

Federal Reserve chairman Alan Greenspan a "political hack"? Political thug is more like it. Greenspan's policies have robbed retirees, poor people, and working people—while bestowing riches on the best off in our society.

Let's start with Greenspan's betrayal of the elderly on Social Security. That's what got Harry Reid, a former boxer, so angry that he took the gloves off.

In 1983, Greenspan chaired the commission that convinced Congress to raise the payroll tax that funds Social Security. He said the tax hike would ensure the Social Security system's solvency for the baby boomer generation and beyond.The higher tax fell heavily on low- and middle-income taxpayers, nearly all of whom pay more in payroll taxes than income taxes. As promised, the tax hike built up a surplus in the Social Security trust fund. With the surplus in place, Greenspan turned around in 2001 and endorsed the Bush administration's tax cuts, whose benefits went overwhelmingly to the richest 1% of taxpayers, those who make more than $373,000 a year. Now that those tax cuts have contributed to soaring budget deficits, Greenspan insists we need to cut Social Security benefits in order to restore "fiscal discipline." Put simply, Greenspan jacked up taxes on working people, adding to the budget surplus, and then endorsed squandering that surplus on giant tax cuts for the top 1%.

It was a masterful bait-and-switch. As *New York Times* columnist Paul Krugman points out, if Greenspan "had tried to sell this package honestly—'Let's raise taxes and cut benefits for working families so we can give big tax cuts to the rich!'—voters would have been outraged."

Future retirees weren't the only ones to fall prey to Greenspan's maneuvers —the poor have taken a drubbing as well. Much of the deficit reduction that Greenspan urged the Clinton administration to carry out came at the cost of low-income families. Robert Pollin, co-director of the Political Economy Research Institute, reports that a majority of the federal budget's swing from deficits to surpluses during the second half of the 1990s came from reducing government spending relative to the size of the economy. Relative to GDP, funding for education was slashed by nearly a quarter, while deep cuts to food stamps, nutrition, and other supports for poor families carved away one-sixth of funding for income security programs.

That Greenspan's true aims were to shrink government and reward the wealthy—and not to enforce fiscal responsibility—became abundantly clear when George W. Bush took office. Despite indications in the administration's early days that he favored "triggers" capping the size of the Bush tax cuts should the budget surplus disappear, Greenspan never made such triggers a precondition for his endorsement of Bush's tax giveaways to the rich. Instead, he assured the Senate in 2001 that "sufficient resources will be available" to undertake both debt reduction and tax cuts. Given the ballooning federal budget deficit, this was either a shockingly poor analysis or pure ideological excess.

Today's monstrous deficits rival those Greenspan insisted must be closed in the early Clinton years, but Greenspan *still* favors making Bush's tax cuts permanent—even in the face of overwhelming evidence that doing so will force massive cutbacks in social spending and core entitlement programs. (Making the 2001 and 2003 tax cuts permanent would cost the U.S. government more than five times the amount that would be necessary to close the projected shortfall in Social Security over the next 75 years, according to the Center on Budget and Policy Priorities, a liberal think tank.)

In other words, Greenspan is the chief enabler of the Republican "starve the beast" strategy for slashing government spending—first enacting tax cuts and then insisting that spending cuts (not tax increases) are necessary to restore budget balance.

When Congress asked him what happened to his concern for fiscal responsibility, Greenspan responded that he had always favored lower taxes, but that he favored lower spending and smaller government as well. And the strategy, at least the government slashing part, is working. In 2004, federal government revenues relative to the size of the economy reached their lowest level since the 1950s.

For all these reasons, the liberal commentator Jonathan Chait has offered up a modification of Reid's insult, calling Greenspan "a Fiscal Policy Hack." His careful choice of words underlines Greenspan's failures in the sphere of fiscal policy, or government spending and taxes. "For the last four years," Chait points out, "Alan Greenspan has cast himself as a champion of fiscal responsibility while lending crucial support to policies that undermine it." Chait insists nonetheless that "Greenspan's views on monetary policy—specifically, his setting of interest rates—"ought to count for a lot." Sadly, this common liberal position turns a blind eye to the role Greenspan's monetary policy plays in perpetuating the searing inequality of today's economy. Greenspan makes monetary policy on behalf those who hold financial assets, not job seekers or workers. And Greenspan's insistence that inflation must be kept low to protect the value of stocks and bonds even if it means keeping a cap on employment growth might count for a lot in the minds of some—but it shouldn't.

Think back to the second half of the 1990s boom. Early on, Greenspan warned that an "irrational exuberance" was igniting a dangerous stock market bubble. In a 1996 Federal Reserve Board meeting, he acknowledged that raising the margin requirement would "get rid of the bubble." The margin requirement is the percent of the purchase price of financial investments, like stocks and bonds, that the buyer must pay for in cash rather than credit. (Since 1974, investors have been required to pay for at least 50% of their stock purchases with cash.) The Fed chair could have raised margins on borrowing to purchase stocks then, cooling off the stock market without sacrificing the whole economy. But, unwilling to confront the monied classes, or uninterested in doing so, Greenspan instead endorsed a huge capital gains tax cut in 1997 that only inflated the bubble more.

Then, in late 1999 and early 2000, with the bubble apparent to everyone, he slammed on the economic brakes, repeatedly hiking interest rates and helping to bring on an economic slowdown just as working people were beginning to see some healthy gains in their paychecks. The recession and the job-barren economic recovery that followed have wiped out much of those gains. Last year, workers' real wages, their purchasing power, actually declined for the first time in 14 years. And today, even *Wall Street Journal* reporter David Wessel warns that "the risk to workers now is that the Federal Reserve, anxious about indications that inflation is returning, [once again] will raise interest rates to slow the economy before the labor market gets strong enough to push wages up."

Outing Greenspan's political thuggery is the first step in the battle for a Federal Reserve Board that serves all of us, not just the rich. No longer the man behind the curtain glorified in *Forbes* magazine billboards, or the Maestro, as establishment journalist Bob Woodward dubbed him, Greenspan might finally be seen for what he is: public enemy number one when it comes to building a more just economy. And once they're accurately translated, "Greenspan-speak," the Fed chair's notoriously obscure mutterings that tighten the screws of class privilege at every turn, will no longer pass for a truthful and disinterested take on the state of the U.S. economy.

*Resources:* "Workers' Wages Trail Growth in Economy," David Wessel, *Wall Street Journal,* April 21, 2005; "Hacking at Greenspan," *Wall Street Journal,* March 7, 2005; "Greenspan, a Fiscal Policy Hack," Jonathan Chait, *Los Angeles Times,* March 18, 2005; "Maestro of Chutzpah," Paul Krugman, *New York Times,* March 2, 2005

# THE DISCOUNT RATE

**BY ELLEN FRANK**
*March/April 2002*

Dear Dr. Dollar:

The Federal Reserve keeps fussing with the "discount rate" and everybody thinks it's important. This is, if I understand it right, the rate banks charge each other for overnight loans. Now presumably someone makes money on the interest that's charged and someone loses money (or makes less) when the rate is lowered. But no one screams. Why not? If it's because the charges among banks just cancel one another out, then why does the rate even matter? Or is it that the Federal Reserve itself charges this interest, in which case the taxpayers lose when the rate it lowered?

—*Peter Marcuse, New York*

To answer your question, it helps to understand how the U.S. Federal Reserve system works. The quasi-public Federal Reserve has two parts, neither of which is actually part of the federal government. First, there are the district banks—12 Federal Reserve Banks scattered across the country, charged with regulating and overseeing the commercial banks in their region and each wholly owned by those banks. Then there is the Board of Governors, a seven-member board with a vast research staff, based in Washington, D.C., and chaired by Alan Greenspan.

Every six weeks, the board and the presidents of the regional banks meet together as the so-called *Federal Open Market Committee* (FOMC), where they set targets for the *fed funds rate*—a rate that commercial banks charge one another for overnight loans. After the fed funds target is announced, the district banks will generally raise or lower the *discount rate*—the rate that commercial banks pay when they borrow from their local Fed—so that the two rates stay roughly equal.

In order to reduce the fed funds rate, the FOMC directs traders at the New

York Federal Reserve Bank to buy U.S. Treasury bills on the financial markets. The Fed creates new money—quite literally, since paper printed by the Fed *is* money—to pay for these bills. When this new money enters the economy, it tends to be deposited in banks that, suddenly awash in cash, must find borrowers for it if they are to earn a profit. (To raise interest rates the FOMC does the opposite, selling U.S. Treasury bills and taking cash out of circulation.)

Since the district banks are owned not by the federal government but by the commercial banks, reductions in the discount rate do not affect the public treasury. And since commercial banks are both borrowers and the lenders in the fed funds market, gains and losses for the banks do tend, as you suspect, to cancel out. The point of reducing the fed funds rate, though, is to drive down other interest rates. If the financial markets are swimming in cheap cash, then competition for borrowers ought to push down rates on auto loans, business loans, mortgages, rates on bonds, and so forth.

Financial firms earn money by charging interest. In general, they prefer high interest rates to low. But they prefer low interest rates to watching their business dry up and their clients default on loans. Banks recognize that in a recession, lower interest rates may be necessary to spur growth and prevent bankruptcies. They accept the Fed's authority to reduce rates and print new money when circumstances warrant it. And they also know that the Fed, traditionally, has been their advocate—if not their mouthpiece—in Washington.

The district banks are owned outright by the finance industry and appointees to the Board of Governors nearly always have close industry ties. Greenspan himself has a well-established record as an "inflation hawk" who tends to err on the side of high interest rates. Moreover, in his nearly 12 years as Fed chair, Greenspan has presided over the slow erosion of the Fed's policy authority, so that a lower fed funds rate often does not translate into lower interest rates for businesses and consumers. Over the past year, for example, the FOMC cut its target fed funds rate from 6.0% to 1.75%, yet rates on home mortgages have fallen by only one percentage point. If the Fed really wanted to bring down long-term interest rates (like mortgage rates), it could sell not only short-term Treasury bills but also long-term bonds. The Fed could use a variety of other means to lower interest rates set in other markets (like the bond market), but such policies could eat into the finance industry's earnings. Instead, the Fed's recent interest rate reductions have meant that banks pay lower rates on deposits, while earning fairly high rates on loans to consumers and businesses.

If the recession persists and competition for credit-worthy customers intensifies, however, lending rates will fall and banks will feel the pinch of the Fed's cheap credit policy. But don't expect to see Citigroup lambasting the Fed on the *New York Times* editorial page or lobbying Congress to oust Greenspan. The banks have a more direct avenue for airing their complaints. Every six weeks, on the day before the FOMC meets to set interest rate policy, the Board meets with the Federal Advisory Council—a group of private bankers from each of the 12 Fed districts—to hear their advice on how high interest rates should be.

Economist Edwin Dickens from Drew University, who has done extensive archival research on the Fed, notes that banks often "are adamant that they can't take the hit in income" if the Fed cuts rates. Records show that they have often thwarted rate cuts, even in recessions. So if lowered rates begin to squeeze financial earnings, the finance industry won't scream. Who needs to scream when you can whisper?

---

## BIG LIES ABOUT CENTRAL BANKING

**BY JOSEPH STIGLITZ**
*June 2003*

An independent central bank focused exclusively on price stability has become a central part of the mantra of "economic reform." Like so many other policy maxims, it has been repeated often enough that it has come to be believed. But bold assertions, even from central bankers, are no substitute for research and analysis.

Research suggests that if central banks focus on inflation, they do a better job at controlling inflation. But controlling inflation is not an end in itself: it is merely a means of achieving faster, more stable growth, with lower unemployment.

These are the real variables that matter, and there is little evidence that independent central banks focusing exclusively on price stability do better in these crucial respects. George Akerlof, who shared the Nobel Prize with me in 2001, and his colleagues have argued forcefully that there is an optimal rate of inflation, greater than zero. So ruthless pursuit of price stability actually harms economic growth and well being. Recent research even questions whether targeting price stability reduces the tradeoff between inflation and unemployment.

A focus on inflation may make sense for countries with long histories of inflation, but not for others, like Japan. America's central bank, the Federal Reserve, is mandated not only to ensure price stability, but also to promote growth and full employment. There is broad consensus in the US against a narrow mandate, such as that of the European Central Bank. Today, Europe's growth languishes, because the ECB is constrained by its single-minded focus on inflation from promoting economic recovery.

Technocrats and financial market players who benefit from this institutional arrangement have done an impressive job of convincing many countries of its virtues, and of the need to treat monetary policy as a technical matter that should be put above politics. That might be the case if all that central bankers did was, say, choose computer software for clearing payments.

But central banks make decisions that affect every aspect of society, including rates of economic growth and unemployment. Because there are tradeoffs, these decisions can only be made as part of a political process.

Some argue that in the long run there are no tradeoffs. But, as Keynes said, in the long run, we are all dead. Even if it were impossible to lower unemployment below some critical level without fuelling inflation, there is uncertainty about what that critical level is. Accordingly, risk is unavoidable: monetary policy that is too loose risks inflation; if it is too tight, it can cause unnecessary unemployment, with all the suffering that follows.

During America's growth boom in the 1990s, the Clinton Administration believed that it was worth risking pushing the unemployment rate lower, especially when the social gains—declining welfare roles, reduced violence—were added to the direct economic benefits. By contrast, the IMF urged tighter monetary policy, because it put far less weight on the cost of unemployment, seemingly no weight on the ancillary social benefits of reducing it, and much greater weight on the costs of potential inflation.

The economic analysis of Clinton's Council of Economic Advisers turned out to be right; the models of the IMF (and the Fed) were wrong. America secured a much lower rate of unemployment without inflation—eventually unemployment fell to below 4%.

But that is not the point: the point is that no one could be sure. A calculated risk is always unavoidable. Who bears it varies with different policies, and that is a decision that cannot—or at least should not—be left to central bank technocrats. While there is a legitimate debate about the degree of independence accorded to central banks and other decision-making bodies, within a democracy, the perspectives of those whose well-being is affected by the decisions taken should be represented in the process.

Workers, for instance, who have much to lose if the central bank pursues an excessively tight policy, do not have a seat at the table. But financial markets—which do not have much to lose from unemployment, but are affected by inflation—are typically well represented. And yet financial markets hardly have a monopoly on technical competency.

Indeed, many in the financial community have little understanding of the intricate workings of the macroeconomic system—as evidenced by their frequent mistakes in managing it. For example, most US recessions since 1945 were caused by the Fed stepping on the brakes too hard. Similarly, central banks adopted monetarism with a fervor in the late 1970's and early 1980's, just as empirical evidence discrediting the underlying theories was mounting.

Whatever the merits of a common currency, those in Europe deliberating about adopting the Euro should consider whether to tie their fortunes to an institutional arrangement whose flaws are increasingly apparent. Likewise, developing countries need to consider not only the central bank's independence, but also its mandate and representativeness. They need to balance concerns about economic efficiency with those of democratic accountability.

In many new democracies, citizens are bewildered. The virtues ofthe new regime are first praised, but then they are told that themacroeconomic policy decisions about which they care most are too important to be left to democratic processes. Citizens are warned against the risks of populism (meaning the will of the people?).

There are no easy answers. But in too many countries, nor is there democratic debate about the alternatives.

*Reprinted with permission from Project Syndicate, June 2003.*

# BERNANKE'S DILEMMA

## BY WILLIAM GREIDER

*November/December 2005*

If Ben Bernanke is unlucky, he may inherit the whirlwind when he succeeds Alan Greenspan as Federal Reserve chairman early next year. The Greenspan Fed is once again pursuing a high-risk strategy while concealing its real intentions from the public: raising short-term interest rates in the name of fighting inflation, but actually aiming to defuse the price bubble in housing. The last time the Fed tried this maneuver, it was hoping to subdue the stock market bubble. That gambit ended badly: shareholders lost $6 trillion, and instead of subsiding gently, the bubble collapsed and the economy went into recession.

This time, as sophisticated financial-market analysts understand, the Fed's true objective is asset deflation—though neither Greenspan nor Bernanke will acknowledge even that a housing bubble exists. Raising short-term rates, the Fed assumes, will induce financial markets to raise rates on long-term loans like mortgages, and higher interest on mortgages would definitely dampen housing prices.

Trouble is, the Fed strategy has so far failed utterly. Long-term rates are not rising. If Bernanke persists with Greenspan's strategy, short-term rates may rise higher than long-term rates. That unnatural condition means the imminent threat of recession, which is what has occurred repeatedly when the Fed has induced this state of inverted short-term and long-term rates.

A recession, as always, imposes the worst pain and loss on the weakest parties—the newly unemployed, families already struggling with debt, and small businesses already squeezed by energy costs and other negatives. Thorstein Veblen called it "the slaughter of the innocents." It's simply wrong for the Fed to put the real, Main Street economy at risk in order to solve a financial problem, the housing bubble, that Greenspan, Bernanke and their colleagues at the Fed won't even acknowledge exists, let alone admit their culpability in creating.

If Bernanke, like Greenspan, is convinced that long-term rates need to rise, there's a better way to do it—an ingenious strategy proposed by Paul McCulley, Fed watcher at PIMCO, the giant bond investment house. Contrary to conventional thinking, McCulley suggests the Fed can effectively force long-term rates to rise if it now starts to *reduce* short-term rates. Inflation vigilantes in the bond market would be alarmed, McCulley explains, believing that the central bank has given in to the return of price inflation that depresses the value of long-term financial assets. In that event, bond-market players would bid up bond rates to protect themselves. Pushing long-term rates up would address the housing bubble; doing so without raising short-term rates would be easier on the Main Street economy.

The logic is persuasive, but don't count on Bernanke to grasp it. Like Greenspan, he belongs to the orthodox school: Markets are logical and efficient, so there should be no need for central bankers to game or surprise market players to induce them to react one way or another. Holding firm to their economic principles—in this case, protecting the interests of the wealth holders and financial markets—is often more important to central bankers than protecting the economic well-being of the overall society.

But perhaps Bernanke will turn out to be a more supple thinker than the excessively admired Greenspan. We will soon find out.

## THE FIGHT FOR TRANSPARENCY AT THE FEDERAL RESERVE

**BY STEPHEN ZARLENGA**

*September/October 2006*

The Federal Reserve banking system is an immensely powerful institution, on a par with a fourth branch of government. As such, it deserves more attention and scrutiny than it now receives, and not just from the financial community trying to divine the direction of interest rates. While most Americans are aware that our monetary system is controlled by the Fed, they remain in the dark on how it operates and whether its actions serve to promote particular interests. But we weaken both democracy and economic justice when we allow the internal workings of the Fed to remain unexamined.

Ben Bernanke's recent appointment to replace Alan Greenspan—for the most part lionized rather than scrutinized by the press during his nearly 20 years as Fed chair—prompted reformer Ralph Nader to put out a call for more transparency at the Fed. However, since Bernanke's ascension to the throne, the Fed has arguably *reduced* transparency by ceasing publication of the M3 money supply statistic. M3 is the broadest measure of the money supply, including cash, savings and checking deposits, travelers checks, large time deposits such as certificates of deposit, and some eurodollar accounts (deposits in foreign banks but denominated in dollars).

The Fed reportedly regarded this statistic as expensive to compute and no longer meaningful, but this ignores its long use by scholars and analysts alike. The widespread reaction to the change among market participants was, "What are they hiding? Is the Fed anticipating inflation that they'd like to keep under wraps?" The Fed should continue to compute and release M3 figures to provide continuity of data for researchers, and if necessary adjust the statistic so that it better reflects what analysts believed it was offering us: the broadest measure of the money supply and thus the best indicator of its rate of growth.

Getting the Fed to continue reporting the M3 figure is just one skirmish in a larger struggle for transparency in the Fed's monetary policymaking. On September

21-24, the second annual Monetary Reform Conference will take place in Chicago, organized by the American Monetary Institute. In addition to developing proposals for broader reforms of the U.S. monetary system, AMI has worked with Rep. Dennis Kucinich (D-Ohio) to prepare draft legislation, the "Monetary Transparency Act," which would require the Fed to make information about its activities available in a way that is understandable for the average newspaper reporter and reader, not just for sophisticated bond traders.

For example, the law would require the Fed to estimate the annual value to commercial banks of their money-creation privilege. When banks take dollars from a depositor and in turn lend them to a borrower, both the depositor and the borrower now "have" those funds. In this way, banks actually add to the money supply; in other words, banks themselves create money. And, of course, banks earn interest on the money the system permits them to create through making loans. This profit is called "seignorage." Its value is estimated at £40 billion for the U.K., and for the United States it may be over $100 billion annually, but we need an authoritative estimate from the Fed itself.

Another key provision of the act would require the Fed to report what share of its reserve lending goes to various activities, such as capital spending, consumer spending, public infrastructure, or leveraged buyouts and mergers. Clear reporting would reveal, for instance, how much of the money the Fed permits banks to create goes into real estate loans (fueling a housing bubble) versus rebuilding crumbling infrastructure (such as the inadequate levees in and around New Orleans)—and these figures in themselves would represent critiques of what the system is doing. Their publication and dissemination would put pressure on the Fed to adjust its operations so as to better serve the public interest and would help lawmakers to shape good public policy.

Passage of the Monetary Transparency Act would represent a significant step toward a more transparent Federal Reserve. And only with a more transparent Fed will activists be able to initiate a genuine, well-informed public debate on monetary policy in the United States.

# MONEY SUPPLY

**BY ELLEN FRANK**

*September/October 2005*

Dear Dr. Dollar:

Of all the mysteries of economics, the one I find the most obscure is the money supply. I know that commercial banks increase the money supply by lending more money than they actually have on hand, but I also hear people worry that the government will cover its deficits by "printing money." Can the government actually do that? When, if ever, is the money supply increased because the government simply prints more of the stuff?

— *Stuart Baker, Tallahassee, Fla.*

Money is whatever a society uses to carry out economic transactions. In the United States, this means cash as well as balances in bank accounts which can be accessed with checks or debit cards (called "demand deposits" because the cash is available to the depositor on demand). Whenever a bank books a loan or pays a vendor for a credit card purchase, it creates a demand deposit and so expands the supply of money. However, in all modern capitalist economies, the money-creating activities of private financial firms are overseen by a government or quasi-government institution called a central bank.

It is this central bank—the Federal Reserve in the United States—that actually prints paper money. (Coins are minted by the U.S. Treasury Department.) However, very little of the Fed's activity involves the actual printing of paper currency; the Fed creates money mostly through so-called open market purchases. Here's how this works:

All federally-chartered banks are required to hold a certain percentage of their deposits in *reserve*—i.e., not to lend them out. When the economy grows, households and businesses spend more and borrow more. People withdraw cash from their accounts, leaving banks with fewer reserves. At the same time, banks are making new loans and creating new deposits—and thus need additional cash to hold in reserve in order to maintain the required reserve ratio.

To ensure that banks have adequate reserves to keep the economy running, the Fed will go into the open market and buy Treasury securities that are currently held by financial institutions or by wealthy individuals. (These securities represent the public debt: funds that the U.S. government had borrowed by selling bonds and notes to the public.) To pay for its purchases, the Fed credits the seller with new cash and the seller's bank with new cash reserves.

Open-market purchases can thus be thought of as liquidating the national government's debt. What was once a non-liquid (meaning it couldn't be used to purchase goods) interest-bearing debt of the Treasury is converted to reserves in the banking system. So the government does routinely increase the money supply by "printing more of the stuff," if not literally. And the way the money gets into the hands of the public is by transforming the government's debt (issued to finance deficits) into cash.

Conservatives in the business press indeed agonize constantly over governments irresponsibly "printing money" to cover their debts. If this is what governments do all the time anyway, why the worry? The answer lies in our definition of government. In the United States, there are two public institutions involved in monetary matters: the Treasury department—part of the executive branch, run by political appointees of an elected president and subject to Congress' power of the purse; and the Federal Reserve, which is a network of quasi-private regional banks overseen by a board of governors, few of whom are beholden to sitting politicians since their terms run for 14 years.

In this set-up, the branch of government responsible for deciding when or whether to increase the money supply (the central bank) is separate from and not directly accountable to the branches of government that decide how much to spend and borrow (the president and legislature). Macroeconomic policymaking is thus split between two institutions, one elected and (at least somewhat) accountable to the public, and one unelected and accountable mostly to large financial institutions.

The United States is hardly alone in this bifurcation of economic policy. The European Central Bank, for example, is probably even less accountable to the public than the Fed; the same is true of the central banks of many of the larger developing countries.

The consequences can be best seen in government responses to unemployment and recession. Elected officials may want to borrow to finance public works and social services so as to alleviate poverty and unemployment—without curbing private spending by raising tax collections. If they do not "print money" to cover the resulting deficits, the increased economic activity could use up bank reserves and push up interest rates, stifling further growth.

An accountable central bank would probably be under pressure to liquidate the debt and keep interest rates low. An unaccountable central bank, however, can thwart the government's social spending by refusing to print money, conducting its own countervailing economic policy. While it is true that runaway inflation can result from excessive printing of money—a concern responsible governments must balance against the need to meet compelling social needs—independent central banks, overly obedient to the financial interests of the wealthy, tend to tap the breaks long before that point.

When conservative financial interests decry "printing money" to pay for government spending, they are really troubled by the possibility that the levers of economic policy will be controlled by those who are accountable to the general public rather than those who are accountable to them.

---

# IS THE FED A CONSPIRACY?

**BY ARTHUR MACEWAN**

*March/April 2007*

Dear Dr. Dollar:

Some of my friends believe that the Federal Reserve and international bankers (Rothschilds, Rockefellers, etc.) run the world. They think the Federal Reserve was formed in secret and is pretty much a conspiracy. This is all hooked up with other conspiracy theories and right-wing views that make me uncomfortable.

What do you think? Isn't the banking system part of the whole capitalist system? How does the Federal Reserve work; does it really have so much power?

—*Carol Brown, New York, N.Y.*

The Federal Reserve is a very powerful institution, and the people who run the world's large banks are a very powerful group of people. No one would claim otherwise. Also, the bankers have common interests, and, like any other group of people with common interests, they do what they can to bring about government policies that favor those interests.

Because the Federal Reserve (the "Fed"), as the central bank of the United States, implements policies that most directly affect the bankers, they of course are quite concerned with what the Fed does, how it is structured, and who runs it. And, like other elite groups, bankers certainly meet in private—in "secret," if one prefers—to figure out how best to get what they want.

With all that said, however, the idea that a small cabal of bankers runs the world through the operations of the Fed is wrong on several counts.

First of all, financial operatives are not the only powerful economic group. There are, for example, the people who run the large oil companies, the Silicon Valley operations, and the pharmaceutical firms, to name a few of the currently important capitalist clusters. These other groups have some common interests with the bankers, and they often all work together, both in private and in public, to achieve their common ends; they do not call in the press every time a few of them meet. (A recent example: when Vice President Cheney held a meeting to formulate the Bush administration's energy policy, the list of attendees—widely assumed to be top energy sector executives—was kept secret.) But to boil down this large class of people to a few bankers both distorts reality and obscures the conflicts that sometimes exist among them.

Second, not only are there often differences among these groups, but there are often contradictions between different things that they want. For example, they want a well-trained work force, but they do not want the high taxes that would be needed to pay for that training; they want freedom from government regulations, but they want the economic stability that often depends on government regulation; they want free access to international markets, but they want special preferences (as compared to foreign companies) within the United States; they want to pay low wages, but they want a populace with enough income to buy their products.

Third, while this set of people is undoubtedly very powerful in affecting the operation of our economic lives and in shaping history, they do not shape history just as they please. They simply can't control everything—as the problem that the Fed has with long-term interest rates illustrates (see below). They cannot control the economy just as they would like and they cannot control the rest of us just as they would like. Formal democracy, however limited, is a useful device. The power that the rest of us have can be a substantial constraint on the actions of big business—bankers, energy executives, and all the others.

But let's return to the Fed. What does it do, and how? The Fed has a variety of functions involving regulation of the banking system, including influencing the amount of money in circulation and interest rates (the price people pay to use other people's money). Of special importance, the Fed can influence the amount of loans that banks issue. When a bank issues a loan, this creates more spending power. This spending power (usually in the form of increasing the amount in the borrower's checking account) is the same thing as more money in circulation. So by influencing banks' loan actions, the Fed influences the money supply.

Right-wingers who view the Fed and the banks as an evil cabal tend to claim that by allowing banks to increase the money supply, the Fed is debasing our currency. The increased money supply lowers the value of money in relation to other goods, and the money prices of other goods rise—i.e., inflation. Moreover, they view this as a way of allowing the government to engage in excessive spending: the government can borrow from the public, but then, because of inflation, can repay in dollars that have less worth.

This fascination of some right-wingers with inflation and the debasement of the currency is ironic because, in fact, the Fed often (although not always) acts in exactly the opposite manner—*limiting* the growth of the money supply and *restricting* inflation. Banks, and businesses generally, like stable prices and stable interest rates. One reason is that a low-inflation policy keeps unemployment rates higher than they otherwise would be, weakening the bargaining power of workers and shifting the distribution of income in favor of capitalists.

A further irony: the Fed is not as powerful as either its proponents or its critics think. The Fed really has control only over short-term interest rates. Long-term interest rates, however, are more important (as they affect major investment decisions) and are influenced by many forces beyond the Fed's control. The expectations of business about future ups and downs of the economy—and about the myriad events that affect those fluctuations—are the central factors determining long-term interest rates. Neither capitalists' behavior nor capitalist economies are so easily controlled. If they were, then there would never be any stock market crashes, burst financial bubbles, or other serious disruptions.

By the way, the Fed was not formed in secret. The Fed was created by legislative action, formally and publicly. But there were certainly private (secret) meetings that laid the groundwork for it. Of course, the same is true of legislative actions affecting the pharmaceutical industry, Silicon Valley, insurance firms, and the list goes on. Nothing that special about the creation of the Fed.

Finally, while I am sure that there are many decent people who see the Fed and the bankers as the source of the world's problems, this view is often part of a larger anti-Semitism. The focus on "Jewish financiers" (the Rothschilds, for example) as the source of our economic and other problems is as old as it is wrong and offensive.

Chapter 2

# THE BANKING AND FINANCE INDUSTRY

## THE U.S. BANKING INDUSTRY IN TRANSITION

**BY WILLIAM K. BLACK**
*November/December 2007*

The U.S. financial system is, once again, in crisis. Or, more precisely, twin crises—first, huge numbers of defaults among subprime mortgage borrowers, and second, massive losses for the holders of new-fangled investments comprised of bundles of loans of varying risk, including many of those subprime mortgages.

These crises should shock the nation. Our largest, most sophisticated financial institutions have followed business practices that were certain to produce massive losses—practices so imprudent, in precisely the business task, risk management,that is supposed to be their greatest expertise, that they have created a worldwide financial crisis.

Why? Because their CEOs, acting on the perverse incentives created by today's outrageous compensation systems, engaged in practices that vastly increased their corporations' risk in order to drive up reported corporate income and thereby secure enormous increases in their own individual incomes. And those perverse incentives follow them out the door: CEOs Charles Prince, at Citicorp, and Stanley O'Neal, at Merrill Lynch, had dismal track records of similar failures prior to the latest disasters, but they collected massive bonuses for their earlier failures and will receive obscene termination packages now. Pay and productivity (and integrity) have become unhinged at U.S. financial institutions.

As this goes to print, Treasury Department officials are working with large financial institutions to cover up the scale of the growing losses. This is the same U.S. Treasury that regularly prates abroad about the vital need for transparency. And a former Treasury Secretary, Robert Rubin, who failed utterly in his fiduciary duty as lead board member at Citicorp to prevent the series of recent abuses, will become Citicorp's new CEO.

To even begin to understand events in the U.S. and global banking industries, you have to look back at the seismic shifts in the industry over the past 30 to 40 years and at the interplay between those shifts and government policy. The story that continues to unfold is one of progressively worse policies that make financial crises more common and more severe.

These policies have their boosters, though. Chief among them are neoclassical banking and finance economists, whose ideology and methodologies lead them into blatant misreadings of the realities of the industry and the causes of its failures. When the history of this crisis-ridden era in global finance is written, the economists will no doubt be given a significant share of the blame.

# I. The U.S. Banking Industry from the 1950s to the 2000s: Vast Transformation

Here is a snapshot of the banking industry fifty years ago. Banks were of two distinct types: commercial banks, which made loans to businesses, and thrifts, for instance savings and loans (S&Ls), which specialized in home mortgage lending. Computers were new and not widely used. Banks were generally limited to operat-

### *THEY JUST NEVER LEARN*

Today's financial crisis offers a superb example of how their methods lead mainstream economists to endorse both private practices and public policies that are perverse. The current crisis exemplifies a variant of accounting control frauds—one in which the CEO and top managers "skim" rather than loot the company—and demonstrates the unrecognized economic costs of obscenely high CEO pay. The incentives created by typical CEO compensation packages in the financial services industry produce bad investment decisions, decisions that increase the CEO's ability to skim, but that expose the financial institution to losses and the nation and world to recurrent financial crises.

Consider the plight of the honest chief financial officer (CFO) in the modern financial world. His counterparts at rival firms are earning record returns by investing in subprime mortgages. Economists trumpet studies showing that banks' income is boosted by practices he questions, including:

- Making more subprime mortgages
- Making more of the worst mortgages such as "Ninja" loans (no verification of income, job or assets), also known as "liars' loans"
- Making subprime loans at particularly high interest rates—which draws in the riskiest borrowers because only the worst credit risks and frauds will apply
- Making loans as quickly as possible
- Growing as quickly as possible
- Reducing internal controls against fraud
- Making loans in cities known to be "hot spots" for mortgage fraud
- Qualifying borrowers by offering "teaser" interest rates that will soon increase substantially
- Making loans in areas with rapidly inflation housing bubbles

ing in a single state; the restrictions on interstate banking helped create a situation in which there were over 20,000 banks in the United States, many of them small. Bank concentration (market power) existed in many rural areas and small towns, but was unusual in medium-sized and large cities.

Banks were generally the only entities permitted to issue checks. Credit cards were introduced in 1951 but did not become common for almost two decades. Checks could take weeks to "clear." Banks often deliberately increased check processing times by using remote centers so that they could profit from the "float" by investing the funds at a profit during the time the funds were unavailable to either the check's recipient or its sender.

Bank failures were rare. There was a consensus—even Milton Friedman agreed—that federal deposit insurance had been a great success, ending the devastating runs on banks that had been a defining element of the Great Depression. Unlike commercial banks, investment banks, which take an ownership interest in the entities they fund, were not insured and were generally unregulated. The Depression-era Glass-Steagall Act required the separation of investment banks from com-

- Purchasing and holding in portfolio high-yield CDOs (collateralized debt obligations, the investment instruments backed by bundles of mortgages and other loans, often of high risk)
- Keeping minimal reserves against losses

When a housing bubble is expanding, these practices dramatically increase fees and other noninterest income, minimize expenses, and produce relatively few losses. (Losses remain low as long as house prices are rising because borrowers who get in trouble can sell their house for more than they owe or else refinance based on its market value.) Note that this pretty income picture requires accounting and securities fraud, though: reserving properly for the future losses inherent in subjecting the financial institution to this vastly increased default risk would remove the fictional accounting gain.

The combination of dramatically increased revenue, moderately reduced expenses, and minimal loss means that financial institutions that invest heavily in subprime mortgages and CDOs must report record profits while the bubble is hyperinflating.

So what is our honest CFO to do? If she does not follow the pack, her company will report substantially lower income. Its stock price will fall relative to its rivals. The CEO's and CFO's compensation and wealth will fall sharply as raises disappear, bonuses decline, and the value of their shares and stock options falls. The CFO may be fired.

The upshot is that modern compensation systems and the short-term perspective of investors and senior managers all result in perverse incentives to make grossly imprudent investments in those assets experiencing the worst bubbles. This creates a destructive cycle in which large numbers of financial institutions follow the same dysfunctional strategy, which in turn extends and inflates the bubble and produces even more accounting control frauds.

mercial banks, which were not allowed to take an equity position in the clients they made loans to. The two kinds of institutions were not allowed to own each other or be affiliates. Glass-Steagall was designed to prevent the conflicts of interest that joint ownership creates and which congressional investigations found to have contributed to the Great Depression.

Limited competition was one key to the era. The federal government regulated the interest rates banks could pay on deposit, preventing competition. This meant that depositors received lower interest rates and that borrowers paid higher interest rates than would be true with greater competition. This made for a golden era for banks, which enjoyed high profits.

Government regulation of the banking business was a patchwork. The Federal Home Loan Bank Board ("the Bank Board") regulated most S&Ls. The FDIC regulated state-chartered S&Ls that were not members of the Federal Reserve System. The Office of the Comptroller of the Currency regulated national banks. The Board of Governors of the Federal Reserve System ("the Fed") regulated bank holding companies and state-chartered banks that were members of the Federal Reserve system. The National Credit Union Administration regulated and insured credit unions. The Securities and Exchange Commission regulated the securities filings of bank and S&L holding companies, but the Bank Board regulated securities filings of publicly traded S&Ls. This combination of state-level chartering and federal insurance was known as the "dual" banking system. The resulting mishmash at times produced confusion, increased costs, and led to inconsistent regulation.

Large corporations sometimes borrowed funds by selling short-term bonds to wealthy individuals, but commercial banks were overwhelmingly the dominant lender to corporations. A few longer-term junk bonds (debt that is either unrated or rated below "investment grade" by credit rating agencies such as Standard & Poors) existed, but they were "fallen angels"—bonds that were originally issued as investment grade and then lost their favorable ratings because of business problems. Original-issue junk bonds did not exist, so commercial banks generally did not face competition from corporations selling them in order to raise long-term funds directly from investors.

Commercial banks loaned overwhelmingly to businesses, rarely to individuals. U.S. corporations borrowed far less in this era, however, than they do now, reducing opportunities for U.S. banks to lend. Still, the combination of government regulation that limited competition on deposit interest rates, limited competition from other lenders, and prosperous, conservative borrowers led to healthy bank profits.

Thrifts (home lenders, S&Ls, and savings banks) also found this to be a golden era. The Great Depression and World War II caused a severe housing deficit. The return of the troops and of prosperity produced sharp upticks in marriages, births (the baby boom), income, and demand for new housing. Affordable Veterans Administration mortgages, the creation of the interstate highway system, and the growing importance of the home mortgage interest and property tax deductions led to the rise of the suburbs and spurred mobility. The G.I. Bill allowed millions to take advantage of postwar prosperity and join the middle class; owning a single-family home was an essential marker of this newfound status. Collectively, these factors produced a sustained housing boom.

This was the era when the long-term, 30-year fixed-rate home mortgage became standard. Mortgage default rates were generally minuscule. The sustained housing boom, limits on the interest rates paid to depositors, and the low mortgage default rate combined to produce broad profitability, and thrift failures were rare. Thrifts held onto the mortgages they originated, only rarely selling them in the so-called secondary market.

This was not, however, a golden era for all financial-services consumers. Discrimination was the norm. Minorities were generally unwelcome in banks and discriminated against at thrifts. Housing segregation was deeply institutionalized. By expressly treating integrated neighborhoods as unduly risky for home loans, the Federal Housing Administration endorsed redlining and created strong incentives for lenders to discriminate. Restrictive covenants banning the sale of homes to minorities were common and were not struck down by the Supreme Court until 1948. Decades later, real estate brokers were still routinely steering homebuyers to areas in which their race predominated. Discrimination against women, whether married or unmarried, was nearly universal. Women's incomes were routinely ignored in evaluating a household's creditworthiness. Women could generally borrow only if a man co-signed the loan. Minority-owned banks were rare. Subprime loans and second mortgages (i.e., home-equity loans) were also rare. Credit was not merely more expensive for minorities and women—it was commonly unavailable.

## Banking Today: An Altered Universe

> Imagine that a banker, economist or policy-maker had been away from civilization for the last fifteen years or so and finally returned. Would he recognize the financial industry that he saw?
>
> —*(Borio and Filosa, 1994)*

Fast forward to the new century. Banks now loan to people, while businesses do much of their borrowing outside of banks. The traditional line between banks and thrifts has blurred; at the same time new kinds of financial-services companies have sprung up. Credit cards are ubiquitous. Large banks have branches in all 50 states.

Banking is heavily computerized. The processing of checks has been greatly speeded up, and federal regulations now require that most checks be paid promptly. Banks, therefore, have reduced profits from float and face increased risk from check frauds.

Over two decades of intense merger and acquisition activity has left a far smaller number of banks, with assets far more concentrated in the largest ones. Between 1984 and 2004, the number of banks on the FDIC's rolls fell from 14,392 to 7,511. While bank failures played a relatively small role in this drop, failures did play a significant role in cutting the number of federally insured thrifts from 3,626 to 1,305 over the same period. The share of the U.S. banking industry's assets held by the ten largest banks rose from 21% in 1960 to nearly 60% in 2005.

Among the factors spurring the high volume of mergers and acquisitions—

and also the historically high number of bank and thrift failures, as we will see—has been the steady deregulation of the industry. For instance, among the regulations modified over the period were the restrictions on banks' geographic expansion across state lines. Laws from 1927 and 1956 had restricted banks from opening branches in other states and bank holding corporations from creating banking subsidiaries in multiple states, respectively. But a few states began allowing the entry of out-of-state banks in the late 1970s; by the mid-1990s most states did so. The 1994 Riegle–Neal Act then overrode all remaining restrictions on interstate banking.

While a number of the regulations contained in the Depression-era Glass-Steagall Act had already been relaxed, its final repeal occurred with the passage of the Gramm-Leach-Bliley Financial Services Modernization Act in 1999, which removed

### *DEPOSIT INSURANCE SPREADS DESPITE ECONOMISTS' PROTESTS*

Banking economists now overwhelmingly criticize deposit insurance. This represents a major change. The prior consensus, shared by Milton Friedman and John Kenneth Galbraith alike, praised deposit insurance for ending the periodic runs on uninsured banks that helped cause the Great Depression. Today, however, the conventional economic wisdom is that deposit insurance may stop runs, but at the expense of encouraging banks to make imprudent loans and take excessive risks. (Neoclassical economists widely view insurance as inherently creating an incentive for insured parties to act in unduly risky ways because of the safety net that insurance provides—a phenomenon termed "moral hazard.")

This claim is dubious: economists do not offer a credible mechanism whereby deposit insurance could lead to the ills they claim it causes. Deposit insurance does not protect the shareholders or the CEO—the two groups (the first, in theory; the second, in practice) that control a bank. It is the depositors who are insured. Thus, they must be the ones who are subject to moral hazard—in other words, the argument against deposit insurance must be based on the claim that it reduces the incentive of depositors to exercise "private market discipline" by pulling their money out of a bank they believe is being poorly run or looted. But there is no credible evidence that depositors are capable of either discerning frauds or avoiding runs on healthy banks based on false rumors. Indeed, studies have shown that even private-sector financial experts who specialize in evaluating the health of banks cannot do so effectively.

Proponents of the view that deposit insurance causes banking failures display an unrecognized logical inconsistency. Their proposed reform is to rely on private market discipline to prevent management from looting the bank or lending imprudently in a bubble. But, if we assume hypothetically that private market discipline is effective against CEOs who would be so inclined, then it should normally be effective despite the presence of deposit insurance. Deposit insurance does not remove private market discipline where the bank is owned by shareholders (unless the CEO owns all the stock) or where the bank issues uninsured subordinated debt. Yet during the S&L crisis, control fraud (the looting of an institution by its own managers or owners) was most common in S&Ls owned in stock form, with the largest losses overwhelmingly among stock S&Ls. In these cases deposit the remaining legal barriers to combining commercial banking, investment banking, and insurance under one corporate roof. The new world of combined financial services is exemplified by the deal, inked (but ostensibly illegal) before the 1999 law was passed, that merged the insurance and investment banking giant Travelers with Citibank, at the time the nation's #1 commercial bank.

Banks now have to compete with many other sources of credit. Investment banks, hedge funds, venture capital funds, and foreign banks and non-bank lenders are all potential sources of business funds. On the consumer credit side, payday lenders, pawn shops, and check cashing businesses all compete with banks. While banks still dominate the credit card market, large retailers continue to look for ways to expand their own consumer credit offerings at the banks' expense.

insurance did not preclude private market discipline; market discipline was simply inadequate to prevent control fraud. Some opponents of deposit insurance proclaim the S&L debacle to be their primary example—a flat misreading of the facts.

The empirical evidence economists use to support their critique of deposit insurance is inconsistent. Moreover, even where the adoption of deposit insurance is correlated with a rise in bank failures, the causal relationship may be just the opposite of what economists claim. Nations with early signs of an impending banking crisis may adopt deposit insurance to reduce the risks of runs. Developing nations tend to adopt deposit insurance in conjunction with privatization—which itself often prompts a banking crisis. More broadly, in part because of the fall of the Soviet Union and the rise of the neoliberal "Washington Consensus," the number of nations adopting deposit insurance increased sharply in the last two decades. Banking crises have indeed been far more common over this same period—precisely because these radical transitions have been occurring in nations with weak institutions, too few regulators with too little experience, patterns of bank ownership that maximize conflicts of interest, and substantial corruption.

In addition, empirical studies rely on subjective coding of different countries' deposit insurance policies, often done by economists who oppose deposit insurance. In countries with no formal deposit insurance, implicit government guarantees for banks are common. There are good theoretical and historical reasons to argue that such implicit guarantees—common in crony capitalism and kleptocracies—create greater moral hazard than explicit deposit insurance does because they can be structured to bail out a bank's shareholders and CEO as well as its creditors (as was done in Chile). But there is no way to code accurately for whether there was an implicit guarantee (or whether bank CEOs believed there was an implicit guarantee) in a particular country at a particular time.

Despite these weaknesses in both evidence and analysis, World Bank economists draw firm conclusions, opposing the adoption of deposit insurance in any nation and clearly hoping for its elimination. But the world has rejected their advice. By 2006, 95 countries had deposit insurance, over four times the number in 1983. Moreover, economists' suggestions on how to "improve" deposit insurance (require banks to issue subordinated debt, charge variable rates for deposit insurance, or require private insurance of accounts) are rarely adopted and have proven unsuccessful in practice.

What the United States still does not have as a competitor for small consumer loans is a strong microcredit banking sector. The country has a micro microcredit sector, and there are few signs of potential expansion in the near or intermediate term.

Mortgage lending has been transformed on many levels. For one thing, S&Ls, which used to issue nearly all mortgages, have been joined by commercial banks and non-bank home loan companies in the mortgage sector. Home mortgage lenders no longer typically hold a mortgage for its duration. Instead, they sell it, often to Freddie Mac, Fannie Mae, or Ginnie Mae, the massive quasi-governmental organizations that buy mortgages and package them as collateral for bonds called "mortgage backed securities" (MBS) that they in turn resell. The MBS market is enormous, with over $4.5 *trillion* outstanding. Both Freddie Mac and Fannie Mae have recently engaged in accounting abuses that raised questions but are not believed to seriously threaten their financial health.

Mortgage products have changed in ways both desirable and dubious. Although 30-year fixed-rate mortgages are still the norm, adjustable rate mortgages (ARMs) have become widespread. Then there are the newer mortgage products that are generating the most concern and controversy, including subprime loans and various no- or even negative-amortization loans.

Subprime loans, those designed for borrowers whose low incomes and/or poor credit histories would disqualify them for a standard loan, bear a higher interest rate. Some subprime loans are "interest-only" or "negative-amortization" loans, which set a low monthly payment level that does not pay down the loan principal at all. This allows homebuyers to qualify for a bigger loan than they otherwise would. And sometimes lenders qualify lower-income borrowers by starting loans out at a very low initial ("teaser") interest rate which then jumps up. Each of these loans offers greater affordability at the beginning, but at the cost of greater risk down the road: risk that interest rates and therefore monthly payments will rise sharply; risk that a borrower will be unable to sell or refinance the house when the time comes to pay the principal.

Proponents argue that these new mortgage products represent a major advance because they open up homeownership opportunities for those previously excluded. But critics suggest several problems. One is that in markets with sharply rising home prices, some subprime lenders are alleged to make loans to borrowers they know are likely to default so that the lender can acquire the home through foreclosure and profit on its resale. Another is that these loans are riskier for both lender and borrower, prompting concern that an economic downturn could cause a surge of failures—a fear now to some extent being realized.

Rival savings and investment opportunities have proliferated since the 1970s. At that time, market interest rates were rising, but government controls kept the interest rates banks and thrifts paid to depositors low. This made uninsured money market funds, which were not subject to interest rate controls, particularly attractive for middle-class savers.

Discrimination against minorities in the provision of credit and other financial services is far less severe than it was 50 years ago; the same is true for women. The United States now has very strong anti-discrimination laws relative to other nations, along with some regulatory structures designed to enforce them. However, studies continue to show discrimination in lending. For example, black and Latino mortgage applicants are more likely to get high-cost subprime loans or else be turned down entirely than white applicants with equivalent credit qualifications. Some apparently neutral credit screens, such as whether a borrower has a high credit score or has had a credit card for two years will, in practice, disproportionately exclude black applicants. World Savings of Oakland, Calif., found that using an alternative credit screening device of checking whether the borrower had a good record of paying utility bills on time worked well and did not exclude nearly as many black borrowers.

Estimates put the number of people with no relationship to banks or other mainstream financial-services institutions at 50 million or more. Poor Americans—disproportionately minorities—end up paying grossly higher interest rates to payday lenders, pawn shops, check cashing services, and rent-to-own outfits, in some cases because banks locate fewer branches in low-income neighborhoods. This represents an immense banking failure. U.S. banks could undercut these competitors and make greater profits, but generally fail to do so—in some cases because the banks themselves own or fund the fringe lenders.

All in all, banking has entered a new world, one with a proliferation of players and products, expanded opportunities in some respects for lenders, borrowers, savers, and investors, and heightened risk throughout the sector.

## II. Misinterpreting Crisis, Facilitating Fraud: Banking Economics in the New Era

The transformational changes in domestic banking outlined above, along with the related effects of economic globalization both in the United States and abroad, have produced recurrent crises in the financial sector. Indeed, the current era has seen over 100 major banking crises, in countries around the globe. Thomas Hoenig, head of the Kansas City Federal Reserve Bank, emphasized the remarkable and disturbing facts in a meeting with fellow heads of supervision:

> A 1996 survey by the IMF [International Monetary Fund] … found that 73 percent [133 of 181] of their member countries had experienced significant banking problems during the preceding 15 years. Many of these problems led to substantial declines in GDP [and] serious disruptions in credit and capital markets … .

To date none of these crises has led to a global Great Depression. Only a few were larger in absolute terms than the 1980s S&L debacle in the United States. Yet many imposed a much greater relative cost, measured as a percentage of the country's GDP. Some caused severe, depression-like economic problems in the affected nation. Some produced contagion effects that caused severe crises in other nations. And acute banking crises can cause long-term harm. Japan is a rich nation and can afford a 15-year banking crisis—but the world economy cannot. The crisis cut Japan's economic growth to near-zero for a decade, in turn creating contagion effects in the many countries for whom Japan was a major trading partner or a significant source of capital investment. Tens of millions of people remain in poverty in Asia and Africa as a result.

The recurrent banking crises have come as a shock to the United States, given the dearth of bank failures over the first three decades after World War II. The first severe postwar U.S. banking crisis was stemmed from the large loans that top U.S. banks made to sovereign borrowers (i.e., nations), largely in Latin America. The banks had claimed that sovereign loans offered high returns with minimal default risk because the nation could always repay the loan by printing more money. Citibank head Walter Wriston notoriously implied that countries could not go broke. The claim was absurd. However, banking regulators took no effective action to restrain this lending.

The 1982 Mexican default led to contagion and fears of an international meltdown, but the Federal Reserve and the Bank for International Settlements (BIS) took effective action. Brazil experienced a long economic slowdown that contributed to an imminent default on its loans from major U.S. banks. A Brazilian default could have rendered several of our largest banks insolvent. The banks were rescued by a combination of bailouts to Brazil through the IMF and the World Bank and flawed (albeit permissible under so-called Generally Accepted Accounting Principles, or GAAP) "troubled-debt restructuring" to cover up the losses. Brazil used the bailouts to pay minimal interest on the U.S. bank loans and ultimately recovered; while several U.S. banks took serious losses, none failed.

On the heels of this crisis came the savings and loan crisis, an unprecedented debacle which saw the collapse of some 1,000 S&Ls and which cost U.S. taxpayers about $125 billion dollars—primarily the cost of repaying to depositors money that criminal S&L heads had literally stolen from their institutions.

The causes of these crises are varied. They typically occur, however, when large banks are in essence looted by their owners and managers (a phenomenon known as "control fraud") or when there are financial bubbles in which assets become massively overvalued.

Economists who conduct case studies of banking crises commonly report the existence of substantial control fraud. Looting played a prominent role in the S&L debacle. Here is the conclusion of the National Commission on Financial Institution Reform, Recovery and Enforcement (NCFIRRE):

> The typical large failure was a stockholder-owned, state-chartered institution in Texas or California where regulation and supervision were most lax .... The failed institution typically had experienced a change of control and was tightly held, dominated by an individual with substantial conflicts of interest.... In the typical large failure, every accounting trick available was used to make the institution look profitable, safe, and solvent. Evidence of fraud was invariably present as was the ability of the operators to "milk" the organization through high dividends and salaries, bonuses, perks and other means. In short, the typical large failure was one in which management exploited virtually all the perverse incentives created by government policy.

### *OFFSHORE BANKS*

One particularly dark side of globalization is the rise of new offshore banks. While Switzerland now has reasonably workable procedures for tracking the funds of kleptocrats and drug traffickers, several small nations have adopted extreme forms of bank secrecy designed to cater to the needs of criminals and tax evaders. Corporations often incorporate in a tax haven because of the extremely low tax rates. In the late 1990s, the Organisation for Economic Co-operation and Development, an organization of the world's industrialized countries, created an initiative to try to curtail these abuses. Conservative think tanks sought to kill the OECD plan and convinced President Bush to block its implementation as one of his earliest actions. The administration reduced its opposition to the OECD initiative after the 9/11 attacks, when it became clear that terrorists used the offshore banks as their preferred means to move funds.

Looting has played a significant role in banking crises around the world. It became so prevalent in the states of the former Soviet Union that it inspired a new term of art, "tunneling," to describe the process of the CEO and owners converting a company's funds to their private benefit.

In addition to the national banking crises, fraud has caused spectacular failures of large banks. The Bank for Credit and Commerce International (BCCI—known informally as the "Bank for Crooks and Criminals International"), Barings Bank, and Continental Bank all stunned the public when they failed. BCCI was the largest bank in the developing world, Barings was England's oldest bank, and Continental was America's third largest bank. Each one collapsed with minimal public warning.

And, of course, more recently control fraud played a role in a number of spectacular business failures outside of the banking industry including Enron, WorldCom, and Tyco. This fact makes it obvious that the conventional economic wisdom, which blames this era's wave of bank failures and banking crises on regulation and deposit insurance (which are specific to the banking industry) is just wrong. Despite this, mainstream economists persist in their diagnosis, rarely scrutinizing the deregulation and privatization that many observers believe in fact triggered these crises.

## ...They First Make Proud

Economists have dominated the creation of public policies to prevent banking crises. Their track record has been abysmal. They designed and implemented the disastrous deregulation that produced the U.S. S&L debacle, they praised Japan's and East Asia's banking structures just before they collapsed, and they designed the IMF's crisis intervention strategy that intensified losses and human misery. They also designed and praised privatization programs in many transition economies that led to banking crises; they planned (and in some cases profited from) the catastrophic failure of "shock therapy" in Russia. The irony is that when financial experts were most confident in their consensus, they erred the most grievously. As Mark Twain remarked: "It's not the things you *don't* know that cause disasters; it's the things you *do* know, *but aren't true.*"

This record of failure is disappointing and has caused great human suffering. Remarkably, the economists' hubris is unaffected by it. They are now engaged in a war against deposit insurance and regulation. At this juncture, they are losing that war, but they are persevering in their effort to reclaim their domination over banking policy.

Neoclassical banking economists are failing in this arena for three reasons. First, they neither study nor understand fraud mechanisms and the institutions that are essential to limit fraud and corruption. Second, they are shackled by an ideology that *presumes* that unfettered markets always produce the best outcomes and that government intervention is always bad. For instance, in their writings many of the World Bank's banking economists display a passionate contempt for democratic government and banking regulators. Third, they are mono-disciplinary. They rarely cite (and no doubt rarely examine) the literature in other relevant fields such as political science, sociology, and white-collar criminology.

Indeed, although it should be central to their study of crisis prevention, they rarely even cite the work of economist and 2001 Nobel Prize winner George Akerlof. Based on their study of the S&L crisis, which found that looting was a major cause of total S&L losses, Akerlof and Paul Romer developed an economic model of the looting control fraud.

Looters use accounting fraud to make a company *appear* extraordinarily profitable. Consider the S&L crisis. The worst S&L control frauds were the ones reporting the highest profitability. Moreover, the control frauds were routinely able to get a Big 8 audit firm to give them "clean" GAAP (or Generally Accepted Accounting Principles, the official standard of review in the U.S. accounting industry) opinions for false financial statements.

Economists, in turn, relied on *reported* accounting profits and share prices (which rose along with reported profits) to determine whether a given S&L was well run. But relying on reported accounting earnings or stock prices *must* lead to perverse results when a wave of looting control frauds is expanding. Thanks to their fraudulent accounting, whatever strategies control frauds follow will look profitable, and hence praiseworthy. In the S&Ls, this led economists to praise (1) domination by an owner/CEO; (2) extremely rapid growth; (3) changes of control; and (4) large investments in acquisition, development, and contruction (ADC) loans and direct investments. Lo and behold, these factors turned out to characterize the worst failures. In other words, standard econometrics techniques led economists to praise that which was fraudulent and fatal. The error was so great that they identified the worst S&L in the nation as the best.

Worse, economists persist in the same error. During the recent expansion of the even larger wave of looting control frauds such as Enron, economists touted (1) conflicts of interest at the top audit firms (which they euphemistically restyled as "synergies"); (2) using a top-tier auditor; (3) rapid growth; and (4) granting the CEO greater stock options as positive factors that were leading to increased profits and higher share prices. It was only after the looters began to collapse that variables like these reversed their sign (from a positive to a negative correlation) and displayed their true relationship to business failure. Economists are doomed to repeat these mistakes until they adopt statistical techniques that cannot be gamed by accounting fraud.

## The Economists' War against Banking Regulation

In keeping with their skewed analysis of the recent wave of bank failures and banking crises, banking economists, including those at the World Bank and the IMF, have been waging a war against banking regulation. It is a curious assault that rests on implicit and false dichotomies between market and regulation and between types of regulation.

The World Bank economists recognize that regulation is vital to mandate accurate disclosure of corporate financial information and aid private market enforcement, but appear to believe that regulatory strength is unnecessary to induce banks to provide accurate information. That view is illogical and incorrect. Obtaining accurate information about banks is the heart of banking examination. Regulators use their powers primarily to pry out accurate information from the fraudulent; control frauds do not cooperate voluntarily.

Economists' rationale for opposing strong banking regulators typically rests on public choice theory, which holds that the actors in political systems act to maximize their own self-interest. This analysis paints politicians as corrupt and regulators as "captured" by the industries they are supposed to be regulating. World Bank economist Thorsten Beck and his colleagues summed up this view in 2003 and 2006 working papers:

> Politicians may induce banks to divert the flow of credit to politically connected firms, or powerful banks may "capture" politicians and induce official supervisors to act in the best interest of banks...
>
> Government solutions to overcome market failures ... have been proven wrong in Bangladesh as across the developed and developing world. ... Indeed, powerful regulators are worse than futile—they are corrupt and harmful.

Again, this analysis is nonsensical. If banks can dominate politicians and strong regulators, they can certainly dominate the design of the disclosure standards they face. In that case, pursuant to the economists' own logic, the banks will submit, and politicians beholden to them will permit, deceptive financial reports that grossly overstate banks' value. (This has, in fact, been done in many cases.) Accounting fraud, in turn, renders markets deeply inefficient and causes private market discipline to become perverse. The looters report record profits. Credit is supposed to flow to the most profitable banks. So private markets *aid* the CEOs looting their banks by providing them with the funds to expand rapidly. Again, the failure to understand bank accounting fraud mechanisms, which have been well explained by Akerlof and his colleague Paul Romer, leads to a deeply flawed analysis. (In lieu of Akerlof and Romer, the anti-regulation economists frequently cite work sponsored by Michael Milken's institute. Milken was the notorious junk-bond king and looter who caused large losses during the S&L crisis by recruiting and funding several of the worst control frauds, such as Charles Keating. Today, Milken's institute blames the S&L debacle on regulation and seeks to rehabilitate his reputation.)

This overarching logical error, their hostility to democracy, and their view of public officials as inevitably rapacious leads economists to a claim that only *private* parties should exert discipline against banks. The view has a number of problems. First, it is overstated. Regulators in some nations do resist political pressure. In the S&L crisis, many regulators did their job despite intense political pressure and saved over a trillion dollars in the process. On the other hand: if, over time, people are taught to believe that it is normal and rational for public officials to be rapacious, this can become a self-fulfilling prophecy as those who aim to enrich themselves sign on to become officials.

Moreover, the argument proves too much. If the banks (or politicians) are powerful enough to act illegitimately *through* regulators, they are powerful enough to act illegitimately *without* regulators to achieve the same result. The argument is also based on a fundamental misunderstanding of control frauds. It is not the "powerful banks" Beck and his coauthors refer to that put pressure on regulators or politicians—it is the CEOs or their agents who do. They do not coerce regulators "to act in the best interest of banks." They coerce them in an attempt to act to help the CEO loot the bank.

In fact, the evidence shows that private parties are *more* subject to capture than public officials. Looting control frauds are routinely able to get top-tier audit firms to give their blessing to massive accounting fraud. The ratings agencies do no better against control fraud. Our most prestigious law firms have helped CEOs loot and destroy their clients. Private deposit insurance funds for thrifts used to exist in many states. None do now. The Maryland, Ohio, and Utah funds were each destroyed by the very first thrift that collapsed in their state thanks to control fraud. No private insurer made more than a feeble effort to exercise discipline. Instead, they acted as boosters for the CEOs who looted and destroyed their own thrifts and brought down the insurance funds with them.

Finally, the empirical studies on banking regulation rely on coding of data by economists who typically oppose regulation, rendering the results unreliable. The risks of subjective bias are acute. There is no objective measure of "strong" regulation, or capture, or "rent seeking behavior." We know that economists have claimed that the Bank Board under Chairman Edwin Gray was captured during the S&L crisis. Not so. In fact, *private* experts were routinely captured by the S&L control frauds. Plus, the studies focus on formal supervisory power, yet informal banking supervision is widespread and often a regulator's most effective tool.

Overall, empirical studies find that better quality regulation (again, to be fair, a subjective concept) reduces banking losses.

## International Convergence

Despite the flawed logic and lack of empirical support for their views, conventional banking economists, including those at the World Bank, continue to voice opposition to the creation of strong supervisory agencies. For now, however, their call has been rejected.

In the 1980s, the U.S. government reacted to Japan's emergence as the new (apparent) dominant financial power by claiming that Japan gained an unfair advantage because its banks were permitted to operate with lower capital reserves. If all other factors are held constant, a bank held to a lower capital reserve requirement can grow more quickly, lend more cheaply, and finance greater economic growth. Complaining that the playing field was not level, the United States insisted on an international agreement to set minimum bank capital standards. The U.S. effort succeeded in 1988, when the largest industrial nations adopted the Basel Accord. More recently, the accord was revised and expanded ("Basel II") to include more closely calibrated minimum capital requirements as well as a supervisory strategy of "prompt corrective action" against banks that fail to meet the capital requirements and a strategy to make private market discipline more effective by requiring banks to disclose more information.

The Basel Accord was a major step towards greater international uniformity of banking regulation ("convergence") among developed nations. The expansion of the European Union is another major force for convergence, as candidate nations must adopt modern banking laws and regulatory structures meeting the EU's minimum standards.

Banks are also subject to an increasing number of international treaties designed to restrict money laundering and bribery. There are, however, very few enforcement actions or prosecutions, so enforcement does not appear to be effective at this time. In addition, offshore banks remain an enormous loophole limiting the effectiveness of convergence.

New banking crises have diminished substantially in nations complying with the Basel accords. Of course, it is too early to judge whether the Basel process is responsible for this success. However, we do have cross-country evidence showing that weak regulation leads to recurrent waves of control fraud. Tests of Basel's effectiveness by one of the World Bank economists find positive relationships between stronger regulation and bank health. (These tests employed a methodology that posed less risk of subjective bias by the economists conducting the studies, but they remain inherently subjective.)

The economists' frustration, however, is understandable. They are skilled research scientists for whom econometric studies are the epitome of proof. Contrary case studies are mere "anecdotal evidence" that are fully encompassed within their data and, therefore, require no refutation. Moreover, their worldview is shaped by public choice theory. They view banking regulators as corrupt, "rent seeking" parasites who merely pretend to virtue. Alternatively, in their "capture" model, regulators are cowards who roll over to aid the control frauds. They have not been banking regulators, so they are uncontaminated and can see the truth as the empirical data reveal it to them.

Regulators, however, dominate much of the Basel process. They view the economists' disdain as an inaccurate and insulting caricature that indicates their ignorance of the real-world banking business. Regulators tend to believe in their experiences, which overwhelmingly teach that control frauds exploit regulatory weaknesses and that normally honest, sober bankers act like frat boys on spring break during financial bubbles. Imprudent lending is the norm in bubbles. Regulators have seen many econometric "proofs" of propositions they know to be false from experience. Some of them have a reasonably sophisticated understanding of the illusion of precision in empirical work and the many opportunities for subjective coding to lead even the best scholars into error. To date, the regulators have staved off the economists' war against banking regulation, and even the World Bank's economists have had to concede that the *initial* results of the Basel process are extremely positive.

Basel II does have a worrying component. It encourages the large banks to value their assets (which implicitly means evaluating their risk) using their own proprietary models. It is easy for these models to be designed so as to dramatically overstate asset values. The problem is compounded by the nature of proprietary models: they are secret, complex, and (perhaps) subject to frequent adjustment. That makes them a nightmare to try to regulate. And in what is essentially a form of control fraud, modern compensation systems, especially in the United States, create powerful incentives for top managers to overstate banks' asset values in order to puff up their own pay packages. Such abuse is so common that instead of "mark to market," the usual term for bringing the valuation of an asset into line with its market price, the process is often known to insiders as "mark to myth."

In the United States, the word "deregulation" still has a positive ring for many despite the disastrous results of this country's experiment in loosening the reins on the banking industry. So perhaps it is ironic that it was the United States that instigated an international effort to develop convergent banking regulations worldwide. International convergence is moving forward, and for now the pace of new financial crises has slowed. The Basel process is indeed leveling the playing field among financial services companies around the world. But what kind of field will emerge? Does the Basel process offer any hope of reshaping the new world of banking into one that better meets consumer needs and better serves the broader public interest? If the banking economists, with their ideological commitment to oppose any regulation, are kept at bay, then at least we may find out.

*Resources:* C.E.V Borio and R. Filosa, "The Changing Borders of Banking: Trends and Implications," BIS Working Paper 23, 10/94; Ctr for Intl Private Enterprise, "Financial Reform: Paving the Way for Growth and Democracy," *Econ Reform Today,* 1995; J. Bisignano, "Precarious Credit Equilibria: Reflections on the Asian Financial Crisis," BIS Working Papers, 3/99; W. K. Black, *The Best Way to Rob a Bank is to Own One,* 2005; L.J. White, *The S&L Debacle: Public Policy Lessons for Bank and Thrift Regulation,* 1991; Federal Home Loan Bank Board, *Agenda for Reform: A Report on Deposit Insurance,* 1983; K. Calavita et al., *Big Money Crime: Fraud and Politics in the Savings and Loan Industry,* 1997; W. K. Black et al., "The Savings and Loan Debacle of the 1980's: White-Collar Crime or Risky Business?" *Law & Policy* 17; G. Akerlof and P. M. Romer, "Looting: The Economic Underworld of Bankruptcy for Profit," *Brookings Papers on Econ Activity,* 1993; M. Mayer, *The Greatest-Ever Bank Robbery,* 1990; T. Curry and L. Shibut, "The Cost of the Savings and Loan Crisis: Truth and Consequences," *FDIC Banking Review*, Fall 2000; W. K. Black, "Reexamining the Law-and-Economics Theory of Corporate Governance," *Challenge,* 1993; C-J Lindgren et al., *Bank Soundness and Macroeconomic Policy,* IMF, 1996; T. M. Hoenig, "Exploring the Macro-Prudential Aspects of Financial Sector Supervision," speech to the Meeting for Heads of Supervision, BIS, Basel, Switzerland, 4/27/04; V. A. Atanasov et al., "The Anatomy of

Financial Tunneling in an Emerging Market," McCombs School of Business, Research Paper Fin-04-06; N. Passas, "The Genesis of the BCCI Scandal," *J Law and Soc,* 3/66; P. L. Zweig, *Belly Up: The Collapse of the Penn Square Bank,* 1986; R. J. Herring, "BCCI & Barings: Bank Resolutions Complicated by Fraud and Global Corporate Structure"; H.R. Davia et al., *Accountant's Guide to Fraud Detection and Control* (2nd ed.), 2000; P. Blustein, "The Chastening: Inside the Crisis that Rocked the Global Financial System and Humbled the IMF," *Public Aff,* 2001; W. K. Black, "A Tale of Two Crises," *Kravis Leadership Inst Rvw,* Fall 2002; Federal Reserve Bank of San Francisco, *Economic Letter,* 3/06; B. H. Soral et al., "Fraud, banking crisis, and regulatory enforcement: Evidence from micro-level transactions data," *Euro J Law and Econ,* 4/06; J. L. Pierce, *The Future of Banking,* 1991; E. J. Kane, *The Gathering Crisis in Federal Deposit Insurance,* MIT Univ Press, 1985; A. Demirguc-Kunt and E. Detragiache, "Does Deposit Insurance Increase Banking System Stability? An Empirical Investigation," *J Monetary Econ,* 10/02; D. Pyle, review of "The Gathering Crisis in Federal Deposit Insurance" in *J Econ Lit,* 9/86; J. Santos, "Bank Capital Regulation in Contemporary Banking Theory: A review of the literature," in *Financial Markets, Institutions & Instruments,* 2001; A.B. Ashcraft, "Does the Market Discipline Banks? New Evidence from Regulatory Capital Mix," 10/2/06; T. Beck et al., "Bank Supervision and Corporate Finance," World Bank Policy Research Working Paper, 5/03; D. R. Brumbaugh, Jr, *Thrifts Under Siege: Restoring Order to American Banking,* 1988; T. Beck et al., "Bank Supervision and Corruption in Lending," 9/3/05; A. Demirguc-Kunt et al., "Banking on the Principles: Compliance with Basel Core Principles and Bank Soundness," IMF Working Paper 10/06; R. La Porta et al., "Related Lending," *Quarterly J Econ,* 2003; S. Johnson et al., "Tunnelling," *Am Econ Assoc Papers & Proceedings,* 2000; R. Haselmann et al., "How Law Affects Lending," Columbia Law and Economics Working Paper, 9/06; J. D. Edwards and J. H. Godwin, "Why Sound Accounting Standards Count," *Econ Reform Today,* 1995; J. R. Barth, *The Great Savings and Loan Debacle,* 1991.

---

# HARD TIMES FOR BANKERS: INNOVATION, POOR JUDGMENT, AND DEREGULATION BRING DOWN BANKS

**BY JOHN MILLER**

*September/October 1991, revised October 1999*

Bankers are a breed apart. Unlike the financial cowboys, outright crooks, and takeover artists behind the financial excesses of the 1980s and 1990s, bankers are stodgy, stiff, invariably conservative dressers, and prudent investors. Heck, bankers, especially Yankee bankers, are downright tightfisted.

Bankers were surely immune to the '80s fever and the feeling that the good times would roll on forever. They must have looked past the short-term profit taking and seen the financial disaster awaiting the gamblers and risk takers.

Right?

Wrong.

For over a decade, bankers feverishly crammed their portfolios with risky loans to Third World debtors, commercial property developers, and financial raiders. That reckless lending, plus increased competition from other financial institutions for what was traditionally only banks' business, combined to bring down a record number of banks across the nation in the second half of the 1980s.

Over 1,000 banks failed from 1985 to 1990. That's more bank failures than occurred between 1934, the year the Roosevelt administration established the Federal Deposit Insurance Corporation (FDIC), and 1985.

Those losses all but exhausted the FDIC insurance fund. At the end of 1990, the fund held $8.4 billion, or less than 40 cents for every $100 of insured deposits in the United States — an all-time low far below the $1.25 level regulators consider safe. Even the FDIC boss, William Seidman said at the time that, unless the fund was replenished, it would become insolvent sometime in 1992, if not before.

The banking industry's problems went well beyond the unprecedented number of bank failures. Profitability in banking declined steadily during the 1970s and 1980s. So did banks' share of the financial business of the United States. A 1991 special report on "The Future of Banking," in *Business Week* concluded that, "the banking industry, at least as we know it, is dying." And despite shoring up the profitability of banks and other financial corporations, the 1990s boom has done little to revive traditional banking.

The problems of the banking industry are, unfortunately, our problems. As each bank fails, the probability rises that taxpayers will be called on to at least partially bail out the FDIC. More importantly, the declining power of banks has left a financial vacuum in the economy. Commercial banks are the "department stores of finance." They make a wide variety of loans to consumers and businesses and offer savings and checking accounts insured by the FDIC for up to $100,000. In return for their public charter and the federal bank deposit insurance program, banks are expected to meet the credit needs of their local communities, including low- and moderate-income neighborhoods. They are the only financial institutions obligated by law to do this. Without active local banks, neighborhood housing and businesses suffer, and residents do not have easy access to checking services.

On the national level, the decline of U.S. banks has coincided with the rise of other financial institutions less tied to their communities and more focused on short-term speculation and financial investment. Hyman Minsky, the financial theorist, use to call today's economy "money market capitalism" — capitalism financed by mutual funds, pension funds, and insurance companies. This turn towards short-term profits and financial investments, in evidence throughout the economy, pulled investments away from new businesses, harming the real economy that produces goods and services. Successful banking reform, as opposed to the law passed by Congress in 1999 that will only further deregulate the financial sector, must strengthen banks' role in community development. That means more public control of the banking industry. Not less.

## Bad Days at the Bank

How did banks get into trouble a decade ago? Stagflation and rising interest rates, financial innovations such as mutual and money-market funds, and deregulation left commercial banks with a dwindling share of U.S. financial business, especially their core business — commercial and industrial loans.

In the mid- and late-1970s, stagflation, a combination of slow economic growth and high inflation, and the Federal Reserve Board's decision to monitor the money supply, rather than interest rates, drove market interest rates to double-digit levels. This was well above the maximum rate banks were allowed by law to pay on deposits. Even government securities such as Treasury bonds, an extremely conservative investment, offered rates of return well above the regulated interest rates banks were limited to paying.

At the same time, advanced technology also empowered competitors to banks. New information and computer systems allowed other financial corporations, such as Fidelity Investments and T. Rowe Price, to create attractive personal investment alternatives. Money-market mutual funds (which invest in short-term bonds and stocks and offer checking services), and stock and bond mutual funds (which sell shares in large stock funds) blossomed. Depositors followed the higher returns and deserted banks. In response, Congress struck down the cap on bank interest rates in the early 1980s, freeing banks to set the interest rates they pay their depositors. Almost immediately, banks began paying depositors more on all types of accounts, decreasing their profit margins.

Because of their lower overhead, and not having to pay FDIC insurance premiums, money-market mutual funds began to out-compete banks and replace them as sources of finance capital for large corporations. These funds made attractive short-term, large-denomination loans to credit-worthy corporations by purchasing a corporation's "commercial paper" (large short-term bonds). These corporate loans grew rapidly. Between 1960 and 1990, the ratio of outstanding commercial paper to bank loans increased from less than 10% to better than 75%, as banks' share of short-term loans to corporations also dropped.

Financial innovations have also eaten into bank profits from their loan business, including consumer, mortgage, and business loans. Prior to the 1980s, banks and thrifts made almost all mortgage loans. In return for assuming the risk of holding these loans for many years, banks charged a margin that kept their profits high. But a new financial development, "securitization," lured non-bank companies, such as pension funds and insurance companies, into the business, breaking banks' control of the lending business. Securitization, or bundling, places a mortgage into a pool with several thousand other mortgages, allowing banks and other lenders to sell shares of the cash flow from the pool. By 1990, over one-third of all residential mortgages in the United States were bundled in this way. Not only did non-bank companies compete for consumer and mortgage loans, the increased competition lowered interest rates on loans, reducing the return that once accrued to banks for making long-term loans.

Finally, non-bank companies — such as General Electric, Sears Roebuck, and General Motors — began offering a wide range of bank-like services in the 1970s. The 1980s allowed these companies to capture an even larger share of the business.

All told, from 1970 to 1990, bank profits suffered a disastrous decline. By the end of this period, banks' return on assets were but one-eighth of what they were 20 years earlier. In 1990, banks earned a 7.7% return on equity, compared with an almost 13% return earned by the 10 largest non-bank finance companies. Large banks, with more than $1 billion in assets, were even harder hit. These big troubles, not big plans, drove some of the largest banks to merge. In a prelude to the current megamergers, New York's Chemical Bank and Manufacturer's Hanover merged in 1991 to form what was then the second largest bank in the nation.

## Desperately Seeking Profits

With the higher costs of obtaining deposits and stiffer competition within the loan business, bankers desperately began seeking new, more profitable, investments. Stagflation, however, had also brought slower growth and fewer investment opportunities. Beginning in the mid-1970s, bankers ventured deeper into riskier territories — international lending, loans for corporate takeovers, and commercial real estate — and accepted a higher level of risks in their asset portfolios. As a result, cash and investment securities, mainly government, corporate, and foreign bonds, the most secure forms of bank assets, decreased from 36% to 27% of total bank assets during the 1970s and 1980s. Meanwhile, loans, a riskier category of assets, increased from 54% to 61%, an additional $700 billion in bank loans.

In the 1970s, bankers poured loans into Third World economies. Lured by the potential profits of variable interest rates that could be adjusted to inflation rates, comforted by the countries' alleged ability to repay loans by taxing their citizens, and lulled further by economic forecasts about potential oil revenues they had little ability to evaluate, bankers jumped to lend money to Mexico, Brazil, and other developing countries. After a decade of periodic defaults, U.S. banks had to repeatedly devalue these loans as assets and place the equivalent of 25% to 30% of them in special loan loss reserves.

Back in the United States, bankers participated in financing the leveraged buyouts and takeovers that reshuffled $1.3 trillion of corporate assets during the 1980s. While high-interest junk bonds financed many of these deals, banks also joined in lending liberally to over-leveraged corporate raiders. By 1990, 11 major U.S. banks had $3 billion or more in loans outstanding to companies that got into deep debt during the roaring eighties.

Real estate provided bankers another opportunity to prosper, and to fail, during the 1980s. In 1982, the Garn-St. Germain Act, embraced by both the Reagan White House and Congress, eliminated restrictions on the percentage of real estate loans in a bank's portfolio and allowed banks to loan to developers with little equity. Banks rushed in. During the 1980s, banks' construction loans and commercial mortgages nearly doubled as a percentage of bank assets. Bankers rode the boom for all it was worth, hoping to restore their lost profits. Fully 32% of all the existing office space in the nation was built in the 1980s.

During the building craze, bankers used questionable lending practices. In New Hampshire, for example, bankers pumped cash into fast-appreciating commercial real estate and resort projects, often lending 110% and 120% of the developers' needs. But the boom crashed. Rising office vacancies and falling property values stuck banks with more and more bad loans. In 1990, almost 10% of real estate loans were unlikely to be repaid. In the District of Columbia and Massachusetts, and for troubled banks like Citicorp, the largest real estate lender in the country, the percentage was almost twice that high.

## New England Stories

Outside of Texas, nobody knows the banking story of the 1980s better than New Englanders. In January 1991, Massachusetts residents suffered the first run on a large bank since the Great Depression. Depositors withdrew more than $1 billion from the Bank of New England (BNE) over one weekend immediately before a FDIC takeover. The takeover curbed the run on money, but did not stem growing concern over the health of New England's banking industry. According to Veribanc Inc., a bank rating company, in 1991 New England housed 11 of the nation's 29 troubled banks that posed the greatest threat to the bank insurance fund.

BNE was once a conservatively managed bank called New England Merchant National Bank. Under the leadership of Roderick MacDougall, the Boston-based bank grew into a premier lending institution with a portfolio long in commercial and industrial loans, the staple of old-line banking. In 1982, MacDougall sold the bank for an attractive sum to Connecticut Bank and Trust, a large retail lender, and retired to serve as Harvard University's treasurer. Walter Connolly, a prototypical go-go banker of the roaring 1980s, headed the Connecticut bank. In 1983, he came to Boston to direct BNE, the holding company formed from the merger. He immediately began to expand the bank aggressively. Connolly told underlings "The market is share driven. Get the share and the profits will follow." He instructed managers to "grow it, grow it." Grow it they did. In just three years BNE acquired 23 other banks to become the second largest bank in the region at the time. BNE often paid top-dollar and questionable prices for its acquisitions. The largest, Conifer Group of Worcester, Mass., cost Connolly $656 million, nearly $100 million more than the next highest bid.

BNE binged on New England's superheated real estate market of the mid-1980s. According to the *Boston Globe*, "BNE never met a real estate deal it didn't like." At one point real estate accounted for 37% of BNE's loans — a higher concentration of money in real estate than any other bank in the country. When the New England real estate market collapsed in 1989, bad loans overwhelmed BNE.

At the time of its failure, BNE had $22 billion in assets, making it the fourth largest bank failure in U.S. history. Some 15% of its remaining assets were non-performing.

Following its "too big to fail doctrine," the FDIC protected every penny of every deposit in the bank, including uninsured deposits over $100,000 and deposits in BNE's foreign branches (virtually all in the Bahamas). The bailout cost the insurance fund more than $2.5 billion.

It didn't have to cost this much. If the FDIC had honored only 45% of uninsured accounts, as it did when Freedom National Bank, one of the nation's largest black-owned banks, failed a few years earlier, it could have reduced the cost of the bailout by hundreds of millions.

Tighter supervision by bank regulators would also have cut down the cost of the bailout. According to Representative Henry Gonzales, then chair of the House Banking Committee, bank regulators knew as early as 1988 that BNE's real estate loans were a possible "time bomb." Despite citing the bank in 1986 and 1987 for underwriting problems, insufficient loan-loss allowances, and poor asset quality, regulators never pressed BNE to take action or to limit the growth of its loans.

Some New England bankers, however, did not succumb to the '80s fever, yet still prospered. Take Woodbury C. Titcomb, chairman of People's Bancorp of Worcester. He told the *Wall Street Journal* that "some incredibly foolish requests crossed my desk in the past few years." Unlike many of his competitors, he turned them down. And his solidly profitable bank almost doubled in size during the 1980s.

Unlike Walter Connolly, Woodie Titcomb was not about to invest recklessly merely because deregulation and a lack of supervision freed him to do so. An old-line banker, Titcomb was trained in the 1950s and early 1960s by bankers with vivid memories of the financial panics of the Depression. He worried "about the worst-case scenarios for the New England economy" and invested accordingly. "Woodie is conservative — a belt and suspenders man," said Corine Turner, a director of People's Bancorp.

## Bushed Bank Reform

But making all bankers as conservative a lender as Woodie Titcomb is not the answer to creating a more stable banking industry that tries to promote the long-term interests of the United States. Nor was the Bush administration's proposal in the early 1990s or the nearly identical Clinton administration proposals of the late.

The Bush administration prescribed further deregulation and freer financial markets as a cure-all for the ailing banking industry. Much like the law passed by Congress in 1999, the Bush administration would have granted banks new powers to expand across state lines and to move into investment banking — selling securities, insurance, and mutual funds.

These reforms would not have nursed the banking industry back to health in the early 1990s nor would they do much good for the more profitable banking industry of the late 1990s. Leaving banking unregulated and subject to market forces has been a sure formula for financial panic. In fact, modern banking regulation came into being in the 1930s to curb the speculative excesses of earlier free-market banking. In addition, whenever banks have gotten into new areas, like commercial real estate in the 1980s, the results have been calamitous.

Ultimately, these reforms will fail because they don't address the root causes of the banking crisis of the 1980s and the disappearance of traditional banking in the 1990s. Favorable economic conditions and successful regulation helped produce the stable banking of the postwar boom. Slower economic growth and higher inflation during the late 1970s and 1980s ate away at the profitability of banking as it ate away at the profitability of other industries. While a deteriorating economy and changing financial markets made the regulatory schemes imposed 50 years earlier work less well, the slow-to-adjust regulation did not compel bankers to make "bad loans." Nor will repealing "bad regulation laws," the goal of both the Bush and Clinton administrations, turn go-go bankers like Walter Connolly into prudent investors like Woodie Titcomb. Rather, unregulated bankers will be able to make more bad loans and reckless investments than those made by bankers who were inhibited by government regulation.

Sound banking requires a sound economy. Only financial restructuring that creates an authentic public control over the banking industry will bring about both. That must begin with new regulations for banks: honest and public reporting of banking practices, more demanding capital requirements and limits on loans for all banks, and stricter public supervision of troubled banks' investment and dividend policies. It would also demand that banks respond to the needs of their local community, particularly the low-income housing market — something Phil Gramm, the arch-conservative Senator from Texas, seems bound and determined to eliminate from the current bank reform proposals.

But most importantly, a stable banking industry and a stable economy require an industrial policy immune to the speculative frenzies of the 1980s. Progressive industrial policy would substitute democratic planning of investment for our current reliance on financial elites — like large bankers and Wall Street bond dealers — who have proven themselves to be unfit custodians of the long-term interests of the economy.

*Resources:* James Barth, R. Dan Brumbaugh, and Robert Litan, "Bank Failures are Sinking the FDIC," *Challenge*, March/April 1991; *Business Week*, "The Future of Banking," April 22, 1991; L.J. Davis, "The Problem with Banks? Bankers." *Harpers*, June 1991.

# RETURN FROM THE DEAD: THE BANKING INDUSTRY FLIES HIGH

**BY JIM CAMPEN**
*March/April 1997*

Fifty billion dollars. Who would have thought that bank profits would reach this record height in 1996? Just six years earlier, experts were dismissing banks as financial dinosaurs unable to compete with the mutual funds, investment firms, and finance companies that were stealing their best customers. As late as 1993, the *Wall Street Journal* featured a former head of the Federal Deposit Insurance Corporation (FDIC) saying that "The banking industry is becoming irrelevant economically, and it's almost irrelevant politically."

There appeared to be good reason for the pessimism. The two main measures of bank profitability had both been trending downward for a decade. Households were increasingly investing their savings in pension funds or mutual funds rather than depositing them in banks. Borrowers ranging from home buyers to major corporations were finding that they could get cheaper loans elsewhere.

Even worse, many borrowers were not repaying their loans. The result was that banks were collapsing at an epidemic rate — more than 1,100 failed between 1985 and 1991. Most ominously, by the end of 1991 the FDIC itself had become insolvent. Taxpayers were threatened by the prospect of a clean-up bill even higher than that for the $200 billion savings and loan debacle that was still fresh in their memories.

The current mood could hardly be more different. As bank profits have soared to record levels in each of the last four years, pessimism has been replaced by an optimism bordering on euphoria. At almost exactly the same time last December that Federal Reserve Chairman Alan Greenspan expressed his concern about the "irrational exuberance" of the stock market, the Wall Street Journal noted that the prices of bank stocks had been "rising twice as fast as the overall market for more than two years." Investors' mood swings may be excessive, but the recovery of the banking industry is real.

Perhaps surprisingly, the banks' return to health is good news for lower-income people and those involved in small businesses. Large corporations, the wealthy, and the middle class all have alternative ways of obtaining the credit and services that banks provide. But for those in small companies or with lower incomes — whether located in inner-city neighborhoods, small towns, or rural areas — there often is no good alternative. Healthy banks mean that more small firms are able to get the credit they need, and that fewer low-income people are forced into the clutches of check-cashers, pawnshops, rent-to-own stores, sub-prime lenders, and other elements of the exploitative, high-cost world of fringe banking.

Yet the news is not all good. Banks' dramatic diversification into new lines of financial business has created the current prosperity. But this transformation raises

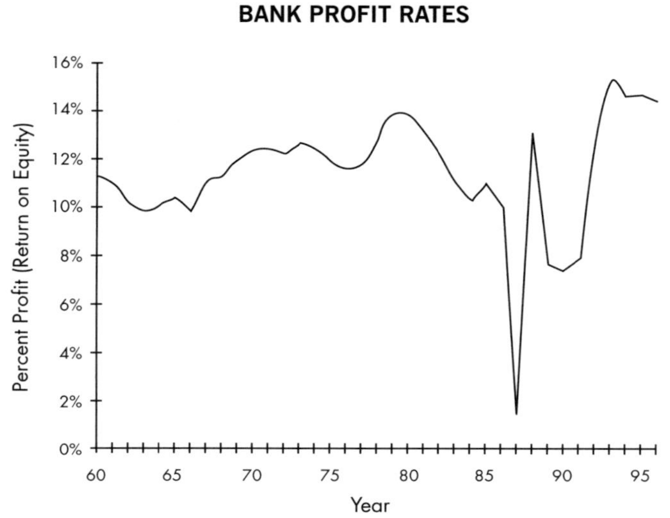


*Source: FDIC Division of Research & Statistics*, Jan. 1997.

threats to the future well-being of the banks themselves, the overall economy, and the rest of us. Threats to the stability of the banking system are greater than at any time since the Great Depression. Mergers are giving large banks greater abilities to wield economic and political power, with consequences such as higher fees for consumers, especially those with low incomes. And banks whose operations spread across the nation will be far less responsive to the needs of local communities, including residential and small-business borrowers.

## Reversal of Fortune

As the decade opened, the most threatening aspect of the banking crisis was the rash of bank failures. In each of the last three years of the 1980s more than 200 banks failed, and the annual number remained in triple digits through 1992. These were shocking numbers for an industry where failures averaged less than four per year — and never reached even double digits in any single year — during the three decades between the end of World War II and the middle of the 1970s. Just a few years later, however, the number of bank failures has returned to single digits. Only six banks failed in 1995, and the same number last year.

The main reason that banks were failing at such a high rate was that bankers had made massive numbers of loans to finance real estate speculation during the late 1980s. When the real estate boom collapsed, many of those who had borrowed the money were unable to repay their loans, and banks found themselves the not-so-proud owners of downtown office towers, suburban malls, and luxury condominium developments that were worth only a fraction of the amount they had loaned.

In hundreds of cases, the losses from these bad loans were big enough to force the banks into failure.

By the beginning of the 1990s banks had stopped making such ill-advised loans, but they could do nothing to stop the accumulating losses from the loans they had previously made. As real estate prices continued to collapse during the recession of the early 1990s, there was no end in sight to the epidemic of bank failures.

At this point, the Federal Reserve Board — whose primary concern is protecting the health of the banking system — decided to take dramatic action. During 1991, the Fed cut the key interest rate directly under its control (the so-called "discount rate") on four separate occasions — from 6.5% at the beginning of the year to just 3.5% by the year's end. Other interest rates dropped accordingly, the lower rates jump-started the stalled economy, and the number of borrowers who were unable to repay their bank loans dropped substantially. Thanks to the Fed, the banks were on the road to recovery.

In fact, virtually all of the increase in bank profits from the depths of 1991 to the heights of 1995 can be accounted for by the drop in bad loans written off by the banks. These fell from $55 billion to $12 billion, thereby raising after-tax profits by $29 billion (assuming an average corporate tax rate of 33%). The actual rise in the industry's profits during this period was an almost identical $30 billion, from $18 billion in 1991 to $48 billion in 1995.

But stopping the avalanche of loan losses dealt only with the immediate crisis that the banks faced at the start of the 1990s. There was also a long-run problem. Since 1979, a decade before speculative real estate loans caused massive losses, banks' share of the economy's total financial assets had been falling as other kinds of financial firms took away their most profitable customers. In order to survive and prosper in a changed environment, the banking industry needed to transform itself. Accomplishing this was complicated by the outmoded regulatory system, established almost sixty years before, within which banks had to operate.

## The Post-Depression Regulatory Structure

During the Great Depression more than 9,000 banks failed — almost 40% of the country's total. As a result, the federal government, led by President Franklin D. Roosevelt, established a new system of rules for banking that was designed to prevent such a disaster from recurring.

Central to the new system was deposit insurance, guaranteeing that depositors would get their money back even if their bank failed. By promoting depositor confidence, insurance eliminated the bank runs that had brought down thousands of otherwise healthy banks. The three other key features of the new regulatory structure were designed to protect banks from the destabilizing effects of competition.

First, the kinds of accounts that banks could offer were restricted, and the maximum rate of interest that banks could pay their depositors was strictly limited. For example, no interest at all could be paid on checking accounts. Second, the law separated the financial industry into distinct compartments, with each type specializing in one or more products and protected from competition with the others. Banks offered checking accounts and business loans, S&L's specialized in savings accounts and home mortgages, investment banks helped corporations raise money by issuing stocks and bonds, and insurance companies sold insurance. Third, individual banks were allowed to operate only in limited geographic areas.

Under this system, which made banking one of the most heavily regulated of all industries, the banking industry flourished for the first three decades following World War II. Bank profits were steady, even if not spectacular. And the banking system provided the financing necessary to fuel the "golden age" of U.S. capitalism. But eventually technological developments and economic changes created problems for the banks.

One major change was the surge in interest rates in the early 1970s. By 1974, the interest rate on U.S. Treasury bills (which cost $10,000 each) rose to over 8%, well above the 5% maximum that banks were allowed to pay their depositors.

Accordingly, money began to flow out of the banks and into T-bills and other high-interest investments. The flow became a flood when investment companies like Fidelity and Merrill Lynch began to offer money market mutual funds. This new product pooled together the money of many small investors, thereby making it easy for the non-wealthy to share in the high "money market" interest rates. Starting from nothing in the mid-1970s, the money in these funds grew to over $220 billion in the early 1980s.

For banks to hold on to a substantial share of the savings of U.S. households, the first key element of the regulatory system had to be abandoned. Accordingly, Congress in the early 1980s removed restrictions on the interest rates that banks could pay to their depositors.

Soon afterwards the geographic limits on banks crumbled. One tactic that banks used to get around the law limiting individual banks to a single state was to create "bank holding companies." These entities collected a number of legally separate banks, in different states, under one corporate parent. Then in 1994 the Riegle-Neal Interstate Banking and Branching Act removed the ability of states to prevent such holding companies from buying banks within their borders, and allowed the holding companies to merge all their subsidiaries into a single bank. When this law is fully phased in by mid-1997, geographic limits on banks will be virtually extinct.

The confinement of bank activities to taking in deposits and making business loans has also been substantially eroded, although this aspect of deregulation is not yet complete. Banks have mounted major counter-offensives against the insurance companies, brokerage firms, and mutual funds that had been stealing their customers. Most large banks now offer their customers insurance policies, mutual funds, and investment services in addition to consumer, real estate, and business loans.

Although the contending groups are still struggling over the details of pending legislation, it seems certain that banks will soon offer the entire range of financial services. This will mark the final step in the demolition of the regulatory system that defined the banking system for the first quarter-century after World War II.

## Banking Today

Making use of the flexibility provided by a dismantled regulatory structure, banks have responded to the rapid changes in technology and economics in ways that have changed banking almost beyond recognition, including:

> ***Multi-state operations*** – Since the barriers that restricted banks to operating in a single state began to fall in the mid-1980s, many banks have spread their operations over large areas of the country. The most extensive single bank network, as of early 1997, is that of NationsBank, which has more than 2,600 branches in a 16-state area bounded by New Mexico, Iowa, Maryland and Florida. In eight of these states it ranks first in deposits. KeyCorp, which owns banks in 12 northern states, will consolidate them into a single new bank that will operate "KeyCenters" in 28 cities ranging from Albany to Seattle. Their corporate goal, according to spokesman Bill Murschel, is to "transform Key away from an organization of a bunch of state-oriented companies to one more like Sears or McDonald's that really operates the same from coast to coast." It seems highly likely that further mergers will lead to one or more truly national banks within the next few years.
>
> ***Consolidation*** – Bank holding company acquisitions across state lines have fueled the expansion of interstate banking. But the continuing wave of bank mergers has also involved major banks that were formerly competitors in the same market. For example, the four largest banks in California combined into two (Bank of America and Security Pacific, Wells Fargo and First Interstate); the four biggest banks in Boston also paired off (Fleet and Shawmut, Bank of Boston and BayBank); and three of the four biggest New York banks were reduced to one (as Chemical acquired Manufacturers Hanover before combining with Chase Manhattan to form the biggest U.S. banking company, with over $300 billion in assets.)

As the mergers proceed, the biggest banks control an ever-larger share of the industry's total deposits. Between 1980 and early 1996, the deposit share of the 50 biggest banking companies rose from 37% to 57%.

New products and services – Banks have reacted to the loss of customers in their traditional lines of business by turning to activities that generate revenue in the form of fees rather than interest. As a result, taking in deposits and making loans is providing a progressively smaller part of bank revenues. For example, many banks now quickly sell almost all of their mortgage, auto, and credit card loans to investors. In this system, interest payments go to the investors, while the banks pocket fees that they charge borrowers to make the loan.

New ways of earning fees range from providing sophisticated financial services for large corporate customers to mass-marketing a wide array of financial products such as insurance, mutual funds, or investment management. Norwest's CEO Richard Kovacevich, saying that "We're not in the banking business — there's not enough revenue in the old-time banking business to make it a success," regards his company as a "retailer," and its branches as "stores" where staff trained in sales techniques focus on selling as many products as possible to each new or existing customer.

Under the headline "For More Bankers 'Bank' is a Dirty Word," the *Wall Street Journal* reported last November that some large banks have stopped using the word "bank" in their advertising and, in some cases, even their names, because they regard the term as "dated" and "limiting." One KeyCorp executive, for example, said "In the world of financial services branding, the word 'bank' doesn't cut it."

New delivery systems – the proliferation of ATM's and 24-hour telephone centers, and the growing use of personal computers for electronic-banking, mean that more and more bank customers rarely set foot in a bank office at all. Others do their banking at one of the thousands of bank branches that now exist in supermarkets and other large stores. And as automated mortgage review systems proliferate, even loans to purchase or refinance a home can be made without human contact.

## Paradise Gained — Not!

Stopping the epidemic of bank failures that raged at the beginning of the 1990s was essential. But the primary reason for investors' current optimistic assessment of the banking industry's prospects is their perception that banks have shown that they can prosper in an environment characterized by continual change and relentless competition.

The banks' success, however, has come at a heavy price for bank workers. As in other industries, competition and change have created stress, speed-up, and insecurity. Layoffs have proliferated as banks have introduced ever-greater automation, downsized in the quest for lower costs, and consolidated operations in the wake of mergers. It is hardly a coincidence that total employment in banking has fallen as profits and stock prices have soared. Between 1990 and 1995, bank employment fell 10%, from 2.25 million to just over 2.0 million, while overall employment rose by about 8%.

Furthermore, the transformation of banking creates potential threats to the economic well-being of everyone. Although banks would like to see deregulation pushed even further, there are three critical reasons why regulation should be strengthened. Because banks are at the heart of the nation's financial system, their actions profoundly affect not only particular groups and communities, but also the stability of the overall economy.

The primary worry of the Fed and other bank regulators is the possibility of another massive financial crisis like that which ushered in the Great Depression. The failure of one or a few major banks could destabilize the entire financial system. The system of bank regulation established in the 1930s was designed with this danger in mind, and the dismantling of that structure makes the banking system more vulnerable. As banks develop new products and expand into new businesses in search of greater profits, they also expose themselves to larger and more spectacular losses.

Second, concentration of economic power within huge banks poses great dangers, including excessive political influence. Popular resistance to such power has been a recurring feature of U.S. history, and is the main reason why banks faced strict limits on geographic expansion. The unprecedented consolidation within the banking industry is made even more threatening by the prospect that mergers among banks, insurance companies, and investment firms will create huge financial conglomerates.

When a banking market is more concentrated it is easier for banks to increase the fees and interest rates that they charge while reducing the rates that they pay to their depositors. A recent study by the U.S. Public Interest Research Group (U.S. PIRG), for example, found that bank fees increased at twice the rate of inflation from 1993 to 1995. Banking regulators and the anti-trust division of the Justice Department, both of which must approve or disapprove proposed mergers, need to more aggressively oppose excessive concentrations of banks' economic power.

A third major worry is that banks operated from distant headquarters will be unable and unwilling to respond effectively to local needs. Historically, locally-based banks have been at the center of local economic and civic life in almost every city and town, possessing detailed knowledge of people and companies and the power to act on this knowledge. Although these banks often failed to serve equally all of the neighborhoods and groups in their local communities (see box), they did recognize that their own well-being was tied to the prosperity of the local economy.

When, for example, NationsBank does business in a 16-state region from its headquarters in Charlotte, North Carolina, the situation is dramatically transformed. Lending for local economic development or affordable housing construction simply cannot be standardized like fast food or discount store operations. Responsiveness to specific local needs inevitably suffers when local bank personnel must defer to faceless decision-makers in regional headquarters. More and more communities, including cities as big as San Diego, have seen control of their biggest banks change from local hands to out-of-state corporations. By the end of 1995, out-of-state bank holding companies controlled more than half of bank assets in 23 states and the District of Columbia. In the transformed world of banking, we need more vigilant and effective oversight to ensure that banks respond to the needs of local communities.

What former Fed Chairman Arthur Burns identified ten years ago as "the ongoing revolution in American banking" cannot be stopped. But it needs to be shaped and directed, by a reinvigorated, and democratically controlled, regulatory structure, so that banks will operate in a safe, efficient, and responsive manner that serves the interests of all of us.

*Resources: Transforming the U.S. Financial System: Equity and Efficiency for the 21st Century*, G. Dymski, G. Epstein, and R. Pollin (editors), Economic Policy Institute, 1993; *The Bankers: The Next Generation*, Martin Mayer, 1997; *Quarterly Banking Profile*, Federal Deposit Insurance Corporation, various issues.

# IT'S A BANK-EAT-BANK WORLD

**BY JIM CAMPEN**
*January/February 1999*

Los Angeles may be the nation's second largest city, but it no longer hosts a major bank. Nor do Houston, Philadelphia, San Diego, Phoenix, San Antonio, or Dallas — the U.S. cities ranked fourth through ninth in population.

In the aftermath of the latest round of banking merger-mania, none of these seven cities is home to any of the country's seventy-five largest banks. The largest bank still based in any of these cities is Frost National Bank of San Antonio, whose parent company, Cullen/Frost Bankers, ranked 79th in mid-1998 with $6.4 billion in assets.

This is just the tip of the iceberg. All across the country, hundreds of cities and towns of all sizes are finding that control over local loans to businesses and residents — the economic lifeblood of any community — has shifted from locally based banks to the distant corporate headquarters of a new breed of mega-banks.

## The Megamergers of '98

Six megamergers in 1998 have escalated the ongoing consolidation of the banking industry to a whole new level (see chart). Three years ago, Citicorp, the parent corporation of Citibank, was bumped from its longstanding position as the country's biggest bank when Chase Manhattan and Chemical banks of New York merged to form the first $300 billion U.S. bank. This year it reclaimed its number one standing by combining with the Travelers Group of insurance and investment companies to form the new Citigroup, with almost $700 billion in assets.

Within banking itself, NationsBank's takeover of Bank of America's operations — and its name — joined the third and fifth largest banking companies in the country to create a giant based in NationsBank's home state of North Carolina. With $580 billion in assets, the megabank's reach now stretches through 22 states from Alaska to Florida. Its 4,800 branches hold more than 8% of the nation's total bank deposits. In eight states, including California, Texas, Florida, and Washington, the new BankAmerica has more deposits than any other bank.

Meanwhile, in the "thrift" industry (S&Ls and savings banks are called "thrifts," and are kept separate from banks in most statistics) the largest single institution, Seattle-based Washington Mutual, took over the second largest, Home Savings, of California. Just a year earlier, Washington Mutual had outbid Home Savings to acquire Great Western Savings, another California insitution, and the country's third largest thrift. When the dust finally clears, Washington Mutual will have $150 billion in assets, more than all but eight banking companies, and more than three times as much as the second largest thrift.

The 1998 mega-mergers are the latest and largest instances of a merger wave

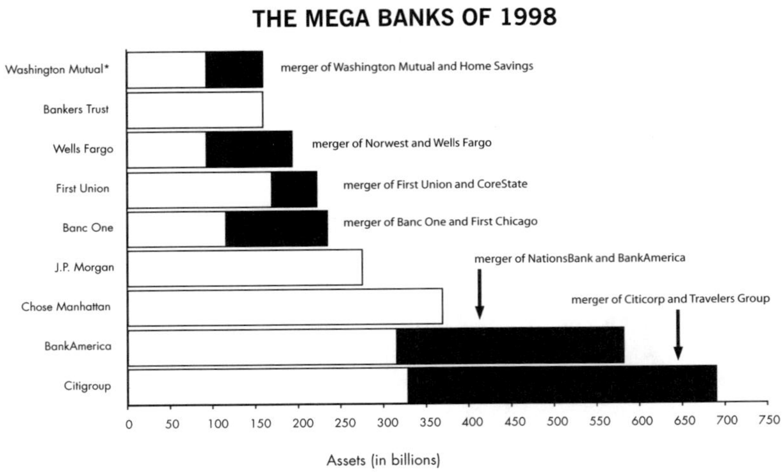


There are now nine U.S. banking companies with assets of over $150 billion, six of which have expanded substantially as a result of 1998 mergers. The estimated size of each megabank, and of each of the major partners in the year's megamergers, is based on total 3/31/98 assets.

*Washington Mutual, as a "thrift," is often omitted from lists of the largest banks.

Source: Federal Financial Institutions Examinations Council (www.ffiec.gov) and the EDGAR database of the Securities and Exchange Commission (www.sec.gov)

that has cut the number of U.S. banks by more than a third since 1984, leaving 8,984 in mid-1998. The number of thrifts has fallen even more — down 53% since 1986 to just 1,728 in mid-1998. In 1990, only one banking company had assets over $150 billion — Citicorp. Now there are nine (see chart).

Ellen Seidman, head of the Treasury Department's Office of Thrift Supervision, told the House Banking Committee last April that the then pending megamergers would, if all completed, result in the nation's top ten banking companies controlling an unprecedented 44% of total industry assets, and the top ten thrifts controlling 36% of all thrift assets. All those mergers are now completed.

## The Reasons Why

Many of the megamergers seem driven more by the empire-building dreams of bank CEOs with outsized egos, or by the maniacal momentum of the merger movement itself, than by economic rationality. Indeed, in the frenzied bank-eat-bank world that now exists, the failure of a merged bank merely serves as the excuse for an even bigger takeover, rather than leading to a slowing of the trend.

For example, the San Francisco-based Wells Fargo botched its 1996 acquisition of First Interstate, another California-based bank, failing to achieve predicted profit levels largely because of computer snafus that wreaked havoc on accounts, alienating tens of thousands of customers on the West Coast. As a result, it was transformed from predator to prey, and taken over this year by the slightly smaller Norwest, a Minneapolis-based bank. And the lackluster performance of the Cleveland-based KeyCorp after merging with Society Corp. in 1994 has, according to the *Wall Street Journal,* caused that bank to be "widely viewed as takeover bait."

In spite of its excesses, however, the merger wave is driven by real political and economic forces that make its continuation seem all but certain. The Riegle-Neal Interstate Banking and Branching Act of 1994 marked the final move in an almost complete dismantling of long-standing legal barriers to the geographic spread of banks. Federal and state laws dating to the 19th and early decades of the 20th century restricted almost all banking companies to a single state in part to curb their power. Banks began their serious campaign to repeal these laws in the 1970s.

The banks' merger wave has been aided by fast-paced changes in communications and computer technology, making it possible to manage massive, far-flung organizations with millions of customers. In such areas as processing credit card accounts or servicing mortgage loans, highly sophisticated computer facilities reduce costs. But the investment needed is so massive that only a handful of banks can afford it, and most others are forced to leave the business.

More ominously, the new technology increases the ability of the biggest banks to compile vast amounts of personal financial data on individual customers — including their buying habits as revealed by credit card and checking account records, and private details exposed on loan applications. Consumer groups are concerned about the possible misuse of this information. Bankers, however, want to use the accumulated information on each customer to fine-tune their marketing of a new range of financial services — since they are now moving beyond checking accounts and loans to selling mutual funds, investment advice, and insurance. The U.S. Public Interest Research Group is sounding the alarm about the Travelers/Citicorp merger because no law prevents the bank side of the business from consulting the health insurance records of Travelers in evaluating loan requests. Presumably a bank would not look kindly on a mortgage application from someone struggling with a potentially fatal illness.

Given current trends, within the next few years between five and ten truly national banking companies could emerge whose branches and ATMs will be as familiar from coast to coast as McDonalds restaurants, Staples office supply outlets, or Exxon gas stations. Although thousands of smaller banks are likely to survive as well, the ascendancy of the mega-banks promises to have profound impacts.

One danger is that dramatically larger banks could lead to dramatically larger bank failures, with consequences as far-reaching as the operation of the megabanks themselves. The meltdown of a single giant bank could bankrupt the Federal Deposit Insurance Corporation. Already, Bank of America alone has deposits almost ten times greater than the FDIC's entire fund balance of less than $30 billion. Another major worry is that the financial power of the megabanks will give rise to concentrated political clout that will make it even harder for government officials at the state and national level to defend the public interest from the banks' profit-oriented agendas.

## Threatening Local Communities

Bank megamergers also pose serious threats to the well being of local communities all across the nation. In the aftermath of major mergers, banks often trim their networks of branch offices, with a disproportionate number of the closings in lower-income neighborhoods. And banks enlarged through mergers use their increased economic clout to charge higher bank fees, increase the interest rates charged on loans, and cut the interest paid on deposits. Federal Reserve Board Member Laurence Meyer, testifying to Congress in April about what he termed the "sometimes breathtaking consolidation of our banking system," noted "substantial evidence that banks that are part of multistate organizations tend to charge higher fees in general than do banks that are not."

Perhaps most significantly, shifting decision-making power to a distant headquarters reduces a bank's knowledge of and sensitivity to local circumstances and needs. This threatens to reduce credit for small businesses, lending to innovative programs promoting community economic development, and support for local civic and philanthropic projects.

Commenting in April on NationsBank's proposed takeover of BankAmerica, the California Reinvestment Committee's Alan Fisher observed, "No one sitting in an office in Charlotte, North Carolina, can understand the credit needs of California's diverse communities. The new bank will be a monolith that is distant from everyday people and their needs." Fisher's concern turned out to be well-founded. Less than one month after the September 30th completion of the merger, the new Bank of America forced the resignation of top community reinvestment officials at the old Bank of America with whom the California Reinvestment Committee had formed good working relationships in recent years. This underscored to the Californians that all important decisions would be made by Charlotte-based executives.

## A Coordinated National Response

In response to the threats posed by the bank megamergers, organizations are mobilizing nationwide. The groups first demanded that regulators stop approving mergers until the consequences were fully studied and understood. That went nowhere, so the groups are now asking regulators to approve only those mergers of banks that guarantee they will meet the needs of lower-income and minority neighborhoods for loans and other banking services.

The Community Reinvestment Act, a 1977 law designed to ensure banks serve the needs of the low-income communities they long ignored, requires Federal Reserve and other regulators to consider a bank's record in poor communities before approving a merger. This gives merging banks a powerful incentive to reach agreements with community groups. Otherwise, community groups can file formal protests with regulators detailing a bank's weak performance in meeting the needs of lower-income and minority borrowers and neighborhoods.

Now that mergers are creating nation-spanning banks, community responses must be on the same scale. Recognizing this, the National Community

Reinvestment Coalition (NCRC), an umbrella for more than 680 organizations, convened a meeting in May of groups from across the country to share information and debate strategies.

The forty organizations represented agreed to pressure merging banks — and federal bank regulators — to develop detailed and specific community reinvestment plans for each area where the megabank would operate. In order to reflect the particular needs of each area, banks must develop these plans through good faith discussions with local community representatives and public officials, NCRC argues. And in order to be credible, the plans need to take the form of signed agreements filed with bank regulators rather than simply announcements in self-congratulatory press releases. The banks' usual habit of issuing vague pledges of nationwide goals is not enough.

"Banks must commit to regional and local community advisory committees that monitor progress toward meeting their pledges," says Gene Ortega of the Home Education Livelihood Program in Albuquerque, New Mexico, who serves as NCRC's chairperson.

Activists point to the $120 billion ten-year community reinvestment commitment announced in May by Washington Mutual as a model for such agreements. The plan — which includes provisions for low-cost bank accounts, more bank branches in lower-income and minority communities, and expanded lending for small businesses, community development, and affordable housing — was developed through discussions with community-based organizations in each area where Washington Mutual operates. Contrasting Washington Mutual's plan with the unilateral announcements made by NationsBank/BankAmerica and Citigroup, the California Reinvestment Committee's Alan Fisher notes that "the commitment is real because the bank is filing it with the regulators — not just with the wire services."

The community reinvestment activists also are calling upon federal regulators to hold public hearings on the proposed mergers in all of the regions that will be affected and to make approval of the mergers conditional upon the banks' offering such community reinvestment plans.

In some of the megamergers of 1998, banks such as Banc One and NationsBank/BankAmerica offered only vague and unilateral plans — without sitting down with community groups for serious discussions. They received the Fed's OK nevertheless.

In other cases, like that of Washington Mutual, community groups achieved considerable success. Strong community protests also led elected officials to bring intense pressure to bear on First Union as it sought approval to take over CoreStates — a merger that left Philadelphia as another major city with no large local bank. In April, Pennsylvania Attorney General Mike Fisher concluded a legal agreement with First Union that guarantees no-fee checking accounts and waiver of ATM fees for many low-income households, provides that new job openings will be available to displaced workers first, and ensures that First Union will honor a promise wrested from it by the Philadelphia Low-Income Housing Coalition and the Philadelphia Association of Community Development Corporations that it would keep a number of particular inner-city bank branches open for at least several years.

It remains to be seen how this story will play itself out as the consolidation of the banking industry continues in the years ahead. But Chris Bohner was right on target back in January 1996 when he observed in these pages that "the march toward the mega-bank will not go unchallenged [by] a vibrant social movement of community-based organizations...pushing for more democratic control of banking."

---

# CREDIT CARD PUSHERS PUMP UP PROFITS — AND RISK

**BY ABBY SCHER**
*November/December 1998*

Tell your friends and relatives you're writing an article on credit cards and see what happens. Everybody has a horror story. Here are only two I've heard recently.

A friend who pays off her credit card balance every month received a letter over the summer from her credit card company, Providian Financial, saying it was closing her account "primarily because you have not been using it." Of course, she has been using her card. She, like a third of all card holders, merely avoids generating any interest charges by paying her balance in full every month. Providian, a California-based specialist in "high risk" customers, doesn't like that. It, like all credit card companies, makes most of its revenue on interest charges and penalties. Having my thrifty friend as a customer just wasn't worth Providian's while.

Another friend's story is a bit more painful. He's a graduate student who used his student loan to clear all of his credit card debts earlier this year. Within eight months, he'd racked up another $18,000 on his credit cards. You might call him a nut, or just an underpaid adjunct professor trying to get by, but what about the credit card companies? They fall all over themselves to keep him as a customer, upping his credit limits, plying him with cards... The credit card industry hopes he'll overspend — and because they delay the pain, credit cards make that easy to do. Somehow money becomes even more unreal when it's plastic.

Since the early 1990s, banks have gone wild, upping credit limits on their customers' credit cards by more than a third, blanketing the country with 3 billion offers in 1997 alone, reaching further and further beyond their core customers in the middle class. Among the beneficiaries of banks' desperate search for credit card profits are men at a Waltham, Massachusetts homeless shelter who, though unable to afford rent, regularly find credit card offers in their mailbox with come-ons like "Receive the Credit You Deserve."

In an era of fraying safety nets and increasing inequality, banks shamelessly peddle plastic as the way for those left behind to live the good life, even if that means

**AMERICANS DROWN IN CREDIT CARD DEBT**

Americans owe more and more on their credit cards, and more and more of what they owe is to credit card companies.

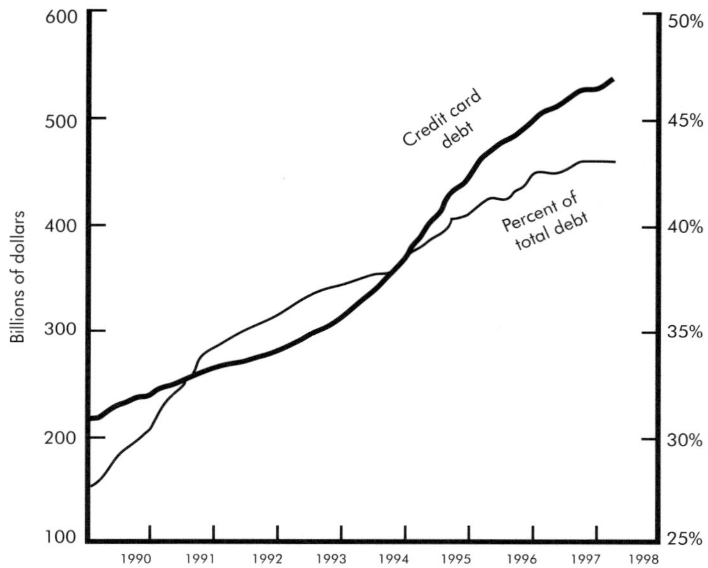


*Source:* Federal Reserve Bank of Cleveland *Economic Trends* (July 1998)

using credit to buy groceries. More poor families have credit cards and it should come as no surprise that their credit card debt is growing as the welfare net is eroding. While only 20% of poor families had a credit card in 1983, 40% did in 1995. Their balances are higher than ever, exceeding $1,300 on average in 1995, up from $700 in '83 (calculated in '95 dollars). Deeper in debt compared to their overall income than wealthier cardholders, they are left with no cushion if crisis strikes.

Because there are no sober-faced bankers dissecting our credit histories before approving our loans, it is hard to remember that's exactly what we are doing when we toss that shiny plastic to the shoe saleswoman — taking out an instant loan from a bank. At least, that's what we're doing if we don't pay off the balance right away. But some low- income newcomers to the world of credit cards, like the students in an adult literacy program I know in Brooklyn, treat their card as if it were an old fashioned installment plan. Until a class discussion set them right, they proudly sent in a check each month for the minimum payment, not realizing it was possible — let alone beneficial — to pay off the whole balance in one lump sum.

These new customers, plus the middle class who are going further into credit card debt, are giving the pinstriped pushers just what they want. Credit card debt rose 23.5% in just over a year, from January 1997 to March 1998, and more of it is owed by lower-income cardholders. Sixty-three percent of all U.S. households now owe money on their credit cards, and last year they spent $70 billion in interest charges and fees. Credit card debt now accounts for 43% of all consumer loans and is growing far faster than all other types of household borrowing, including home mortgages or auto loans. The average household now owes an amount equal to 95% of their yearly income. That's up from 60% in 1960 and 75% in 1980. And the more borrowers owe on all types of loans, the greater their risk of bankruptcy if they suffer even a minor financial setback or lose their job.

With the Providians and Citibanks alike going after more lower-income customers, the credit card companies also may be exposing themselves to greater risk. "The new card holders are different and potentially riskier," wrote two economists with the New York Federal Reserve Bank in a recent study. People denied a card in 1989 qualified for one in 1995. They typically carry more debt from auto loans and the like on top of their credit card balances. Furthermore, they are more likely to be unskilled laborers working in on-again, off-again jobs with erratic income. They are more in debt relative to their income than wealthier cardholders and more likely to miss a payment. But as we will see, ballooning consumer debt threatens not just desperate lower income cardholders or a bank's bottom line, but the whole economy.

## The Banking Industry

How can banks afford their drive into the lower income market, making riskier and riskier loans? With credit cards' declining profit margins, perhaps the banks are asking how they can afford not to. Credit card operations are still lucrative, especially compared to other parts of the banking business right now, but cost a lot to keep going. During the 1970s, when credit cards still were relatively new, banks sunk a lot of money into upgrading already high tech processing operations, and only made their money back in the 1980s, according to a history of the industry by Joseph Nocera. Even before that, the credit card business walked a slow and volatile road toward profitability.

Visa began as BankAmericard in 1958 (changing its name in 1976), the first charge card ever that aimed to be accepted not just by a single department store, like a Sears card, or by restaurants, like Diners Club. The postwar consumer boom was built on an explosion of buying on credit; but at first customers were paying for their new refrigerators and sofas through store installment plans, paying retailers directly, month by month. BankAmerica wanted those customers for itself, so it invested in Bank Americard's expensive start-up. Bank salesmen blanketed California, recruiting businesses one by one to accept the card, and recruiting cardholders with mass mailings. Then BankAmerica developed a network of banks to do the same nationwide, building a customer base and a retail base at the same time. (This same process is now being pushed globally. Until the recent crisis, the world's largest credit card issuer, Citibank, was busily exporting the consumer dream of buying on plastic to Asia's new monied classes.)

In the United States today, Mastercard and Visa operate as networks of banks — and increasingly since the early 1990s of nonbanks like Providian — that issue cards under their imprint. They operate almost like coops, sharing in the expense of keeping the system going. And the costs are high. While most of the cost of a home mortgage is the money a bank lends, much of the cost of a credit card loan is the paperwork. Credit card companies have all the expenses of sending a zillion piece mailings for new customers, processing the credit card receipts, reimbursing the local merchants' bank, and maintaining the powerful computers that approve or disapprove your credit card within seconds of being swiped by a salesperson. That high overhead exerts pressure on banks to really put that expensive infrastructure to use once it's in place, and try to suck more and more interest-paying customers into the system.

Banks and freestanding credit card companies like Providian cover the risk by keeping their interest rates high even while interest rates are dropping elsewhere in the economy. The flood of nonbank players into the business in the 1990s was supposed to heighten competition and put a damper on those interest rates. That didn't happen. Instead 3,000-plus credit card pushers all trying to steal each other's customers just cut into all of their profits, saturating the "market," forcing small players out of the game, and making it harder to charge annual fees. Fees in 1991 provided as much as 24% of their revenue. Now, only 10% of their revenue comes from annual fees and the small charge to the retail store or other business accepting your card for a purchase. Interest charges of 16% — or even 24% for the unlucky customers who've missed a few payments — bring in all the bucks these days, along with shortened grace periods, and new and improved penalties of $25 a pop for everything from exceeding your credit limit to paying late. Some cards have eliminated the grace period entirely, charging interest from the day you make a purchase. Rates are so steep that even on the average card, as Doug Henwood points out in a recent Left Business Observer, it would take 34 years to pay off a $2,500 balance if you paid only the bank's suggested minimum.

While credit card loans were always risky — banks "wrote off" five times more credit-card than commercial loans as uncollectible — they are writing off even more today. Last year, banks wrote off $20 billion in credit card loans — 5.5% of the total debt outstanding. The norm was 3% until the mid-90s. The banks' exposure is serious enough that the federal government's Comptroller of the Currency warned credit card banks to improve their credit standards.

Banks claim new and improved computer programs now allow them to isolate out risky prospects from sound ones. But they really seem to be containing their risk by changing the rules of the game. For instance, they are not "writing off" the customers who defaulted on their credit card debt. Instead, they've invented a new credit card for them. "Secured" credit cards are one of the fastest growing products in the business, designed for people like yet another friend of mine who defaulted on his student loans and is now eager to return to the fold of creditworthy Americans. For an annual fee, a hefty initial processing charge and a $90 deposit paid to Providian, one of the largest issuers of secured cards, my friend won the right to charge his card up to a whopping $400 credit limit.

Banks are also trying to contain their risk, not by scrutinizing who deserves higher credit lines, but by campaigning for bankruptcy reform that will restrict consumers' access to more favorable bankruptcy laws (see box). If reform is enacted, the banks could become even worse pushers, argues Stephen Brobeck, executive director of the Consumer Federation of America: "By allowing creditors to collect more debt, bankruptcy reforms would encourage credit card banks to market and extend credit more aggressively."

## Debt For Sale

With credit card debt riskier and at a new high, how can banks carry so many loans on their balance sheets? After all, by law they must keep on hand capital amounting to about 6% of their outstanding loans, and there's $500 billion in credit card debt out there. The quick answer is they don't. Since 1987, when First Boston invented the practice, the big players have removed some of their credit card debt from their balance sheets by selling it off to investors, much as they sell off home mortgages. Together the major credit card banks — Citibank, First Chicago, NationsBank (which just merged with Bank America) — and other credit card issuers sell off the right to collect on about $40 billion worth of their credit card debt to investors. This maneuver gives them more money on hand to loan out, pumping up their desire to find new, perhaps riskier, customers, while removing the loans from their balance sheets and ultimately increasing the bubble of debts left unpaid.

## Who's the Victim?

Like most capitalist enterprises, banks' desperate pursuit of credit card profits is not a victimless crime. There are plenty of victims littered along the road, and many are low income. "Jesse" is in Debtor's Anonymous now after racking up $93,000 in credit card debt after losing her job at a warehouse and failing to apply for unemployment benefits. Her sister almost lost her home after paying for the birth of her son on a credit card — her husband was working temp jobs at the time, and they had no health insurance.

Like Jesse and her sister, the new lower income customers tend to use credit cards when their income drops, not just for convenience like many middle class customers, according to a study published by the Institute for Research on Poverty at the University of Wisconsin. For instance, while the better off tend to cut their credit card use during a recession, the poor and near poor use them even more.

With stagnating middle class incomes, however, the middle class also might be caught in more credit card debt than they expected. Unlike lower and upper income Americans, they are the only group whose incomes have not yet returned to their pre-recession, 1989 level, and some may have charged up their credit cards expecting more of a rebound to help them pay off their bills. Brobeck of the Consumer Federation even blames credit cards (as opposed to stagnating incomes, steep housing prices, lost health insurance or erratic job markets) for the skyrocketing bankruptcy rates: "Mounting credit card debt was the most important reason for the rise in personal bankruptcies (1.3 million in 1997)," he says.

## Unstable Economy

The other victim of credit card companies' desperate strategies is the economy as a whole. In good Keynesian fashion, consumers have been driving economic growth.

But in a period of income stagnation, and with greater access to credit, consumers have been doing their spending more and more with debt. This creates a "consumer debt-driven business cycle" that creates new dynamics — and longterm problems — for the economy.

"The great fear is, if we go into recession, we'll be saddled with record levels of debt," says Tom Palley, an economist with the AFL-CIO. In 1997, consumer debt peaked to record levels, created not just by credit cards but by home equity and other loans.

## Let the Debtor Beware

Even those like Brobeck of the Consumer Federation who are critical of the banking industry's greedy pursuit of lower income credit card holders hesitate to call for a halt to the practice. The New York Federal Reserve Bank economists say that as long as banks "cover any extra risks they are taking, and as long as borrowers understand the price they are paying," both sides can benefit. The problem is that credit card companies do everything they can to ensure customers don't know the price they are paying. At the very least, bank regulators must force credit card companies to reveal right on our monthly bills how much it will cost us in interest charges by the next month and by the end of the year if we don't pay the bill in full right away (the Senate approved a mild version of this in its recent bankruptcy bill).

Congress must also stop credit card companies from offering ridiculously high lines of credit that delude us into thinking we can carry heavy amounts of debt. Credit limits tap into our deep sense of power as consumers and distort our sense of our wealth. Jesse from Debtor's Anonymous reveals, "I used to see credit cards as an asset. If they give you a credit line, it increases your sense of importance." Credit card companies should enforce reasonable credit limits instead of using them as yet another opportunity to profit from those who exceed them.

If they actually do this, the credit card companies need not cover their risk by charging high interest rates and hidden penalties. Such usury is another form of "fringe banking," almost as bad as those rent-to-own stores targeting low income folks for double the usual price of a television set in "easy" monthly installments. Congress might also cap the interest rates the companies can charge, a move Rep. Joseph Kennedy pondered a few years back. A cap need not force the companies to dump their new, high risk, customers, as they direly warned when faced with the prospect. They need only do their jobs as bankers and enforce reasonable credit limits.

If nothing else, this quandary of how best to stop credit card companies from feeding off the economic insecurity of lower income Americans reveals how urgently we need to develop less exploitative ways of raising people's incomes and easing their credit crunch. America's economic health must be built on more than easy credit so those slipping through the safety net don't end up desperately trying to charge their way back to financial stability.

*Resources:* Stephen Brobeck, "Recent Trends in Bank Credit Card Marketing and Indebtedness," Consumer Federation of America (July 1998); Sandra E. Black and Donald P. Morgan, "Risk and the Democratization of Credit Cards," Federal Reserve Bank of New York Research Paper 9815 (June 1998); Edward J. Bird, Paul A. Hagstrom and Robert Wild, "Credit Cards and the Poor," Univ. of Wisc. Institute for Research on Poverty Discussion Paper 1148-97 (October 1997); "U.S. Credit Card Industry: Competitive Developments Need to Be Closely Monitored," General Accounting Office Report GGD-94-23 (April 1994); Federal Reserve Bank of Cleveland *Economic Trends* (July 1998).

# U.S. BANKS AND THE DIRTY MONEY EMPIRES

**BY JAMES PETRAS**
*September/October 2001*

Washington and the mass media have portrayed the United States as being in the forefront of the struggle against narcotics trafficking, drug-money laundering, and political corruption. The image is of clean white hands fighting dirty money from the Third World (or the ex-Communist countries). The truth is exactly the opposite. U.S. banks have developed an elaborate set of policies for transferring illicit funds to the U.S. and "laundering" those funds by investing them in legitimate businesses or U.S. government bonds. The U.S. Congress has held numerous hearings, provided detailed exposés of the illicit practices of the banks, passed several anti-laundering laws, and called for stiffer enforcement by public regulators and private bankers. Yet the biggest banks continue their practices and the sums of dirty money grow exponentially. The $500 billion of criminal and dirty money flowing annually into and through the major U.S. banks far exceeds the net revenues of all the information technology companies in the United States. These yearly inflows surpass the net profits repatriated from abroad by the major U.S. oil producers, military industries, and airplane manufacturers combined. Neither the banks nor the government has the will or the interest to put an end to practices that provide such high profits and help maintain U.S. economic supremacy internationally.

## Big U.S. Banks and Dirty Money Laundering

"Current estimates are that $500 billion to $1 trillion in illegal funds from organized crime, narcotics trafficking and other criminal misconduct are laundered through banks worldwide each year," writes Senator Carl Levin (D-MI), "with about half going through U.S. banks." The senator's statement, however, only covers proceeds from activities that are crimes under U.S. law. It does not include financial transfers by corrupt political leaders or tax evasion by overseas businesses, since in those cases any criminal activity takes place outside the United States. Raymond Baker, a leading U.S. expert on international finance and guest scholar in economic studies at the Brookings Institution, estimates the total "flow of corrupt money ... into Western coffers" from Third World or ex-Communist economies at $20 to $40 billion a year. He puts the "flow stemming from mis-priced trade" (the difference between the price quoted, for tax purposes, of goods sold abroad, and their real price) at a minimum of $80 billion a year. "My lowest estimate is $100 billion per year by these two means ... a trillion dollars in the decade, at least half to the United States," Baker concludes. "Including other elements of illegal flight capital would produce much higher figures."

The money laundering business, whether "criminal" or "corrupt," is carried out by the United States' most important banks. The bank officials involved in money laundering have backing from the highest levels of the banking institutions. These are not isolated offenses perpetrated by loose cannons. Take the case of Citibank's laundering of Raúl Salinas' $200 million account. The day after Salinas, the brother of Mexico's ex-President Carlos Salinas de Gortari, was arrested and his large-scale theft of government funds was exposed, his private bank manager at Citibank, Amy Elliott, said in a phone conversation with colleagues (the transcript of which was made available to Congressional investigators) that "this goes [on] in the very, very top of the corporation, this was known ... on the very top. We are little pawns in this whole thing."

Citibank is the United States' biggest bank, with 180,000 employees worldwide, operating in 100 countries, with $700 billion in known assets. It operates what are known as "private banking" offices in 30 countries, with over $100 billion in client assets. Private banking is the sector of a bank which caters to extremely wealthy clients, with deposits of $1 million or more. The big banks charge customers for managing their assets and for providing the specialized services of the private banks. These services go beyond routine banking services like check clearing and deposits, to include investment guidance, estate planning, tax assistance, off-shore accounts, and complicated schemes designed to secure the confidentiality of financial transactions. Private banks sell secrecy to their clients, making them ideal for money laundering. They routinely use code names for accounts. Their "concentration accounts" disguise the movement of client funds by co-mingling them with bank funds, cutting off paper trails for billions of dollars in wire transfers. And they locate offshore private investment corporations in countries such as the Cayman Islands and the Bahamas, which have strict banking secrecy laws. These laws allow offshore banks and corporations to hide a depositor's name, nationality, the amount of funds deposited, and when they were deposited. They do not require any declarations from bank officials about sources of funds.

Private investment corporations (PICs) are one particulary tricky way that big banks hold and hide a client's assets. The nominal officers, trustees, and shareholders of these shell corporations are themselves shell corporations controlled by the private bank. The PIC then becomes the official holder of the client's accounts, while the client's identity is buried in so-called "records of jurisdiction" in countries with strict secrecy laws. The big banks keep pre-packaged PICs on the shelf awaiting activation when a private bank client wants one. The system works like Russian matryoshka dolls, shells within shells within shells, which in the end can be impenetrable to legal process.

Hearings held in 1999 by the Senate's Permanent Subcommittee on Investigations (under the Governmental Affairs Committee) revealed that in the Salinas case, private banking personnel at Citibank – which has a larger global private banking operation than any other U.S. bank – helped Salinas transfer $90 to $100 million out of Mexico while disguising the funds' sources and destination. The bank set up a dummy offshore corporation, provided Salinas with a secret codename, provided an alias for a third party intermediary who deposited the money in a Citibank account in Mexico, transferred the money in a concentration account to New York, and finally moved it to Switzerland and London.

Instead of an account with the name "Raúl Salinas" attached, investigators found a Cayman Islands account held by a PIC called "Trocca, Ltd.," according to Minority Counsel Robert L. Roach of the Permanent Committee on Investigations. Three Panama shell companies formed Trocca, Ltd.'s board of directors and three Cayman shell companies were its officers and shareholders. "Citibank controls all six of these shell companies and routinely uses them to function as directors and officers of PICs that it makes available to private clients," says Roach. Salinas was only referred to in Citibank documents as "Confidential Client No. 2" or "CC-2."

Historically, big-bank money laundering has been investigated, audited, criticized, and subjected to legislation. The banks have written their own compliance procedures. But the big banks ignore the laws and procedures, and the government ignores their non-compliance. The Permanent Subcommittee on Investigations discovered that Citibank provided "services," moving a total of at least $360 million, for four major political swindlers, all of whom lost their protection when the political winds shifted in their home countries: Raúl Salinas, between $80 and $100 million; Asif Ali Zardari (husband of former Prime Minister of Pakistan), over $40 million; El Hadj Omar Bongo (dictator of Gabon since 1967), over $130 million; Mohammed, Ibrahim, and Abba Sani Abacha (sons of former Nigerian dictator General Sani Abacha), over $110 million. In all cases Citibank violated all of its own procedures and government guidelines: there was no review of the client's background (known as the "client profile"), no determination of the source of the funds, and no inquiry into any violations of the laws of the country where the money originated. On the contrary, the bank facilitated the outflow in its prepackaged format: shell corporations were established, code names were provided, funds were moved through concentration accounts, and the funds were invested in legitimate businesses or in U.S. bonds. In none of these cases did the banks practice "due diligence," taking the steps required by law to ensure that it does not facilitate money laundering. Yet top banking officials have never been brought to court and tried. Even after the arrest of its clients, Citibank continued to provide them with its services, including moving funds to secret accounts.

Another route that the big banks use to launder dirty money is "correspondent banking." Correspondent banking is the provision of banking services by one bank to another. It enables overseas banks to conduct business and provide services for their customers in jurisdictions where the bank has no physical presence. A bank that is licensed in a foreign country and has no office in the United States can use

### *INVESTMENT BANKING GLOSSARY*

**Firewall** is a non-legal delineation between investment banking and brokerage activities (respectively the creation and the distribution of securities).

**Brokers**, or salespeople, facilitate the buying and selling of securities for investors. In that capacity, they work on the public side of the firewall. SEC laws dictate that they advise investors based on their specific needs and financial situation. But, often brokers get paid a higher commission to sell the securities their banks want sold.

**Analysts** study individual companies, often specializing in a particular industry, and make buy and sell recommendations. Investors may rely on these recommendations to make investment decisions. Analysts can act on both sides of the firewall but are not supposed to let their different roles collide. (The recent spate of scandals proved this to be an impossibility.) On the "public" side, they worked with brokers explaining the merits (but rarely drawbacks) of a stock being recommended to a customer. On the other side of the firewall, analysts worked with investment bankers. They met with corporations about to issue new stock or bonds, or merge or acquire other corporations, to glean information that could be used in the subsequent marketing of new deals or newly created securities. This is referred to as the "private" side of the wall, because all conversations take place in a "planning" stage, before the general public is made aware of the deals. The settlement will supposedly prohibit analysts from performing both private and public roles, except in the presence of intermediaries, like lawyers or compliance officers.

**Investment Bankers** may be lower down in the firm's hierarchy than the senior executives, but senior bankers are still quite powerful. They create the terms, nature, and timing of the deals between banks and corporations, thus facilitating mergers, acquisitions, or corporate restructurings. They also arrange underwriting agreements for corporations issuing securities. Investment bankers worked closely with stock analysts like Jack Grubman to ensure that when a deal got off the ground, there was enough positive publicity on the public side of the firewall—with the investor base—to ensure the highest degree of profit back to the corporation, and fees to the bank.

**Senior Executives** (like the CEO, CFO, or President) run the banks or large divisions within them. They are thus in the position of deciding which client firms receive favored status or service. Senior executives escaped the recent period of scandals, untarnished.

correspondent banking to attract and retain wealthy criminal or corrupt clients interested in laundering money in the United States. Instead of exposing itself to U.S. controls and incurring the high costs of locating in the U.S., the bank will open a correspondent account with an existing U.S. bank. By establishing such a relationship, the foreign bank (called the "respondent") and its customers can receive many or all of the services offered by the U.S. bank (called the "correspondent"). Today, all the big U.S. banks have established multiple correspondent relationships throughout the world so they may engage in international financial transactions for themselves and their clients in places where they do not have a physical presence. The largest U.S. and European banks, located in financial centers like New York or London, serve as correspondents for thousands of other banks. Most of the offshore banks laundering billions for criminal clients have accounts in the United

States. Through June 1999, the top five correspondent bank holding companies in the United States held correspondent account balances exceeding $17 billion; the total correspondent balances of the 75 largest U.S. correspondent banks was $34.9 billion. For billionaire criminals an important feature of correspondent relationships is that they provide access to international transfer systems. The biggest banks specializing in international fund transfers (called "money center banks") can process up to $1 trillion in wire transfers a day.

## The Damage Done

Hundreds of billions of dollars have been transferred, through the private-banking and correspondent-banking systems, from Africa, Asia, Latin America, and Eastern Europe to the biggest banks in the United States and Europe. In all these regions, liberalization and privatization of the economy have opened up lucrative opportunities for corruption and the easy movement of booty overseas. Authoritarian governments and close ties to Washington, meanwhile, have ensured impunity for most of the guilty parties. Russia alone has seen over $200 billion illegally transferred out of the country in the course of the 1990s. The massive flows of capital out of these regions – really the pillaging of these countries' wealth through the international banking system – is a major factor in their economic instability and mass impoverishment. The resulting economic crises, in turn, have made these countries more vulnerable to the prescriptions of the IMF and World Bank, including liberalized banking and financial systems that lead to further capital flight.

Even by an incomplete accounting (including both "criminal" and "corrupt" funds, but not other illicit capital transfers, such as illegal shifts of real estate or securities titles, wire fraud, etc.), the dirty money coming from abroad into U.S. banks amounted to $3.5 to $6.0 trillion during the 1990s. While this is not the whole picture, it gives us a basis for estimating the significance of the "dirty money factor" in the U.S. economy. The United States currently runs an annual trade deficit of over $400 billion. The gap has to be financed with inflows of funds from abroad – at least a third of which is "dirty money." Without the dirty money the U.S. economy's external accounts would be unsustainable. No wonder the biggest banks in the United States and Europe are actively involved, and the governments of these countries turn a blind eye. That is today's capitalism – built around pillage, criminality, corruption, and complicity.

*Resources*: "Private Banking and Money Laundering: A Case Study of Opportunities and Vulnerabilities," Permanent Subcommittee on Investigations of the Committee on Governmental Affairs, United States Senate, One Hundred Sixth Congress, November 9-10, 1000; "Report on Correspondent Banking: A Gateway to Money Laundering," Minority Staff of the U.S. Senate Permanent Subcommittee on Investigations, February 2001.

# THE NEW OLD WALL STREET SETTLEMENT

**BY NOMI PRINS**
*July/August 2003*

You may have experienced a sense of déjà vu soaking in the media fanfare surrounding the recent Wall Street settlement, a $1.4 billion wrist-slap levied on the investment banking industry in the name of reform. That's because the headlines that accompanied the finalization of the "global" agreement were recycled versions of the ones that came out in December 2002, when the settlement was first publicized.

On April 28, the Securities and Exchange Commission (SEC), the New York Stock Exchange (NYSE), the National Association of Securities Dealers (NASD), and New York State Attorney General Eliot Spitzer settled "enforcement actions" with 10 top Wall Street banks and two star 1990s research analysts. The banks—including Citigroup-Salomon Brothers, JPM Chase, Goldman Sachs, Merrill Lynch, and Morgan Stanley—were charged with deliberately misleading investors with biased stock research that exaggerated the virtues of key client corporations.

The process leading up to the settlement started two years ago when Spitzer's office began investigating conflicts of interest on Wall Street. In April 2002, regulators at the SEC hopped on board with a joint investigation into the "undue influence of investment banking interest on securities research at brokerage firms."

The settlement makes three main changes to banking practices. First, it will insulate (or "firewall") research analysts from the influence of investment bankers by demanding that analyst pay be set with no input from the investment-banking department. Second, it requires that investment banks and brokerage firms provide independent research purchased from external sources to their clients (but only for the next five years—not exactly a permanent fix) and it makes analyst opinions public 90 days after they have been issued privately. Third, it bans firms from practicing hot IPO "spinning," or doling out initial public offering stock to the senior executives of client companies.

According to Spitzer's statement, the settlement "implements far-reaching reforms that will radically change behavior on Wall Street." But nothing in the settlement poses a serious threat to the status quo.

It's quite telling that no Wall Street firm has complained about the settlement. That's because it doesn't impact how they do business.

***Here are the top 10 reasons this settlement is a smokescreen:***

**#1** The fines are tiny. If you remove the $513 million thrown in for spurious investor research and education activities—banks will distribute research from independent firms *that they select*—you're left with less than a billion bucks in fines. Putting that into perspective, the top 10 Wall Street firms made $62 billion in fees alone over the four years in which their activities are in question.

The fines amount to just 1.5% of fee revenue. And that's not to mention the $1 trillion in other revenues these banks garnered over the same period. The settlement fines are so miniscule they are unlikely to deter future wrongdoing.

**#2** Individual investors will see little of the settlement money. Spurred by class-action lawyers, Spitzer et al. established 10 different distribution funds for customers whose claims are "deemed appropriate" by the federal court at some future date. About $387.5 million of the $1.4 billion will go to the funds. But with thousands misled by brokers (*brokers*, not just analysts), it will take years to divvy up that cash.

**#3** It is not a global settlement even though it was spun as such. It's a U.S. settlement, and about as global as the World Series. Even the original 2002 SEC press release put the word "global" in quotes. Though most of the named firms are international, their practices outside the United States don't fall under SEC jurisdiction. And foreigners who bought stock under misleading information won't receive compensation.

**#4** No bank admitted any wrongdoing. This is, unfortunately and consistently, par for the course with all SEC corporate corruption settlements. There is never an admission of any culpability.

**#5** Acting contrite is no substitute for being held to account. And banks are not even managing to act contrite. At an investor conference held days after the settlement announcement, the *New York Times* reported Morgan Stanley CEO Philip Purcell saying, "I don't see anything in the settlement that will concern the retail investor about Morgan Stanley. Not one thing." (He's right, but that's because the settlement doesn't say anything meaningful at all, not because Morgan Stanley was above the fray.) SEC chairman William Donaldson shot off an irate response, concerned that those remarks were "evidence [of] a troubling lack of contrition." It is totally hypocritical for Donaldson to accuse Purcell of not acting sorrier. If that's the best our new SEC head can do, we're in trouble. Plus, back to #4, why should he be sorry if he didn't admit any wrongdoing to begin with?

**#6** The hardship of being prohibited from spinning hot IPOs, in a dead stock market environment when nothing's hot anyway, is a non-starter. There is no such thing as a hot IPO right now. And, when IPOs become hot again, there are myriad simple ways to get around the ban. Just wait and see. As a ban, this IPO ruling is as robust as, well, a Wall Street firewall.

**#7** The increased insulation, or "firewalls," mandated by the settlement—like prohibiting investment bankers and analysts from joint business trips with clients or ensuring a few extra lawyers are present at potentially questionable internal meetings—are cosmetic changes.

Many top analysts are now switching to jobs as investment bankers or salespeople. As a result, they'll be able to say anything to customers, anyway. It just won't be called research. Wall Street firms are not about to physically relocate their analyst staffs to separate buildings. (And even that wouldn't be sufficient.) If you're on the same e-mail system, share the same limos home and get your food from the same cafeteria, you're connected.

**#8** This settlement does nothing to change the deeply institutionalized incentive systems (and cultures) within financial firms. As a managing director at one of the fine-paying firms put it, "Hey, it's not like junior analysts in training are now being told they'll get penalized for bringing in deals." Without a deeper revision of the system, there will always be someone at a high level who will find ways to ensure someone lower doesn't publicize negative views on a company with whom the firm is about to do a large deal.

**#9** The settlement scapegoats analysts while leaving senior executives and investment bankers unscathed. The central problem with Wall Street aconflicts of interest is not former Citigroup-Salomon Brothers' star telecom analyst, Jack Grubman, and is even less Merrill Lynch's Internet analyst Henry Blodget (paying $15 million and $4 million in fines respectively). These people were tools who played their roles in the whole system exceedingly well, while the media promulgated their cheerleading

The settlement criminalizes analysts for extolling the virtues of their top client corporations, but does nothing to reform the more troublesome—and clandestine—behavior of senior executives and investment bankers who created the deals and issued the stock that analysts were paid to market

Instead of penalizing analysts who don't even close investment-banking deals, the priority should be to pry apart and isolate corporate executives and investment bankers, and their corporate customers, starting at the top—with the board. Citigroup CEO Sandy Weill was on AT&T's board when Citigroup-Salomon's chief telecom analyst Grubman inflated AT&T's rating. AT&T CEO Michael Armstrong was also on Citigroup's board at the time (and still is). E-mails uncovered by Spitzer suggest that Weill had asked Grubman to upgrade AT&T's rating as a personal favor. Grubman upped AT&T's rating just before Citigroup bagged the deal to do an IPO for AT&T's wireless division. Citigroup reaped profits from doing and distributing the AT&T IPO, all the while duping investors. Yet while Grubman was banned from ever working as an analyst again, and has to pay a multimillion dollar fine, Weill remains at Citigroup's helm, his wallet untouched by the settlement.

**#10** There has been no mention of bringing back the Glass-Steagall Act, which prohibited commercial banks from owning brokerages. The repeal of Glass-Steagall in November 1999 unleashed a spate of bank mergers that resulted in many firms combining investment, broker activities, and commercial banking under the same roof.

The New Deal-era act was passed in 1933 to resolve the rampant conflicts of interest and fraud in the 1920s that led to the 1929 crash. Though hacked at for years since, Glass-Steagall was the one piece of legislation that kept the same banks that merged companies, issued debt, and created stock IPOs from touting them to the public via retail brokerage arms and commercial bank accounts.

Real reform would reinstitute strong, Glass-Steagall-type separation between investment and commercial banking activities. And it would regulate conflicted senior investment banking and corporate relationships. Key to any real reform would be regulation of the widespread practice of loan-tying, or giving cheap credit to corporate clients in exchange for profitable banking business (like IPOs and mergers). Loan-tying is a practice made easier by Glass-Steagall repeal. Citigroup became the largest issuer of Ford debt after Citigroup director and former Treasury secretary Robert Rubin joined Ford's board of directors. Because of Rubin's relationship with Ford, Citigroup gave the company preferential terms, offering to issue debt (in the form of bonds) for Ford more cheaply than other banks would. The net result was that Ford issued more debt because it was so cheap. Yet, under all that debt weight, Ford's stock price and ratings plummeted this past year, taking along jobs and pensions with them.

Of course, there's a good reason points eight, nine, and ten haven't been brought to light—they are remedies that would actually make a difference.

# CHASE: A BANK FOR THE NEW CENTURY

## BY JOSEPH PLUTA
*Spring 2007*

Here are a few items from the recent corporate history of JPMorgan Chase & Company:

***October 2001:*** Chase quietly pays $1 million to settle Securities and Exchange Commission charges that it filed false reports while acting as a transfer agent for bond issues.

## *Chase and Enron*

In 2000 and 2001, Chase and other investment banks became involved in a scheme which inflated Enron's reported profits and hid large amounts of its corporate debt. By April of 2002, Chase was the target of both Securities and Exchange Commission (SEC) charges and a class-action shareholder lawsuit, with the University of California as lead plaintiff. Both suits contended that the bank assisted Enron in maintaining its fraudulent image as a profitable firm. Their allegations were numerous and specific: First, Chase loaned Enron $65 million to help a company subsidiary buy Enron assets and thereby make its 1999 profits look higher than they actually were. Formed by Merrill Lynch, this subsidiary was named LJM2—perhaps one of the many Enron offshoots with Star Wars-inspired names. In December of 2000, Mahonia Ltd., a firm controlled by Chase and located on the Channel Islands off the coast of England, purchased oil and gas contracts from Enron. Chase later sold these contracts back to Enron, which treated the dollar value of its repurchase as revenue.

But Chase was not only facilitating Enron's creation and manipulation of legally questionable partnerships. At the same time, the company was also selling Enron stock to investors—despite possessing insider information that would have given pause to any honest investment adviser. Chase and other banks, therefore, were charged with instigating fraud by helping Enron hide debt in off-balance-sheet partnerships and by providing false information to the public about Enron stock they knew was shaky.

Later in 2002, more federal and shareholder charges followed. The CEO of Chase was accused of lobbying Moody's Investor Service not to downgrade Enron's ratings while Chase tried to arrange a merger between Enron and Dynegy, Inc. The resulting false appearance of Enron's financial strength misled the public into investing billions of dollars. Three of Chase's "special purpose entities" (Choctaw Investors, Cherokee Finance, and Zephyrus) engaged in unusual lending transactions with Enron subsidiary Sequoia Financial Assets. These "loans" were repaid in full on the last day of the month, only to be loaned again the next day. The arrangement apparently was designed to allow Enron to covertly borrow hundreds of millions of dollars in undisclosed loans.

In June of 2005, Chase agreed to pay $2.2 billion to settle the class-action lawsuit over its role in assisting Enron in accounting fraud that cheated investors out of billions of dollars. (One month earlier, Chase agreed to pay $2 billion to settle similar claims by shareholders of WorldCom.) The $2.2 billion amount represents the largest settlement deal among all of Enron's criminal accomplices. During the following fourteen months, Chase also agreed to pay $80 million to settle regulatory charges that some of its employees helped Enron cook its books as well as another $350 million as part of a lawsuit Enron filed against ten banks. While Chase management still arrogantly denied any wrongdoing, most industry observers took the bank's willingness to pay such healthy sums as an implicit admission of guilt. Perhaps more importantly, these bank actions were a convenient way of avoiding lengthy court proceedings during which even more adverse information could have come to light.

***April 2002:*** Chase comes under investigation by the National Association of Securities Dealers (NASD) for charging customers extraordinarily large commissions for selling shares in initial public offerings—up to $3 a share, versus a typical fee of five cents a share—and is eventually fined.

***2003-2004:*** Following large-scale job cuts in New York, Indianapolis, Tampa, Fla., and Findlay, Ohio, the company faces lawsuits alleging race and age discrimination in the layoffs.

***January 2005:*** Chase is fined $400,000 by the NASD for illegal late trading of mutual fund shares and for falsely recording customer trading orders—the largest fine ever imposed for this type of violation.

***January 2005:*** A Chase vice president pleads guilty to charges that he arranged to have the company pay $50,000 to a close friend of the Philadelphia mayor in order to seek favor with the city administration.

***November 2005:*** Chase faces accusations of overcharging active-duty military personnel on loans, in direct violation of the Servicemembers Civil Relief Act, a 2003 law passed to ensure that military families could obtain low-interest loans to cover expenses while their service member is serving in a war zone.

***March 2006:*** The Tokyo branch of JP Morgan Securities Asia is fined an undisclosed amount by Japan's Financial Services Agency for breaking securities laws. Accused of manipulating futures contracts, the Tokyo branch is also ordered to suspend its stock-futures trading temporarily.

This brief roster offers just a glimpse of the full range of Chase Bank's brushes with the law since 2000. And there is good reason to take a look at what megabanks such as Chase have been up to in the past seven years. The new century was ushered in by what may have seemed an obscure piece of legislation, but one that is significant in its impact on the U.S. financial system: the Gramm-Leach-Bliley Act, signed by Bill Clinton in November 1999. The new law repealed the remaining regulations of the 1933 Glass-Steagall Act and related Depression-era laws that had created a range of banking-industry regulations designed to prevent future financial meltdowns.

From the standpoint of the big bankers, the 1999 law meant their industry had finally turned a corner. Opponents of Glass-Steagall within the banking industry had sought its repeal for over six decades. While earlier laws had chipped away at its regulatory regime, the 1999 law finally reversed the most critical regulations.

Free to expand and diversify in new ways, many banks reacted cautiously. But not Chase. In September 2000, Chase Manhattan merged with JP Morgan to form J.P. Morgan Chase & Co. Then, in July 2004, Chase merged with Bank One, under the new name JPMorgan Chase & Co. (Yes, the same name minus some periods and spaces.) The roster of Chase's dubious practices over these seven years is one piece of the puzzle in coming to understand the new, post-Glass Steagall banking regime. Chase has clearly been a more frequent target of legal action in recent years than any other large bank, so it may not be typical—or perhaps fewer of the crimes and misdemeanors of the other megabanks have come to light. Either way, a portrait of the new 21st-century Chase bank illustrates the kinds of business practices that megabanks can now pursue.

## Deregulation Dilemmas

Probably the most significant change the 1999 law made was to allow commercial banks to pursue investment banking activities. Inevitable conflicts of interest arise when the same financial institution can engage in both commercial and investment banking, a point clearly understood by the Depression-era policymakers who wrote Glass-Steagall.

On its commercial banking side, a bank accepts deposits from customers and presumably looks out for their best interests, for instance, when it recommends various savings options. On its investment banking side, however, a bank has an incentive to downplay to customers the risks of investments such as stocks because it receives a brokerage commission when it buys stock for a customer—and when it resells a customer's stock as well, even if that stock has substantially plunged in value. There may be an even sharper conflict of interest when an investment bank is recommending specific stocks to individual investors while at the same time consulting for those same corporations and negotiating merger overtures for them.

Perhaps not surprisingly, many of the ethically-suspect actions Chase has been caught in since 2000 involve the interface between commercial and investment banking. Chase's involvement in the Enron scandal is the most prominent example: in 2002 Chase became the target of Securities and Exchange Commission (SEC) charges and a class-action shareholder lawsuit, both stemming from the myriad ways the bank had allegedly helped Enron maintain its fraudulent image as a profitable firm. (See "Chase & Enron," at right for more detail.)

Chase's new investment businesses engaged in some smaller-scale corporate misbehavior as well. The acquisition of J.P. Morgan in 2000 was intended to be part of Chase's move into investment banking, although ironically Morgan was another commercial bank, not an investment bank, and thus not likely to be a source of the kind of expertise Chase was seeking. So perhaps the company's problems with Texas customers beginning in 2000 were only a matter of inexperience. At that time, a number of investors in central Texas purchased mutual funds with a Chase investment services branch. In an effort to lure these customers away from their commercial banks, the investment advisors encouraged them to open checking and savings accounts with Chase as well. Soon afterward, these customers began getting charged service fees because of supposedly inadequate balances. The checking and savings accounts, however, were backed by the money in their individual investment accounts, in some cases as much as several hundred thousand dollars. While the fees were removed when customers complained, the annoyance factor severely damaged the bank's reputation. The claim of a computer error for eight consecutive months in one case suggests ineptness, indifference, or both.

Alternatively, this behavior could be part of a larger pattern of extracting revenues intensively from small investors (as in the NASD investigation of Chase's exorbitant trading commissions noted above). Moreover, the performance of the mutual fund accounts was abysmal, with some losing more than a third of their value in less than a year. During this time, money managers serving the accounts in Texas changed frequently. None of the new managers contacted customers about possible concerns. All were difficult to reach and reluctant to meet with customers when they sought advice. When meetings finally occurred, investors were treated rudely and criticized for their alleged lack of knowledge about the complexities of the world of finance. Predictably, investors began withdrawing funds at the earliest available opportunity.

Chase has engaged in plenty of questionable behavior (and gotten into plenty of legal scrapes) on other fronts as well. For one thing, it is the silent partner to a whole range of businesses—such as payday lenders, pawn shops, and check cashing stores—that prey on low-income households with little or no access to mainstream financial services. These businesses are part of a fringe banking system that has propped up the profits of Chase and the other "legitimate" financial corporations that finance the shabby storefronts. Consumer groups have criticized Chase for closing bank branches in low-income neighborhoods—South Bronx, for example—and then financing check cashing stores in those same neighborhoods.

Chase also engages heavily in subprime lending in low- and moderate-income neighborhoods—not only mortgages, but also auto, home equity, and other loans. Banks typically portray subprime loans as a legitimate attempt to provide credit to borrowers whose income or credit history prevent them from qualifying for loans at lower interest rates. But in many instances, the story is a shadier one. According to studies conducted by Inner City Press, a nonprofit watchdog group based in New York City, for instance, Chase disproportionately excludes blacks and Latinos from its conventional mortgage lending, a practice which has *worsened* since 1999. In the Boston area in 2002, for example, Chase's denial rates were nearly nine times greater for blacks and over six times greater for Latinos than for whites. Chase's lending in Washington, D.C., San Francisco, St. Louis, Little Rock, Detroit, Milwaukee, and Dallas shows a similar pattern, with variations in denial rates that far exceed the differences in income and credit history between the groups. Inner City Press reports thousands of consumer complaints against Chase on issues ranging from racially motivated loan denials to arrogant and indifferent treatment by bank personnel. Denied conventional mortgages, these home buyers have little choice but to turn to the subprime market, where Chase stands ready to "serve" them.

And then there are the charges of outright fraud. In 2001, a group of homeowners in the Poconos region of Pennsylvania went so far as to file a federal civil racketeering suit against Chase. Their complaint: local developers, in collusion with appraisers and Chase's mortgage division, had sold them houses overpriced by two-thirds or more. Unable to either sell or refinance, numerous homeowners ended up in foreclosure. In 2003 Chase faced a similar suit in Ohio. According to the complaint in the Ohio case:

> *Rather than jeopardize its lucrative mortgage business, the Chase Defendants chose to ignore their own independent appraiser's warning and continued to purchase the*

*Raintree mortgages [Raintree was the mortgage originator. —Ed.], knowing that they would be able to promptly "flip" the loans to Freddie Mac and Fannie Mae before the Raintree customers began to default.*

Chase vigorously denied the allegations in both the Pennsylvania and Ohio cases. In the Poconos, though, the company later acknowledged buying loans that it knew were based on fraudulent, inflated assessments and offered to reduce the mortgages of hundreds of homeowners by amounts ranging up to $50,000.

## Bigger and Bigger

Federal regulators had an opportunity to scrutinize Chase's record in 2004, when it sought to merge with Bank One. But in July of that year federal authorities approved the merger, despite the objections of consumer groups and the reduction in competition which the merger would inevitably cause. The newly created banking giant now has, for example, a nearly 50% market share in key areas of Texas, including Houston. It is remarkable that the Department of Justice did not challenge this merger on antitrust grounds. Merger guidelines established in 1982 under the Reagan administration were designed to prevent such a high local concentration level. They also were supposed to block proposed horizontal mergers (i.e., mergers of firms that were previously direct competitors in the same industry) between firms with individually large *national* market shares in an industry that is already highly concentrated. Banking clearly fits this category. The only plausible explanation is that it never hurts to have friends in high places. The Bush administration has routinely pursued policies favorable to corporate interests, even if those policies include lax enforcement of federal merger guidelines and antitrust laws.

Ironically, despite the wide regulatory latitude given to Chase in recent years, the banking giant has largely been a bottom-line basket case. In 2001, returns on its $800 billion asset base were barely positive and only one-sixth the industry average, and the bank's stock lost a third of its value. In the third quarter of 2002, profits fell 91% to one cent per share—a drop far exceeding those of other major banks. Then-CEO William B. Harrison admitted that Chase had made loans to some of the biggest business failures in history, including Enron, Kmart, and telecom carrier Global Crossing. (This undistinguished record did not stop the company from lavishing Harrison with multimillion dollar pay packages, however.)

Hard times have continued to plague Chase since the Bank One merger as well. For instance, the company experienced a 30% fall in profit during the second quarter of 2005—and that was before the Enron settlement was charged to the books in the third quarter.

## The Future of Banking?

Is corporate chicanery an inevitable result of mega mergers like the ones that have made Chase into a financial services colossus? Big is not necessarily supposed to mean bad; in theory, ethical behavior may find a way to exist in a world of giant firms. In reality, however, *mergers confer power*, especially when two mammoth firms are involved. The substantial caches of funds which flow to such firms enable relatively easy payment of fines and out-of-court settlements that are often structured so as to minimize adverse publicity. These war chests also make possible advertising counteroffensives aimed at influencing broader public opinion. Chase has already undertaken a huge public relations blitz, with full-page ads in several large newspapers that offer statements from prominent corporate executives supporting Chase despite its many legal fiascos. It is possible, therefore, for a company like Chase to maintain a generally positive public image by paying handsome sums which smaller firms with more ethical management do not possess.

Behind the PR façade, however, the financial and political power of a megabank like Chase facilitates a culture of corporate greed—with a whole range of negative consequences for consumers and communities—that is far less likely to exist among smaller, more competitive firms.

*Resources:* Inner City Press, "J.P. Morgan Chase Watch," 2001-07, www.innercitypress org/jpmchase.html; H. Timmons, "The Besieged Banker," *Business Week*, 4/22/02; E. Sanders, "Bankers Under Fire," *Austin Am. Statesman*, 7/24/02; ongoing *New York Times* coverage; numerous online company press releases.

# NO EXPENSE TOO GREAT: A HISTORY OF THE SAVINGS & LOAN BAILOUT

**BY DORENE ISENBERG AND VINCE VALVANO**

*May 1989 (revised June 1993)*

The savings and loan (S&L) crisis has led to new regulations and regulators, and to dramatic changes in the S&L industry. But the $200 billion taxpayer-financed bailout is not a response to our needs for low-interest mortgage loans and stable community lenders. Many of those who produced and profited from the crisis have crafted the bailout, and so it bears all the limitations of its creators.

The explicit costs of the bailout are captured in the $200 billion figure, but there are many other costs that can't be calculated. The restructuring and decline of S&Ls has caused massive losses in jobs, economic growth, and well-being. The bailout bears partial responsibility for the stagnant economy of the early 1990s.

Though the S&L crisis emerged early in the 1980s, it took until 1989 for the government to plan and finance a bailout. In the intervening years several attempts were made to address the evolving problem, but it was a politically unpopular topic. The Bush and Reagan administrations preferred to let the regulators and insurers grapple with it.

Even after the bailout legislation was passed, most politicians knew that too little money had been allocated to save the industry. With government deficits taking center stage, federal spending of tens of billions of dollars to salvage risk-hungry S&Ls was not the type of program that voters would be wild about supporting. To hide their dilemma, Congress and succeeding presidents based bailout funding on unrealistically hopeful predictions. Since these predictions have not come to pass, each president has returned to Congress almost annually with requests for additional tens of billions of dollars. The crisis has peaked but the bailout's costs continue to escalate.

## Financial Stability

The financial disruptions of the Great Depression led to greater regulation of the financial sector. One of the key elements designed to promote stability was deposit insurance. In 1933, Congress created the Federal Savings and Loan Insurance Corporation (FSLIC), a private corporation that is government sponsored. Federally chartered S&Ls (thrifts) bought insurance which covered their deposits. The size of the deposit covered has increased over time, with accounts of up to $100,000 covered since 1980.

The purpose of deposit insurance was to stem the fear of a "run." Should a thrift go belly up due to bad loans or investments, FSLIC guaranteed that the institution's losses would not wipe out any insured deposits. Were the federal government, through the FSLIC, to delay, let alone refuse, to pay off depositors at bankrupt S&Ls, it would risk creating a massive run on thrifts and, possibly, commercial banks — leading to a full-scale financial panic.

In return for deposit insurance protection, S&Ls accepted close supervision by federal regulators and pledged to limit their activities to a safe and socially useful business: making long-term home mortgage loans at relatively low interest rates. In contrast to the Wall Street side of the financial sector, the S&L side shunned risk and the search for big profits.

## Deregulation

This low-risk policy succeeded — until the 1980s, S&L failures averaged less than ten per year. The system, however, began to unravel in the late 1970s and early 1980s. Many thrifts were hurt when high inflation pushed up interest rates and thus the cost of their funds (deposits), while earnings remained tied to long-term, low-interest mortgages.

During the same period, new types of financial instruments evolved, such as money market mutual funds, that offered individual depositors much higher interest rates than were available from traditional savings accounts. This forced thrifts to compete more vigorously for funds in the financial markets. The new competition caused an outflow of deposits from the S&Ls in the early 1980s, weakening the industry's financial health.

In response, the S&Ls pressed Washington to relax its regulatory hold over the industry. Congress and Reaganite bank regulators willingly obliged. They allowed the thrifts to offer higher interest rates to attract deposits, leading in turn to the demise of affordable home mortgages. Thrifts were also permitted to invest in a wider range of assets: commercial real estate, financial futures contracts, and junk bonds, among other high-risk projects. Conflict-of-interest rules governing lending were also eased, providing incentives for developers and other entrepreneurs to buy thrifts and use them to finance their own deals.

The federal government deemed such deregulation necessary because the S&Ls were no longer assured a steady supply of low-cost deposits. Now they needed the leeway to make loans and investments that would produce higher returns than standard home mortgages. By definition, however, such projects were considerably riskier than the home mortgage business. And S&L loan officers didn't have much collective experience in evaluating these more complex projects.

With the end of restrictions on the interest rates that S&Ls could pay on deposits, it became extremely easy for any thrift, no matter how obscure, to attract funds. As long as it was willing to offer a premium interest rate, a thrift could attract large sums of Wall Street money. These so-called "brokered deposits" would be broken into $100,000 chunks to qualify for government deposit insurance. Of course, if a thrift was paying a premium for its deposits, it naturally had to invest the money in riskier projects in order to turn a profit. Moreover, brokered deposits were inherently unstable — they could disappear just as quickly as they arrived, lured by higher interest rates elsewhere.

Despite the increasing financial shakiness of the industry, deposits poured into the newly liberated thrift sector. Between 1980 and 1989, they grew from less than 1% of total deposits to 7%. Thrifts that were already in bad shape tended to be the ones that relied most on brokered deposits. The autopsies on many failed thrifts showed 50% of their deposits to have been brokered. The ballooning of S&L deposits after deregulation dramatically increased the potential liabilities facing the FSLIC insurance fund.

Meanwhile, Reagan administration deregulators repeatedly denied requests by the Federal Home Loan Bank Board (FHLBB) — the regulator of federally chartered thrifts — for funding for more thrift examiners. In the face of a rapidly growing and increasingly complex industry, the FHLBB was unable to monitor the financial condition of many thrifts. The Bank Board reacted to this situation by relaxing its supervision of the industry and loosening capital requirements, making it easier for impaired thrifts to continue operating.

A transformation was taking place in the financial sector. Deregulation, coupled with inflation, recession, financial innovations, and increased competition among all the banks and thrifts produced hundreds of sick and dying S&Ls. These impaired S&Ls created a new set of problems. Neither the regulators nor the industry were ready or able to cope with these changes.

## The Dead and Brain Dead

By definition, a thrift dies (it becomes bankrupt or insolvent) when its liabilities (customer deposits) exceed the value of its assets (loans and various investments). Unlike other businesses, however, when a thrift becomes insolvent it is not forced by its creditors to shut down, thanks to the miracle of deposit insurance. A broke thrift can continue indefinitely to generate from depositors the cash it needs to stay in business — so, functionally, it's only brain dead.

Most of those involved with S&Ls don't have much of an incentive to demand that a bankrupt thrift close down. Depositors, who need not worry about losing their money (as long as their account at any one thrift doesn't exceed $100,000), don't pay close attention to the financial condition of any particular thrift. Equity owners know that by the time an S&L has gone over the edge, its stock has lost most of its value, so they can't lose much more if the thrift keeps operating at a loss. Managers often have an ownership stake in the thrift, so they have a more pronounced interest in its continued operation. They can continue to collect often hefty salaries and perks, and hope for a turnaround.

In this environment, the decision to close a failing thrift rests largely in the hands of federal regulators. Once a thrift becomes insolvent, the way to minimize taxpayer costs is for regulators to close it down, pay off the depositors from FSLIC's coffers, and sell the thrift's assets to recoup as much of the deposit liability as possible. The problem with this process (besides the disruption it causes to the local community), known as liquidation, is that it requires FSLIC to lay out cash up front to pay depositors.

For example, say the Longhorn Savings and Loan of Houston (fictitious) becomes insolvent. To liquidate the thrift, the FSLIC would have to pay its depositors $500 million right away. Longhorn's assets at that point are worth, at most, only $300 million and many of those assets aren't easily converted into cash. It would take a lot of time and effort by the FSLIC to sell assets such as commercial or residential property in order to partially recoup its payments to depositors.

In the early 1980s, FSLIC was faced with hundreds of Longhorn S&Ls, but instead of shutting them down, it allowed them to stay in business. The number of "brain dead" thrifts quickly outpaced the ability of regulators to liquidate them. The insurance fund was simply not large enough for the job. In 1980, the number of operating insolvents was 17; by 1986, it had soared to 468. This increase, the result of FSLIC's own insolvency, is mirrored by the decline in thrift shutdowns. They peaked in 1982, at 252, while in 1986 only 83 thrifts were closed.

## The Southwest Plan

In the fall of 1988, as thrift losses climbed ever higher, the FHLBB embarked on a more aggressive strategy, dubbed the "Southwest Plan," to tackle S&L insolvencies. Strapped for cash and unable to liquidate S&Ls on its own, FHLBB negotiated the sales of 220 bankrupt thrifts, primarily in the Southwest, to private investors. In return for putting up small amounts of capital, these investors received big tax breaks and a guaranteed rate of return on their assets.

Congress and many others criticized these sales for continuing the tradition of putting S&Ls into the hands of financial speculators, while providing generous government guarantees. For example, one group of thrifts was sold to a corporate raider who put $300 million of capital, only $65 million of which was his own, into the deal and walked away with $900 million in tax breaks. The FHLBB argued that this was the best it could do, given its lack of cash in hand to liquidate insolvent thrifts.

Aside from the complaints of overly generous terms for investors, critics also charged that the Bank Board was underestimating the cost to insurers (soon to be taxpayers) of these sales. The Bank Board members believed that in the long run the revenue from the sales would exceed the cost of liquidation. But, instead, by 1989 $40 billion was needed to pay off the FSLIC notes issued to finance the Southwest Plan. These expenses added significantly to the overall cost of the S&L crisis.

## The Bailout

Finally, the government acknowledged the bankruptcy of FSLIC and the hundreds of "brain dead" S&Ls by passing the Financial Institutions Reform, Recovery and Enforcement Act of 1989 (FIRREA). This legislation signed FSLIC's death certificate along with that of hundreds of S&Ls. It created an institution for liquidating "brain dead" S&Ls, procured money to liquidate them, and reconfigured the thrifts' industrial and regulatory structure.

The Resolution Trust Corporation (RTC) was set up to sell, merge, or liquidate the "brain dead" thrifts. Like the Southwest Plan before it, the purchasers received big tax breaks and, in many cases, a guaranteed rate of return on their assets. Initially, Congress gave the RTC $50 billion, with which it took over 267 of the failed thrifts. Many more insolvents, however, continued to operate because the funds and staffing were insufficient to completely resolve the problem. While the $50 billion was in addition to the $40 billion required to settle the Southwest Plan's outstanding balance, both were a drop in the bucket compared to what was needed.

In addition to the RTC, Congress also created a new insurance corporation, the Savings Association Insurance Fund (SAIF). SAIF, in contrast to the FSLIC, is a part of the Federal Deposit Insurance Corporation (FDIC), the insurer of commercial banks.

In the early 1980s, deregulation attempted to homogenize the depository institutions. Instead of allowing each institution to maintain and further define its special area of expertise, the government pushed to erase the differences between the thrifts and banks. By merging the insurance funds into one corporation, the loan specializations that used to differentiate the S&Ls from commercial banks — an emphasis on home mortgage loans versus commercial lending — were being eradicated.

Further evidence of this move is the RTC policy, and prior to it the FSLIC policy, that promotes commercial bank acquisitions of failing S&Ls. As of July, 1992, of the 651 resolutions, 383 S&Ls were acquired by banks and only 180 were acquired by other S&Ls. These 383 S&Ls represented 58% of the total assets resolved by the RTC.

## The Continuing Crisis

With FIRREA's passage the financial crisis in the savings and loan industry was addressed, but not solved. The RTC has closed 651 thrifts and taken 60 more under conservatorship. These thrifts had $111 billion in assets most of which were low quality, and thus less marketable. The higher quality assets were usually sold off before the RTC takeover. The annual number of failing S&Ls has slowed, but in 1992 the Congressional Budget Office (CBO), a non-partisan government organization, estimated that as many as 700 more institutions may fail by 1997.

Even as the rate of failures is declining, the cost of the bailout is climbing. Congress' initial $50 billion funding in 1989 was followed by $30 billion in 1991 and $25 billion in 1993. According to the FIRREA action plan, the RTC should have all of the "brain deads" resolved by September 1993. The CBO's estimate of more insolvent thrifts on the horizon, however, coupled with the RTC's generous asset return policy (in many cases if an acquired asset fails to perform as expected, the RTC must buy it back) portends a longer life for the RTC and a need for more taxpayer money.

The total current cost of the S&L bailout is estimated at $205 billion. This will become about $500 billion over time if we include 30 years of interest payments on the U.S. Treasury bonds sold to finance the cost. The current cost averages out to an $800 payment by every living American.

These are the explicit costs. The alterations that the financial sector continues to undergo are producing numerous costs that are not as easily quantified. The thrifts that remain after the shakeout are larger, but fewer in number, so they serve fewer communities. Their offerings of financial services have grown, but their old specialty, the home mortgage loan, is now only one of their many services and is harder to obtain.

The cheap home mortgage loan that U.S. financial policy made available in earlier decades has been eliminated by the various Congressional acts that have deregulated and then reregulated the S&L industry. While the low market interest rates of the early 1990s have made home mortgages relatively affordable for the moment, the regulations which ensured that S&Ls would provide low cost loans have been wiped off the books. S&Ls still make home loans, but less of them, and mortgage rates are now tied to general market interest rates — so they can rise again at any time. Partial responsibility for the decreased affordability of housing lies here. Additionally, home mortgage lending pumped deposits from thrifts back into their local communities. With fewer S&Ls, and with home mortgages being a smaller percentage of their assets, local institutions have reduced their investment in communities.

## Financial or Economic Stability?

The post-Great Depression S&L regulatory structure aided in producing stable financial institutions and inexpensive funds for mortgage lending. The current restructuring has kept the savings and loan crisis from blossoming into a full-scale depression, but has greatly contributed to the economy's sustained recession since 1990.

The restructuring has also shifted the cost of the crisis. Instead of the S&L industry, its stockholders, and the depositors paying for the bailout, a larger group, taxpayers, is paying for the thrift crisis. This expands the size of the group sharing the bailout's cost, and extends the period over which it will be born to 20-30 years. As a result, the impact on each individual will be smaller than in previous financial crises such as the Great Depression.

Shifting this burden produces two problems, however. The greater tax burden could depress household spending, which may foster a period of extended stagnation. Also, like the earlier Chrysler and Continental Illinois bailouts, the government's policy uses public money without giving people a voice in how the money is used. Taxpayers were never asked whether they supported the S&L bailout or how it should proceed. The blame for the thrift mess is easy to spread around. Congress, the Reagan and Bush administrations, the S&L industry, regulators, and a variety of fast-buck entrepreneurs who bought up S&Ls for use as personal money machines all contributed to the crisis. Unfortunately, this same group of interested parties has produced the new industrial and regulatory structure. Will the new structure provide a financial environment that helps to stabilize the economy, or is it merely a boondoggle in which taxpayers shoulder the burden?

The Clinton administration's proposal for a system of community development banks and credit unions is an acknowledgment of the disastrous mess this financial crisis has made in our communities. While such a system would be a good first step, the need for loans to homebuyers and community businesses far outdistances the paltry $354 million in funding over 1993-97 that Clinton proposed in his original economic plan. This level of spending can't begin to remedy the financial and productive disruptions we have experienced throughout the past 15 years. What remains to be seen is whether the whole fiasco will spark renewed grassroots pressure for public accountability, social responsibility, and a democratic voice in the financial sector.

*Resources:* The Greatest Ever Bank Robbery, M. Mayer, 1992; "Staff Report of the Committee on Banking, Finance, and Urban Affairs," U.S. House of Representatives, December 1992; "Taking the Measure of the Resolution Trust Corporation," RTC Review, August 1992; "Thrift Industry Crisis: Causes and Solutions," R. Brumbaugh, Jr. and A. Carron, Brookings Papers on Economic Activity, 2:1987.

# Chapter 3

# THE STOCK MARKET

## RECESSION TIME! THE HOUSING BUBBLE BURSTS THE ECONOMY

**BY DEAN BAKER**
*September 2007*

The downturn in jobs reported last month by the Labor Department provided evidence of an economic downturn that even the economy's greatest cheerleaders could not ignore. Healthy economies do not shed jobs.

During the core periods of the upturns in the eighties and nineties, there were three months in which the economy lost jobs. In two of these, the loss was attributable to major strikes. (The jobs of striking workers are not counted in the survey.) That leaves a grand total of one month in more than twelve years of recovery in which the economy lost jobs. In other words, the August job loss leaves the economic optimists somewhat less credible than the deniers of global warming.

The backdrop for the August job loss is the collapse of the subprime mortgage market. Millions of low- and moderate-income homeowners are now looking at the resetting of interest rates on adjustable rate mortgages to levels that they cannot afford. While the Fed chairman and other leading economists assured the public that the problems would be restricted to the subprime segment of the housing market, this assertion was always ridiculous on its face.

Subprime mortgages accounted for one-fourth of all mortgages issued in 2006. The equally troubled Alt-A mortgage category accounted for another 15 percent. With segments that account for 40 percent of the mortgage market going into convulsion, there was no way that the housing market as a whole would not be affected. Of course, record supplies of unsold new homes and vacant homes also ensured that there would be substantial downward pressure on house prices.

The excess supply and constriction of mortgage credit is now affecting prices. Prices in the cities that had been the hottest bubble markets, such as San Diego, Las Vegas, Phoenix, and Miami, are declining at double-digit rates. Prices in slightly less bubbly markets, such as New York City, Washington, DC, and Boston, are falling at single-digit rates. These declines are likely to continue and quite possibly accelerate as the turmoil in the mortgage market further constrains demand.

This process will set in motion a downward spiral, as declines in house prices lead to more mortgage defaults. This will both place more foreclosed homes on the market and further constrain mortgage credit as the risk of default rises. The weakness in the housing market will be further reinforced by the weakening of the job market.

The job loss will first show up in the housing-related sectors. More than 50,000 layoffs have already been announced in the mortgage banking industry. This job loss has not shown up yet in the jobs data, since these workers were still employed when the August survey was taken. Construction and real estate will also see sharp declines in employment in the months ahead.

However, the direct impact on the housing sector is just the tip of the iceberg. The housing bubble created more than $7 trillion in housing wealth. Homeowners have used this bubble wealth to support a surge in consumption over the last five years, pushing the saving rate to near zero. They borrowed against their home equity to pay for vacations, new cars, or just to meet necessary expenses. As this bubble wealth disappears, consumption of all forms will be cut back, slowing growth and leading to more job losses.

In addition, declining construction-related fees and property tax revenue will constrict state and local budgets. This will lead to pressure for tax increases, just as the economy is going into a downturn, and to cutbacks in government spending and employment. This will further reinforce the downward spiral.

The growth of the housing bubble made this sort of collapse inevitable, just as the crash of the stock bubble was inevitable. The only question was when the bubble would finally burst and the exact form that the collapse would take.

It was incredibly negligent for the Federal Reserve Board and the Bush administration to allow the housing bubble to grow unchecked, and especially to allow the sort of mass fraud perpetrated against moderate-income homebuyers in the subprime market. At this point, there is probably no way to avoid a recession. If those making economic policy show no better judgment going forward than they have in the recent past, it is likely to be a long and painful recession.

*Reprinted from Truthout.org*

# TOO MUCH OF THE BUBBLY ON WALL STREET?

**BY DEAN BAKER**

*July/August 1999*

As the Dow Jones soared to record heights, most of the nation, which still has little or no direct stake in the stock market, watched with a combination of envy and amusement. Both sentiments are understandable. But more careful analysis suggests a third sentiment, alarm. Although most of the nation stands to gain little from Wall Street's raging bull, it may lose big in the subsequent bust. There may be no easy way to offset the impact of a crashing market, but we should at least know the problems we face up the road.

## The Logic of Stock Prices

First, some simple truths about the market's climb. The value of the Standard and Poor's 500, a broad measure of the stock market, increased nearly 400% over the last decade. After adjusting for inflation, the increase is still close to 250%.

In principle, the value of stock shares is supposed to be determined by the profits companies are expected to earn in the future. Since 1988, the after-tax profits of corporations have risen by almost 80% after adjusting for inflation — this is nowhere near the 250% run up in stock prices. As a result, the ratio of stock prices to corparate earnings is at a record high.

Historically, the ratio of the price of a share to corporate earnings per share has been slightly less than 15 to one. This means that if a company earned one dollar of profit for each share of stock it had issued, then the price of a share would be just under $15. Right now, the "price-to-earnings ratio" is about 33 to one. This means that the shares of a company that has one dollar of profit for each share of stock it issued would sell for $33.

What could justify paying so much more for a dollar of corporate earnings in 1999, than in the 1960s, '70s, or '80s? One answer is that people expect earnings to grow rapidly in the future. Suppose earnings were to double in the next five years. If stock prices didn't rise at all in that time, then the price to earnings ratio would fall to just above 16 to one — close to the historic average. If this scenario is indeed expected to materialize, then current stock prices might not be too unrealistic.

The problem with this story is that virtually no serious economic analyst expects profits to even come close to doubling. The Congressional Budget Office projects that corporate profits will be just 15.7% higher in 2004 than they are today. Once inflation is taken into account, there is almost no change at all. With profit rates already at post-war highs, it is difficult to imagine that they could rise much higher.

If the Congressional Budget Office's projections for profit growth are accurate, and stock prices don't rise in five years, the ratio of stock price to earnings will still be near record levels. If prices don't rise, someone holding stock throughout this five-year period would only receive the annual dividend payment from the corporation as their return. Currently the annual dividend payment on a share of stock averages less than 1.5% of the share price. By comparison, it is possible to get a 30-year government bond that pays 5.7% annual interest. If investors expect stock prices to stay roughly constant, then they would be far better off holding completely safe government bonds.

If stock prices do go higher in the future, and profits don't rise, then the ratio of stock prices to earnings will become even more out of line with its historic level. This is the story of a classic speculative bubble. People buy the asset (in this case stock), not because of its intrinsic value, but because they believe that someone else will come along willing to pay more for it. As long as someone else comes along, speculators in these markets can profit and get rich. But, inevitably, the bubble collapses as the market runs short of suckers.

## Blowing Bubbles

The history of capitalism is full of such speculative bubbles. During the tulip bulb mania in Holland in the 17th century, people bet millions that the price of tulip bulbs would soar without limits. At the beginning of the 18th century, there was the "South Sea Bubble" in England, where people expected to make a fortune in the stock of the South Sea Trading Company. The 19th century saw a series of speculative bubbles in both England and the United States around the stock of railroad companies. And of course, earlier in this century we had the huge run-up in the stock market that led to the 1929 crash and the Great Depression.

In each case, people made enormous fortunes on paper, as the price of their tulips or stock kept getting higher. The smart or lucky ones got out before the crash, and managed to pocket these gains. However, for every investor who got out in time, many more held on, hoping that the market would just keep rising. These people took big losses, in many cases their life savings.

What should we expect from a collapsing stock bubble at the end of the millennium? First, we must face the magnitude of the decline that could happen. If stock prices fell back enough to maintain their historic relationship to profits, then the decline would be approximately 55%. On average, people would lose more than half the money they have in the stock market.

There is some reason to believe that the historical relationship between stock prices and earnings may have permanently changed. Mutual funds that hold a broad index of stocks make it less risky for regular folks to be in the market, thus there are more people holding stocks. Under these circumstances, the dividend yield for any one stockholder goes down, suggesting that a price to earnings ratio of 20 to one is a more appropriate benchmark than the historic average of 15 to one. This still implies that stock prices could decline about 40% on average from their current levels.

Of course in many cases the declines would be much larger. There are Internet companies, with stock valuations in the tens of billions of dollars, which have never earned a penny. Their stock may end up being totally worthless. People usually aren't willing to pay much money for a company that only knows how to lose money.

## The Downside to the Nineties Expansion

Even counting those who own stock in mutual funds through their retirement accounts, just over half of the population has no money in the stock market (according to the Federal Reserve Board). Why should the typical worker care if yuppies get burned by their foolish gambling? It turns out that, while most workers don't stand much to gain by having the market go up, they have a lot to lose when it goes down.

Throughout the '90s expansion, and over the last three years in particular, the economy has been driven primarily by a consumption boom. As people buy more, household savings rates have hit record lows. The savings rate was actually negative in the first quarter of 1999. People are far more indebted relative to their income than ever — even compared to the last peak right before the last recession.

This consumption boom in turn is driven by the boom in the stock market. As people see the value of their stock holdings rise, they feel more comfortable spending their whole paycheck. In many cases, they feel they can even borrow against their home or run up credit card debt because of the wealth they have accumulated in the stock market.

While a stock boom can drive a consumption boom, a stock bust will lead to plunging demand. The conventional wisdom among economists is that a one dollar increase in stock wealth leads to a three cent increase in consumption. If stock prices fall enough to bring the price to earnings ratio down to 20 to one, this would mean a loss of $5 trillion dollars of wealth, and a subsequent drop in consumption of $170 billion. A decline of this magnitude would lower economic output (GDP) by at least 2.5%, and probably lead to an increase in the unemployment rate of at least 2%.

If price-to-earnings ratios fell back even further to their historic levels, it would mean a loss of $7.7 trillion in wealth and a $230 billion reduction in consumption. This would reduce GDP by at least 3.5%, and probably cause the unemployment rate to rise by more than three percentage points as growth slows and companies lay off workers. A stock market crash will throw the economy into a serious recession that hurts even those who don't own stocks.

## The Stock-Market Boom and Economic Policy

The fact that the stock market is significantly over-valued is widely recognized by economists. The International Monetary Fund even warned about the impact of a stock market crash in its last two reports on the United States. Yet, little is done to try to slow the run-up and avoid the inevitable economic fallout from a plunging market.

The reason is quite simple. For politicians and central bankers, it is easiest to do nothing and hope that the crash doesn't happen on their watch. This allows President Clinton and Federal Reserve Board Chairman Alan Greenspan to bask in the glow of a booming economy. With any luck, they'll both be in retirement by the time the market comes back down to earth.

It is also not clear exactly what they should have done to prevent the stock market boom. As governments have discovered through the years, there is no simple way to influence the direction of financial markets. Nonetheless, it is possible that continued statements by someone as respected in financial markets as Alan Greenspan could have prevented this run-up. While Greenspan did warn of the market's "irrational exuberance," this was a one-time warning issued more than two years ago, when the market was at about half its current level. A bit more concerted effort may have met with more success.

Of course, Wall Street is not just a place where stock prices move up and down. It's also an industry that has been incredibly profitable as trading has risen eight fold in the last decade. Politically connected Wall Street investment bankers and brokerage firms did not want to hear politicians trashing their business. A central banker, or a president, who warned of the dangers of an over-valued market would have faced considerable hostility from the financial industry. Clearly the current group of office holders was not prepared to pay this price.

Nor has the economics profession done much to warn the public of the dangers of an overvalued market. This is particularly ironic because mainstream economists are so obsessed with the failure of people to save money. For some reason, they seem more upset when the spending is by mothers on welfare, Social Security beneficiaries, or government employees than when the big spenders are yuppies with booming stock portfolios, partners in Goldman Sachs, or the latest Internet billionaire. Consistency is apparently not a common practice among economists.

## The Post-Crash Rubble

Even workers who never invested a dollar in the market will suffer from the the unemployment that would certainly follow any stock market crash. But many moderate income workers do have a direct stake in the market now that the vast majority of their pensions take the form of tax sheltered retirement accounts such as a 401(k). These plans provide no guaranteed benefit to workers. At her retirement, a worker gets exactly what she has managed to accumulate in these accounts.

Right now, a large percentage of the assets in these retirement accounts is in stock funds. In some cases this is due to the deliberate decision of workers to take an additional risk with their money. In other cases, it is due to the deceptive practices of fund managers who get extra commissions by pushing people into the stock market. Regardless of the reason, after the crash, some of these accounts will lose 40%, or more, of their value. Millions of workers will find that they have much less money to retire with than they had expected and be forced to delay their retirement by several years.

In short, the post-crash world is not likely to be a pretty one. The people who take the biggest losses will undoubtedly be wealthy speculators who should have understood the risks. The Yuppie apostles of the "new economy" will also be humbled by a plunging stock market. But these people can afford large losses on their stock holdings and still maintain a comfortable living standard. The real losers from a stock market crash will be the workers who lose most of their pensions, and the workers who must struggle to find jobs in the ensuing recession. Once again, those at the bottom will pay for the foolishness of those at the top.

# THE GREAT STOCK ILLUSION

**BY ELLEN FRANK**
*November/December 2002*

During the 1980s and 1990s, the Dow Jones and Standard & Poor's indices of stock prices soared ten-fold. The NASDAQ index had, by the year 2000, skyrocketed to 25 times its 1980 level. Before the bubble burst, bullish expectations reached a feverish crescendo. Three separate books—Dow 36,000, Dow 40,000 and Dow 100,000—appeared in 1999 forecasting further boundless growth in stock prices. Bullish Wall Street gurus like Goldman's Abby Cohen and Salomon's Jack Grubman were quoted everywhere, insisting that prices could go nowhere but up.

But as early as 1996, skeptics were warning that it couldn't last. Fed chair Alan Greenspan fretted aloud about "irrational exuberance." Yale finance professor Robert Shiller, in his 2001 book titled Irrational Exuberance, insisted that U.S. equities prices were being driven up by wishful thinking and self-fulfilling market sentiment, nourished by a culture that championed wealth and lionized the wealthy. Dean Baker and Marc Weisbrot of the Washington-based Center for Economic and Policy Research contended in 1999 that the U.S. stock market looked like a classic speculative bubble—as evidence they cited the rapidly diverging relationship between stock prices and corporate earnings and reckoned that, to justify the prices at which stocks were selling, profits would have to grow at rates that were frankly impossible.

In 1999 alone, the market value of U.S. equities swelled by an astounding $4 trillion. During that same year, U.S. output, on which stocks represent a claim, rose by a mere $500 billion. What would have happened if stockholders in 1999 had all tried to sell their stock and convert their $4 trillion into actual goods and services? The answer is that most would have failed. In a scramble to turn $4 trillion of paper gains into $500 billion worth of real goods and services, the paper wealth was bound to dissolve, because it never existed, save as a kind of mass delusion.

## The Illusion of Wealth Creation

Throughout the 1990s, each new record set by the Dow or NASDAQ elicited grateful cheers for CEOs who were hailed for "creating wealth." American workers, whose retirement savings were largely invested in stocks, were encouraged to buy more stock—even to bet their Social Security funds in the market—and assured that stocks always paid off "in the long run," that a "buy-and-hold" strategy couldn't lose. Neither the financial media nor America's politicians bothered to warn the public about the gaping disparity between the inflated claims on economic output that stocks represented and the actual production of the economy. But by the end of the decade, insiders saw the writing on the wall. They rushed to the exits, trying to realize stock gains before the contradictions inherent in the market overwhelmed them. Prices tumbled, wiping out trillions in illusory money.

The case of Enron Corp. is the most notorious, but it is unfortunately not unique. When Enron filed for bankruptcy protection in November of 2001 its stock, which had traded as high as $90 per share a year before, plummeted to less than $1. *New York Times* reporter Jeffrey Seglin writes that the elevators in Enron's Houston headquarters sported TV sets tuned to CNBC, constantly tracking the firm's stock price and acclaiming the bull market generally. As Enron stock climbed in the late 1990s, these daily market updates made employees— whose retirement accounts were largely invested in company shares—feel quite wealthy, though most Enron workers were not in fact free to sell these shares. Enron's contributions of company stock to employee retirement accounts didn't vest until workers reached age 50. For years, Enron had hawked its stock to employees, to pension fund managers, and to the world as a surefire investment. Many employees used their own 401(k) funds, over and above the firm's matching contributions, to purchase additional shares. But as the firm disintegrated amid accusations of accounting fraud, plan managers froze employee accounts, so that workers were unable to unload even the stock they owned outright. With employee accounts frozen, Enron executives and board members are estimated to have dumped their own stock and options, netting $1.2 billion cash—almost exactly the amount employees lost from retirement accounts.

Soon after Enron's collapse, telecommunications giant Global Crossing imploded amid accusations of accounting irregularities. Global Crossing's stock, which had traded at nearly $100 per share, became virtually worthless, but not before CEO Gary Winnick exercised his own options and walked away with $734 million. Qwest Communications director Phil Anschutz cashed in $1.6 billion in the two years before the firm stumbled under a crushing debt load; the stock subsequently lost 96% of its value. The three top officers of telecom equipment maker JDS Uniphase collectively raked in $1.1 billion between 1999 and 2001. The stock is now trading at $2 per share. An investigation by the *Wall Street Journal* and Thompson Financial analysts estimates that top telecommunications executives captured a staggering $14.2 billion in stock gains between 1997 and 2001. The industry is now reeling, with 60 firms bankrupt and 500,000 jobs lost. The Journal reports that, as of August 2002, insiders at 38 telecom companies had walked away with gains greater than the current market value of their firms. "All told, it is one of the greatest transfers of wealth from investors—big and small—in American history," reporter Dennis Berman writes. "Telecom executives … made hundreds of millions of dollars, while many investors took huge, unprecedented losses."

Executives in the energy and telecom sectors were not the only ones to rake in impressive gains. Michael Eisner of Disney Corp. set an early record for CEO pay in 1998, netting $575 million, most in option sales. Disney stock has since fallen by two-thirds. Lawrence Ellison, CEO of Oracle Corp., made $706 million when he sold 29 million shares of Oracle stock in January 2001. Ellison's sales flooded the market for Oracle shares and contributed, along with reports of declining profits, to the stock's losing two-thirds of its value over the next few months. Between 1999 and 2001, Dennis Kozlowski of Tyco International sold $258 million of Tyco stock back to the company, on top of a salary and other compensation valued near $30 million. Kozlowski defended this windfall with the claim that his leadership had "created $37 billion in shareholder wealth." By the time Kozlowski quit Tyco under indictment for sales tax fraud in 2002, $80 billion of Tyco's shareholder wealth had evaporated.

Analyzing companies whose stock had fallen by at least 75%, Fortune magazine discovered that "executives and directors of the 1035 companies that met our criteria took out, by our estimate, roughly $66 billion."

## The Illusion of Retirement Security

During the bull market, hundreds of U.S. corporations were also stuffing employee savings accounts with corporate equity, creating a class of captive and friendly shareholders who were in many cases enjoined from selling the stock. Studies by the Employee Benefit Research Council found that, while federal law restricts holdings of company stock to 10% of assets in regulated, defined-benefit pension plans, 401(k)-type plans hold an average 19% of assets in company stock. This fraction rises to 32% when companies match employee contributions with stock and to 53% where companies have influence over plan investments. Pfizer Corporation, by all accounts the worst offender, ties up 81% of employee 401(k)s in company stock, but Coca-Cola runs a close second with 76% of plan assets in stock. Before the firm went bankrupt, WorldCom employees had 40% of their 401(k)s in the firm's shares. Such stock contributions cost firms virtually nothing in the short run and, since employees usually aren't permitted to sell the stock for years, companies needn't worry about diluting the value of equity held by important shareholders—or by their executive option-holders. Commenting on recent business lobbying efforts to gut legislation that would restrict stock contributions to retirement plans, Marc Machiz, formerly of the Labor Department's retirement division, told the *Wall Street Journal*, "business loves having people in employer stock and lobbied very hard to kill this stuff."

Until recently, most employees were untroubled by these trends. The market after all was setting new records daily. Quarterly 401(k) statements recorded fantastic returns year after year. Financial advisers assured the public that stocks were and always would be good investments. But corporate insiders proved far less willing to bank on illusory stock wealth when securing their own retirements.

Pearl Meyer and Partners, an executive compensation research firm, estimates that corporate executives eschew 401(k) plans for themselves and instead negotiate sizable cash pensions—the average senior executive is covered by a defined-benefit plan promising 60% of salary after 30 years of service. Under pressure from the board, CEO Richard McGinn quit Lucent at age 52 with $12 million in severance and a cash pension paying $870,000 annually. Lucent's employees, on the other hand, receive a 401(k) plan with 17% of its assets invested in Lucent stock. The stock plunged from $77 to $10 after McGinn's departure. Today it trades at around $1.00. Forty-two thousand Lucent workers lost their jobs as the firm sank.

When Louis Gerstner left IBM in 2002, after receiving $14 million in pay and an estimated $400 million in stock options, he negotiated a retirement package that promises "to cover car, office and club membership expenses for 10 years." IBM's employees, in contrast, have been agitating since 1999 over the firm's decision to replace its defined benefit pension with a 401(k)-type pension plan that, employee representatives estimate, will reduce pensions by one-third to one-half and save the firm $200 million annually. Economist Paul Krugman reports in the *New York Times* that Halliburton Corp. eliminated its employee pensions; first, though, the company "took an $8.5 million charge against earnings to reflect the cost of its parting gift" to CEO Dick Cheney. *Business Week*, surveying the impact of 401(k)s on employee retirement security, concludes that "CEOs deftly phased out rich defined-benefit plans and moved workers into you're-on-your-own 401(k)s, shredding a major safety net even as they locked in lifetime benefits for themselves."

Since 401(k)s were introduced in the early 1980s their use has grown explosively, and they have largely supplanted traditional defined-benefit pensions. In 2002, three of every four dollars contributed to retirement accounts went into 401(k)s. It is thanks to 401(k)s and other retirement savings plans that middle-income Americans became stock-owners in the 1980s and 1990s. It is probably also thanks to 401(k)s, and the huge demand for stocks they generated, that stock prices rose continuously in the 1990s. And it will almost certainly be thanks to 401(k)s that the problems inherent in using the stock market as a vehicle to distribute income will become glaringly apparent once the baby-boom generation begins to retire and liquidate its stock.

If stocks begin again to rise at historical averages—something financial advisors routinely project and prospective retirees are counting on—the discrepancy between what the stock market promises and what the economy delivers will widen dramatically. Something will have to give. Stocks cannot rise faster than the economy grows, not if people are actually to live off the proceeds.

Or rather, stock prices can't rise that fast unless corporate profits—on which stocks represent a legal claim—also surpass GDP gains. But if corporate earnings outpace economic growth, wages will have to stagnate or decline.

Pension economist Douglas Orr believes it is no accident that 401(k)s proliferated in a period of declining earnings and intense economic insecurity for most U.S. wage-earners. From 1980 until the latter half of the 1990s, the position of the typical American employee deteriorated noticeably. Wages fell, unemployment rose, benefits were slashed, stress levels and work hours climbed as U.S. firms "downsized" and "restructured" to cut costs and satiate investor hunger for higher profits. Firms like General Electric cut tens of thousands of jobs and made remaining jobs far less secure in order to generate earnings growth averaging 15% each year. Welch's ruthless union-busting and cost-cutting earned him the nickname "Neutron Jack" among rank-and-file employees. GE's attitude towards its employees was summed up by union negotiator Steve Tormey: "No matter how many records are broken in productivity or profits, it's always 'what have you done for me lately?' The workers are considered lemons and they are squeezed dry." Welch was championed as a hero on Wall Street, his management techniques widely emulated by firms across the nation. During his tenure, GE's stock price soared as the firm slashed employment by nearly 50%.

The Institute for Policy Studies, in a recent study, found that rising stock prices and soaring CEO pay packages are commonly associated with layoffs. CEOs of firms that "announced layoffs of 1000 or more workers in 2000 earned about 80 percent more, on average, than the executives of the 365 firms surveyed by *Business Week*."

Throughout the 1980s and 1990s, workers whose jobs were disappearing and wages collapsing consoled themselves by watching the paper value of their 401(k)s swell. With labor weak and labor incomes falling, wage and salary earners chose to cast their lot with capital. In betting on the stock market, though, workers are in reality betting that wage incomes will stagnate and trying to offset this by grabbing a slice from the profit pie. This has already proved a losing strategy for most.

Even at the peak of the 1990s bull market, the net wealth—assets minus debts—of the typical household fell from $55,000 to $50,000, as families borrowed heavily to protect their living standards in the face of stagnant wages. Until or unless the nation's capital stock is equitably distributed, there will always be a clash of interests between owners of capital and their employees. If stocks and profits are routinely besting the economy, then either wage-earners are lagging behind or somebody is cooking the books.

Yet surveys show that Americans like 401(k)s. In part, this is because savings accounts are portable, an important consideration in a world where workers can expect to change jobs several times over their working lives. But partly it is because savings plans provide the illusion of self-sufficiency and independence. When retirees spend down their savings, it feels as if they are "paying their own way." They do not feel like dependents, consuming the fruits of other people's labor. Yet they are. It is the nature of retirement that retirees opt out of production and rely on the young to keep the economy rolling. Pensions are always a claim on the real economy—they represent a transfer of goods and services from working adults to non-working retirees, who no longer contribute to economic output. The shift from defined-benefit pensions to 401(k)s and other savings plans in no way changes the fact that pensions transfer resources, but it does change the rules that will govern how those transfers take place—who pays and who benefits.

Private defined-benefit pensions impose a direct claim on corporate profits. In promising a fixed payment over a number of years, corporations commit to transfer a portion of future earnings to retirees. Under these plans, employers promise an annual lifetime benefit at retirement, the amount determined by an employee's prior earnings and years of service in the company. How the benefit will be paid, where the funds will come from, whether there are enough funds to last through a worker's life—this is the company's concern. Longevity risk—the risk that a worker will outlive the money put aside for her retirement—falls on the employer. Retirees benefit, but at a cost to shareholders. Similarly, public pension programs, whether through Social Security or through the civil service, entail a promise to retirees at the expense of the taxpaying public.

Today, the vast majority of workers, if they have pension coverage at all, participate in "defined-contribution" plans, in which they and their employer contribute a fixed monthly sum and invest the proceeds with a money management firm. At retirement, the employee owns whatever funds have accrued in the account and must make the money last until she dies. Defined-contribution plans are a claim on nothing. Workers are given a shot at capturing some of the cash floating around Wall Street, but no promise that they will succeed. 401(k)s will add a huge element of chance to the American retirement experience. Some will sell high, some will not. Some will realize gains. Some will not.

Pearl Meyer and Partners estimate that outstanding, unexercised executive stock options and employee stock incentives today amount to some $2 trillion. Any effort to cash in this amount, in addition to the stock held in retirement accounts, would have a dramatic impact on stock prices. American workers and retirees, in assessing their chances for coming out ahead in the competition to liquidate stock, might ponder this question: If, as employees in private negotiations with their corporate employers, they have been unable to protect their incomes or jobs or health or retirement benefits, how likely is it that they will instead be able to wrest gains from Wall Street where corporate insiders are firmly in control of information and access to deals?

# STOCK VOLATILITY

**BY ELLEN FRANK**
*May/June 2002*

Dear Dr. Dollar:

During the course of a single day, a stock can go up and down frequently. These changes supposedly reflect the changing demand for that stock (and its potential resale value) or changing expectations of a company's profitability. But this seems too vague to me. How can these factors be so volatile? Who actually decides, or what is the mechanism for deciding, when a stock price should go up or down and by how much?

*—Joseph Balszak, Muskegon, Michigan*

Let's start with your last question first—how are stock prices determined? Shares in most large established corporations are listed on organized exchanges like the New York or American Stock Exchanges. Shares in most smaller or newer firms are listed on the NASDAQ—an electronic system that tracks stock prices.

Every time a stock is sold, the exchange records the price at which it changes hands. If, a few seconds or minutes later, another trade takes place, the price at which that trade is made becomes the new market price, and so on. Organized exchanges like the New York Stock Exchange will occasionally suspend trading in a stock if the price is excessively volatile, if there is a severe mismatch between supply and demand (many people wanting to sell, no one wanting to buy) or if they suspect that insiders are deliberately manipulating a stock's price. But in normal circumstances, there is no official arbiter of stock prices, no person or institution that "decides" a price. The market price of a stock is simply the price at which a willing buyer and seller agree to trade.

Why then do prices fluctuate so much? The vast bulk of stock trades are made by professional traders who buy and sell shares all day long, hoping to profit from small changes in share prices. Since these traders do not hold stocks over the long haul, they are not terribly interested in such long-term considerations as a company's profitability or the value of its assets. Or rather, they are interested in such factors mostly insofar as news that would affect a company's long-term prospects might cause *other traders* to buy the stock, causing its price to rise. If a trader believes that others will buy shares (in the expectation that prices will rise), then she will buy as well, hoping to sell when the price rises. If others believe the same thing, then the wave of buying pressure will, in fact, *cause* the price to rise.

Back in the 1930s, economist John Maynard Keynes compared the stock market to a contest then popular in British tabloids, in which contestants had to look at photos and choose the faces that *other contestants* would pick as the prettiest. Each contestant had to look for photos "likeliest to catch the fancy of the other competitors, all of whom are looking at the problem from the same point of view." Similarly, stock traders try to guess which stocks other traders will buy. The successful trader is the one who anticipates and outfoxes the market, buying before a stock's price rises and selling before it falls.

Financial firms employ thousands of market strategists and technical analysts who spend hours poring over historical stock data, trying to divine the logic behind these price changes. If they could unlock the secret of stock prices, they could arm their traders with the ability to always buy low and sell high. So far, no one has found this particular holy grail. And so traders continue to guess and gamble and, in doing so, send prices gyrating.

For small investors, who do hold stock for the long term and will need to cash in their stocks at some point to finance their retirements, the volatility of the market can be a source of constant anxiety. Every time a share in, say, General Electric is traded, the new price is used to revalue all outstanding shares—just as the value of your home appreciates when the house down the block sells for more than a similar house sold last week. But the value of your home wouldn't be so high if every house on your block were suddenly put up for sale. Similarly, if all ten billion outstanding shares of General Electric—or even a small fraction of them—were put up for sale, they wouldn't fetch anywhere near the current market price. Small investors need to keep in mind that the gains and losses on their 401(k) statements are just hypothetical paper gains and losses. You won't know the true value of your stocks until you actually try to sell them.

# TEACHING ABOUT STOCKS FOR FUN AND PROPAGANDA

**BY MARK MAIER**

*March/April 2001*

Every year, more than a million U.S. primary, middle, and high school students play the stock market at school. They use pretend money and imaginary trades, but students experience the feel of real-world finance, tallying their gains as they buy and sell stock at prices relayed electronically from the real-life stock exchanges. These stock market simulations come with complete lesson plans, worksheets, professional advice from real stockbrokers, and even cash prizes. No wonder they are so popular. Melissa, a secondary school student, raves, "We are all having a blast and no one has even skipped class." Teachers, too, are pleased. A middle school computer teacher in West Bend, Wisconsin, notes, "The very first thing in the morning, before the pledge of allegiance, they want to check their stocks."

But stock market games and their accompanying curriculum guides present a rosy, one-sided picture of Wall Street, in which everyone starts out rich and all that matters is short-term profits. Omitting the less attractive side of the stock market fits conveniently with the corporate underwriters' viewpoint, but it is poor training for future citizens and investors.

## $100,000 is a Nice Start

The most popular stock market games are played on the web using a variety of internet sources. The oldest and still most commonly adopted is The Stock Market Game, a program trademarked by an affiliate of the Securities Industry Association. Teachers often use it in conjunction with a curriculum distributed by the National Council on Economic Education (NCEE), a nonprofit organization of education, business and labor leaders. Increasingly, teachers are turning to commercially produced stock market games that are free of charge. Commercial games sometimes offer complex stock trades, as well as research assistance that is unavailable at nonprofit sites. Commercial games are designed to attract students and other individuals to the web site's advertisements, usually for the company's real-life, paid stock transactions.

Nearly all games follow a common script. Students begin with a tidy sum, usually $100,000, with no reference to the source of this initial endowment – although one curriculum offers the unlikely scenario that students have inherited money from "Uncle Mort," who helped Brazilian Indians profit from rain forest products. Since everyone starts out with the same amount of money, the games perpetuate the idea that individual effort is the reason that some people get rich and others do not.

Of course, in real life the starting line isn't even. Fewer than one out of ten households owns $100,000 in *total* financial assets, including not only stocks but also bonds, bank accounts, and retirement accounts. And stocks themselves are distributed in a very lopsided manner, with 10% of shareholders owning 90% of all

### *STOCK MARKET LINGO*

***Financial assets***– Items of wealth, such as stocks and bonds, that represent a paper claim to a future flow of income (differentiated from other assets such as real estate, factories, or patents).

***Risk***– The probabilities of various outcomes for a financial asset: How likely is it that the asset will lose a lot? A little? Nothing?

***Portfolio***– A collection of assets owned by an individual, business, or fund. The main purpose of owning a portfolio – instead of one asset – is to diversify and therefore reduce risk.

***Diversification***– Experts recommend that investors reduce a portfolio's risk by including assets that tend to move up and down at different times. For example, an investor may want to own stock in oil producers that do well when fuel prices rise, in order to counterbalance utilities that may be in trouble if fuel prices go up.

***Mutual funds***– The pooling of investor assets in order to benefit from less expensive diversification and professional management than a single investor could afford. The largest mutual funds include Fidelity Investments and the Vanguard Group.

***Stocks and bonds***– Technically, stocks are units of ownership in a corporation, but most shareholders do not influence corporate policy; instead, they hold stock simply for its potential dividends and increases in price. Bonds are long-term loans to businesses or government that do not involve ownership. Usually bonds provide a set interest payment for a set number of years.

***Random stock market***– Economists use this term to explain why it is so difficult to make above-average profits in the stock market. In this view, stock prices appear to move randomly because information about a corporation's prospects is already reflected in its current price.

***Bubble***– Sometimes the price of a single stock, the entire stock market, or a national currency will spiral upwards simply because many investors buy into the expectation of even higher prices. When these expectations collapse, the bubble bursts, and the price falls calamitously for those still holding the asset.

stock, while the top 1% owns more than half of all shares. Unequal distribution of stocks goes unmentioned in teaching guides such as the New York Stock Exchange's *The Stock Market Wants You,* or the NCEE's *Learning from the Market.* Instead, these manuals emphasize the recent broadening of stock ownership, so that 50% of households now own stock. A true-to-life stock market simulation would show that, while it is true that more U.S. households own some stock than in the past, ownership has become even more unequal: The rich now own an even larger percentage of all stock than they did 20 years ago.

## Shortsighted and Risky

Even for the small number of students who one day will own a substantial amount of stock, the games are poor practice for real-world investing. The short time period during which students buy and sell stocks – typically eight to 12 weeks to fit comfortably in a school term – means that students focus on short-term gains. Professional advisors recommend a much longer-term perspective, holding stock for a decade or more in order to avoid periodic downturns in stock prices.

### *"PLAY" THE MARKET ON THE WEB*

Stock market simulations are so sophisticated that they look just like actual trading. Participants can choose from nearly all available stocks, mutual funds, margin purchases, short selling – all at prices delayed usually only a few minutes from actual stock market prices. Many schools use *The Stock Market Game*, sponsored by the Securities Industry Association but commercial-free. However, in recent years non-profit simulation games have been displaced by explicitly commercial sites such as CNBC's *Student Stock Tournament* (now used in more than 10,000 schools), *Final Bell* from Sandbox, *MarketPlayer.com*, and *Virtual Stock Exchange*. Because of advertising, these stock competitions are free. Also, they offer cash prizes, as well as links to research that is unavailable in the traditional, non-profit world. Some web sites have extended the simulations to the "buying" and "selling" of predictions about events other than the stock market, including athletes' performances at *Wall Street Sports* and film earnings at the *Hollywood Stock Exchange.*

In addition, stock market games reward students who take excessive risks. Analysis of game winners shows that the best strategy is for students to ignore diversification – owning stock in a variety of corporations, which is the starting point for all prudent investment. By focusing on a few stocks known to swing wildly in price, some students, either through blind luck or an ill-advised risky portfolio, will end the game with big winnings, beating students who took the safer, diversified route. When it became apparent that students with such careless investments consistently won stock market competitions, some games forced students to invest in at least four stocks and to make a minimum number of trades. But the winning strategy remains to gamble as much as possible.

Most students take a naïve approach, choosing portfolios based on brand names they know – McDonalds, Colgate-Palmolive, and Disney in one typical Boston seventh-grade classroom. The training manuals accompanying the best-selling games tell students that they will win if they carefully study these corporations. Several games use McDonalds as an example, suggesting that if students saw the burger chain introduce a popular new menu item, then this would be a good time to buy McDonalds stock.

No expert would agree. If McDonalds' profitability improves because of a new menu item, then other stock investors would have already purchased McDonalds stock, pushing up the price to a point where further gains are unlikely. Economists debate the full impact of this effect. It may be possible for a few experts, or those with privileged access to new information, to buy and sell stock with above-average success. Alternatively, the stock market may behave irrationally, not following the wisdom of any investor. But it is well proved that the strategy recommended for students – buying and selling stocks based on readily available information – is no better than a random choice of stocks and, on average, will cause students to lose because profits are reduced by broker's fees.

In a typical classroom, the stock market's random fluctuations will ensure that a handful of students will do well, tallying high profits and winning prizes put up at commercial web sites. Pride in such gains is misplaced. Students with losing stocks may feel an undeserved sense of personal failure, wrongly perceiving themselves as less clever than the game winners. When they are adults, students may expect the same returns earned by the lucky few, a lesson no more valid than if students practiced betting on horses.

The stock market game's easy profits also might make students more receptive to recommendations to privatize Social Security. After all, if investing is simple and fun, wouldn't we be better off making individual decisions about our retirement funds? In the real world, privatization would be inequitable, risky, and more costly than a simulation game in which everyone starts off with the same $100,000 and there are no penalties for a losing investment strategy.

It is easy to see why teachers want to take advantage of student interest in stocks. Algebra teacher Tony Smith explains: "I have never seen kids so excited to come to class." Stock market simulations grab students' attention with real-world applications of math and research skills. The games can also be used to teach economics. However, rather than asking students to pick a winning portfolio, teachers should use the stock market to show students the actual workings of corporate America. For example, reading the stock pages could help students to see corporate ownership behind popular name brands. Beginning with Oscar Meyer wieners, a student will learn that they are produced by Philip Morris, the same corporation that owns Marlboro, Miller beer, and Velveeta cheese. These examples would show students the power over food marketing held by corporations such as the Philip Morris-Kraft conglomerate, and the problems of its recent merger with Nabisco foods.

## Up with Stocks

The instructor's manuals that accompany stock market games puff up the importance of stock markets in the U.S. economy, implying incorrectly that stocks are the source of most new corporate investment. Instead, retained profits or bank loans, not new stock issues, are the preferred source of funding for new plant and equipment. In fact, U.S. corporations have been buying back their own stock in order to keep stock prices high. As a result, the stock market is an overall *drain* on corporations' ability to build for the future.

Stock market games also teach that buying stock gives one "ownership" of a corporation, that is, voting rights in decision-making. As one student put it, "I thought it was so cool I owned a part of McDonalds." The reality is that corporate governance is a complex process, with decision-making split between management and those with large numbers of shares. Sometimes a major shareholder will intervene in corporate decision-making. For example, in January, when the Gateway computer company was doing poorly, Ted Waitt – who owned nearly a third of the stock – took over as chief executive. But small shareholders, even when they act collectively, rarely influence company policy. Instead of perpetuating the myth of shareholder democracy, a better curriculum would ask students to find out how a local corporation decides to introduce a new product or move its production facilities.

## The Casino Economy

Finally, stock market games almost never explore the problems caused by speculation. A 15-year-old Mamaroneck, New York, high school student explained: "It was so cool… my money could make money without me doing anything!" This attitude, held by real-world investors as well, worries many economists who predict that the current bubble will burst, bringing down stock prices and likely causing a recession. Remarkably, such possibilities are not mentioned in any of the leading teacher manuals. Instead, the stock market is portrayed as a wise judge, rewarding those who make the right choices. An accurate curriculum would point out that speculation is not only risky for individual investors but also potentially harmful for the entire economy, since it might divert funds from socially useful purposes.

One can easily imagine an exciting simulation game that includes the real-world possibility of prices first rising irrationally, only to fall when investors lose confidence. Students might buy and sell stocks as quickly as they can, passing the hot stock to someone else – until the bubble bursts and the stocks are worthless.

For some purposes like teaching math, stock market games provide a dose of reality. Brad, a sixth grader in Pasadena, California, points proudly to the stock chart he keeps at home: "It *wasn't* math; we used percentages and multiplication to figure out how much we made." It might be too much to expect schoolteachers to pass up such an easy way to spice up a humdrum class. Certainly, the lure of a compelling game, along with glitzy corporate-sponsored lesson plans, is attractive to overworked teachers. But if students are to learn how the economy actually works, then teachers need to use stock market games with great caution, supplementing them with alternative activities to show the real world of unequal resources, impotent small shareholders, and reckless speculative bubbles.

*Resources: The Stock Market Game* <www.smgww.org>

---

# LABOR'S CAPITAL: PUTTING PENSION WEALTH TO WORK FOR WORKERS

**BY ADRIA SCHARF**
*September/October 2005*

Pension fund assets are the largest single source of investment capital in the country. Of the roughly $17 trillion in private equity in the U.S. economy, $6 to 7 trillion is held in employee pensions. About $1.3 trillion is in union pension plans (jointly trusteed labor-management plans or collectively bargained company-sponsored plans) and $2.1 trillion is in public employee pension plans. Several trillion more are in defined contribution plans and company-sponsored defined benefit plans with no union representation. These vast sums were generated by—and belong to—workers; they're really workers' deferred wages.

Workers' retirement dollars course through Wall Street, but most of the capital owned *by* working people is invested with no regard *for* working people or their communities. Pension dollars finance sweatshops overseas, hold shares of public companies that conduct mass layoffs, and underwrite myriad anti-union low-road corporate practices. In one emblematic example, the Florida public pension system bought out the Edison Corporation, the for-profit school operator, in November 2003, with the deferred wages of Florida government employees—including public school teachers. (With just three appointed trustees, one of whom is Governor Jeb Bush, Florida is one of the few states with no worker representation on the board of its state-employee retirement fund.)

The custodians of workers' pensions—plan trustees and investment managers—argue that they are bound by their "fiduciary responsibility" to consider only narrow financial factors when making investment decisions. They maintain they have a singular obligation to maximize financial returns and minimize financial risk for beneficiaries—with no regard for broader concerns. But from the perspective of the teachers whose dollars funded an enterprise that aims to privatize their jobs, investing in Edison, however promising the expected return (and given Edison's track record, it wasn't very promising!), makes no sense.

A legal concept enshrined in the 1974 Employee Retirement Income Security Act (ERISA) and other statutes, "fiduciary responsibility" does constrain the decision-making of those charged with taking care of other people's money. It obligates fiduciaries (e.g., trustees and fund managers) to invest retirement assets for the exclusive benefit of the pension beneficiaries. According to ERISA, fiduciaries must act with the care, skill, prudence, and diligence that a "prudent man" would use. Exactly what that means, though, is contested.

The law does *not* say that plan trustees must maximize short-term return. It does, in fact, give fiduciaries some leeway to direct pension assets to worker- and community-friendly projects. In 1994, the U.S. Department of Labor issued rule clarifications that expressly permit fiduciaries to make "economically targeted investments" (ETIs), or investments that take into account collateral benefits like good jobs, housing, improved social service facilities, alternative energy, strengthened infrastructure, and economic development. Trustees and fund managers are free to consider a double bottom line, prioritizing investments that have a social payoff so long as their expected risk-adjusted financial returns are equal to other, similar, investments. Despite a backlash against ETIs from Newt Gingrich conservatives in the 1990s, Clinton's Labor Department rules still hold.

Nevertheless, the dominant mentality among the asset management professionals who make a living off what United Steelworkers president Leo Gerard calls "the deferred-wage food table" staunchly resists considering any factors apart from financial risk and return.

This is beginning to change in some corners of the pension fund world, principally (no surprise) where workers and beneficiaries have some control over their pension capital. In jointly managed union defined-benefit (known as "Taft-Hartley") plans and public-employee pension plans, the ETI movement is gaining ground. "Taft-Hartley pension trustees have grown more comfortable with economically targeted investments as a result of a variety of influences, one being the Labor Department itself," says Robert Pleasure of the Center for Working Capital, an independent capital stewardship-educational institute started by the AFL-CIO. Concurrently, more public pension fund trustees have begun adopting ETIs that promote housing and economic development within state borders. Most union and public pension trustees now understand that, as long as they follow a careful process and protect returns, ETIs do not breach their fiduciary duty, and may in certain cases actually be sounder investments than over-inflated Wall Street stocks.

## Saving Jobs: Heartland Labor Capital Network

During the run-up of Wall Street share prices in the 1990s, investment funds virtually redlined basic industries, preferring to direct dollars into hot public technology stocks and emerging foreign markets, which despite the rhetoric of fiduciary responsibility were often speculative, unsound, investments. Even most collectively bargained funds put their assets exclusively in Wall Street stocks, in part because some pension trustees feared that if they didn't, they could be held liable. (During an earlier period, the Labor Department aggressively pursued union pension trustees for breaches of fiduciary duty. In rare cases where trustees were found liable, their personal finances and possessions were at risk.) But in the past five years, more union pension funds and labor-friendly fund managers have begun directing assets into investments that bolster the "heartland" economy: worker-friendly private equity, and, wherever possible, unionized industries and companies that offer "card-check" and "neutrality." ("Card-check" requires automatic union recognition if a majority of employees present signed authorization cards; "neutrality" means employers agree to remain neutral during organizing campaigns.)

The Heartland Labor Capital Network is at the center of this movement. The network's Tom Croft says he and his allies want to "make sure there's an economy still around in the future to which working people will be able to contribute." Croft estimates that about $3 to $4 billion in new dollars have been directed to worker-friendly private equity since 1999—including venture capital, buyout funds, and "special situations" funds that invest in financially distressed companies, saving jobs and preventing closures. Several work closely with unions to direct capital into labor-friendly investments.

One such fund, New York-based KPS Special Situations, has saved over 10,000 unionized manufacturing jobs through its two funds, KPS Special Situations I and II, according to a company representative. In 2003, St. Louis-based Wire Rope Corporation, the nation's leading producer of high carbon wire and wire rope products, was in bankruptcy with nearly 1,000 unionized steelworker jobs in jeopardy. KPS bought the company and restructured it in collaboration with the United Steelworkers International. Approximately 20% of KPS's committed capital is from Taft-Hartley pension dollars; as a result, the Wire Rope transaction included some union pension assets.

The Heartland Labor Capital Network and its union partners want to expand this sort of strategic deployment of capital by building a national capital pool of "Heartland Funds" financed by union pension assets and other sources. These funds have already begun to make direct investments in smaller worker-friendly manufacturing and related enterprises; labor representatives participate alongside investment experts on their advisory boards.

"It's simple. Workers' assets should be invested in enterprises and construction projects that will help to build their cities, rebuild their schools, and rebuild America's infrastructure," says Croft.

## "Capital Stewardship": The AFL-CIO

For the AFL-CIO, ETIs are nothing new. Its Housing Investment Trust (HIT), formed in 1964, is the largest labor-sponsored investment vehicle in the country that produces collateral benefits for workers and their neighborhoods. Hundreds of union pension funds invest in the $2 billion trust, which leverages public financing to build housing, including low-income and affordable units, using union labor. HIT, together with its sister fund the Building Investment Trust (BIT), recently announced a new investment program that is expected to generate up to $1 billion in investment in apartment development and rehabilitation by 2005 in targeted cities including New York, Chicago, and Philadelphia. The initiative will finance thousands of units of housing and millions of hours of union construction work. HIT and BIT require owners of many of the projects they help finance to agree to card-check recognition and neutrality for their employees.

HIT and BIT are two examples of union-owned investment vehicles. There are many others—including the LongView ULTRA Construction Loan Fund, which finances projects that use 100% union labor; the Boilermakers' Co-Generation and Infrastructure Fund; and the United Food and Commercial Workers' Shopping Center Mortgage Loan Program—and their ranks are growing.

Since 1997, the AFL-CIO and its member unions have redoubled their efforts to increase labor's control over its capital through a variety of means. The AFL-CIO's Capital Stewardship Program promotes corporate governance reform, investment manager accountability, pro-worker investment strategies, international pension fund cooperation, and trustee education. It also evaluates worker-friendly pension funds on how well they actually advance workers' rights, among other criteria. The Center for Working Capital provides education and training to hundreds of union and public pension fund trustees each year, organizes conferences, and sponsors research on capital stewardship issues including ETIs.

## Public Pension Plans Join In

At least 29 states have ETI policies directing a portion of their funds, usually less than 5%, to economic development within state borders. The combined public pension assets in ETI programs amount to about $55 billion, according to a recent report commissioned by the Vermont state treasurer. The vast majority of these ETIs are in residential housing and other real estate.

The California Public Employees' Retirement System (CalPERS) is an ETI pioneer among state pension funds. The single largest pension fund in the country, it has $153.8 billion in assets and provides retirement benefits to over 1.4 million members. In the mid-1990s, when financing for housing construction dried up in California, CalPERS invested hundreds of millions of dollars to finance about 4% of the state's single-family housing market. Its ETI policy is expansive. While it requires economically targeted investments earn maximum returns for their level of risk and fall within geographic and asset-diversification guidelines, CalPERS also considers the investments' benefits to its members and to state residents, their job creation potential, and the economic and social needs of different groups in the state's population. CalPERS directs about 2% of its assets—about $20 billion as of May 2001—to investments that provide collateral social benefits. It also requires construction and maintenance contractors to provide decent wages and benefits.

Other state pension funds have followed CalPERs' lead. In 2003, the Massachusetts treasury expanded its ETI program, which is funded by the state's $32 billion pension. Treasurer Timothy Cahill expects to do "two dozen or more" ETI investments in 2004, up from the single investment made in 2003, according to the *Boston Business Journal.* "It doesn't hurt our bottom line, and it helps locally," Cahill explained. The immediate priority will be job creation. Washington, Wisconsin, and New York also have strong ETI programs.

In their current form and at their current scale, economically targeted investments in the United States are not a panacea. Pension law does impose constraints. Many consultants and lawyers admonish trustees to limit ETIs to a small portion of an overall pension investment portfolio. And union trustees must pursue ETIs carefully, following a checklist of "prudence" procedures, to protect themselves from liability. The most significant constraint is simply that these investments must generate risk-adjusted returns equal to alternative investments—this means that many deserving not-for-profit efforts and experiments in economic democracy are automatically ruled out. Still, there's more wiggle room in the law than has been broadly recognized. And when deployed strategically to bolster the labor movement, support employee buyouts, generate good jobs, or build affordable housing, economically targeted investments are a form of worker direction over capital whose potential has only begun to be realized. And (until the day that capital is abolished altogether) that represents an important foothold.

As early as the mid-1970s, business expert Peter Drucker warned in *Unseen Revolution* of a coming era of "pension-fund socialism" in which the ownership of massive amounts of capital by pension funds would bring about profound changes to the social and economic power structure. Today, workers' pensions prop up the U.S. economy. They're a point of leverage like no other. Union and public pension funds are the most promising means for working people to shape the deployment of capital on a large scale, while directing assets to investments with collateral benefits. If workers and the trustees of their pension wealth recognize the power they hold, they could alter the contours of capitalism.

# DOW'S ALL-TIME HIGH INCONSEQUENTIAL FOR MOST AMERICANS

**BY SYLVIA ALLEGRETTO**

*Spring 2007*

In April the Dow Jones Industrial Average rose above 13,000 for the first time ever, an event marked with great fanfare in some quarters. "Dow 13,000" may be a milestone on Wall Street, but it is a relatively insignificant blip on the radar screen of average working families. Fostered by the constant focus and widespread attention given to the performance of the stock market, conventional wisdom has it that everyone in the United States is heavily invested in the stock market—and so is poised to benefit when stock prices rise. However, the data tell a different story.

In recent decades the share of U.S. households owning any stock, whether directly (owning shares in a particular company) or indirectly (owning shares through a mutual fund or a retirement account) has indeed increased. But the most recent triennial data from the Survey of Consumer Finances show that this trend has actually reversed course: just over half of households (51.9%) owned any stock in 2001, but just under half (48.6%) in 2004—the first such decline on record (see Figure 1). In 2004, only about a third of U.S. households had stock holdings valued at more than $5,000.

The distribution of stocks by value is heavily tilted to the wealthiest Americans, as shown in Figure 2. In 2004, the wealthiest 1% of households owned 36.9%

**FIGURE 1**
**SHARE OF HOUSEHOLDS OWNING STOCK, 1989 TO 2004**

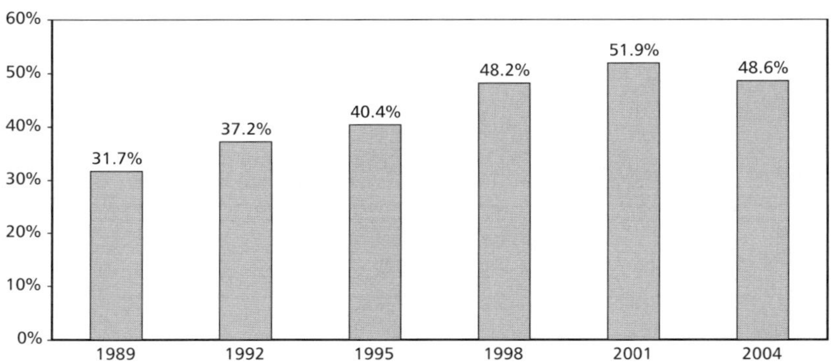


Source: The State of Working America 2006/2007

**FIGURE 2**
**DISTRIBUTION OF STOCK MARKET WEALTH BY WEALTH CLASS, 1989 TO 2004**

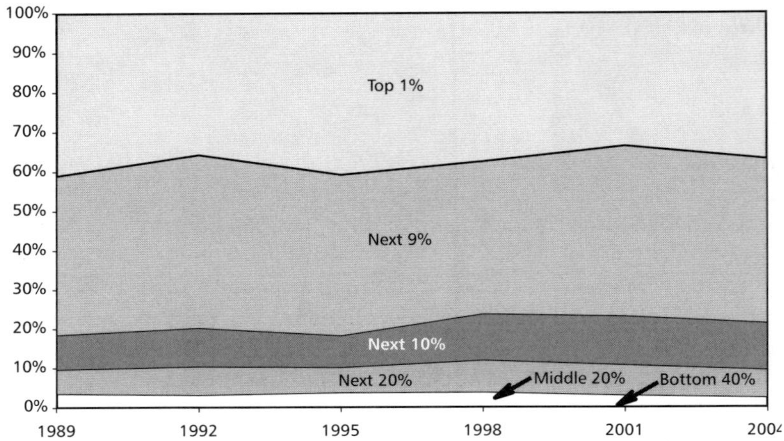


Source: The State of Working America 2006/2007.

of the value of all stocks, while the next 9% owned 41.9%. Hence, the wealthiest 10% owned about 80% of all wealth in stocks. Between 2001 and 2004, while the wealthiest 1% of households increased their share of total stock value, the share held by the bottom 80% fell from just above 10% (10.7%) to just below (9.4%).

For the most part, lower-, middle-, and even upper-middle-income working-age households depend on their paychecks, not stock portfolios, to meet their everyday needs. Typical working families that own stock do so in retirement plans that are costly to turn into cash. So higher stock prices do little to help them make ends meet at a time when inflation-adjusted wages for most workers have been stagnant for many years now.

# BAD NEWS ON MAIN STREET IS GOOD NEWS ON WALL STREET

**BY JOHN MILLER**
*July/August 2003*

One May 2, the Bureau of Labor Statistics announced that the U.S. economy lost 48,000 jobs in April, pushing the unemployment rate up to 6% and matching the eight-year high. The stock market promptly rallied. The Dow Jones Industrial Average of blue-chip stocks shot up 158 points to close at 8,582, its highest level in months. And the battered Nasdaq average of high-tech stocks gained 30 points, breaking the 1,500 barrier for the first time since June, 2002.

This uptick in the stock market in reaction to what he called "miserable" economic news left David Johnson, a Dallas stockbroker and commentator on National Public Radio's business program "Marketplace," perplexed.

"A lot of times you look at the market reactions," Johnson confessed to his radio listeners, "and it looks like the market always tries to do whatever it can to confound the greatest number of people." Johnson's reaction was typical of mainstream and business reporters, who commonly express surprise when the unemployment rate and the Dow rise in tandem.

Indeed, it might seem like a contradiction that stock prices can go up when the unemployment rate is rising. After all, a soft labor market suggests slower economic growth and dimmer prospects for corporate profits—what investors are buying shares of in the stock markets. During severe economic downturns—for example, the Great Depression—rising unemployment and a collapsing stock market do go hand in hand. But it's really no puzzler: bad news for workers on Main Street can often add up to good news for investors on Wall Street.

It's all about class conflict. Low unemployment gives workers greater bargaining power to press for higher wages and benefits. Businesses can either absorb these higher labor costs by cutting profits or pass them along by raising prices. Either way, investors lose out. If corporate profits decline, the value of investors' stock holdings is diminished. If prices rise, greater inflation cuts into the value of their assets. On the other hand, higher unemployment eats away at the bargaining power of workers, keeping their wage growth in check. And with labor costs under control, inflation remains low and corporate profit margins wide.

A closer look at current economic numbers bolsters this view. April's rising unemployment rate confirmed that the current, jobless economic recovery is doing little to empower workers, push up wages, or threaten corporate profits. In fact, since the recession officially began in March 2001, the economy has shed some 2.7 million jobs. An economic recovery that continues to destroy jobs two years after the onset of the recession is jobless in the extreme. Were this a typical post-World War II recovery, the economy would have been gaining jobs for nearly a year by now and would already have added back three-quarters of the jobs lost during the recession.

Continued job losses have put the kibosh on wages. Real weekly earnings have fallen in each of the past four quarters for the median full-time worker 25 years of age or older—the longest continuous decline in this group's real earnings since 1990.

The flip side of this jobless recovery is rapid productivity growth. Corporate restructuring, layoffs, and little rehiring have produced rapid increases in productivity—the economy's output per hour of labor. Since the fourth quarter of 2001, the hourly output of U.S. workers has gone up at a 4.2% annual rate, exceeding the "new economy" productivity growth rate of 2.4% from 1995 to 2001. And for the first time in a postwar recovery, productivity is growing faster than the economy. Rapid productivity gains have allowed companies to expand production without hiring new workers. For example, despite improving factory orders, manufacturers laid off 95,000 workers in April. That marked the 33rd consecutive month of declines in factory jobs, the longest string of manufacturing layoffs since the Great Depression.

In this way, what financial analysts call positive fundamentals—rising productivity and declining unit labor costs, improved competitiveness, and low inflation rates—have meant fewer rehires, continued layoffs, and deteriorating real wages on Main Street. For those pounding the pavement in search of work or forced to produce more in fewer hours with little or no improvement in pay, this is all bad news.

But that is not how Wall Street sees it. Higher unemployment rates boost stock prices. That should not really be surprising. For Wall Street remains, as Woody Guthrie once put it, "the street that keeps the rest of us off Easy Street."

*Resources:* Jared Bernstein & Lawrence Mishel, "Jobless Recovery Catches Up with Wages, Stifles Growth," Economic Policy Institute *Issue Brief* #193, May 2003; "Marketplace," Minnesota Public Radio/PRI, May 2, 2003, transcript at <www.marketplace.org>.

# SOCIALLY RESPONSIBLE INVESTING COMES OF AGE

**BY STEVE FAHRER**

*July/August 1998*

Tracy and Tom Hamilton needed a loan to enlarge their organic chicken farm in New Mexico. But though they logged years of success with their crops, the local banks, unfamiliar with organic farming methods, turned them down flat. Today their farm is flourishing because their local community development corporation came through with a much needed loan.

When the owners of a Chicago restaurant decided to sell because Latinos were moving into the neighborhood, waitress Lucia Montealvo saw her chance to go into business for herself. But though she, her husband, and their extended family pooled all their money, it still was not enough to buy the eatery. As immigrants, with no collateral, where could they go for a loan? Montealvo bought the restaurant with the help of a microenterprise loan from Acción International.

These entrepreneurs reaped the benefits of community investing, a growing movement that provides low-cost capital to businesses that serve social needs, such as neighborhood development and affordable housing. Along with shareholder activism and "screened" mutual funds, community investing is one of the growing methods of "socially responsible investing" (SRI) — activities that try to challenge irresponsible corporate behavior and channel investment where the market does not want to go.

According to the Social Investment Forum, a non-profit membership organization of more than 400 investment practitioners and institutions, over $1.2 trillion, or 10% of all investment, was engaged in SRI in some form in 1997. SRI has become more acceptable and leaders in the field are increasing their efforts to expand its reach.

SRI operates within a framework that accepts great inequalities of power and wealth in the financial markets. Even with the best of intentions, SRI alone will not stop companies from polluting the environment or discriminating at the workplace. But as an educational tool, used in conjunction with other forms of social activism, SRI can have an impact.

## Screening

SRI grew out of opposition to the Vietnam War. Dow Chemical, the maker of Napalm (used for firebombs) became a vilified corporate symbol for many and the target of corporate actions. The South Africa divestment movement followed, in which activists challenged universities and pension funds to get rid of their stock in companies with investments in South Africa. Nelson Mandela credits the pressure created by worldwide divestment campaigns with helping to rid South Africa of apartheid.

The divestment campaigns taught investors a valuable lesson. If you can divest from South Africa, why not divest from environmental polluters, companies that discriminate, and producers of weapons, nuclear power, tobacco, and alcohol? When possible, why not invest in companies that have useful products, treat their workers fairly, place women and minorities on their boards, or make charitable contributions to the communities where they are located?

Screening investment portfolios was not a new idea. For decades many religious investors avoided investing in the sin stocks — tobacco, alcohol, and gambling. But interest rose in the 1980s because of the drastic shift toward self-funded retirement plans in the United States. Fewer working people rely on union pensions or pensions controlled by their employer, and many more now have 401(k)'s or other retirement plans where they manage their own investments.

This new management responsibility can be intimidating, but it also provides an opportunity for self-education, organizing, and action. Fifteen years ago there were few avenues for those who did not want to invest in tobacco, weapons, or nuclear power, but in the past few years the number of socially screened mutual funds has tripled to more than 140. Socially responsible investing has become acceptable, and even the large brokerage firms and mutual fund companies have entered the field. Currently $529 billion, or 5% of all the money invested in the United States, is screened in some fashion.

Screening is a way to make retirement savings more consistent with one's values, such as investing in a mutual fund that will avoid owning shares of Shell Oil. There have been numerous consumer and labor campaigns against Shell Oil since the 1980s because of the company's investments in South Africa, its environmental practices, and most recently its collusion in the Nigerian government's repression of the Ogoni people. If you have participated in a boycott of Shell, it is inconsistent to own Shell stock in your 401(k) plan.

The campaign to force institutional and government portfolios to divest their tobacco stocks is probably the most active one right now. Just last April, San Francisco's Pension Fund became the first major municipal pension fund to vote to divest from tobacco stock. Earlier in the year, Oakland, Calif. voted to remove its short term investments from money market funds which own tobacco stocks. "If we're heading a campaign against tobacco billboards, it doesn't make any sense to invest money in the same industry we are trying to discourage," said City Councilwoman June Bruner. And the city of Arcata, Calif. voted to withdraw $6.2 million from the state government's $10 billion Local Agency Investment Fund, because the fund does not exclude companies that pollute the environment, produce tobacco products, or violate worker rights.

## Community Investments Expand

Community investments make social benefits, not profit maximization, their main concern. Today investors have put about $4 billion into financing local development initiatives, affordable housing, and small business lending in poor urban and rural areas. The need for such investment continues to grow as the government cuts its support of community development.

Most of this financing is done through community development financial intermediaries (CDFIs), such as community development loan funds and credit unions. For these loans to be effective they often carry a below-market rate, which is made possible by lenders who are willing to provide capital at even lower rates.

Because community investing has traditionally had low returns and high minimum investments, it has been the domain of wealthy investors and charitable institutions. Despite the success of CDFIs in meeting credit gaps, the pool of community capital available remains small. CDFIs are not well known and have had a hard time attracting capital, particularly outside of major metropolitan areas.

But this may be changing. Efforts are underway to attract a wider range of investors to community investing by reducing the risks and the minimum amount of money needed. For example, Calvert Group, the largest family of socially responsible mutual funds, has been placing 1% of its money into community investments since 1990, one of the only mutual funds to do so.

In order to expand the pool of available capital, Calvert has recently begun offering "Community Investment Notes," which are similar to bank certificates of deposit (CDs), but without a government guarantee of repayment. Both the Hamiltons and Lucia Montealvo got loans from CDFIs that Calvert's Notes had helped to fund.

Calvert has used the combined $16 million pool of social capital from the mutual funds and the Notes to make 140 below-market rate investments in seventy-five non-profit community groups. These investments support low-income housing and small business development in the United States and abroad, such as as the Environmental Enterprises Assistance Fund, Institute for Community Economics, and the Self Help Ventures Fund/Credit Union.

The Community Investment Notes are offered for as little as $1,000, for terms of one to five years, and investors can choose interest rates of 0% to 4%. The low minimum, large pool of projects receiving loans, and existence of a reserve fund to cushion losses from project failures are designed to make the Notes attractive to small investors as well as wealthy individuals and institutions.

Community funding intermediaries are also financing efforts around the world. The Environmental Enterprises Assistance Fund (EEAF), for example, is a nonprofit that provides long-term risk capital to environmental businesses in developing countries. It makes investments of $100,000 to $750,000, primarily in Central America, including projects in agriculture, nature tourism, renewable energy, and recycling. EEAF has managed investments for a waste water treatment facility in Costa Rica, an aluminum recycling company in Honduras and supported the expansion of a solar leasing business based in the Dominican Republic.

These innovations are positive developments, but it is important not to overstate their impact. Community development strategies cannot provide enough jobs and services to substitute for welfare and the social safety net. Nor can investment funds make up the great disparity of wealth between the developed world and countries in Asia, Africa and Latin America.

## Shareholder Activism

Shareholder activism, the form of socially responsible investing with perhaps the most visible impact, is growing fast. Last year, institutional investors leveraged $736 billion worth of stocks in shareholder resolutions, and the leading campaigner, the Interfaith Center for Corporate Responsibility (ICCR), sponsored 159 shareholder resolutions involving 116 companies.

ICCR is a coalition of 275 religious institutional investors who "expect companies to pursue the social and environmental bottom line as vigorously as they pursue profits," says Tim Smith, its executive director. Forty of the resolutions spurred companies either to agree to the shareholder requests or enter a dialogue with them. Smith listed some of this year's successes: Sara Lee's divestiture of its tobacco business; Coca Cola and Baxter International's endorsements of the Coalition of Environmentally Responsible Economic Principles (CERES) designed to regulate corporate environmental behavior; and Allstate's breaking ranks with the insurance industry and acknowledging that global climate change is a real threat to people and property.

The groups of shareholders who initiate resolutions at corporate annual meetings rarely win the votes. That's because most shares of major corporations are held by institutions and mutual funds that want to maximize profits without regard to social concerns. But even when the votes go against them, the pressure of resolution campaigns, including adverse publicity, still can change corporate behavior.

Working with the ICCR, my own firm, Progressive Asset Management (PAM), has initiated resolutions on behalf of its clients which addressed: Pacific Telesis stop the use of clearcut rainforest timber for paper in phonebooks; International Paper and Union Camp, to eliminate the chlorine and dioxins in paper production; and Unocal, to prevent the San Francisco Bay from becoming more polluted.

PAM and its allies scored an impressive victory at the Walt Disney Company shareholder meeting in 1997. Disturbed by scenes of Haitian sweatshop workers making Disney pajamas, our resolution asked the company to take responsibility for monitoring the labor practices of the 4,000 suppliers it contracts with. The resolution won the support of 39 million shares (8.5% of the total). After first issuing denials, Disney eventually acknowledged the problem and agreed to issue a code of conduct governing child and forced labor, discrimination, compensation, and environmental protection. Disney also agreed to post the code in factories in the language of the country where the plant was situated, to monitor compliance with the code, and to pay the prevailing wage.

The resolution succeeded because it was part of a grassroots protest campaign against the publicity-shy company. The National Labor Committee, along with many other groups, organized protests at Disney stores nationwide, raising awareness of Disney's sweatshops. The shareholder resolution provided another avenue for action because consumer-oriented corporations do not want negative publicity.

Any success is bound to be noticed, and the SEC, which oversees corporate governance and security laws, recently tried to hamper activists by issuing rules giving corporations the right to disallow some shareholder resolutions, and making it harder to resubmit resolutions. A coalition of pension funds, endowments, and social issue groups challenged the SEC's proposed rules and for the moment have thwarted efforts to raise the threshold required to resubmit shareholder resolutions. Republicans in Congress have also proposed legislation to restrict labor unions from filing shareholder resolutions.

Community investing, shareholder activism, and screened investments are all part of a greater struggle to control how capital is used. And with millions more people investing their retirement money, SRI is a growing arena for action. While it is beginning to open new avenues for challenging corporate behavior, it cannot substitute for other forms of social change activism we might employ as workers, citizens, or community residents.

To become a truly political force the practitioners of socially responsible investing will have to take on the big questions like saving social security, reinstituting progressive taxation, and challenging trade and investment policies that allow corporations to privatize profits and socialize costs. This is new ground, and it starts with each individual educating themselves as to what is being done with their capital — however large or small.

*Resources:* Interfaith Center for Corporate Responsibility (iccr.org), Progressive Asset Management (progressive-asset.com), Social Investment Forum (socialinvest.org)

## Chapter 4

# RETIRMENT FINANCE

## SOCIAL SECURITY ISN'T BROKEN

**BY DOUG ORR**

*November/December 2004*

Federal Reserve Chairman Alan Greenspan told Congress earlier this year that everyone knows there's a Social Security crisis. That's like saying "everyone knows the earth is flat."

Starting with a faulty premise guarantees reaching the wrong conclusion. The truth is there is no Social Security crisis, but there is a potential crisis in retirement income security and there may be a crisis in the future in U.S. financial markets. It's this latter crisis that Greenspan actually is worried about.

Social Security is the most successful insurance program ever created. It insures millions of workers against what economists call "longevity risk," the possibility they will live "too long" and not be able to work long enough, or save enough, to provide their own income. Today, about 10% of those over age 65 live in poverty. Without Social Security, that rate would be almost 50%.

Social Security was originally designed to supplement, and was structured to resemble, private-sector pensions. In the 1930s, all private pensions were defined-benefit plans. The retirement benefit was based on a worker's former wage and years of service. In most plans, after 35 years of service the monthly benefit, received for life, would be at least half of the income received in the final working year.

Congress expected that private-sector pensions eventually would cover most workers. But pension coverage peaked at 40% in the 1960s. Since then, corporations have systematically dismantled pension systems. Today, only 16% of private-sector workers are covered by defined-benefit pensions. Rather than supplementing private pensions, Social Security has become the primary source of retirement income for almost two-thirds of retirees. Thus, Congress was forced to raise benefit levels in 1972.

What has happened to private-sector defined benefit pensions? They've been replaced with defined-contribution (DC) savings plans such as 401(k)s and 403(b)s. These plans provide some retirement income but offer no real protection from longevity risk. Once a retiree depletes the amount saved in the plan, their retirement income is gone.

In a generous DC plan, a firm might match the worker's contribution up to 3% of his or her pay. With total contributions of 6%, average wage growth of 2% a year, and an average return on the investment portfolio of 5%, after 35 years of work, a retiree would exhaust the plan's savings in just 8.5 years even if her annual spending is only half of her final salary. If she restricts spending to just one-third of the final salary, the savings can stretch to 14 years.

At age 65, life expectancy for women today is about 20 years, and for men about 15 years, so DC savings plans will not protect the elderly from longevity risk. The conversion of defined-benefit pensions to defined-contribution plans is the source of the real potential crisis in retirement income. Yet Greenspan did not mention this in his testimony to Congress.

## No Crisis

Opponents of Social Security have hated it since its creation in 1935. The first prediction of a Social Security crisis was published in 1936! The Heritage Foundation and Cato Institute are home to many of the program's opponents today, and they fixate on the concept of a "demographic imperative." In 1960, the United States had 5.1 workers per retiree, in 1998 we had 3.4, and by 2030 we will have only 2.1. Opponents claim that with these demographic changes, revenues will eventually be insufficient to pay Social Security retirement benefits.

The logic is appealingly simple, but wrong for two reasons. First, this "old-age dependency" ratio in itself is irrelevant. No amount of financial manipulation can change this fact: all current consumption must come from current physical output. The consumption of all dependents (non-workers) must come from the output produced by current workers. It's the overall dependency ratio—–the number of workers relative to all non-workers, including the aged, the young, the disabled, and those choosing not to work—that determines whether society can "afford" the baby boomers' retirement years. In the 1960s we had only 0.62 workers for each dependent, and we were building new schools and the interstate highway system and getting ready to put a man on the moon. No one bemoaned a demographic crisis or looked for ways to cut the resources allocated to children; in fact, the living standards of most families rose rapidly. In 2030, we will have 0.98 workers per dependent. We'll have more workers per dependent in the future than we did in the past. While it is true a larger share of total output will be allocated to the aged, just as a larger share was allocated to children in the 1960s, society will easily produce adequate output to support all workers and dependents, and at a higher standard of living.

Second, the "demographic imperative" ignores productivity growth. Average worker productivity has grown by about 2% per year, adjusted for inflation, for the past half-century. That means real output per worker doubles every 36 years. This productivity growth is projected to continue, so by 2040, each worker will produce twice as much as today. Suppose each of three workers today produces $1,000 per week and one retiree is allocated $500 (half of his final salary)—then each worker gets $833. In 2040, two such workers will produce $2,000 per week each (after adjusting for inflation). If each retiree gets $1,000, each worker still gets $1,500. The incomes of both workers and retirees go up. Thus, paying for the baby boomers' retirement need not decrease their children's standard of living. A larger share of output going to retirees does not imply that the standard of living of those still working will be lower. Those still working will have a slightly smaller share of a much larger pie.

So why the talk of a Social Security crisis? Social Security always has been a pay-as-you-go system. Current benefits are paid out of current tax revenues. But in the 1980s, a commission headed by Greenspan recommended raising payroll taxes to expand the trust fund in order to supplement tax revenues when the baby boom generation retires. Congress responded in 1984 by raising payroll taxes significantly. As a result, the Social Security trust fund, which holds government bonds as assets, has grown every year since. As the baby boom moves into retirement, these assets will be sold to help pay their retirement benefits.

Each year, Social Security's trustees must make projections of the system's status for the next 75 years. In 1996, they projected the trust fund balance would go to zero in 2030. In 2000, they projected a zero balance in 2036 and today they project a zero balance in 2042. The projection keeps changing because the trustees continue to make unrealistic assumptions about future economic conditions. The current projections are based on the assumption that annual GDP growth will average 1.8% for the next 75 years. In no 20-year period, even including the Great Depression, has the U.S. economy grown that slowly. Each year the economy grows faster than 1.8%, the zero balance date moves further into the future. But the trustees continue to suggest that if we return to something like the Great Depression, the trust fund will go to zero.

Opponents of Social Security claim the system will then be "bankrupt." Bankruptcy implies ceasing to exist. But if the trust fund goes to zero, Social Security will not shut down and stop paying benefits. It will simply revert to the pure pay-as-you-go system that it was before 1984 and continue to pay current benefits using current tax revenues. Even if the trustees' worst-case assumptions come true, the payroll tax paid by workers would need to increase by only about 2% points, and only in 2042, not today.

If the economy grows at 2.4%—which is still slower than the stagnant growth of the 1980s—the trust fund never goes to zero. The increase in real output and real incomes will generate sufficient revenues to pay promised benefits. By 2042, we will need to lower payroll taxes or raise benefits to reduce the surplus.

The claim that benefits of future retirees must be reduced in order to not reduce the standard of living of future workers is simply wrong. It is being used to drive a wedge between generations and panic younger workers into supporting Bush's plan to destroy Social Security. Under the most likely version of his privatization proposal, according to Bush's own Social Security Commission, the guaranteed benefits from Social Security of a 20-year-old worker joining the labor force today would be reduced by 46%. That Commission also admitted that private accounts are unlikely to make up for this drop in benefits. An estimate made by the Goldman-Sacks brokerage firm suggests that even with private accounts, retirement income of younger workers would be reduced by 42% compared to what they would receive if nothing is done to change the Social Security system. Private accounts are a losing proposition for younger workers.

## The Real Fear: An Oversupply of Bonds

So why did Greenspan claim cutting benefits would become necessary? To understand the answer, we need to take a side trip to look at how bonds and the financial markets affect each other. It turns out that rising interest rates reduce the selling price of existing financial assets, and falling asset prices push up interest rates (see box "How Does the Bond Market Work?").

For example, in the 1980s, President Reagan cut taxes and created the largest government deficits in history up to that point. This meant the federal government had to sell lots of bonds to finance the soaring government debt; to attract enough buyers, the Treasury had to offer very high interest rates. During the 1980s, real interest rates (rates adjusted for inflation) were almost four times higher than the historic average. High interest rates slow economic growth by making it more expensive for consumers to buy homes or for businesses to invest in new infrastructure. The GDP growth rate in the 1980s was the slowest in U.S. history apart from the Great Depression.

But high interest rates also depress financial asset prices. A five percentage point rise in interest rates reduces the selling price of a bond (loan) that matures in 10 years by 50%. It was the impact of the record-high interest rates of the 1980s on the value of the loan portfolios of the savings and loan industry that caused the S&L crisis and the industry's collapse.

Greenspan is worried because he sees history repeating itself in the form of President Bush's tax cuts. In his testimony, Greenspan expressed concern over a potentially large rise in interest rates. This is his way of warning about an excess supply of bonds. Starting in 2020, Social Security will have to sell about $150 billion (in 2002 dollars) in trust fund bonds each year for 22 years. At the same time, private-sector pension funds will be selling $100 billion per year of financial assets to make their pension payments. State and local governments will be selling $75 billion per year to cover their former employees' pension expenses, and holdings in private mutual funds will fall by about $50 billion per year as individual retirees cash in their 401(k) assets. Private firms will still need to issue about $100 billion of new bonds a year to finance business expansion. Combined, these asset sales could total $475 billion per year.

This level of bond sales is more than double the record that was set in the 1980s following the Reagan tax cuts. But back then, the newly issued bonds were being purchased by "institutional investors" such as private-sector pension funds and insurance companies. After 2020, these groups will be net sellers of bonds. The financial markets will strain to absorb this level of asset sales. It's unlikely they will be able to also absorb the extra $400 billion per year of bond sales needed to cover the deficit spending that will occur if the new Bush tax cuts are made permanent. This oversupply of bonds will drive down the value of all financial assets.

In a 1994 paper, Sylvester Schieber, a current advisor to President Bush on pension and Social Security reform, predicted this potential drop in asset prices. After 2020, the value of assets held in 401(k) plans, already inadequate, will be reduced even more. More importantly, at least to Greenspan, the prices of assets held by

### *HOW DOES THE BOND MARKET WORK?*

A bond is nothing more than an IOU. A company or government borrows money and promises to pay a certain amount of interest annually until it repays the loan. When you buy a newly issued bond, you are making a loan. The amount of the loan is the "face value" of the bond. The initial interest rate at which the bond is issued, the "face rate," multiplied by this face value determines the amount of interest paid each period. Until the debt is paid back, events in the financial markets affect the bond's value.

If market interest rates fall, prices of existing bonds rise. Why? Suppose you buy a bond with a face value of $100 that pays 10%. You then collect $10 per year. If the current interest rate falls to 5%, newly issued bonds will pay that new rate. Since your bond pays 10%, people would rather buy that one than one paying 5%. They are willing to pay more than the face value to get it, so the price will be bid up until interest rates equalize. The price at which you could sell your bond will rise to $200, since $10 is 5% of $200.

But changes in bond prices also affect interest rates. If more people are selling bonds than buying them, an excess supply exists, and prices will fall. If you need to sell your bond to get money to pay your rent, you might have to lower the price of the bond you hold to $50. Because the bond still pays $10 per year to the owner, the new owner gets a 20% return on the $50 purchase. Anyone trying to issue new bonds will have to match that return, so the new market interest rate becomes 20%.

corporations to fund their defined benefit pension promises will fall. Thus, pension payments will need to come out of current revenues, reducing corporate profits and, in turn, driving down stock prices.

It's this potential collapse in the prices of financial assets that worries Greenspan most. In order to reduce the run-up of long-term interest rates, some asset sales must be eliminated. Greenspan said, "You don't have the resources to do it all." But rather than rescinding Bush's tax cuts, Greenspan favors reducing bond sales by the Social Security trust fund. Doing that requires a reduction in benefits and raising payroll taxes even more.

Framing a question incorrectly makes it impossible to find a solution. The problem is not with Social Security, but rather with blind reliance on financial markets to solve all economic problems. If the financial markets are likely to fail us, what is the solution? The solution is simple once the question is framed correctly: where will the real output that baby boomers are going to consume in retirement come from?

The federal budget surplus President Bush inherited came entirely from Social Security surpluses resulting from the 1984 payroll tax increase. Bush gave away revenues meant to provide for workers' retirement as tax cuts for the wealthiest 10% of the population.

We should rescind Bush's tax cuts and use the Social Security surpluses to really prepare for the baby boom retirement. Public investment or targeted tax breaks could be used to encourage the building of the hospitals, nursing homes, and hospices that aging baby boomers will need. Such investment in public and private infrastructure would also stimulate the real economy and increase GDP growth. Surpluses could be used to fund the training of doctors, nurses and others to staff these facilities, and of other high skilled workers more generally. The higher wages of skilled labor will help generate the payroll tax revenues needed to fund future benefits. If baby boomers help to fund this infrastructure expansion through their payroll taxes while they are still working, less output will need to be allocated when they retire. These expenditures will increase the productivity of the real economy, which will help keep the financial sector solvent to provide for retirees.

Destroying Social Security in order to "save" it is not a solution.

*Resources:* Dean Baker and Mark Weisbrot, *Social Security: The Phony Crises*, University of Chicago Press, 1999; William Wolman and Anne Colamosca, *The Great 401(k) Hoax*, Perseus Publishing, 2002; Sylvester J. Schieber and John B. Shoven, "The Consequences of Population Aging on Private Pension Fund Saving and Asset Markets," National Bureau of Economic Research, Working Paper No. 4665, 1994.

---

# SOCIAL SECURITY Q & A: SEPARATING FACT FROM FICTION

**BY DOUG ORR**
*May/June 2005*

*The president just completed his 60-day, 35-state tour to spread fear over the financial solvency of the Social Security system and promote his plan to allow workers to divert nearly a third of the 12.4% Social Security payroll tax into private investment accounts.*

*At a stump speech in West Virginia in early April, Bush pointed to a filing cabinet stuffed with paper representing government IOUs and said, "A lot of people in America think there is a trust—that we take your money in payroll taxes and then we hold it for you and then when you retire, we give it back to you. But that's not the way it works. There is no trust 'fund'—just IOUs…." On April 28, Bush proposed indexing high-income workers' benefits to inflation, a move he described as "progressive." If these and other administration statements about Social Security leave you scratching your head, you're not alone.*

*With all the fear-mongering falsehoods flying around, it can be difficult to separate fact from fiction. Below, Doug Orr helps D&S readers do just this, withclear, at times surprising, answers to many common Social Security-related questions. Congress is expected to vote on Social Security "reform" in June.*

*—Eds.*

Has the president actually lied to the public about Social Security? Yes. President Bush has repeatedly said that those who put their money in private accounts are "guaranteed" a better return than they'll receive from the current Social Security system. But every sale of stock on the stock market includes the disclaimer: "the return on this investment is not guaranteed and may be negative"—for good reason. During the 20th century, there were several periods lasting more than 10 years where the return on stocks was negative. After the Dow Jones stock index went down by over 75% between 1929 and 1933, the Dow did not return to its 1929 level until 1953. In claiming that the rate of return on a stock investment is guaranteed to be greater than the return on any other asset, Bush is lying. If an investment-firm broker made this claim to his clients, he would be arrested and charged with stock fraud. Michael Milken went to jail for several years for making just this type of promise about financial investments.

In fact, under the most likely version of the Bush privatization proposal, a 20-year old worker joining the labor force today would see her guaranteed Social Security benefits reduced by 46%. Bush's own Social Security commission admitted that private accounts are unlikely to make up for this drop in guaranteed benefits. The brokerage firm Goldman Sachs estimates that even with private accounts, retirement income of younger workers would be reduced by 42% compared to what they would receive if no changes are made to Social Security.

President Bush also misrepresents the truth when he claims that Social Security trustees say the system will be "bankrupt" in 2042. Bankruptcy is defined as "the inability to pay ones debts" or, when applied to a business, "shutting down as a result of insolvency." Nothing the trustees have said or published indicates that Social Security will fold as a result of insolvency.

Until 1984, the trust fund was "pay-as-you-go," meaning current benefits were paid using current tax revenues. In 1984, Congress raised payroll taxes to prepare for the retirement of the baby boom generation. As a result, the Social Security trust fund, which holds government bonds as assets, has been growing. When the baby boomers retire, these bonds will be sold to help pay their retirement benefits.

If the trust fund went to zero, Social Security would simply revert to pay-as-you-go. It would continue to pay benefits using (then-current) tax revenues, and in doing so, it would be able to cover about 70% of promised benefit levels. According to analysis by the Center for Economic and Policy Research, a 70% benefit level then would actually be higher than 2005 benefit levels in constant dollars (because of wage adjustments). In other words, retirees would be taking home more in real terms than today's retirees do. The system won't be bankrupt in any sense. On this point, President Bush is "consciously misrepresenting the truth with the intent to deceive." That is what the dictionary defines as lying.

**Is it true that the trust fund is just a bunch of government IOUs and therefore worthless?**

The trust fund does just contain IOUs, but they're not worthless. If they are, someone should tell that to the very smart and very rich people who bought $475 billion in government bonds last year to finance the deficits President Bush and Congress created, and to the central banks of Japan, China, and many other countries that hold a large share of their assets in U.S. government bonds.

When the trust fund was created in 1935, the law stipulated that any excess revenues coming into the Social Security system must be used to purchase federal government bonds. (At the time, the stock market had just lost over 75% of its value and was understood to be unsafe.) Federal bonds are absolutely safe; the government of the United States has never defaulted on any bond obligation. President Bush appears to be ready to break this tradition.

If the president wants the Treasury to "selectively default" on the bonds in the Social Security trust fund, it means he feels the United States doesn't have to meet its obligation to the working people of America the way it meets its obligations to ultra-wealthy bondholders. His suggestion that the U.S. government might not be willing to repay its debt obligations is remarkable.

**What will happen when the assets held in the trust fund are needed to help pay for benefits?**

The trust will start selling the bonds. Currently it has to sell them back to the Treasury, although the law could easily be changed to allow sales to the same people, institutions, and governments who were buying U.S. bonds this past year. But let's assume the government has to buy them back.

If the government were running a surplus, as it did for the last four years of the Clinton administration, it would use that surplus to pay for them. If, on the other hand, the government were running a balanced budget but not a surplus, it would need to issue new Treasury bonds to pay for the bonds it would buy from the trust fund. In finance, this is called "rolling over" debt, and every major corporation in the world does it every day. At no point would the government need to roll over more than $300 billion in any given year to pay for the trust fund bonds. We already know the federal government can easily sell $475 billion per year in bonds, because it did that last year and interest rates did not even go up—in fact, they remained relatively low.

**So there's no problem, right?**

Actually, there is one thing that could cause a problem: the government running a massive deficit, as it now does. In that case, selling more bonds could put a very real strain the financial system's ability to absorb the creation of this new debt.

This is the issue that Federal Reserve chairman Alan Greenspan has been trying to raise for the past three years. Unfortunately, Greenspan speaks in financial jargon, so it's hard for the general public to understand what he's trying to say.

**Even if the Social Security system isn't going to go bankrupt by 2029, 2042, or 2058, won't the Social Security trust fund begin cashing in the IOUs from the federal government as early as 2018?**

The contributions to Social Security will become less than the benefits paid out in 2018, based on the trustees' overly pessimistic assumptions. (See "Social Security Isn't Broken" and "The SSA's Cracked Crystal Ball," *D&S* November/December 2004, at <www.dollarsandsense.org>.) But that doesn't mean that the Social Security Administration will need to start selling bonds at that point. The interest income from the existing bonds will be sufficient to make up the difference until 2028. *If* the trustees' pessimistic assumptions are true, they will need to start selling bonds in 2028 and the trust fund will be reduced to zero in 2042. At that point, as I mentioned above, the Social Security system would simply revert back to pure pay-as-you-go, operating just as it did successfully from 1936 to 1983.

**Shouldn't we consider benefit cuts today to help prevent a potential shortfall in the future?**

Congress, correctly, has not been willing to cut benefits. They don't need to, and they shouldn't. Telling your kids today they only get to eat one plate of rice each day and they have to get their clothes at Goodwill, because there is a *chance* that you might lose your job 40 years from now, would be irrational. It would be equally irrational to implement benefit cuts immediately on the *chance* that the trust fund might go to zero in 2042—especially when future recipients would still be getting more in real terms than recipients do today.

**What would it mean to index Social Security benefits to prices rather than to wages as is done now? David Brooks of the *New York Times* and others say this would prevent the system from going broke.**

Right now, the formula for Social Security benefits in the first year of retirement is based on an average of the worker's wages over a 35-year period, accounting for productivity increases and for inflation. Productivity is figured in by adjusting the worker's earnings by the change in average annual wages. In effect, the worker's own 35-year average wage is recalculated as if it had been earned in the three years before retirement. The reason for this adjustment is simple: With more education and more and better machines, labor productivity (what each worker can produce in an hour's time) rises. Thus, each worker produces more real output and, assuming that wages rise with productivity, workers' standards of living improve. If workers contribute more to society's output, they deserve more in return. This is how market economies are supposed to work.

If productivity rises by 3% a year, the standard of living should go up by 3% a year. But what if inflation is also 3%? In that case, if wages rise by just 3%, workers would not be able to purchase any more real output than the year before. That's why the wage increase must also be adjusted for inflation. To correct for this, wages would need to rise by 6% (3% for productivity and 3% for inflation).

When the Bush administration proposes indexing initial Social Security benefits only to price increases, it is really suggesting stripping out the part of wage increases that results from rising productivity and only allowing for inflation. It's the equivalent of linking your retirement benefits to the very first job you take, rather than the job you hold at retirement. It freezes your retirement standard of living at whatever the standard of living was when you entered the workforce. According to President Bush's own commission, if this "price indexing" approach were implemented, future retirees would see their retirement income drastically reduced—if you retire in 2022, benefits would be 10% lower, in 2042, 26% lower, and in 2075, 54% lower.

Currently, once you retire, your benefit is adjusted annually for inflation but not for the change in wages. This cost of living adjustment (COLA), based on the inflation rate, helps maintain retirees' standard of living at the level they had when they retired, although their standard of living slowly falls behind that of the rest of society as the overall standard of living rises with productivity. Without the COLA, the individual's standard of living would fall even below what it was when he or she retired. With the private accounts plan proposed by President Bush, the reduced benefit levels would still rise with prices but the income from private accounts would not, so inflation would erode retirees' income.

**So what does Bush mean by "progressive" indexing?**

This is just applying price indexing to only some workers. It would change the current indexation of benefits for "high" income and "middle" income individuals, leaving the current formula in place for the bottom 30% of wage earners. The highest wage earners' benefits would be adjusted for inflation, but not for productivity growth. Middle wage earners (those between 30% and 70%) would have their benefits only partially adjusted for productivity growth.

When he talks about his tax cuts, Bush defines "middle income" as $200,000, which is actually in the top 5% of income. In this case, though, he defines middle income as $36,500 in 2005, and high-income as $58,400. Under his plan, the retirement benefits of all workers would ultimately be reduced to match those of low-income workers regardless of how much they contributed to the system. This would result in a massive increase in poverty among the elderly, undermine political support for the system, and destroy Social Security. This does not fit the definition of a "progressive" policy.

**What impact will Bush's plan have on the national debt?**

Unless taxes are raised, the government will have to borrow up to $4 trillion over the next 20 years to make up the money that is drained out of the system by private accounts. Bush and Congress already racked up a $475 billion deficit in Bush's first term. Social Security privatization will raise the size of the government's deficit to nearly $700 billion per year for the next 20 years, almost tripling the size of the national debt.

**How will the rest of the U.S. economy be affected if the president's plan is enacted?**

Put simply, moving to a system of private accounts would not only put retirement income at risk—it would likely put the entire economy at risk.

The current Social Security system generates powerful, economy-stimulating multiplier effects. This was part of its original intent. In the early 1930s, the vast majority of the elderly were poor. While they were working, they could not afford to both save for retirement and put food on the table, and most had no employer pension. When Social Security began, elders spent every penny of that income. In turn, each dollar they spent was spent again by the people and businesses from whom they had bought things. In much the same way, every dollar that goes out in pensions today creates about 2.5 times as much total income. If the move to private accounts reduces elders' spending levels, as almost all analysts predict, that reduction in spending will have an even larger impact on slowing economic growth.

The current Social Security system also reduces the income disparity between the rich and the poor. Private accounts would increase inequality—and increased inequality hinders economic growth. For example, a 1994 World Bank study of 25 countries demonstrated that as income inequality rises, productivity growth is reduced. Market economies can fall apart completely if the level of inequality becomes too extreme. The rapid increase in income inequality that occurred in the 1920s was one of the causes of the Great Depression.

**Won't having people invest in stocks strengthen the business sector?**
There is a commonly accepted myth that buying stock in the stock market provides funds directly to businesses that they can use for new investment. This is completely incorrect. Only when someone buys stock that is part of an initial public offering (IPO) does the money go directly to the firm. If you were to buy a share of General Motors stock tomorrow, the money you pay would go to the stockowners and not to General Motors. If a large number of people were to suddenly enter the stock market, it would drive up the selling price of stock and create a windfall for those who currently own stock, but it would not provide a penny to the firms whose stock is traded. Economists Dean Baker and Bob Pollin did a study a decade ago during the IPO boom that illustrates this distinction. They found that for every $113 in stocks traded, only $1 actually went to businesses to finance real investment.

Your question does point to a change that could greatly strengthen Social Security in the future. Many economists, both conservative and liberal, support the idea of a tax on speculation in the stock market. This is often called a "Tobin tax" after one of its proponents. The tax rate would not have to be very high to have a big impact. Using data from 1992, a tax rate of just 0.5% on stocks that are held for less than five years would generate revenues of more than $15 billion per year. If this revenue were allocated to the Social Security trust fund, the shortfall projected by the trustees would be completely eliminated.

**Given that England initiated private accounts in 1984 that failed miserably, what guarantee is there that the Bush plan won't also fail?**
The British experiment with private accounts has indeed failed to provide an adequate and stable retirement income for the majority of citizens. The United Kingdom is now trying to figure out how to switch back to a defined-benefit system of retirement insurance. The problem is that the trillions of pounds that were diverted into the stock market can't be brought back into the defined-benefit system.

Chile's system is one that President Bush often mentions. His proposal is likely to be similar because one of his advisors, José Piñera, designed the system in Chile for the Pinochet military dictatorship. Under that government, workers were encouraged to opt out of the system of pension insurance and into private accounts. Over the past 25 years, the return on stocks in Chile has averaged over 10%—a higher return than we can expect in the U.S. stock market over the next 25 years. Yet, even with that extremely high rate of return, the average Chilean retiree relying on private savings will receive a benefit less than one-half as large as someone who had remained in the old system, and that benefit lasts only 20 years. If a retiree is "unlucky" enough to live longer than that, he will simply run out of retirement income. Those in the old system not only receive a higher benefit, but the benefit lasts as long as they live, and continues to provide benefits to their surviving spouse.

A recent survey shows that 90% of Chileans who opted for the private accounts wish they had remained in the old system. The only people who have benefited by the new system are the wealthiest top 2% of the population.

The United States' Social Security system is the most efficiently run insurance program in the world, with overhead of only 0.7% of annual benefits; for every $100 paid into the system, $99.30 is paid out in benefits to retirees. In the British and Chilean systems, at retirement, workers convert their private accounts to annuities provided by private insurance companies. In the United States, overhead for annuities provided by private firms averages about 20%; for every $100 paid in, $20 gets siphoned off. And almost no annuities are indexed for inflation.

There is a third important experiment with "private accounts" to consider: the United States' own experiment with defined-contribution retirement plans. Since 1975, corporations have been phasing out their old defined-benefit pensions and replacing them with private savings accounts such as 401(k)s. In 1975, 39% of private-sector workers were covered by defined-benefit pensions, and only 6% by defined-contribution savings plans. By 1998 the share covered by real pensions had plummeted to just 18% and the percent relying on private accounts had risen to 38%. What has this rapid reversal done to retirement income security?

A 2002 study by New York University economist Edward Wolff defines retirement income insecurity as having less than half of your final working income in your first year of retirement. In 1989, less than 30% of workers aged 47 to 64 faced retirement income insecurity. Yet by 1999, after the shift to greater reliance on private accounts, even after the most rapid run-up in stock values in U.S. history, almost 43% of workers in this age group faced retirement income insecurity. We don't have to look to other countries to see the results of a shift to private accounts. That experiment has already been tried in the United States, and it failed.

**How large is the employer's contribution for every dollar put into the system by the wage earner? What happens to the employer's contribution to Social Security under the Bush proposal?**

The employee pays a payroll tax of 6.2% on every dollar earned, up to an income level of $90,000. The maximum amount of tax paid annually is $5,580. The employer pays a tax that is exactly equal to that paid by the employee.

It's difficult to answer the second part of the question precisely, since the president has refused to detail his actual proposal. While the plan developed by Bush's first-term Social Security advisory commission does not speak to this issue directly, in his first term he suggested that employer contributions should be reduced by the same amount as employee contributions. If Bush gets what he said he wanted, employers would see their portion of payroll taxes drop from 6.2% to 2.2% (a reduction of 64.5%). This would be a windfall for corporations.

**Other economics writers, such as *Newsweek*'s Robert Samuelson, believe the**

> ### *PRIVATIZATION ADVOCATES*
>
> Powerful advocates for privatization include libertarian and conservative think tanks and advocacy groups such as the Cato Institute, the Heritage Foundation, Americans for Tax Reform, and Citizens for a Sound Economy, all driven by an ideological commitment to the abolition of federal social programs.
>
> Wall Street too is thirsty for the $1.4 trillion that privatization would funnel into equities if the taxes collected to support the Social Security system were invested privately rather than reinvested in federal government bonds. That's not to mention the windfall of fees privatization would deliver for banks, brokerage houses, and investment firms.
>
> Just after he took office, President Bush appointed a commission to examine privatizing the Social Security system. The commission could not figure out how to maintain payments to current recipients while diverting tax dollars to the savings of current workers, nor could it resolve how to cover the benefits of the disabled or resolve issues surrounding survivors' benefits. Although the president did not succeed in carrying out Social Security privatization in his first term, he has made the partial privatization of Social Security retirement accounts the top priority of his second-term domestic agenda.

**system does need revision, and suggest reforms including raising the eligibility age and lowering benefits to wealthy people. What, if any, changes do you think need to be implemented?**

I do not think either of those changes should be implemented.

Raising the retirement age is simply a benefit reduction, because retirees would receive benefits for fewer years, and fewer workers would live to see retirement. As I mentioned before, there is no reason to cut benefits out of fear of the remote possibility of a shortfall 47 years from now.

Lowering benefits for the wealthy is also a bad idea. That's like proposing that, after an accident, someone who drives a Lexus should only get half of the replacement value of their car, while someone who drives a Ford Focus should get the full replacement value. Social Security is a universal insurance system. This change would make the system less universal and pit one group of workers against another.

In answer to the last part of your question, I mentioned the possibility of a "Tobin tax" above. Another change would be to remove the cap on the Social Security payroll tax. Payroll taxes take 6.2% of every worker's first $90,000. Income above $90,000 is not subject to the tax. For the nine out of 10 Americans who will never make more than $90,000, this represents a constant financial burden. But those who make more than $90,000 per year pay progressively smaller percentages of their total income, as their incomes rise. Eliminating the cap and subjecting high-income salaries to the same tax rate paid on lower incomes would make the system fairer. The actuaries of the Social Security administration estimate that removing the cap on all wage and salary income would eliminate 90% of the projected shortfall. Those same actuaries found that raising the cap to just $147,000 would eliminate more than 57% of the shortfall.

Finally, Social Security funding currently relies on taxing only wage and salary incomes. Over the past two decades, as corporations have driven down the real wages of the vast majority (80%) of employees, the share of total national income going to wages and salaries has declined, and the share going to capital income (from financial assets) has gone up. This erosion of the wage share of total income has reduced the share of total income flowing into the Social Security system, which explains a large part of the projected shortfall. The retirement systems of the rest of the industrialized world are funded out of general tax revenues. The logic is that everyone in society benefits from the efforts of workers, so all should contribute to the support of retired workers. So another possible change to the system would be to expand the Social Security tax to cover all forms of income. If this were done, the tax rate could be significantly lower. This would provide an enormous benefit to small businesses and the self-employed as well as to everyone who works for wages and salaries.

**President Bush's top five campaign donations last year were from large brokerages. For instance, Morgan Stanley gave $600,480 and was the largest contributor to the Bush campaign. Do these brokerages stand to benefit financially from the privatization of Social Security?**

This industry was the biggest contributor to President Bush in both the 2000 and 2004 campaigns. How much it stands to gain depends on how many people decide to opt for the private accounts; estimates range from $40 billion to $80 billion per year.

It's likely that only the 16 brokerage firms that are allowed to interact with the Federal Reserve Bank would be permitted to manage private accounts. Divide $40 billion by 16 and you get $2.5 billion for each firm. A $2.5 billion annual return on a $600,000 "investment" in the Bush campaign is pretty amazing!

**The reason so many Enron employees lost so much is that they forgot the first step of investing—diversify! Isn't diversification the key?**

You are correct that history shows that diversified investing provides the best opportunity for success. But it does not guarantee success.

My research, and that of others, addresses this issue directly. If the amount contributed to Social Security by a median-income worker had been put into a diversified portfolio, and if that individual were to live 20 years into retirement, and if the economic outcomes (real wage and stock market growth rates) of any 10-year period during the 20th century were applied to that portfolio, only the period of the 1990s would result in higher retirement income from the portfolio than the existing Social Security system.

If that person were to live longer than 20 years, even the decade of the 1990s would not have outperformed Social Security. The only reason that anyone is willing to look seriously at private accounts is because of the aberrant behavior of the stock market during the 1990s.

Today, most retirees relying on 401(k) plans have significantly lower retirement income than those who were able to hold on to their old defined-benefit pension plans. It is not only workers at bankrupt companies like Enron who have been hurt; Enron highlights the level of risk imposed upon all workers by private accounts. We've been told repeatedly that if we diversify our holdings in private accounts sufficiently, we don't face much risk. But when the stock market goes down significantly (e.g., 45% in 2001-2002), diversification does not provide much protection.

Bush Social Security advisor Sylvester Scheiber, who works for the corporate benefits consulting firm the Wyatt Group, wrote an article in 1994 predicting that the financial markets are likely to lose as much as half of their value as the baby boom generation retires and starts to sell its financial assets to pay for food and rent. This is why he has been advising his corporate clients for decades to replace their real defined-benefit pension plans with 401(k) plans. It shifts the cost of a financial collapse from the corporation to the employees.

**How important are the assumptions being made about economic growth and stock market returns to Bush's privatization proposal?**

The growth numbers underlying the talk of a shortfall in the trust fund are extremely pessimistic, while the stock market projections behind the privatization proposal are extremely optimistic. Bush assumes that long-term GDP growth will be only 1.8%, yet claims the return on stocks will be 7% per year. Other than the Great Depression, the slowest decade of growth in U.S. history was the 1980s, with a growth rate of 2.4%. If the economy grows at 2.4%, the Social Security trust fund never goes to zero.

But what if we use Bush's own assumptions? In 2004, the GDP was almost $12 trillion, and the value of publicly traded stock was about $40 trillion, a ratio of 3.3 to 1. If, as in the past, half of the return on stocks takes the form of an increase in stock prices, in 60 years the value of the stock market will be a lopsided nine times the size of the economy. If the other half of the return came from dividends, fully one-third of GDP would need to be paid out in dividends at that time. This scenario is impossible. The assumptions don't make sense.

**Young people say they want more control over their Social Security investments. How do you explain the purpose of Social Security to today's young workers?**

The best way to explain Social Security is to say what it is. It's an insurance system that protects your income when you retire or face disability, and provides income to your children if you die. President Bush wants you to look at Social Security as an investment—but it is a form of insurance that guarantees you a constant stream of income in retirement or in case of disability, adjusted to protect against inflation, for as long as you live.

Social Security can be compared to other types of insurance such as home insurance. You insure your home because if it should burn down, you would not be able to afford to rebuild it with your personal income alone. If your house never burns down, you will pay into the insurance fund and never get a penny back. But fire insurance isn't a "bad investment" because it *isn't* an investment *at all.* You are purchasing security.

Unlike fire insurance, Social Security inevitably gives most of us our money back. But the fact that we get money back does not change the fact that Social Security is a form of insurance, not an investment. Only the richest of the rich can afford not to have insurance and to rely solely on their own savings and investments to fund their retirement or risk of disability.

Young people must also understand that financial investments are inherently risky. Many investments fail, and when they do, you lose all of the money you invested. Today's 25 year olds have only seen the stock market go up, except for one (very large) drop. But you don't have to go back to the 1930s to see a different picture: If you put money into the stock market in 1970 and waited until 1980 to take it out, you would have lost money. There is absolutely no guarantee that stock investors will see the high returns Bush is falsely promising.

*Parts of these questions and answers are derived from an online chat posted at <www.spokesmanreview.com>.*

# AFRICAN AMERICANS AND SOCIAL SECURITY: WHY THE PRIVATIZATION ADVOCATES ARE WRONG

**BY WILLIAM E. SPRIGGS**

*November/December 2004*

Proponents of Social Security privatization are trying to claim that the current program is unfair to African Americans and that a privatized program would serve African Americans better. This argument lends support to the privatization agenda while at the same time giving its advocates a compassionate gloss. But the claims about African Americans and Social Security are wrong.

The Old Age Survivors and Disability Insurance Program (OASDI), popularly known as Social Security, was put in place by Franklin Roosevelt to establish a solid bulwark of economic rights for the public—specifically, as he put it, "the right to adequate protection from the economic fears of old age, sickness, accident, and unemployment." Most Americans associate Social Security only with the retirement—or old age—benefit. Yet it was created to do much more, and it does.

As its original name suggests, Social Security is an insurance program that protects workers and their families against the income loss that occurs when a worker retires, becomes disabled, or dies. All workers will eventually either grow too old to compete in the labor market, become disabled, or die. OASDI insures all workers and their families against these universal risks, while spreading the costs and benefits of that insurance protection among the entire workforce. Currently, 70% of Social Security funds go to retirees, 15% to disabled workers, and 15% to survivors.

Social Security is a "pay as you go" system, which means the taxes paid by today's workers are not set aside to pay their own benefits down the road, but rather go to pay the benefits of current Social Security recipients. It's financed using the Federal Insurance Contribution Act (or FICA) payroll tax, paid by all working Americans on earnings of less than about $90,000 a year. While the payroll tax is not progressive, Social Security benefits are—that is, low-wage workers receive a greater percentage of pre-retirement earnings from the program than higher-wage workers.

In the 1980s, recognizing that the baby boom generation would strain this system, Congress passed reforms to raise extra tax revenues above and beyond the current need and set up a trust fund to hold the reserve. Trustees were appointed and charged with keeping Social Security solvent. Today's trustees warn that their projections, which are based on modest assumptions about the long-term growth of the U.S. economy, show the system could face a shortfall around 2042, when either benefits would have to be cut or the FICA tax raised.

Those who oppose the social nature of the program have pounced on its projected shortfall in revenues to argue that the program cannot—or ought not—be fixed, but should instead be fundamentally changed (see "Privatization Advocates.") Privatization proponents are seeking to frame the issue as a matter of social justice, as if Social Security "reform" would primarily benefit low-income workers, blue-collar workers, people of color, and women. Prompted by disparities in life expectancy between whites and African Americans and the racial wealth gap, a growing chorus within the privatization movement is claiming that privatizing Social Security would be beneficial to African Americans.

Opponents attack the program on the basis of an analogy to private retirement accounts. Early generations of Social Security beneficiaries received much more in benefits than they had paid into the system in taxes. Privatization proponents argue those early recipients received a "higher rate of return" on their "investment" while current and future generations are being "robbed" because they will see "lower rates of return." They argue the current system of social insurance—particularly the retirement program—should be privatized, switching from the current "pay-as-you-go" system to one in which individual workers claim their own contribution and decide where and how to invest it.

But this logic inverts the premise of social insurance. Rather than sharing risk across the entire workforce to ensure that all workers and their families are protected from the three inevitabilities of old age, disability, and death, privatizing Social Security retirement benefits would enable high-wage workers to reap gains from private retirement investment without having to help protect lower-wage workers from their (disproportionate) risks of disability and death. High-wage workers, who are more likely to live long enough to retire, could in fact do better on average if they opt out of the general risk pool and devote all their money to retirement without having to cover the risk of those who may become disabled or die, although they would of course be subjecting their retirement dollars to greater risk. But low-wage workers, who are far more likely to need disability or survivors' benefits to help their families and are less likely to live long enough to retire, would then be left with lower disability and survivors' benefits, and possibly no guaranteed benefits. This is what the Social Security privatization movement envisions. But you wouldn't know it from reading their literature.

And when the myths about Social Security's financial straits meet another American myth—race—even more confusion follows. Here is a look at three misleading claims by privatization proponents about African Americans and Social Security.

## Myth #1

Several conservative research groups argue that Social Security is a bad deal for African Americans because of their lower life expectancies. "Lifetime Social Security benefits depend, in large part, on longevity," writes the Cato Institute's Michael Tanner in his briefing paper "Disparate Impact: Social Security and African Americans." "At every age, African-American men and women both have shorter life expectancies than do their white counterparts. … As a result, a black man or woman earning exactly the same lifetime wages, and paying exactly the same lifetime Social Security taxes, as his or her white counterpart will likely receive a far lower rate of return." Or as the Americans for Tax Reform web site puts it: "A black male born today has a life expectancy of 64.8 years. But the Social Security retirement age for that worker in the future will be 67 years. That means probably the majority of black males will never even receive Social Security retirement benefits."

The longevity myth is the foundation of all the race-based arguments for Social Security privatization. There are several problems with it.

First, the shorter life expectancy of African Americans compared to whites is the result of higher morbidity in mid-life, and is most acute for African-American men. The life expectancies of African-American women and white men are virtually equal. So the life expectancy argument can really only be made about African-American men.

Second, the claim that OASDI is unfair to African Americans because their expected benefits are less than their expected payments is usually raised and then answered from the perspective of the retirement (or "old age") benefit alone. That is an inaccurate way to look at the problem. Because OASDI also serves families of workers who become disabled or die, a correct measure would take into account the probability of all three risk factors—old age, disability, and death. Both survivor benefits and disability benefits, in fact, go disproportionately to African Americans.

While African Americans make up 12% of the U.S. population, 23% of children receiving Social Security survivor benefits are African American, as are about 17% of disability beneficiaries. On average, a worker who receives disability benefits or a family that receives survivor benefits gets far more in return than the worker paid in FICA taxes, notwithstanding privatizers' attempts to argue that Social Security is a bad deal.

Survivors' benefits also provide an important boost to poor families more generally. A recent study by the National Urban League Institute for Opportunity and Equality showed that the benefit lifted 1 million children out of poverty and helped another 1 million avoid extreme poverty (living below half the poverty line).

Finally, among workers who do live long enough to get the retirement benefit, life expectancies don't differ much by racial group. For example, at age 65, the life expectancies of African-American and white men are virtually the same.

President Bush's Social Security commission proposed the partial privatization of Social Security retirement accounts, but cautioned that it could not figure out how to maintain equal benefits for the other risk pools. The commission suggested that disability and survivor's benefits would have to be reduced if the privatization plan proceeds.

This vision is of a retirement program designed for the benefit of the worker who retires—only. A program with that focus would work against, not for, African Americans because of the higher morbidity rates in middle age and the smaller share of African Americans who live to retirement.

## Myth #2

African Americans have less education, and so are in the work force longer, than whites, and yet Social Security only credits 35 years of work experience in figuring benefits. Tanner says, "benefits are calculated on the basis of the highest 35 years of earnings over a worker's lifetime. Workers must still pay Social Security taxes during years outside those 35, but those taxes do not count toward or earn additional benefits. Generally, those low-earnings years occur early in an individual's life. That is particularly important to African Americans because they are likely to enter the workforce at an earlier age than whites…."

This claim misinterprets the benefit formula for Social Security. Yes, African Americans on average are slightly less educated than whites. The gap is mostly because of a higher college completion rate for white men compared to African-American men. But the education argument fails to acknowledge that white teenagers have a significantly higher labor force participation rate (at 46%) than do African-American teens (29%). The higher labor force participation of white teenagers helps to explain why young white adults do better in the labor market than young African-American adults. (The racial gaps in unemployment are considerably greater for teenagers and young adults than for those over 25.)

These differences in early labor market experiences mean that African-American men have more years of zero earnings than do whites. So while the statement about education is true, the inference from education differences to work histories is false. By taking only 35 years of work history into account in the benefit formula, the Social Security formula is progressive. It in effect ignores years of zero or very low earnings. This levels the playing field among long-time workers, putting African Americans with more years of zero earnings on par with whites. By contrast, a private system based on total years of earnings would exacerbate racial labor market disparities.

## Myth #3

A third claim put forward by critics of Social Security is that African-American retirees are more dependent on Social Security than whites. Tanner writes: "Elderly African Americans are much more likely than their white counterparts to be dependent on Social Security benefits for most or all of their retirement income." Therefore, he concludes, "African Americans would be among those with the most to gain from the privatization of Social Security—transforming the program into a system of individually owned, privately invested accounts." Law professor and senior policy advisor to Americans for Tax Reform Peter Ferrara adds, "the personal accounts would produce far higher returns and benefits for lower-income workers, African Americans, Hispanics, women and other minorities."

It's true that African-American retirees are more likely than whites to rely on Social Security as their only income in old age. It's the sole source of retirement income for 40% of elderly African Americans. This is a result of discrimination in the labor market that limits the share of African Americans with jobs that offer pension benefits. Privatizing Social Security would not change labor market discrimination or its effects.

Privatizing Social Security would, however, exacerbate the earnings differences between African Americans and whites, since benefits would be based solely on individual savings. What would help African-American retirees is not privatization, but rather changing the redistributive aspects of Social Security to make it even more progressive.

The current formula for Social Security benefits is progressive in two ways: low

### *FEDERAL POLICY FOR DEFINED-BENEFIT PLANS*

For almost a century, the U.S. government has promoted defined-benefit pension plans because they increase productivity and reinforce the employment relationship while stabilizing retirement income. In 1919, the federal government was faced with a melt-down of the defined-benefit plans of legacy railroads that struggled in competition with small, low-cost start-ups that didn't provide pensions to their young workers. This is analogous to regional air carriers like Jet Blue decimating United Airlines and other legacy airlines today. In response, the mandatory, industry-wide Railroad Retirement system was established in 1935, a decade before Social Security, requiring all railroads to pay into a multi-employer pension fund.

During World War II and in the post-war period, court cases and tax laws favored rapid growth in defined-benefit plans. An unusually large pension default at the Studebaker automobile corporation in South Bend, Ind., in 1964, led Congress to pass comprehensive pension regulatory legislation, the Employee Retirement Income Security Act (ERISA), in 1974. ERISA established the PBGC to insure firms' defined-benefit pensions in the event of bankruptcy (which, even before 1974, happened infrequently; one out of 1,000 defined-benefit sponsors had defaulted in 10 years). Since its creation in 1974, the PBGC has operated without ever missing a payment it owes, despite having an overall balance-sheet deficit in most years, using the premium income that every plan sponsor (single employers, multiple employers, or unions) pays to carry the agency through normal cyclical downturns.

In creating an insurance structure, the legislation required companies to fund their defined-benefit promises over time, anticipating "moral hazard" problems (when an insured entity becomes lax, relying on another body to bail it out). ERISA intended companies to have flexibility, contributing more in good times and less in bad. Originally, companies had 40 years to reach 100% funding, using wage, investment returns, and interest-rate projections. In the late 1980s and 1990s, faster funding was required of plans that were less than 70% funded. (A pension's funded status refers to its ratio of assets to liabilities. If a plan is more than 90% funded, that is, if its current assets amount to 90% of the present value of promises, including expected future promises, made to its participants, it is considered fully funded.)

earners get a higher share of their earnings than do higher wage earners and the lowest years of earning are ignored. Changes in the formula to raise the benefits floor enough to lift all retired Social Security recipients out of poverty would make it still more progressive. Increasing and updating the Supplemental Security Income payment, which helps low earners, could accomplish the same goal for SSI recipients. (SSI is a program administered by Social Security for very low earners and the poor who are disabled, blind, or at least 65 years old.)

The proponents of privatization argue that the heavy reliance of African-American seniors on Social Security requires higher rates of return—returns that are only possible by putting money into the stock market. Yet given the lack of access to private pensions for African-American seniors and their low savings from lifetimes of low earnings, such a notion is perverse. It would have African Americans gamble with their only leg of retirement's supposed three-legged stool—pension, savings, and Social Security. And, given the much higher risk that African Americans face of both death before retirement and of disability, it would be a risky gamble indeed to lower those benefits while jeopardizing their only retirement leg.

Privatizing the retirement program, and separating the integrated elements of Social Security, would split America. The divisions would be many: between those more likely to be disabled and those who are not; between those more likely to die before retirement and those more likely to retire; between children who get survivors' benefits and the elderly who get retirement benefits; between those who retire with high-yield investments and those who fare poorly in retirement. The "horizontal equity" of the program (treating similar people in a similar way) would be lost, as volatile stock fluctuations and the timing of retirement could greatly affect individuals' rates of return. The "vertical equity" of the program (its progressive nature, insuring a floor for benefits) would be placed in greater jeopardy with the shift from social to private benefits.

Social Security works because it is "social." It is America's only universal federal program. The proposed changes would place Social Security in the same political space as the rest of America's federal programs—and African Americans have seen time and again how those politics work.

# TAKING ONE FROM THE BUSH TEAM

**BY DEAN BAKER**

*November/December 2002*

Implausible as this may seem, President Bush's Social Security commission came up with a good idea. While no single proposal could possibly fix all the problems of the private pension system, the commission designed a scheme that could get part of the way there.

Granted, the members of the "President's Commission to Strengthen Social Security" were selected by the Bush administration for their allegiance to the myth of the Social Security crisis and their support of privatization. The commission's 2001 final report was remarkable not so much for its recommendation of partial privatization (that came as little surprise) but for its cynical errors and omissions of fact. For example, its inflated stock return projections conflict with the slow economic growth rates projected by the Social Security trustees. The commission's case for an imminent Social Security meltdown, and for partial privatization, is founded on fiction.

But one commission idea merits serious consideration. It proposed establishing a national system of pension accounts for every worker in the country. Of course, Bush's commission wanted to *divert* a portion of the Social Security payroll tax from Social Security into these accounts. This would not only place at risk the only guaranteed income many Americans can bank on having at retirement. It would more than double the administrative costs of the current Social Security system, and strain Social Security finances (which despite the hyperbole are on sound footing at present).

The commission has it backwards. Its proposed system of individual accounts makes no sense as a replacement for Social Security. It does make sense, however, as a supplement to Social Security. *Without* drawing on Social Security payroll deductions, a system similar to that envisioned by the Bush commission could serve as a nationwide alternative to private 401(k) plans. (See "401(k) Defined" on page 33.)

A bare bones 401(k)-like pension modeled after the Thrift Savings Plan for federal employees, the national pension plan would offer workers three or four basic funds (for example, a stock index, bond index, and money market) and allow them to divide their accounts among these funds and to switch their holdings periodically. The accounts would be administered by a central authority.

## A Universal Solution

The benefits from such a system would be substantial. Currently, about half of the nation's workers have no access to a pension. Coverage rates for low-wage workers are far lower. Only about 13% of workers in low-income households are eligible for employer-sponsored pensions. Among the hardest hit are people who work for small businesses and short-term and part-time workers. Under a national pension system, every individual in the country would immediately have access to a low-cost, fully portable, retirement plan. This means that workers could contribute to the fund on their first day at a job, even in part-time or temporary positions. They could also keep the same account no matter how frequently they changed jobs.

Employers would have the option to contribute to this fund on behalf of their workers, just as they do now with 401(k) plans. Because the plan would be low-cost and simple, many employers would probably replace their existing 401(k) plans with the national system. Small businesses that now see pension administration as burdensome might begin to make contributions to their workers' accounts at very little administrative cost. In this sense, a national voluntary 401(k)-type system may actually prove to be something of a boon to small businesses, since they would be able to offer the sort of pensions provided by larger companies.

The fact that a national pension system will cost far less to administer than the current system will also bolster workers' asset accumulations. The Bush commission estimated (probably optimistically) that the administrative fees on a national pension system would average 0.3% of the account values, more than 1.1 percentage points below the cost of a typical employer-sponsored 401(k) plan at present. Over time, the fee reduction (whatever the exact amount) would have a large impact on the size of retirement wealth.

Taking the commission's fee estimate at face value for the moment, if a worker puts $1,000 per year for thirty years into a typical 401(k), the account would grow to just $50,000. But with the lower-cost national system, it would grow to more than $60,000 (at a 4% rate of return). Over a forty-year period the difference would grow still larger: $80,000 under the existing system, compared to $104,000 under the national system.

A national pension system will not address all or even most of the problems of the existing system. There are tens of millions of workers just making ends meet now. Most low-income workers will not be able to contribute to a national pension system regardless of how good a deal it is. Once a national pension system were put in place, it would be imperative for working people to push for a federal subsidy or tax reimbursement, similar to the one President Clinton proposed in 1999 and Vice President Gore proposed in his 2000 presidential campaign. Under Gore's proposal, federal government contributions would be paid into the accounts of low-income individuals. Such a federal match could amount to a sizable transfer of wealth to the working poor.

It is also worth noting that this system of accounts need not be established at the national level to reap economies of scale. A relatively large state would have enough workers to push down the costs close to that of the national system. (As the number of workers in a system gets larger, the costs per worker decline.) Since most workers don't often move across state borders, they could expect to stay with a single fund for much of their working career. Already, there is substantial interest in the Washington State legislature for setting up a system of "Washington Voluntary Accounts." If Washington or any other state successfully adopted a centralized system of accounts, it could serve as a model for other states and for the nation.

As a side benefit, a national system of voluntary accounts should provide a bit of a shake-up to the financial industry in a time when the public doesn't think very highly of Wall Street. The banks and brokerage houses that have been charging workers administrative fees equal to 1.4% of 401(k) holdings will suddenly be forced to compete with a system that charges less than one quarter of this amount. In order to keep their place in the market, the banks and brokerage houses would have to reduce their fees. Such a reduction in fees would benefit all workers with 401(k)s, even those who opt not to take part in the national system.

In short, a national pension system could be a good first step toward repairing the holes in the private pension system. (And a federal match or tax reimbursement for low-income workers' contributions would be better still.) There seems little not to like about the Bush commission's plan for a national system of pension accounts, so long as it has *nothing* to do with Social Security.

# HIJACKING THE FUTURE: HOW WALL STREET IS TAKING OVER WORKERS' PENSIONS

**BY JAMES RIDGEWAY**
*September/October 1999*

In the Huntingdon, Pennsylvania, fiberglass plant owned by the French firm, Groupe Porcher, workers in their off moments are encouraged to use nearby computer terminals and check out the stock market.

Like those in thousands of other plants and offices across the nation, the 450 workers here at the former Owens Corning plant are in the midst of a seismic change. They are being nudged — some would say pushed — into a new-fangled 401k pension scheme and away from the old reliable pension plan. Under the old plan workers were assured of a set payment every month. Under the new scheme, the payment depends upon how well they can play the market. If they're smart, maybe they can make a million and retire. But if they're like most people, plodding along, then they'll just get by. And if they have bad luck and the market crashes, that's their problem. In fact, it's all very much their problem.

Baffled by the new arrangement, representatives from UNITE, the union which represents the Porcher workers, are pouring over the books, reading nearly incomprehensible pension filings made with the government, scouring the newspapers to help the local figure out how to proceed. The local itself has hired a consultant and already unearthed "administration" fees charged to its members without their knowledge. The payment of these fees has become the basis of a union grievance.

UNITE is grappling with one of the most dramatic changes in the American economy over the last decade: The quiet elimination of the pension, long regarded by organized labor as a virtual worker's right, and its transformation into a Wall Street speculation device. This is an extraordinary public relations triumph for corporate leaders and a huge potential defeat for labor. Basically, the modern corporation, with only recent and sporadic opposition from labor or government, has shifted the costs of retirement from employers onto the workers. The signposts along the way to this revolution are few and far between.

## A Brief Moment in Time

Employers shouldered the burden of paying pensions to their non-salaried workers for only a brief moment in U.S. history. In the 1940s, powerful unions began negotiating company pensions for their workers — or, like the Teamsters, they demanded that employers pay into a union pension fund. They won these concessions from employers through collective bargaining after retreating, defeated, from promoting a broader agenda at the federal level — an agenda that would have enacted national health insurance and expanded public pensions for all workers, not just their own members.

The company pension schemes now being supplanted by 401ks are far from perfect. For instance, a parent company is under no obligation to pay the debts of a subsidiary that goes under. And through shell companies and slick lawyers, some multinationals avoided paying out pensions to rustbelt workers left jobless by the plant closings of the 1970s and 1980s. In Which Side Are You On?, labor lawyer Thomas Geoghegan tells of securing only $14 million out of the $65 million in pension money that International Harvester owed those who once worked for its bankrupt subsidiary Wisconsin Steel.

The shift to 401ks provides a host of other opportunities to milk workers of their pensions. This time, the milking is done as much by Wall Street as by the company.

### 401k Pension plans

One of every four Americans has a 401k, with 200,000 employers offering plans whose assets have grown from $91 billion in 1984 to $1 trillion today. The share of employers offering 401k plans jumped from 34% in 1981 to 75% in 1996, according to a recent study by Teresa Ghilarducci, an economics professor and pension expert at Notre Dame. A great deal of this money ends up in the stock market where it is invested through mutual funds — pools of stocks and bonds managed by professionals — that increasingly dominate this new pension industry.

---

## WHEN BAD THINGS HAPPEN TO GOOD PENSIONS

**BY TERESA GHILARDUCCI**

*May/June 2005*

February was a momentous month for American workers' retirement security. Just days after President Bush called for the partial privatization of Social Security, his administration proposed major modifications to the system that guarantees employer-sponsored defined-benefit pensions. Both initiatives break with longstanding "insurance" models of old-age income security and accelerate the use of individual accounts.

Defined-benefit pensions, like Social Security, provide a modest but steady stream of income for the duration of a retiree's life. Both systems are based on collective risk sharing: they gather premium contributions from populations facing similar risks—such as old age or disability—and provide a guaranteed stream of income to individuals when those risks befall them.

Much as the administration is using a financing problem in the Social Security system as an excuse to demand big changes that would endanger Social Security itself, it's using a deficit in the agency that insures defined-benefit pensions to call for "reforms" that would imperil those very pensions.

Both of Bush's proposals would undermine the retirement security of working people and their families. But the two proposals also deeply contradict each other. By making the puzzling claim that the Social Security trust fund, which holds only U.S. Treasury bonds, owns no "real money," the Social Security proposal urges younger workers to divert Social Security contributions into individual accounts. On the other hand, most independent analysts believe the administration's proposed pension reform would lead corporations to load up on bonds in order to stabilize their asset portfolios—and their credit ratings—and over time drive them out of the defined-benefit system altogether. The Social Security proposal is based on the premise that individuals don't own enough stock; the pension proposal is based on the premise that pension funds fall short because they own too much.

The administration's proposals place us at a crossroads. We can either hasten the end of group and social insurance and move toward individual accounts—personal savings accounts and 401(k)s—or we can save Social Security and expand incentives for employers to provide defined-benefit pensions to workers.

## Why Defined-Benefit Plans Should Be Strengthened—Not Undermined

Unlike defined-contribution plans like 401(k)s, which yield benefits—or losses—based on the contributions and investment prowess of the individual worker, defined benefits are predictable; they're usually based on a worker's pay rate and length of employment. For the median worker, defined-benefit wealth is higher than defined-contribution account wealth, and because the former is paid as an annuity, workers collect for as long as they live. (See Table 1 on next page for the risks associated with defined-benefit versus defined-contribution plans.)

Defined-benefit plans offer another, frequently overlooked, benefit to society: they serve as an equalizing force. For over 40 years, American retirement policies have reduced income inequality between the top tier and the rest, narrowing consumption gaps as people age. Social Security and defined-benefit plans set an income floor underneath the working class that does not fluctuate with the financial markets. Among current retirees (Americans born between 1926 and 1935), the ratio of the income that goes to the top 20% versus the middle 20% of the income distribution is 234%. For retired boomers (workers born between 1946 and 1956), the gap will be 285%, and it will continue to rise for subsequent generations. This growth in inequality is tied to the decline of defined-benefit pensions and the rise of defined-contribution plans as shares of the income of elderly households. Current retirees have 20% of their income coming from defined-benefit plans while future retirees are projected to have only 11%.

Under the current system, companies with defined-benefit pensions pay insurance premiums to the Pension Benefit Guaranty Corporation (PBGC), a government corporation created in 1974 to insure pension assets. If a pension plan fails, the PBGC takes control of it and continues to pay covered workers' retirement

**TABLE 1**
**COMPARISON BETWEEN DEFINED BENEFIT AND DEFINED CONTRIBUTION PLANS:THE RISKS FOR THE EMPLOYEE**

| | *Defined Benefit plans* | *Defined Contribution plans* |
|---|---|---|
| Chance that pension benefit will be larger than expected (Investment Benefit) | No (unless union and/or employer increases benefits) | Yes (if investments exceed expectations) |
| Risk that pension fund investments will fall short (Investment Risk) | No | Yes (if individuals make investment mistakes or investments unpredictably fail) |
| Risk that retiree will outlive their benefits. (Longevity Risk) | No | Yes |
| Risk that inflation will diminish the pension's buying power (Inflation risk) | Yes | Yes |
| Risk that a plan sponsor's bankruptcy will diminish the pension (Employer Bankruptcy Risk) | Some (only very high paid DB participants aren't fully insured by the PBGC) | Yes (almost half of all 401(k) assets are in employer stock) |
| Risk that administration costs can increase and diminish returns) | Borne by employer | Borne by employee |
| Ease of pension portability between jobs | No | Yes |

benefits up to a cap. The PBGC receives no federal tax dollars, relying instead primarily on insurance premiums paid by employers and unions who sponsor defined-benefit pensions.

## Bush's Pension Proposal

On February 7 [2005], the Bush administration unveiled a sweeping rewrite of federal pension law in the form of a proposal it calls "Strengthen Funding for Single-Employer Pension Plans." The administration claims to want to strengthen pensions by fixing the problem of "underfunded plan terminations"—which, it argues, "are placing an increasing strain on the pension insurance system."

The proposal is tailored to an imagined reality where most companies grossly underfund their plans, and it ignores fundamental problems caused by the rise of risky defined-contribution plans and the one-time contraction of the steel and airline industries. If enacted, it would destroy the very system the administration claims it wants to save.

The plan dramatically increases PBGC premiums for single-employer defined-benefit sponsors, doubling premiums for "at risk" firms (those with unfunded liabilities that are likely to default) and tripling premiums for healthy firms (see Table 2).

**TABLE 2**
**THE EFFECT THE BUSH PROPOSALS WILL HAVE ON PREMIUMS OF UNHEALTHY AND HEALTHY COMPANIES SPONSORING DB PLANS**

| Category of firm | Total PBGC premiums paid by firms as a percent of the expected losses imposed on the PBGC | | |
|---|---|---|---|
| | *Actual in 2004* | *Proposed under Bush plan* | *Percent increase in premiums* |
| Below Investment Grade Firms | 8% | 16% | 113% |
| Above Investment Grade Firms | 66% | 340% | 240% |

*Source:* Coronado and Schieber, 2005

Whereas today, healthy firms pay premiums equal to 66% of their "expected losses" (meaning the amount they would owe to current and future retirees if they defaulted), the Bush plan would raise healthy firms' premiums to 340% of their expected losses. It thus penalizes healthy companies for sponsoring defined-benefit pensions.

For the first time, a company's ability to provide such pensions to its workers would be linked to the company's own creditworthiness. The plan divides companies into two groups: those above and those below "investment grade." Companies that fall below investment grade face large premium rate hikes and have just five years to reach a 90% pension-funding level. (See "Federal Policy for Defined-Benefit Plans" for more on pension funding requirements.) An estimated one-fourth of the nation's largest firms, including Delta Air Lines, Goodyear Tire and Rubber, United States Steel, and Lucent Technologies, are currently below investment grade. In this way, the plan intensifies the funding obligations of companies already experiencing financial difficulties. At the same time, it prohibits firms from building up a cushion of credit during flush periods. For decades, companies have contributed more during boom years so as to lighten their funding obligations during slow periods. The Bush plan takes away that flexibility.

What's more, firms would be required to value their plan assets according to their market value, rather than using an average or smoothed valuation of assets, as they do now. This change will produce greater year-to-year volatility in asset prices and funding obligations. Measures of liability (the amount a plan owes to current and future beneficiaries) would also become more volatile: The plan requires firms to use a complex method to calculate the present value of future liabilities. Firms now use a single interest rate in the calculations; under the Bush plan their interest rates would be pegged to when their workers are expected to retire. Firms with younger employees would use a higher interest rate tied to a long-term bond, while firms with older employees would use a low rate, which would make their liabilities soar. These accounting changes will hurt older plans in blue-collar manufacturing and make contributions more uncertain.

Bush claims the changes would result in "increased accuracy." But he fails to mention that they will make defined-benefit plans more expensive for companies to offer, required contributions less predictable, and valuations much more complicated to compute—something companies, especially small and medium sized ones, complain about.

The volatility produced by the new accounting framework would force firms to shift their pension investments from stocks to bonds. In fact, bonds, with their predictable rates of return, would become the only reasonable investment to include in a corporate pension fund. But bonds' low yields would drive up the cost of providing a plan—and hasten the elimination of the defined-benefit pension.

The Bush proposal starts from the wrong premise. It assumes that many firms purposefully underfund their plans because they know that the PBGC will pick up the shortfall if they go bankrupt. (Economists call this the "moral hazard" problem.) Similarly, it reduces employer flexibility in the belief that firms will use the flexible rules to "game the system." It anticipates bad faith behavior rather than mixing protections against bad behavior with positive incentives for promoting and strengthening the system, which, in reality, most companies deal with in good faith and want to keep strong.

## Why the Shortfall?

There's no question that the PBGC is facing a serious shortfall. In 2004, its budget plummeted into a $23 billion hole from a 2000 (stock-swollen) surplus of $10 billion. The dramatic fall was caused by crippling mass bankruptcies and defaults in the steel and airline industries. The agency was designed to cope with isolated cases of default, not sector-wide crises. Since 2002, about 70% of the $8 billion the PBGC has absorbed in pension losses was related to steel and airline defaults. It is expected to absorb another $6.6 billion from United Airlines. The independent monitoring organization Center for Federal Financial Institutions (COFFI) projects a program deficit of $16.2 billion in 2013. According to its founder, former Treasury staffer Douglas Elliot, the PBGC might require a program bailout of $56 to $100 billion by 2020 under certain scenarios.

The Bush proposal may have been prompted by the PBGC's deficit, but it does not address the two most fundamental causes of the agency's financing troubles: First, its premium base is shrinking thanks to the financial industry and to government regulations that privilege defined-contribution plans over defined-benefit plans; second, two industries recently caused unusual PBGC outlays. (In 2004 less than 5% of all defined-benefit participants constituted over two-thirds of the claims—see Table 3.) Underfunding of plans, the problem the Bush plan targets, is rare; a minority of companies underfund, and most are not at risk of defaulting.

***Fewer DB Plans***— The number of private defined-benefit plans peaked in the mid-1980s at 112,000, when they covered 40% of the U.S. work force. By 2004, just 31,000 remained, covering only 20% of workers. New economy companies like Microsoft and Wal-Mart never adopted the plans and old economy companies such as GE and IBM (along with 18% to 20% of other long-time sponsors) are freezing and terminating their plans.

When I served on the PBGC advisory board during the Clinton administra-

**TABLE 3**
**STEEL AND AIRLINES CONSTITUTE MOST OF THE PBGC'S CLAIMS**

| | Percentage of PBGC-insured Plan Participants and Claims on the PBGC from its Inception to 2004 | |
|---|---|---|
| | *Steel* | *Airlines* |
| Participants (all workers covered by a defined benefit pension) | 3% | 2% |
| Claims | 56% | 17% |

*Source:* PBGC Annual Report, 2004

tion, we used to say "pension plans aren't created—they're sold." Vendors, brokers, money management firms, and mutual funds charge more for individual account management than defined-benefit management, so they actively market 401(k)-type programs to employers. Employers find these plans attractive because they can subcontract record keeping and paperwork to vendors while passing administration costs on to their workers. Under employer-sponsored defined-benefit plans, employers bear the administrative costs—and the long-term liability. Moreover, the decline of unions, the shrinking of the manufacturing sector, and the erosion of durable employment relationships more generally have all combined to cut the number of defined-benefit pensions.

As more companies replace their guaranteed defined-benefit pensions with defined-contribution plans, the PBGC's financial position erodes because defined-contribution sponsors don't pay premiums to the PBGC. For a while, the effects of these long-term problems were masked by the stock market bubble, but no longer.

A glimmer of evidence suggests the decline is slowing. Four major companies, SBC, UMC, UK Barclays, and TransCanada, adopted defined-benefit plans in 2004. And public-sector employees are fending off muscular attempts, the latest one by California Governor Arnold Schwarzenegger, to convert their defined-benefit plans to defined-contribution plans.

***External Industry Factors***— The second threat to the defined-benefit pension has nothing to do with the pension system's internal flaws, but with outside economic and political events and trends, namely the dramatic acceleration in the off-shoring of U.S. manufacturing; strong dollar policies that boosted cheap imports; the 9/11 attacks; and fuel price hikes. These combined factors have pummeled the airline and steel sectors. Bethlehem Steel, Delta Airways, US Airways, and the giant United Airlines, plus one large company in another sector, Polaroid, have all offloaded some of their pension liabilities onto the PBGC within the past few years. In doing so, the steel and airline sectors brought down some of America's largest pension plans. The pension losses in these two industries have overwhelmed the PBGC. Given the exceptional confluence of factors at work here, Congress should not expect the

PBGC to absorb the impacts of two major industry collapses with its own premium revenues.

The Bush administration is simply wrong in assuming that corporate moral hazard and poor funding lie behind the PBGC's woes. Most firms actually behave as though they are committed to their plans. My survey of over 700 firms over a 19-year period (1981–1998) shows that when rates of return of defined-benefit pension funds were high—in good times—firms contributed more to both their defined-benefit and defined-contribution plans, just as the 1974 pension law known as ERISA intended. The airline and steel industries alone stopped contributing recently when both industries, facing crises, altered course and cut back their contributions when the defined-benefit plans were earning high rates of return. (There are two explanations, not mutually exclusive, for this reversal. One is that these industries decided to offload their liabilities onto the PBGC and workers; the other is that when the rest of the economy was doing all right, these industries were experiencing their own sector-specific recessions.) This is an unusual behavior pattern—the exception, not the rule. Beyond these sectors, far fewer firms withhold contributions to the PBGC during flush periods than the Bush administration contends.

## Toward Secure Retirement Income

Raising pension funding standards as aggressively as the Bush administration proposes tightens the rules to the point where plan sponsors could no longer afford or want to afford most of the defined-benefit pensions they now offer. According to Pensions and Investments, Ron Gebhardtsbauer, senior pension fellow at the American Academy of Actuaries, predicts, "Instead of investing their pension assets in stocks, companies will simply shut down their pension plans, set up defined-contribution plans and let the employees invest in stocks." Surveys show that when asked what poses a threat to defined-benefit plans, firms point to market downturns and volatility caused by eliminating actuarial smoothing in favor of "mark to market" funding schemes (exactly what Bush plans to implement). Standard & Poor's Ratings Services agrees. Credit ratings would likely fall for defined-benefit sponsors because of increased pension costs and volatility. Given the specter of lowered credit ratings, companies will use bonds to stabilize their fund pension contributions, and their reputation in the finance community, at the same time that the new regulations push them to drop their defined-benefit plans altogether.

There are three chief ways to truly advance defined-benefit pensions. They all involve strengthening the PBGC. The first is to promote cash balance plans, a form of defined-benefit pension typically distributed in some form of annuity for the life of a retiree and spouse. Employers appreciate cash balance plans because, like in a 401(k), the employer contribution is predictable: the employer contributes a defined amount of money to an account every year. But unlike in a 401(k), individuals don't have to manage their own money and they bear no risk—the employer guarantees the rate of return. Because they are a form of defined-benefit pension, cash balance plans are insured by the PBGC. More defined-benefit plans of any type would bring fresh revenues to the PBGC, yet the Bush administration has dragged its feet in forming regulatory rules to make firms feel comfortable with providing them.

Second, Congress should infuse the PBGC with revenue, perhaps from taxes on goods and services tied to the airline and steel industries that have most strained the system. The PBGC's recent losses coincided with windfalls of low prices for steel-made products and air travel. Consumers could help pay some portion of the price of industry dislocation and workers' retirements if Congress imposed a modest tax on airline tickets and tons of steel (domestically produced or imported), and dedicated the revenue to the PBGC. More broadly, reforms to strengthen rather than destroy the defined-benefit system and the PBGC will have to deal with the health of the airline industry and steel industry—like we did almost a 100 years ago with railroads. (See "Federal Policy for Defined-Benefit Plans.")

Third, the PBGC is modeled as insurance; strengthening it requires applying insurance principles. Any proper insurance system distinguishes between catastrophic events and normal ones. Other insurance companies have "reinsurance" to cover catastrophes, recognizing that larger-than-usual claims, if absorbed only by premium payers, can severely damage an entire insurance system. But the PBGC itself currently has no insurance. The need for a bailout should be avoided by correcting this mistake.

Government policy makers recognized long ago that in a competitive capitalist economy, some employers might be driven out of business before they had fully funded the pension benefits they had promised their workers. Congress knew that mandating plan sponsors to back up their benefit promises by requiring them to fund their pension trusts according to a prescribed payment schedule was not enough. It recognized that business failure is a possibility and wisely added the PBGC as a backstop for retirees, should their company fail. It also knew that the defined-benefit system had to renew itself by attracting new sponsors to adopt such plans, and mandated, by statute, that the PBCG encourage and maintain the defined-benefit system and keep premiums as low as possible.

Even as it's lobbying to dismantle the nation's only form of social insurance, Social Security, and drive workers into individual accounts, the Bush administration is taking aim at the only other source of guaranteed retirement income available to millions of working people, the defined-benefit pension. The defined-benefit pension system needs to be strengthened and expanded—not undermined. The president, and officials at the PBGC who are now supporting the president's proposals, are in an awkward position: they are purportedly saving an agency by eliminating its reason to exist.

*Resources:* American Academy of Actuaries, "Analysis of the president's proposals to strengthen the single employer pension funding," 2005, <www.actuary.org/pdf/pension/funding–single.pdf>; Vineeta Anand, "Pension Reform: White House might be in the mood to deal," Pensions and Investments, January 2005; Julia L. Coronado and Sylvester J. Schieber, "Saving Private Pension Insurance: An Evaluation of Current Proposal to Shore up the PBGC," Watson – Wyatt Worldwide, 2005; Center on Federal Financial Institutions, "PBGC Updated Cash Flow Model from COFFI, November 18, 2004; T. Ghilarducci and Weis Sun, "Pension Regulation and Destabilization: Are firms forced to decrease pension funding in an upturn and to contribute in a recession?" University of Notre Dame, Faculty of Economics, 2005; Scott Sprinzen, "Pension Plans and Credit Ratings," *Business Week*, March 31, 2005; Fay Hansen, "Rethinking Employee

Benefits," Business Finance, 2005; Department of Labor, "The administration's single employer defined benefit pension reform proposal," <www.dol.gov/ebsa/pensionreform.html>; James Wooten, The Employee Retirement Income Security Act of 1974: A Political History, California/ Milbank Books on Health and the Public Policy.

---

# THE SOCIAL SECURITY ADMINISTRATION'S CRACKED CRYSTAL BALL

**BY JOHN MILLER**

*November/December 2004*

2042. That's the year the Social Security Trust Fund will run out of money, according to the Social Security Administration (SSA). But its doomsday prophesy is based on overly pessimistic assumptions about our economic future: The SSA expects the U.S. economy to expand at an average annual rate of just 1.8% from 2015 to 2080—far slower than the 3.0% average growth rate the economy posted over the last 75 years.

What's behind the gloomy growth projections? Is there anything to them—or has the SSA's economic crystal ball malfunctioned?

## Flawed Forecast

The Social Security Administration foresees a future of sluggish economic growth in which labor productivity, or output per worker, improves slowly; total employment barely grows; and workers put in no additional hours on the job. (It reasons that economic growth, or growth of national output, must equal the sum of labor productivity increases, increases in total employment, and increases in the average hours worked.)

In its widely cited "intermediate" 1.8% growth scenario, labor productivity improves by just 1.6% a year and workforce growth slows almost to a standstill at 0.2% a year—rates well below their historical averages. (See Table 1.) Under these assumptions, and if average work time holds steady, Social Security exhausts its trust fund in the year 2042, at which point it faces an initial shortfall of 27% of its obligations. After that, Social Security would be able to pay out just 70% of the benefits it owes to retirees.

The problem is not with the logic of the method the Social Security Administration uses to make its projections, but rather with its demographic and economic assumptions. Its forecast of 1.6% annual labor productivity growth is especially

**TABLE 1**
**SOCIAL SECURITY ADMINISTRATION'S PRINCIPAL ECONOMIC ASSUMPTIONS[a]**

| | Annual Percentage Increase | | | |
|---|---|---|---|---|
| *Year* | *Real Gross Domestic Product[b]* | *Productivity (Total U.S. Economy)* | *Total Employment[c]* | *Average Hours Worked* |
| 2004 | 4.4% | 2.7% | 1.7% | 0.0% |
| 2005 | 3.6% | 1.8% | 1.7% | 0.0% |
| 2006 | 3.2% | 1.9% | 1.3% | 0.0% |
| 2007 | 3.0% | 1.9% | 1.1% | 0.0% |
| 2008 | 1.0% | 1.8% | 2.8% | 0.0% |
| 2009 | 2.7% | 1.8% | 0.9% | 0.0% |
| 2010 | 2.6% | 1.7% | 0.8% | 0.0% |
| 2011 | 2.4% | 1.7% | 0.8% | 0.0% |
| 2012 | 2.3% | 1.6% | 0.6% | 0.0% |
| 2013 | 2.2% | 1.6% | 0.6% | 0.0% |
| | Average Annual Percentage Increase | | | |
| 2010 to 2015 | 2.2% | 1.6% | 0.6% | 0.0% |
| 2015 to 2080 | 1.8% | 1.6% | 0.2% | 0.0% |

[a] These are the "intermediate economic assumptions" that the Social Security Administration regards as most plausible. The SSA also reports a "low cost" forecast that projects a 2.6% real growth rate from 2015 to 2080 and a "high cost" forecast that projects a 1.1% real growth rate from 2015 to 2080.

[b] Real Gross Domestic Product is calculated in constant 1996 dollars.

[c] Total employment is the total of civilian and military employment in the U.S. economy.

*Source:* Social Security Administration, 2004 *Annual Report of the Board of Trustees* (March 23, 2004), Table V.B.1 and Table V.B.2, pp. 89 and 94.

suspect. When the nonpartisan Congressional Budget Office (CBO) assessed the financial health of Social Security earlier this year, it assumed that productivity would improve at a rate of 1.9% per year. In the CBO forecast, faster productivity growth, along with a lower unemployment rate, boosts wages—the tax base of the system—allowing Social Security to remain solvent until 2052, 10 years longer than the SSA had projected just a few months earlier.

One doesn't have to buy into the hype about the magic of the new economy to conclude that the CBO came closer to getting the projected productivity growth rates right than the SSA did. The federal government's own Bureau of Labor Statistics estimates that productivity rates in the nonfarm sector improved at a 2.3% average pace from 1947 through 2003. Adjusting for the gap of 0.2 percentage points between the productivity growth of the nonfarm business sector and the economy as a whole still leaves productivity across the economy growing by a healthy 2.1% over the postwar period. That historical record convinces economist Dean Baker, from the Washington-based Center for Economic and Policy Research, that a productivity growth rate of 2.0% a year is a "very reasonable" assumption.

The drastic deceleration of employment growth, from its historic (1960 to 2000) average of 1.78% to 0.2% per year, is also overstated. As the trustees see it, employment will grow far more slowly as the baby-boomers leave the labor force. That is true as far as it goes. But if their projections are correct, the country will soon face a chronic labor shortage. And in that context, the immigration rate is unlikely to slow, as they assume, to 900,000 a year. Rather, future immigration rates would likely be at least as high as they were in the 1990s, when 1.3 million people entered the United States annually, and possibly even higher if immigration laws are relaxed in response to a labor shortage. Faster immigration would boost employment growth and add workers, who would pay into Social Security, helping to relieve the financial strain on the system created by the retirement of the baby-boom generation.

In its own optimistic or "low cost" scenario, the SSA erases the shortfall in the trust fund by assuming a faster productivity growth rate (of 1.9%), a lower unemployment rate (of 4.5% per year), and higher net immigration (of 1.3 million people per year). The still rather sluggish 2.6% average growth rate that results would wipe out the rest of the imbalance in the system and leave a sizeable surplus in the trust fund—0.15% of GDP over the next 75 years.

## Making Short Work of the Shortfall

Even in the unlikely event that the pessimistic predictions the SSA has conjured up actually do come to pass, the Social Security imbalance could be easily remedied.

The Social Security Trust Fund needs $3.7 trillion to meet its unfunded obligations over the next 75 years. That is a lot of money—about 1.89% of taxable payroll and about 0.7% of GDP over that period. But it's far less than the 2.0% of GDP the 2001 to 2003 tax cuts will cost over the next 75 years if they are made permanent. (Many of the tax cuts are currently scheduled to sunset in 2010.) The portion of the Bush tax cuts going to the richest 1% of taxpayers alone will cost 0.6% of GDP—more than the CBO projected shortfall of 0.4% of GDP.

Here are a few ways to make short work of any remaining shortfall without cutting retirement benefits or raising taxes for low- or middle-income workers. First, newly hired state and local government workers could be brought into the system. (About 3.5 million state and local government workers are not now covered by Social Security.) That move alone would eliminate about 30% of the projected deficit.

In addition, we could raise the cap on wages subject to payroll taxes. Under current law, Social Security is funded by a payroll tax on the first $87,900 of a person's income. As a result of this cap on covered income, the tax applies to just 84.5% of all wages today—but historically it applied to 90%. Increasing the cap for the next decade so that the payroll tax covers 87.3% of all wages, or halfway back to the 90% standard, would eliminate nearly one-third of the SSA's projected deficit.

Finally, stopping the repeal of the estate tax, a tax giveaway that benefits only the richest taxpayers, would go a long way toward closing the gap. Economists Peter Diamond and Peter Orszag, writing for The Century Fund, advocate dedicating the revenues generated by renewing the estate tax to the Social Security Trust Fund. They suggest an estate tax set at its planned 2009 level, which would exempt $3.5 million of an individual's estate. The tax would fall exclusively on the wealthiest

0.3% of taxpayers. That alone would close another one-quarter of the SSA's projected shortfall. Returning the estate tax to its 2001 (pre-tax cut) level (with a $675,000 exemption for individuals) would do yet more to relieve any financial strain on Social Security.

Any way you look at it, Social Security can remain on sound financial footing even in the dreariest of economic futures, so long as alarmist reports like those of its trustees don't become an excuse to corrupt the system.

*Resources:* Congressional Budget Office, *The Outlook for Social Security* (June 2004); Social Security Administration, *2004 Annual Report of the Board of Trustees* (March 23, 2004); "What the Trustees' Report Indicates About the Financial Status of Social Security," Robert Greenstein, Center on Budget and Policy Priorities (March 31, 2004); "The Implications of the Social Security Projections Issued By the Congressional Budget Office" Robert Greenstein, Peter Orszag, and Richard Kogan, Center on Budget and Policy Priorities (June 24, 2004); "Letter to Rudolph G. Penner" from Dean Baker, co-director of the Center For Economic and Policy Research (January 26, 2004); *Countdown to Reform: The Great Social Security Debate*, Henry Aaron and Robert Reischauer, The Century Foundation Press, 1998.

---

# THE MYTH OF THE SOCIAL SECURITY TRUST FUND

**BY ELLEN FRANK**
*May/June 1999*

Since the 1980s, American workers have been paying more into the Social Security system than retirees are taking out. These excess payroll taxes, now running at about $100 billion per year, go to the Social Security Trust Fund, "saved" for the coming baby-boom retirement, when there will be as few as two workers for every retiree. The Trust Fund now contains some $900 billion; by 2021, it will be worth nearly $4 trillion dollars.

The Social Security Administration (SSA) — using, it should be noted, very grim forecasts of future economic growth — predicts that sometime early in the 21st century, workers' payroll taxes will equal only three-quarters of the benefits currently legislated for retirees. To cover this potential shortfall, the SSA plans gradually to spend down the Trust Fund, until 10 or 20 or 30 years later, depending on whose numbers you believe, the $4 trillion runs out. This, in a nutshell, is the Social Security "crisis."

Supposedly to make the surplus funds grow faster and last longer, Congressional Republicans propose placing Social Security funds in the stock market. Clinton has put forth a complicated plan (see box) also intended to enlarge the Trust Fund so that it lasts through 2050. Both sides have acceded to gradual cuts in Social Security benefits — achieved by raising the retirement age to 67 and reducing annual cost-of-living adjustments — so that a larger share of today's payroll tax dollars can be saved for the baby-boom Trust Fund.

All of these recommendations, indeed the Trust Fund itself, rest on a deceptive premise. Today's workers are being taxed both to support current retirees and, via Trust Fund surpluses, to partially pre-fund their own retirement. Yet pre-funding a universal public pension plan is neither attainable nor desirable.

Many people, when discussing the Trust Fund, apparently have in mind a great heap of money stacked high in some underground vault. As more boomers retire, the SSA opens the vault, dusts off the cobwebs and doles out the cash. But there is no such pile of money. When excess payroll taxes come into the SSA, the cash is turned over to the Treasury which, in turn, issues interest-bearing bonds to the SSA. The Treasury then spends the cash on welfare, roads, weapons, tax cuts.

When, in 2020 or thereabouts, payroll taxes fall short of retirees' needs, officials at SSA will begin taking their bonds back to the Treasury to redeem them for the cash with which to pay benefits. Where, in 2020, will the Treasury obtain the cash to repay the SSA? They will either have to print it, borrow it, levy additional taxes on the public of 2020 or they will have to cut benefits. There is no getting around this. Treasury, after all, spends the funds as they come in; they are not languishing in a vault. If Social Security benefits remain intact, the government will be liable to raise funds for retirement benefits in 2020. The bonds issued by the Treasury represent nothing more than a promise to do this; the public of the future will either raise the funds and keep this promise or they will renege on the obligation.

The "saving" we are doing today through Social Security does not in any way reduce the need to tax, borrow or cut benefits in the future. If the Trust Fund were to disappear tomorrow nothing would change; the baby boom retirement burden would be made neither heavier nor lighter.

Which raises an obvious question. If the excess payroll taxes being "saved" today can't ease the burden of caring for retirees in the future, why are we paying them? The idea of "saving up," through higher payroll taxes, for the baby-boomer retirement originated with the Reagan Administration — ostensibly proposed to "save" Social Security when the system faced its last "crisis," in the 1980s. The Trust Fund surpluses were small at first, barely noticeable in the deluge of fiscal red ink of the Reagan/Bush era. Sold to the public as a method for pre-funding the impending baby-boom retirement, the Trust Fund's real function was to disguise the shift of federal tax burdens from the wealthy to those with moderate and low incomes. Today, nearly one-third of federal revenues derive from the payroll tax, perhaps the most regressive of all federal taxes. Of this money, about one-fifth is not needed to pay current Social Security benefits. It is credited to the Trust Fund, but is destined, in fact, for general government spending.

Democratic Party defenders of this charade argue that the Trust Fund, though devoid of economic merit, is politically necessary. The Trust Fund may be an empty gesture, but it is not made in bad faith. While admittedly regressive, the funds represent an implicit assurance to current workers that benefits will be there for them tomorrow. The illusion of pre-funding instills confidence among voters that their benefits are "paid up" and thus secure. Further, the surpluses provide a veneer of financial planning which defuses right-wing attacks on Social Security. Excessive payroll taxes, in this view, are a small price to pay for political insurance against Republican attacks.

But this argument is wrong. In fact, as the Social Security surplus has grown in size and significance, public confidence in the system has been shaken and the right-wing assault has taken on new ferocity. Currently, projected federal budget surpluses for the next three years can be attributed entirely to excess Social Security taxes. For anti-government Republicans, these surpluses are a provocation, not a deterrent. They evoke greed and fear: greed for the tax cuts, corporate giveaways, and Wall Street management fees, that Social Security surpluses could pay for without exposing Republican budget politics for the fraud it is. That greed was on display this past winter, but has now been replaced by fear.

The right wing deeply abhors the Trust Fund and fears precisely the implicit contract with the future that it represents. Conservative economists understand all too clearly that the Trust Fund bonds are nothing more than a promise that society will one day be asked to keep. When the bonds come due, they worry, who will pay? Currently, Social Security benefits are financed through a tax on low-and middle-income wage earners, but this group cannot be expected alone to carry the entire burden of the baby-boom retirement.

Who else will be asked to give up income in the future so that retirees can eat? The National Association of Manufacturers, no doubt concerned that its members' profits might be targeted, has endorsed the full and immediate privatization of Social Security, to foreclose the establishment of an uncontrolled "baby boomer entitlement." *Wall Street Journal* columnist Alan Murray writes ominously of the "aging baby-boomer assault on the federal budget" and the threat that "general revenues" (perhaps corporate taxes!) rather than payroll taxes, may one day be used to cover Social Security's "accrued liabilities." Economist Milton Friedman, always a shill for corporate interests, recently proposed in The *New York Times* that the Trust Fund be liquidated and the Social Security system disbanded.

Recently, conservative Republicans have come to fear as well that the excess payroll taxes flowing to Social Security will be exposed for the sham they are and that workers will demand an accounting of funds purportedly saved on their behalf. In recent weeks, Congressional Republicans have been scrambling to "wall off" the Trust Fund from "raids" by the Treasury. Draping themselves in the language of financial prudence, they insist that "every penny" of the surpluses be used "to save Social Security."

In practice, this amounts to using the surpluses to repay federal debt, a ruse which effectively transfers tax dollars from wage-earners to bond-holders. The Cato Institute, alarmed that the public might actually decide to spend its own money, advocates placing Trust Fund revenues in a privately managed money market fund. Above all, Republicans in Congress are terrified that the surplus funds pouring into Social Security might actually be used on the public's behalf.

And this, indeed, is precisely what those who believe in Social Security should be promoting. The mythical image of piles of money squirreled away on behalf of future retirees has become a serious impediment to responsible, even intelligible, discussion of Social Security. As recent Republican proposals should make abundantly clear, the language of saving and financial planning threatens to sink Social Security's supporters into the muck of right-wing economics. It is long past time to shift the terms of the debate. The Social Security debate is not about saving or interest rates or compound 30-year rates of return. It is about who pays taxes in this country, on whose behalf that money is spent and what the obligations of government are to its citizens.

All funds being paid into Social Security will be spent, either on tax cuts, Wall Street investment accounts, debt reduction or something socially useful. The left's task in this debate is to make this point clear and to ask, explicitly, what the money will be spent on, who will spend it and how, exactly, that spending will ease the burden of caring for an aging population.

All the Trust Funds and IRA's in the world cannot change the fact that, in 20 years or so, the task of caring for the growing ranks of the aged will fall, inevitably, to the younger generation and will require their labor, energy and commitment. If the workers of the 21st century are ill-fed and uneducated, if the environment is ravaged, the air unbreathable, the climate hostile to health, the aged will languish, regardless of the money put aside today. As a society, the United States is not well set up to care for an aging population and there is no reason to believe that throwing money at Wall Street will improve this situation. We lack affordable and accessible housing and transportation; pollution and climate change are taking a harsh toll on the elderly; Medicare is riddled with fraud and our nursing homes are a national disgrace.

Imagine what could be done with the $100 billion plus currently flowing into Social Security each year. Imagine how secure our retirees could be made if these funds were used to construct housing, train scientists, cleanup the environment, build public health facilities, and educate future workers. The Social Security surpluses are paid by low- and middle-income workers and should be spent on programs that will benefit them and help their children to care for them as they age. Money earmarked for their future should be spent in securing that future: on schools, parks, infrastructure, the environment, our children.

Unless the funds are spent on their behalf, the bonds piling up in the Social Security Trust Fund today do nothing to help future retirees. They can, however, positively hurt today's workers. If these regressive and excessive tax dollars are squandered, as Democrats and Republicans now propose, to pay down the national debt or reduce (progressive) income taxes, this will amount to a federally sanctioned redistribution of income from wage-earners to the wealthy (see box). Furthermore, by aggravating income inequality, these proposals will worsen, not improve, the long-term accounting imbalances of the Social Security system, since the projected cost of caring for retirees will fall on a workforce whose share of national income is shrinking. How long then before the next "crisis" is announced and further cuts proposed to "save" Social Security?

Many sincere supporters of Social Security are wary of exposing the Trust Fund charade. They fear that without the Trust Fund, the Democratic party's political commitment to Social Security's future will falter and the entire system will gradually collapse under continued right-wing assault. But this may happen with or without the Trust Fund. Early in the 21st century, payroll taxes may fall short of legislated benefits and, at that time, resources will be raised to support retirees or they will not be. Either Americans then will agree to care for the aged collectively or those without children to support them will be forced to work until they die. The battle over the baby-boomer retirement is of vital consequence. It will test the very meaning of our society and democracy, but it cannot, in fact, be won today.

Only today's battles can be won today, and they must focus on who is paying taxes and how the government today can best serve the people. There is no political advantage to be gained from expediency in this debate. Those who wish to inherit a just and humane future must fight for a just and humane present.

*Resources:* Annual Report of the Board of Trustees of the Federal Old-Age and Survivors Insurance and Disability Insurance Trust Funds, 1998; Cato Policy Report, September 1998; "Defusing the Baby-Boomer Time-Bomb," Dean Baker, Economic Policy Institute, 1998; "Clinton Plays to Aging Baby Boomers," Alan Murray, *Wall Street Journal*, 3/29/99.

# SOCIAL SECURITY'S BET ON STOCKS

**BY RICHARD DU BOFF**
*May/June 1999*

Some advocates of privatizing Social Security argue that retirees who depend on Social Security will never get their money's worth out of what they put into it. The only way to provide adequate retirement income for future generations, they say, is to allow people to invest in the stock market, where future returns will be much higher.

What's wrong with this argument? First, this myth treats Social Security as if it were simply an investment fund. It is actually an insurance pool covering practically the entire population, and part of its function is to transfer income from the fortunate to the unfortunate. Social Security provides not only retirement benefits that replace larger portions of low-wage workers' incomes, but also disability coverage and benefits to survivors of workers who die before retirement. For employees, the chances of becoming disabled or dying before age 65 are four in ten. The only disability insurance for three-quarters of all workers comes from Social Security. For each worker, this insurance is equivalent to a $207,000 policy in the private sector.

But even if we think of Social Security simply as a savings vehicle, the right wing is wrong. Since 1926, and apparently since the 1880s as well, common stocks have returned 7% per year on average (through dividends and price appreciation), corrected for inflation. Those who want to privatize Social Security confidently project similar returns in the future. They grant that from one year to the next stocks can swing way above or below normal, but insist that over any period as long as a decade or two, rates of return will, like a homing pigeon, come back to the time-proven 7% trend.

These claims involve two major fallacies about the likely performance of the stock market in future years. One is that slower economic growth will create future deficits for Social Security, forcing it to cut benefits for retirees, but that slower growth will not affect stocks. In fact, stocks have produced 7% returns over the past century when the economy averaged 3% growth per year. But if economic growth slows to 1.4% over the next 75 years, as the Social Security Trustees pessimistically predict, corporate profits will stagnate, and returns to stocks will inevitably fall. If the economy does grow at a faster rate, the stock market will rise at a healthy pace — but Social Security will also have the funds it needs to pay all the benefits that future retirees count on.

Second, privatizers assume that the historical average of 7% never varies much from one decade to the next. The truth is that the long-term averages hide great variation in stock market returns, and individuals face high risk that their returns will be lower than what Social Security provides.

For most people, saving for retirement is concentrated during the last 20 years of their working lives. While some people will be lucky, and be saving during periods when stocks are booming, others will be unlucky and have their prime savings years wiped out by bear markets.

The nation's confidence in stocks may be high because of the great bull market stretching from August 1982 through the present. But during four 20-year periods in this century — 1901-1921, 1929-1949, 1962-1982, and 1964-1984 — average stock returns (in real terms, corrected for inflation) were close to zero, or worse (see the chart). This means, for instance, that investors purchasing stocks in 1929 and holding them for 20 years would have lost money on their investments by 1949.

Similarly, there were many 20-year periods in which the stock market performed worse than the 2% to 3% returns that future retirees are expected to get on the taxes that they pay into Social Security during their working years. If we look at the dashed line in the graph, drawn to show a 2.5% annual return, there were many 20-year periods — more than one-fifth of the total — in which the stock market performed worse than a 2.5% annual return on Social Security.

Another way to look at this history is in terms of how much of their pre-retirement wages workers would be able to get as income after retiring. Typically, this would be done by using one's accumulated savings to buy an "annuity," which is an insurance policy guaranteeing a constant retirement income for as long as a person survives.

Gary Burtless of the Brookings Institution finds that a worker who invested a constant fraction of her earnings in a broad stock market index fund, then retired at age 62 in 1969 (after many years of booming stocks) could have bought an annuity providing 104% of her former annual earnings. By contrast, another worker retiring

**S&P 500, AVERAGE RETURNS FOR PRIOR 20 YEARS**

Note: Each pointon the S&P 500 line is an average of returns for the S&P 500 group of stocks during the prior 20 years. The Social Security line is set at 205%, the average rate of return that future retirees can expect to get on their social security taxes. Both lines are adjusted for inflation using the Consumer Price Index. Data on the S&P 500 line before 1926 comes from the Cowles Commission stock index.

at 62 just six years later (after a period of low stock returns) would have replaced only 39% of her previous income.

And as the Federal Reserve Bank of Chicago recently warned, "the currently high stock market valuation may actually forecast low future returns" for holders of stocks, since profits, and dividends, would have to grow at extraordinarily high rates even "to achieve historical stock returns [of 7% per year] in the future."

Financial analyst John Mueller, who calls himself a conservative Republican, points out that returns on stocks must be adjusted for "volatility risk"—how much above average, and below, stock returns fluctuate over the years. By this measure, says Mueller, the stock market has been four times as risky as the economy (gross domestic product, or GDP) since 1926, so that the risk-adjusted return on common stocks has been lower than the return on Social Security's pay-as-you-go system.

Finally, the return on stocks must be reduced for the administrative costs that investors, particularly those with moderate or low incomes, would have to pay in a partially or wholly privatized system. The costs of running Social Security (collecting taxes, managing investments, disbursing benefits) amount to less than 1% of revenues. Individual savers would face far higher expenses, of two types:

- fees, of 1% a year or more, that mutual funds charge to manage investments;

- fees, ranging from 4% to 6% of accumulated savings, charged by insurance companies to provide retirement annuities that are guaranteed for as long as a retiree lives (and the insurance firm stays solvent).

Between them, these costs would wipe out much of any remaining benefits from investing in the stock market rather than staying with the present Social Security system.

Chapter 5

# FAIR LENDING / PREDATORY LENDING

## LENDING INSIGHTS: HARD PROOF THAT BANKS DISCRIMINATE

**BY JIM CAMPEN**
*January/February 1994 (revised October 1999)*

> "These really are horrifying numbers."
> — *Comptroller of the Currency Eugene A. Ludwigon banks' 1992 record denying mortgages to minorities, Nov. 4, 1993.*

As appalling as it was, the latest annual report on mortgage lending shocked few observers when the Clinton Administration's top regulators unveiled it before the Senate Banking Committee in early November. In keeping with past patterns, black mortgage applicants were turned down more than twice as often as whites in 1992. Indeed, the most closely watched single number indicated that things were getting worse rather than better: The ratio of the black denial rate to the white denial rate rose from 2.16 in 1991 to 2.26 in 1992.

What was different this year was the response to the statistics. Instead of denying the obvious as they have in the past, government officials acknowledged that discrimination is "alive and well in America," as Housing Secretary Henry Cisneros put it. Bank regulators, along with Attorney General Janet Reno, testified that they are intensifying efforts to identify and punish lenders who discriminate.

And bankers, rather than disputing charges that they had discriminated, emphasized their efforts to do better. Since researchers found what one Massachusetts banker referred to as a "smoking gun" in October 1992, bankers have recognized that they can no longer offer credible denials. The crucial evidence, from a study by the Federal Reserve Bank of Boston, finally established beyond a reasonable doubt that banks discriminate along racial lines when making mortgage loans.

The banks' quandary is the triumph of a nationwide grassroots "community reinvestment" movement that for over twenty years has been employing innovative strategies to challenge banks' failure to meet the credit needs of low-income and minority neighborhoods and individuals. That banks discriminate has, of course, long been obvious to those receiving the short end of the stick. But community advocates recognized that obtaining proof of discrimination would be the key to combatting it. So, they fought not only for laws that regulate banks, but also for requirements that banks furnish relevant information on their lending practices. They then used this data to publicize banks' abysmal performances, sparking the public outrage necessary to make banks more responsive to the needs of low-income and minority communities.

Their first major legislative victory was the 1975 enactment of the Home Mortgage Disclosure Act (HMDA — pronounced HUMdah), which required each bank to report the number and dollar amount of the mortgage and home improvement loans by census tract (census tracts are areas a few blocks square, containing a few thousand people, for which detailed demographic and socio-economic data are available). Two years after HMDA took effect, Congress adopted the Community Reinvestment Act (CRA). The CRA declares that banks have an "affirmative obligation" to serve the credit needs of local communities, including low and moderate income areas — which are often communities of color. A lesser-known set of fair lending laws, including the Fair Housing Act of 1968 and the Equal Credit Opportunity Act of 1974, explicitly prohibit racial discrimination. Only very recently, however, have bankers and regulators begun to take the CRA and the fair lending laws at all seriously.

## The Information Game

In the absence of earnest enforcement efforts by bank regulators, it fell primarily to independent community-oriented researchers to document discriminatory lending practices. Their efforts to build this case, beginning with the struggle to enact HMDA, have followed a recurring pattern.

Typically, community groups made charges only to see them dismissed by the banks as unsupported by solid evidence. The groups then struggled to make more data available, so researchers would be able to produce more definitive results. Consistently, though, the banks and their defenders (including, in many cases, the regulatory agencies) criticized the resulting studies as inconclusive. The limited nature of the data available, they argued, made it impossible to rule out other possible explanations of racial disparities in lending patterns. But with this maneuver, the banks backed themselves into a corner: They were now in no position to deny demands from community advocates for additional data to fill out the picture. So another round would begin, as researchers used the more extensive data supplied by the banks to produce results even more suggestive of racial discrimination.

By the end of the 1980s, this cycle had yielded an impressive array of studies that combined HMDA data with Census Bureau information on the racial composition and income level of census tracts in order to document mortgage lending discrimination. The *Atlanta Journal-Constitution*'s Pulitzer Prize-winning series "The Color of Money" (May 1988) compared stable, middle-income neighborhoods that were at least 80% white to those that were at least 80% nonwhite. It found that

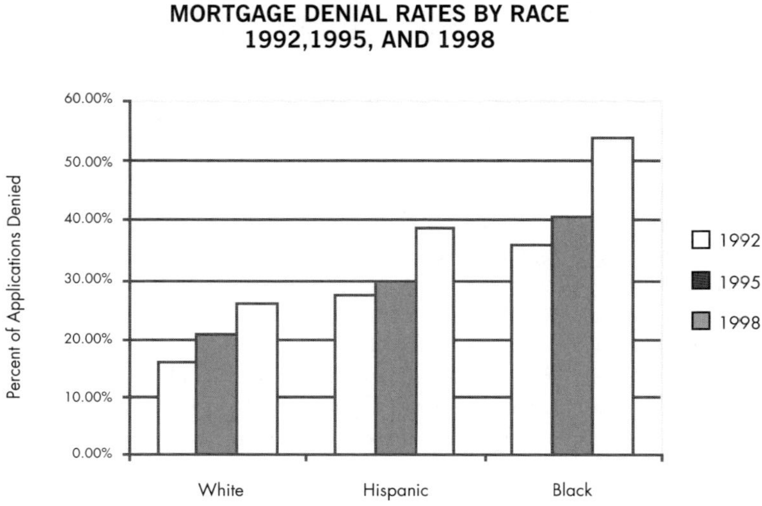


*Source:* Federal Reserve Board; *American Banker*, 11/5/93.

between 1984 and 1986, Atlanta banks and savings & loans (S&Ls) made 4.5 times as many loans per 1,000 single-family structures in white neighborhoods as in comparable black neighborhoods.

In city after city, studies documented similarly dramatic racial disparities in mortgage lending. Between 1981 and 1987 in Boston, for instance, banks made 2.9 times as many mortgage loans per 1,000 housing units in low-income white neighborhoods as in minority neighborhoods with similar incomes. In Detroit, the ratio of the mortgage lending rate (loans per 1,000 homes) in middle-income white neighborhoods to that in middle-income black neighborhoods rose every year between 1981 and 1986, reaching 3.14 to 1 in 1986. Similar patterns appeared in Chicago, Los Angeles, Milwaukee, and New York as well as in 14 cities observed by the Center for Community Change. A survey of 23 studies by Professor Anne Shlay of Temple University showed that all 23 found a negative impact of race on conventional mortgage lending.

Bankers acknowledged that these results were troubling, but argued that they didn't prove that banks were discriminating. First, the bankers suggested that the low level of lending in minority neighborhoods might reflect a low level of applications rather than a high level of bank denials. They also pointed out that the data referred only to the location of the homes being purchased. Since it provided no direct information about the race or income level of the applicants, they argued that the data failed to prove discrimination against minority individuals.

These defensive arguments by bankers helped make it possible for the community reinvestment movement to finally succeed in broadening the scope of HMDA. As part of the S&L bailout bill adopted in August 1989, HMDA was amended to require banks to report on all mortgage applications received, rather than just on loans made. Beginning January 1, 1990, banks had to record the race, income, and sex of each applicant, the result of the application, and the previously required information on the census tract in which the home was located.

In October 1991, the Federal Reserve reported the results of its analysis of the expanded HMDA data for 1990. It was the most extensive set of mortgage lending data ever assembled — more than six million loan applications reported by over 9,000 mortgage lenders. The most striking single result of their analysis was the difference in denial rates for black and white applicants. Overall, 34% of black applications for conventional home mortgages were rejected, compared to a 14% rejection rate for whites. (Hispanics were rejected at a 21% rate; rejection rates for Asians were slightly lower than for whites.) Large differentials persisted even when comparisons were limited to applicants in the same income categories. In many cities, high-income blacks experienced higher denial rates than low-income whites. As the chart indicates, these disparities in denial rates continued through the 1990s.

Lenders could no longer claim that low levels of lending resulted solely from a lack of demand for loans by minority applicants rather than from their own decisions on which applications to accept. They were, however, quick to adopt a fallback position. In its reponse to the grossly unequal denial rates revealed by the expanded HMDA data, the American Bankers Association (ABA) emphasized that the data didn't include "information critical to judging the creditworthiness of loan applicants." It was entirely possible, the bankers suggested, that differences in applicants' credit histories, wealth, job instability, or other economic characteristics accounted for the more frequent rejection of minority loan applicants. ABA chief lobbyist Ed Yingling maintained that "the HMDA numbers don't show a whole lot; they don't mean a whole lot."

These denials persisted in the face of both statistical and tangible evidence of racial discrimination by banks. Court cases and case studies compiled by community-based organizations supplemented the faceless statistical studies with the stories of real human beings. Banks were closing offices in minority neighborhoods while opening them elsewhere, and new surveys revealed that banks had disproportionately few black executives. It would have been perverse, in light of all this evidence, for anybody to doubt that banks were in fact discriminating.

But that did not deter the banking industry from commissioning social scientists to argue that the case for discrimination was based entirely on "circumstantial evidence." They took the position that, according to the standards of statistical research in the social sciences, the conclusion had not been proven beyond a reasonable doubt.

## The "Smoking Gun"

Meanwhile, researchers at the Federal Reserve Bank of Boston — which has been a somewhat liberal outpost in the overwhelmingly conservative Federal Reserve System — were pursuing another path. If conclusions had been limited by missing data, they reasoned, why not collect and analyze all of the data necessary to resolve the issue? Taking advantage of the Fed's status as a banking regulator, they were able to conduct the first study to take into account virtually all of the factors used in mortgage lending decisions. They asked the 131 banks in the Boston area that had received 25 or more mortgage applications in 1990 to review their loan files and gather 38 additional pieces of information for each application from a black or Hispanic (about 1,200 applications) and for a randomly selected set of 3,300 applications by whites. Once again, the banks' attacks on the alleged insufficiency of existing data had led to the gathering of more and better information.

Using a special variant of the standard statistical technique known as multiple regression analysis, the Boston Fed's analysts then sought to explain why minorities in the Boston area were denied mortgages 2.7 times as often as whites. To what extent, the researchers asked, did legitimate factors account for the disparity?

Banks, hoping to be exonerated by the Boston Fed's study, were dismayed at the results. The additional information showed that, as the banks claimed, blacks and Hispanics were on average poorer, had worse credit histories, and requested mortgage loans that were larger relative to their incomes. But it also showed that these and similar factors only told part of the story. Even if black and Hispanic borrowers had been just as creditworthy as the average white applicant with respect to all 38 of the factors considered, they still would have been 56% more likely to be denied a mortgage. Only the applicants' minority status could account for the difference. As Alicia Munnell, who was then the Boston Fed's Research Director, put it, "The study eliminates all the other possible factors that could be influencing decisions." The long-sought "smoking gun" had been found.

## After the Smokescreen Clears

Pushed beyond the stage of denial — in spite of the inevitable, and quickly discredited, objections published by *Forbes*, *Business Week*, and the *Wall Street Journal* — bankers and federal regulators have begun to recognize the value of measures that had been urged on them for years by community advocates. Bank responses have included taking a systematic "second look" at minority loan applications recommended for denial; training bank employees to increase understanding of fair lending issues and sensitivity to cultural differences; hiring more minority loan officers; revising certain traditional credit standards that are biased toward white cultural practices; forging working relationships with realtors and appraisal firms that have positive records in minority communities; developing new mortgage lending products adapted to the special circumstances and needs of minority borrowers; and using internal "testing" programs to identify whether or not bank employees are in fact offering equal treatment to minority applicants.

At the same time, the four federal bank regulatory agencies began taking steps to ensure that banks are complying with fair lending laws. But they acted only after Congressional hearings had brought to light what Deepak Bhargava of the Association of Community Organizations for Reform Now (ACORN) characterized as "a long and sorry record" of regulatory failure. Even New York's Republican Senator Alphonse D'Amato was moved to ask whether the "regulatory agencies [were] asleep at the switch, or worse, turning a blind eye?"

In fact, between 1978 and 1990 three successive directors of the OCC's fair lending office resigned in frustration at the attitude of the agency's leadership, which not only refused to allow them to take the steps they regarded as necessary to enforce the law, but even refused to release reports documenting possible discrimination. A single community organization in one medium-sized Ohio city, the Toledo Fair Housing Center, was able to identify and successfully pursue numerous cases of lending discrimination annually, while all four of the federal bank regulators — taken together — only referred one case of racial discrimination in lending to the Department of Justice in 18 years. And until its September 1992 settlement requiring Georgia's Decatur Federal Savings & Loan to pay $1 million to 48 black applicants denied mortgage loans, the Justice Department had never charged a single bank with racial discrimination in mortgage lending.

## The Power of Disclosure

It remains to be seen whether, and to what extent, this story will have a happy ending. It will be years before we know whether the hard-won gains by community-based groups and their advocates will bring about an actual reduction in lending discrimination.

The Boston Fed study established the fact of discrimination in mortgage lending. But with its narrow focus on data from completed loan applications, the study did not attempt to measure the full extent of discrimination. For example, many potential minority borrowers encounter responses to their initial contacts with banks that discourage them from ever applying, and the property values recorded in loan files may have been furnished by appraisers who systematically undervalue homes in minority neighborhoods.

The community reinvestment movement is right to insist that banks are obliged by the CRA to do more than simply deal fairly with the loan applicants who come through their doors. A whole range of aggressive, affirmative initiatives will be necessary to extend credit and financial services to currently underserved communities. Moreover, without constant pressure from community groups, regulators will likely bow to pressure from banks and fail to enforce community-oriented laws and regulations.

If properly enforced, disclosure laws should continue to be useful. Many aspects of the normal operation of our economic system cannot stand the light of day. With that in mind, the community reinvestment movement has recently been emphasizing its long-standing call for the extension of disclosure requirements to the realm of business lending.

Activists believe that businesses based in low-income communities and those owned by minorities have had an even harder time obtaining credit than minority homebuyers. But until there is something comparable to HMDA for small business lending, it will be impossible to persuasively document the existence and extent of the problem. And as the ongoing struggle for fair mortgage lending has demonstrated, exposing the nature of a problem can go a long way toward forcing its solution.

*Resources:* Alicia Munnell and others, "Mortgage Lending in Boston: Interpreting HMDA Data," Federal Reserve Bank of Boston, October 1992. "Discrimination in the Housing and Mortgage Markets," a special issue of *Housing Policy Debate*, Vol. 3, No. 2, 1992. "Mortgage Lending

Discrimination: A Review of Existing Evidence," Urban Institute, 1999; John Yinger, "Closed Doors, Opportunities Lost: The Continuing Costs of Housing Discrimination," Russell Sage Foundation, 1995; Helen Ladd, "Evidence of Discrimination in Mortgage Lending," *Journal of Economic Perspectives, Spring 1998.*

# THE COMMUNITY REINVESTMENT ACT: A LAW THAT WORKS

**BY JIM CAMPEN**

*November/December 1997*

At an American Bankers Association convention in the early 1980s, bank consultant Ken Thomas was surprised to hear howls of laughter emerge from one of the meeting rooms. He stepped in to find the speaker ending his presentation with a flourish, pointing to the initial letters of the words projected behind him. "In conclusion," he shouted above the laughter and applause, "you can have your Community Reinvestment Act Programs, you can have your Community Reinvestment Act Policies, you can have your Community Reinvestment Act Personnel. But — as you can see — it's all just ... CRAP!"

The bankers' laughter may have been justified at the time, as the Reagan administration and its bank regulators ignored the law that a nationwide grassroots movement of community activists had successfully pushed Congress to enact in 1977. But as the Community Reinvestment Act (CRA) marks its twentieth anniversary this year, no one is laughing at it anymore.

In fact, the CRA is one of the most remarkable success stories of the 1990s. Under strong pressure from a second wave of grassroots activism that began ten years ago, many banks have recognized the potential for profitable business in neighborhoods that they had written off without a second thought not so long ago. Mortgage loans to minority and low-income homebuyers have soared. Hundreds of local partnerships among banks, community-based organizations and government agencies have resulted in tens of thousands of new units of affordable housing.

The CRA has acquired broad and deep support, due to the difference that it has made in hundreds of communities throughout the United States. This support paid off in 1996 when the CRA emerged intact from a determined attempt by congressional Republicans, following their 1994 electoral victory, to gut the law .

In spite of this legislative success and its many accomplishments, the future of the CRA remains uncertain. Its opponents may have lost a battle, but they have not given up the war, and the need for vigilant defense of the CRA will remain. Moreover, the dramatic ongoing transformation of the banking industry poses new challenges to successful implementation of the CRA.

## A Collection of Laws

In fact, the CRA is the centerpiece of several laws that have worked together to increase flows of credit to borrowers and neighborhoods that banks have traditionally neglected. The CRA itself simply says that banks are obliged to serve the credit needs of all the communities where they are located. It requires regulators to examine each bank's record of doing so and to take this record into account when deciding whether or not to approve applications for new branches or mergers with other banks. (Throughout this article, the term "banks" refers to Savings & Loans and other thrift institutions as well as to commercial banks.)

The movement that won passage of the CRA in 1977 was primarily concerned about "redlining" of inner-city neighborhoods by lenders. The term refers to some bankers' practice of actually drawing red lines on maps to indicate areas off-limits for lending. Banks were using deposits collected in these neighborhoods to make loans in the suburbs. Gale Cincotta, of the Chicago-based National People's Action, was probably the most prominent of the many community leaders throughout the country who demanded that this disinvestment be replaced by reinvestment of the community's own money back into the community.

Two years earlier, in 1975, the community reinvestment movement had won passage of the Home Mortgage Disclosure Act (HMDA), which requires each bank to report annually on the number and dollar amount of mortgage loans made in every neighborhood in every metropolitan area. This disclosure made it possible to monitor where banks were and were not making mortgage loans.

Because the driving concern of the community reinvestment movement was saving neighborhoods, both the CRA and HMDA were focused on geographic communities. A separate set of "fair lending laws" prohibits discrimination against individual borrowers on the basis of race, national origin, sex, age and other characteristics. The two most important of these laws, both legacies of the civil rights movement, are the Fair Housing Act of 1968, which prohibits discrimination in the home purchase and home rental process (including lending), and the Equal Credit Opportunity Act of 1974, which outlaws discrimination in all types of lending.

## The Awakening

Until about ten years ago, the government agencies charged with enforcing these laws all but ignored them. U.S. Senate Banking Committee hearings in 1988, for example, revealed that even after a rebuke from the General Accounting Office for inadequate CRA examinations, bank regulators actually reduced the total hours devoted to CRA exams by 68% between 1981 and 1984. Moreover, only nine out of over 50,000 bank applications submitted since the passage of the CRA had been denied on the grounds of inadequate CRA performance. HMDA data were of notoriously poor quality and were frequently inaccessible to community groups. And the 1980s ended with the bank regulators having acted on only one case of lending discrimination during the entire life of the fair lending laws. As Mildred Brown, president of the national grassroots organization ACORN, told the senators, "Banks are breaking the law and the regulators are their accomplices."

Two initiatives by community activists during the second half of the 1980s turned the CRA into an effective anti-discrimination tool. First, activists recognized that the emergence of interstate banking provided a new leverage point, as bank holding companies sought regulatory approval for their expansion plans. Community groups challenged these proposals on the grounds of weak performance in meeting community credit needs. Confronted with the resulting uncertainty and delay, most banks responded by negotiating "CRA agreements" that committed them to expand their lending programs in return for withdrawal of the challenges.

The second initiative was the use of HMDA data to document dramatic disparities between the amount of mortgage lending in minority and white neighborhoods. Most significantly, "The Color of Money," a May 1988 Atlanta Journal-Constitution series, showed that in 1986 banks made 5.4 times as many mortgage loans per 1,000 homes in Atlanta's white neighborhoods as in comparable black neighborhoods. The Pulitzer Prize-winning series sparked investigations that generated similar findings, and publicity, in several other cities, and led to the Senate hearings later that year that highlighted the bank regulators' indefensible neglect of their responsibilities.

In 1989, the CRA and HMDA were strengthened by important amendments that increased public disclosure and accountability for both banks and regulators. Starting the next year, each bank's CRA performance rating became publicly available, along with a written report by its regulator. Furthermore, starting with 1990 applications, HMDA data were expanded to contain information on each application received, including the applicant's race and income and whether the application was approved or denied.

When they were released in the fall of 1991, the expanded HMDA data showed that the mortgage denial rate for blacks was more than twice that for whites. Bankers argued that the higher denial rate for blacks might simply reflect their weaker credit histories, smaller down payments and other factors not included in HMDA data.

But just one year later the Federal Reserve Bank of Boston announced the results of a study that proved the bankers wrong. Using statistical methods that separated out the effects of all other known factors, the study found that racial discrimination was a major reason why blacks and Hispanics were denied mortgage loans more frequently than whites (see "Lending Insights").

## The Fruits of CRA

As publicity and pressure mounted, the laws enacted in the mid-1970s finally began to produce dramatic benefits. Once the spotlight began to shine on mortgage lending patterns, and the Justice Department reached some high-profile settlements in lending discrimination cases, loans to blacks and Hispanics soared. Between 1991 and 1995, while conventional home-purchase loans to whites increased by two-thirds, loans to blacks tripled (from 45,000 to 138,000 a year) and those to Hispanics more than doubled. During the same period, loans in predominantly minority neighborhoods rose by 137%, while loans in areas where the population was almost all white grew by just 37%.

Meanwhile, all of the mega-mergers that have recently transformed the banking industry were vulnerable to CRA challenges. In order to ensure regulatory approval, in each case banks have negotiated agreements with the community to provide more low-income loans. By mid-1997, according to Comptroller of the Currency Eugene Ludwig (the principal regulator of the nation's largest banks), these CRA Agreements had produced total commitments (some extending ten years into the future) for over $215 billion of increased loans and investments in underserved areas.

## Fighting to Survive

While some banks recognized that the increased pressures had pushed them to make what turned out to be profitable loans, most resented the growing scrutiny of their performance and called for rollback of the CRA. When the Republicans gained control of Congress after the 1994 elections, bank lobbyists convinced them to make the Community Reinvestment Act a prime target. The prospects for survival of a meaningful CRA looked bleak as the confident Republicans, led by senators Richard Shelby (Alabama) and Connie Mack (Florida) and Florida Representative Bill McCollum, offered a series of innocuous-sounding "reforms."

A "small-bank exemption" for banks of less than $100 million in assets, coupled with a "self-certification" provision that would have allowed banks with up to $250 million to evaluate their own CRA performance, would have eliminated CRA oversight for 88% of all banks. And a "safe harbors" provision would have prohibited challenges to proposed mergers of banks with a CRA rating of "satisfactory" or better — at a time when more than 95% of all banks, including all of the biggest ones, had such ratings. Any difference between amending the CRA in these ways and repealing it outright would have been purely cosmetic.

The banks' Republican allies offered three arguments to support their position, none of which could withstand serious scrutiny. First, they claimed that the CRA imposed a massive regulatory burden on small banks. While grossly exaggerated in any case, this claim was rendered obsolete by an overhaul of CRA regulations in early 1995. The revised regulations replaced an excessive emphasis on process and paperwork with a focus on actual performance, and drastically streamlined the process for banks with less than $250 million in assets.

Second, CRA opponents claimed that it requires risky loans that could undermine a bank's profitability and threaten its survival. Actually, the reverse is closer to the truth. The 1980s were marked by massive speculative lending to wealthy real estate developers and get-rich-quick schemers that resulted in the failure of more than two thousand banks and S&Ls. Yet not a single bank failure has been caused by making too many bad loans to disadvantaged borrowers.

Recently, Federal Reserve Board researchers found "no evidence of lower profitability" at banks that specialize in mortgage lending to lower-income borrowers and neighborhoods and, in a nationwide survey by the Kansas City Fed, 98% of banks reported that their CRA lending was profitable. A recent investigation by the Comptroller of the Currency found that affordable home loans had "the same level of losses" as standard mortgages.

Overall, the look-the-other-way attitude toward CRA enforcement of the 1980s was accompanied by a steady fall in bank profit rates, while the increasingly serious enforcement of the CRA in the 1990s has coincided with five straight years of record bank profits.

The third argument raised against CRA — that it was ineffective and all of the efforts to enforce it in the 1990s had accomplished little — was contradicted not just by statistics but by massive support from cities and towns around the country attesting to how much had, in fact, been accomplished. One open letter to Congress was signed by over 2,000 community-based organizations and more than 200 mayors.

The swell of grassroots support overwhelmed pressure from industry lobbyists and produced unanimous opposition by congressional Democrats to every proposal that would have weakened CRA. In addition, the Clinton administration never wavered from an early pledge to veto any bill containing such provisions. (Of course, since supporting the CRA required virtually no budgetary resources, it was easier for Clinton to take a strong stance.) When the dust of battle finally cleared at the end of 1996, the CRA emerged intact.

## Challenges Ahead

With this important victory behind it, the community reinvestment movement now faces several important challenges and opportunities — in addition to the need for continuing vigilance against future legislative attacks on the CRA:

- Aiding small businesses and rural households. A major increase in lending to small and minority-owned businesses is needed to support the economic development essential to healthy communities. Because HMDA data played such a central role in generating pressure to remedy the glaring disparities in mortgage lending, activists eagerly anticipate analyzing the data on lending to small businesses that will become available in late 1997 (as mandated by the 1995 revisions to the CRA regulations).

Similarly, community groups in rural areas are looking forward to analyzing this year's HMDA data, which will for the first time include data on mortgage lending outside of metropolitan areas. Both rural and urban groups want to maintain access to banking services by halting wholesale branch closures in lower-income areas — such as the 140 mostly rural branches that KeyCorp announced it will close or the hundreds of branches that Wells Fargo abandoned after its 1996 merger with First Interstate.

- Extending CRA-type obligations to other financial institutions. As banks and other kinds of financial firms enter more and more into each other's businesses, it makes little sense to continue exempting these other firms from responsibilities to serve lower-income and minority communities.

Study after study has demonstrated that mortgage companies devote far smaller shares of their total loans to disadvantaged borrowers and neighborhoods than banks do. Mortgage companies, who now make the majority of mortgage loans, benefit enormously from being able to sell their loans to the government-sponsored enterprises Fannie Mae and Freddie Mac. In order to retain this benefit, the companies should be required to provide for community credit needs.

Regulation of insurance companies takes place at the state level, where the companies benefit from taxpayer-supported guarantee funds that make their policies more attractive to customers. In Massachusetts, community organizations won passage of a law in 1996 that requires property insurers to disclose — HMDA-style — the geographic distribution of their homeowner policies. Activists are now campaigning to require that life insurance companies invest part of their assets in ways that benefit the lower-income and minority neighborhoods where many of their policy-holders live.

- Dealing with the growing dominance of mega-banks. With virtually all restrictions on interstate banking phased out by mid-1997, the rapid consolidation among large U.S. banks will accelerate. Giant banking companies such as NationsBank, KeyCorp, BankAmerica, Wells Fargo and Norwest will continue to expand their geographic scope, homogenize their operations, and centralize their decision-making power.

Although some of the megabanks have excellent overall records of CRA performance, their corporation-wide programs do not match the needs of every city and town. As decision-making authority migrates from local offices to regional or even national headquarters, "it is becoming harder and harder to get the big banks to deal with the specifics of local situations — even though responsiveness to the particular needs of local communities is exactly what CRA is all about," notes Debby Goldberg of the Center for Community Change's Neighborhood Revitalization Project.

- Monitoring discriminatory interest rates on loans. As enforcement of the fair lending laws has increased in the last few years (for example, the Comptroller of the Currency made 23 referrals to HUD and the Department of Justice from 1993 to 1996, compared to just one referral in the preceding quarter-century), most cases have involved racial discrimination either in marketing practices or decisions to deny applications. Recently, however, attention has shifted to the fact that companies charge some borrowers more than others. One exploitative technique — a specialty of the Fleet Financial Group, which has been caught at it more than once — is for a megabank to steer vulnerable loan applicants, who are disproportionately black and Hispanic, to a related finance company where fees and interest rates are higher.

Another method is to use supposedly independent mortgage brokers to negotiate individualized loan terms with vulnerable (often elderly, female and/or minority) borrowers. This arrangement allows the brokers to impose higher interest rates and larger hidden fees of up to 12% of the loan amount into the monthly payments. Such actions cost Long Beach (California) Mortgage Company (formerly Long Beach Bank) a $4 million settlement with the Justice Department when they were caught red-handed. Earlier, Long Beach had received awards for making many loans to minority borrowers — underlining the need to consider loan pricing as well as the number of loans when evaluating a lender's performance.

- Holding the bank regulators accountable. As Rochelle Nawrocki of National People's Action observes, "If our history has taught us anything, it's that only we make CRA work — not bankers, regulators, or Congress." Regulators will enforce the law only when under strong pressure to do so. Currently, CRA activists realize the need to scrutinize how regulators implement the revised CRA examination procedures for big banks that took effect in mid-1997; to question whether the fact that almost one-third of banks examined last year were rated "outstanding" reflects lowered standards; and to ensure that regulatory changes adopted as part of continuing deregulation of banking don't undermine the CRA.

Unless the bank regulators as well as banks are continually held accountable for their actions, the fact that the CRA remains the law of the land may again make no more difference than it did during the Reagan years.

*Resources:* NCRC Reinvestment Compendium, National Community Reinvestment Coalition (ncrc.org); CRA Watch, Center for Community Change (communitychange.org); "CRA and Fair Lending Regulations," Douglas Evanoff & Lewis Segal, Economic Perspectives (Federal Reserve Bank of Chicago), Nov./Dec. 1996; Disclosure, National People's Action (http://www.npa-us.org).

---

# A MATTER OF LIFE AND DEBT: THE IMPACT OF PREDATORY LENDING ON THE BLACK COMMUNITY

**BY JABULANI LEFFALL**
*March/April 2003*

Think of it as a word problem. Problem is the operative word: If "company A" lends $50,000 to "consumer F" at an interest rate 7 points above the prime rate, charging finance fees equal to 10% of the loan and a prepayment penalty, how long would it take for consumer F to pay back the interest, let alone the principal?

Sound complicated? Well it is and that's how the lenders want it to be. The answer to the problem: too long. (As long as possible is also acceptable.) This complex equation is what is known as predatory lending—loans made with abusive terms like hidden or excessive fees and foreclosure defaults. Predatory lending banks use deceptive solicitation and often target borrowers who should qualify for credit on better terms.

While poor people in general are the main quarry in this multi-billion dollar business, it's African Americans who are the biggest losers. "We are targeted more than any other group through aggressive marketing and mail-out campaigns," says Yolanda Clark, a Los Angeles-based black mortgage broker who deals with homebuyers every day.

Although not all subprime (high interest) loans are predatory, almost all predatory loans are subprime. And, according to a November 2002 report by the Association of Community Organizers for Reform Now (ACORN), subprime lenders account for more than half of all housing refinance loans made in predominately black neighborhoods. From 1995 to 2001 the number of subprime purchase loans to African Americans rose 686%.

Large financial concerns and the subprime lending lobby deny that blacks are being targeted. They point out the true fact that whites procure subprime loans in greater number than blacks and that the loans some black consumers get reflect their poor credit.

But even though more whites get subprime loans, the likelihood that these same loans are predatory is higher for blacks, according to another report, "Risk or Race?" issued last year by the Center for Community Change. Its findings dispel the claim that bad credit or poverty explains predatory lending patterns. In fact, the study found that racial inequities increased as homeowners' salaries and creditworthiness went up.

The report, which ranks all 331 metropolitan areas in the nation, finds that:

- African Americans are three times more likely than whites to receive a subprime loan.
- Upper-income African Americans are more likely to receive subprime loans than are lower-income whites.
- Subprime lending and racial disparities are found in all regions and in urban areas of all sizes.

Allen J. Fishbein, general counsel of the Center for Community Change, says the overall racial disparities are due to a lack of mainstream prime lenders in the black community.

Predatory lenders contribute to neighborhood deterioration by stripping homeowners of their equity and overcharging those who can least afford it, adds David Swanson, ACORN's spokesman.

"The circle of debt is killing our community," says Earl Ofari Hutchinson, an author and talk show host for KPFK, a Pacifica affiliate in Los Angeles. "It's peonage and indentured servitude to the loans. Black people in greater and greater numbers are subjected to piracy by legalized thieves."

## Lena J

Lena J, a community resource adviser for United Way and a resident of Inglewood,

Calif.—a predominately black city on the outskirts of Los Angeles—knows the perils of predatory lending all too well.

Ms. J requested that her last name not be used out of fear of reprisal from her lender. She bought her home three years ago for $149,000, with two loans through a neighborhood bank. She pays interest rates of 7.2% and 7.3%. (The prime rate currently hovers slightly above 4%.)

When Ms. J decided she needed a second mortgage, she went to Household International, Inc. subsidiary Beneficial to apply for a personal line of credit to pay off her car loans and provide some extra cash for home improvement.

Beneficial first told her that the loan was denied. Then, out of the blue, she got a call saying it had been approved and was being processed. The total amount of the loan was $52,904 including $3,903 in points and fees at an interest rate of 11.5%. Money is money, she surmised. So she rushed back over to Beneficial and signed up.

Beneficial neglected to mention that there was a prepayment penalty on her loan for five years costing six months interest minus 20% of the loan amount.

Even worse, Beneficial set up her loan as a home equity loan instead of the regular line of credit that she requested.

Beneficial indicated in fine print that it would pay off her second mortgage. But when Ms. J got the checks from Beneficial, they were for the wrong amounts. Even though the loan went through and $21,000 for her second mortgage is listed on page two of her Truth in Lending Disclosure form, Beneficial never paid that amount.

It has to be true if it's on the "Truth in Lending Disclosure" form right? Wrong. While Beneficial did send her a check, the company paid off far less of her mortgage balance than it led her to believe it would. Meanwhile Ms. J thought her second mortgage had been paid in full by Beneficial and so did not submit her second mortgage payments. Late charges hit her like a ton of bricks falling from a "fixer upper."

Ms. J now makes three payments per month when she should only have two. Her monthly payments (on the original housing loans and the Beneficial loans combined) total $1,150. Her monthly net income is less than $2,000.

She joins a host of others forced to pay 60% or more of their net income toward high-interest mortgages. A domino effect ensues, as there is less money for other essentials such as groceries, phone and utilities and car payments. If Ms. J does not make her payments, she pays in a different way—foreclosure.

False and misleading Beneficial information (in both its written and person-to-person communication with Ms. J) were factors in her victimization. Because Ms. J trusted Beneficial and did not suspect a shady deal was brewing, when she found out the loan was approved, she signed on the dotted line. Ms. J cannot take her fight in earnest to the courts—because a signature, even on a confusing loan form, is binding in most cases.

## Definitions

The line between "legal" subprime lending and "predatory lending" is a contested one. Many deny that a clear definition of predatory lending exists. Without a widely understood definition of the term, the enemy remains faceless. People cannot fight what they do not understand.

Although several states and localities have recently passed laws clarifying the scope of illegal lending practices, and recent court settlements may have begun to curb some of the worst fraudulent practices of a few large corporations, a wide scope of deceptive activity remains legal in most of the country.

Further, although predatory lending is a discriminatory practice, most of the media has not defined it as such. It is not treated as a matter of overt racial discrimination the way racial profiling, police brutality, and voter disenfranchisement sometimes are. Instead, too often the Ms. J's of the world are simply labeled "irresponsible" and left to fend for themselves.

Federal Reserve Board Governor Edward M. Gramlich, who has called for additional research to explore the "significance" of predatory lending, gave a vague and unmistakably political take on the definition question.

The Federal Reserve is charged with supervising and regulating banking institutions and protecting the credit rights of consumers. Addressing the Consumer Federation of America, Gramlich said: "Just as with safety and soundness and unfair and deceptive trade practices," there should be no final definition of the term "predatory lending."

Gramlich's remarks are about as clear as what happened to Ms. J. It is evident that he wants to tread lightly until the debate reaches Capitol Hill. When in doubt, commission a study.

The truth of the matter is that a list of predatory lending practices can be named, and the effects of predatory lending can be measured. An independent study on the economic cost of predatory lending in the housing arena by the Durham, N.C.-based Coalition for Responsible Lending identified three clusters of predatory lending practices and analyzed their costs:

1. ***Equity Stripping:*** Charging borrowers exorbitant processing fees, resulting in substantially higher payments that are subtracted from the equity of the home when a borrower refinances or sells his or her house.

2. ***Rate-Risk Disparities:*** Charging borrowers a higher rate of interest than their credit histories would justify.

3. ***Excessive Foreclosures:*** Homeowners struggling to make payments under the combined weight of excessive fees and high interest rates often pay the ultimate price—the loss of their home and all the equity they have accumulated.

The Coalition for Responsible Lending's report goes on to say that the equity of the neighbors of the foreclosed is also reduced as foreclosures start to permeate the neighborhood. "Finally," the study states, "there are significant social costs to the pending wholesale loss of neighborhoods of homeowners, particularly in African-American communities."

And the housing finance arena represents just one branch of the predatory lending industry. Housing finance predatory lenders target consumers of a particular stratum; those with incomes high enough to permit homeownership. More pervasive still are smaller-scale predatory-lending operations geared to personal finance. (See the sidebar for discussion of one such type: the payday loan.)

## High Finance Connections

Predatory lenders have been called "pirates" and "scavengers" by their victims, but while this banking niche is on its face morally reprehensible, these "pirates" are not from some underworld of organized crime. They are among the most respected institutions in the world, companies whose leaders mix with powerful dignitaries as stewards of high finance. Their billboards celebrate the American dream.

But for two groups in particular: Citigroup Inc. and Household International Inc.—better known by their opponents as "Citigrope" and "Chokehold"—the term "high finance" takes on a whole new meaning. Both are mainstream institutions with ties to predatory lending practices.

## "Citigrope"

New York-based Citigroup is the world's second largest financial services concern and is America's largest consumer finance firm. Its 2001 revenue was $112 billion with profits of $14 billion.

Citigroup's chief executive, Sanford Weill, is revered on Wall Street as a banking legend and the "best deal-maker on the planet." Weill presided over the historic 1998 merger between Traveler's Group and Citibank (hence Citigroup) and parlayed his company into the top ten of the Fortune 500.

In 2001's Fortune 500 edition, Fortune magazine said of Weill: "Weill is a star: His shareholders earned an average annual total return of 40.8% (in 2001) a stunning result that only 15 other companies in the list—all of them smaller—beat."

In the years since the article appeared, both Citigroup and Weill have drawn fire for analyst improprieties at Salomon Smith Barney—its investment banking arm—and more recently for the actions of CitiFinancial, its subprime consumer-lending arm.

CitiFinancial sells bill consolidation, debt refinancing and subprime home equity home improvement and personal loans through more than 2,000 offices in North America. It was CitiFinancial's $31 billion acquisition of notorious predatory lender Associates First Capital in 2000 that tarnished Citigroup's reputation. In 2001, The Federal Trade Commission (FTC) alleged that Associates violated the Federal Trade Commission Act through what it called "deceptive marketing practices that induced consumers to refinance existing debts into home loans with high interest rates, costs, and fees, and to purchase high-cost credit insurance."

The FTC also said the company violated the Truth in Lending Act, the Fair Credit Reporting Act, and Equal Credit Opportunity Act, and used unfair tactics in collecting consumers' payments on its loans.

Jodie Bernstein, then the Director of the FTC's Bureau of Consumer Protection, stated in a press release:

> "(Associates) hid essential information from consumers, misrepresented loan terms, flipped loans, and packed optional fees to raise the costs of the loans. What had made the alleged practices more egregious is that they primarily victimized consumers who were the most vulnerable—hard working homeowners who had to borrow to meet emergency needs and often had no other access to capital."

To protect the merger and shield itself from liability and attacks from the press, Citigroup launched a website called "Tell Citibank." The homepage says: "Associates Customer: Are you a customer of Associates First Capital? If so, you already may be a victim of predatory lending."

Despite Citigroup's newly deployed campaign for the little guy, it once again found itself the object of protest late last year. A San Francisco-based advocacy group, The California Reinvestment Committee (CRC), attacked the parent company for discrimination and openly fought the bank's expansion in the western United States.

Said CRC executive director Alan Fisher, "We fear a growing Citigroup presence in California and believe it will be harmful to California communities."

According to the CRC, Citigroup hides behind its subsidiary CitiFinancial, which CRC contends still charges high points and fees on subprime loans, imposes prepayment penalties that trap borrowers into high cost loans, and sets arbitration provisions denying borrowers access to legal recourse.

The CRC further contends that CitiFinancial lends subprime monies to African-American and Latino borrowers, while low-cost lenders are three to four times as likely to deny African Americans as they are white applicants.

"It's the bait and switch," says Donnette Heard, treasurer for the Los Angeles-based Multicultural Real Estate Alliance For Urban Change. "If the big bank denies you, they send you to their subprime lenders who will then contact you. They keep your business and deal with you on their terms."

## "Chokehold"

Such is the case with Chicago-based Household International, Inc. whose Beneficial subsidiary played the bait and switch with Ms. J from Inglewood.

According to Internet business portal Hoovers, Household has "made lending to the little people profitable." With a company slogan that says: "Helping everyday people everyday," it is the second largest consumer finance company behind Citigroup.

Yet for the past several years, consumer advocacy groups and Attorneys General from scores of states have dragged Household through the courts for duping the Ms. J's of America into high-interest hell.

In 2001 Household still managed to post $13 billion in revenues with a profit of $1.9 billion. Moreover, Household caught a break in November of 2002 when powerful British Bank HSBC, led by chairman Sir John Bond, snapped it up in a $14 billion dollar deal. At the time of the deal, Bond assured investors that Household's "aggressive" lending practices were a thing of the past. Bond laughed his way to the bank because Household's legal troubles and bad press helped him acquire the company at a bargain-basement price. It was nevertheless one of the largest acquisitions of 2002.

With assets of more than $100 billion and about 50 million customers at 1,400 retail branches, Household will lift the earnings before taxes of HSBC's North American operation to more than 30% of the conglomerate's total profits. It will also boost HSBC's credit card business, adding about 2 million new Household customers.

This deal, much like Citigroup's acquisition of Associates, is not without controversy. The Bronx, N.Y.-based Inner City Press (ICP), which in the past attacked big banks such as Citigroup, opposes the HSBC-Household deal. ICP revealed data showing that HSBC, even before the acquisition was announced, denied African-American loan applications 2.7 times more frequently than whites' applications. Groups like the ICP believe HSBC will willingly participate in the bait and switch, using Household and its units to trap consumers.

What Citigroup and Household have in common, other than being lenders under fire, is that they both were involved in multi-billion dollar mergers in which subprime lenders sought refuge. The danger of the absorption of subprime lending groups into publicly traded mainstream banks is that the holding companies do not have to submit transparent financial records for private subsidiaries to the Securities and Exchange Commission (SEC) or any other regulatory body. The figures can hide in long, tedious financial statements and be signed off on by accounting firms and lawyers retained by these large companies.

For instance, Associates was absorbed into CitiFinancial, a private arm of Citigroup, which is traded on the New York Stock Exchange. Moreover, now that it has acquired Household and is facing public scrutiny, publicly traded HSBC may clean up the house by burying Household financials deep into the number soup that comprises an SEC filing.

Both Citigroup and Household declined to comment for this article. Company spokespeople did, however, point to the large settlements made to predatory lending plaintiffs.

In the fall of 2002, Citigroup put up almost $250 million and Household about $484 million. The combined settlement money represents the largest sum in American history paid to settle a consumer lending complaint.

But considering that since 1995 predatory lending institutions have raked in almost $100 billion, the $734 million is, in layman's terms, chump change.

Citigroup settled with the FTC to shake the shame off its merger with Associates. In the case of Household, regulators and attorneys general from 20 states had accused it of violating state laws by misrepresenting loan terms and failing to disclose material information. "We could have litigated, but the headline and litigation risk over an extended period would have been worse for the company," said Household's Chief Executive William Aldinger in a conference call with analysts last October. "We made a call to get it over with quickly." Household said it would record a $330 million charge in the third quarter as a result of the settlement and that its earnings for 2003 would miss Wall Street expectations.

Since the settlement, Citigroup and Household have issued "best practices guidelines" that they say can further prevent future exploitation of borrowers with

### *"GHETTO" BANKING*

Pick an inner-city, any inner-city, and take a drive. If you keep your eyes open you'll see large neon signs: "Instant Cash Advance," "Currency Exchange," and "Pay Day Loans." The signs are pervasive in places where poor people live. They call to mind the lyrics from the theme song of a popular black sit-com, "Good Times." Residents of these neighborhoods are "Keeping their heads above water" and subjected to "easy credit rip-offs."

Predatory lending is not limited to the home financing and refinancing lending markets. It's even more prevalent in the realm of personal finance. With small storefronts that residents dub "Ghetto Banks," profit- seeking financial institutions catch desperate and impoverished people in their crosshairs.

Over ten million American families lack formal bank accounts. They are an easy mark for the check cashing stores, collateral loan companies, and pay day lenders that siphon almost as much from their wages—up to 20 cents on the dollar—as F.I.C.A. These entities are able to take advantage of consumers because there are often no other financial service providers present in low-income areas.

These "ghetto," or what consumer advocates call "shadow" banks are in effect the siblings of the mainstream banks that fund them. The kicker is that the large banks that deny loans and accounts to low-income people are the same ones that end up doing business with poor folks, albeit indirectly.

For example, Wells Fargo, the seventh largest bank in the country, has arranged more than $700 million in loans since 1998 to three of the nation's largest check cashing companies: Ace Cash Express, EZ Corp., and Cash America. Moreover, many check cashers and payday lenders have sought to lease national bank charters to avoid legislative interference and circumvent state usury laws.

In Chicago, the country's ninth most segregated metropolitan area, small loan and check cashing outlets saturate the streets. One of them is Illinois Title Lenders Inc., where applicants put their cars up for collateral in exchange for loans. The lender holds the vehicle title and keeps the car in the event of default. In some cases, the lender reposseses the vehicle even if the loan is less than the car's value.

Far from the "fringe" of the banking industry, Illinois Title Lenders Inc. has partnered with the American Chartered Bank (one of the twenty-five largest banks in the state of Illinois). Other mainstream lenders have also profited from the "alternative" loan arena. Bank of America, PNC Bank, LaSalle National Bank, Finova Capital Corp., and Providian have all been involved at one time or another in Illinois' "alternative" loan sector. Banks

low-incomes or weak credit histories.

One promise they have made is to reform up-front points and fees. In the opinion of ACORN's David Swanson, Household should lower its cap on up-front points and fees from 5% of the loan amount to 3%. Citigroup already caps them at 3%.

Yet a cap on points and fees does not help if there is no limit to how high a basic interest rate can go. If a lender still really wants to bilk a borrower, it can lower the points and raise the interest rate. For example, if maximum points are 3% of the loan instead of 5 or 6%, a lender can raise a rate to 12 or 13% and be satisfied with a 3% cap on points.

There are also stipulations in both Household's and Citigroup's guidelines that like these issue payday loans that bind consumers to unreasonable terms and require them to waive their rights to legal recourse.

To see how exploitative payday loans can be, one need not look further than the loan application at a franchise called "Instant Cash Advance: Chicago's answer for fast cash." Applicants are asked to sign a pledge in fine print at the bottom of the page, effectively signing away their consumer rights in three ways:

- The applicant is pegged for direct mail and other marketing schemes including possible mail fraud and identity theft: *I fully release all parties, companies their subsidiaries & employees, past or present, from any and all liability for any damage that may result. My signature below indicates that for purposes of verification and qualification, I have voluntarily waived the protection of all rights to privacy laws.*
- The applicant forfeits the ability to fight back if ripped off: *Furthermore, I also voluntarily waive my right to pursue or take any legal action against Instant Cash Advance, employees past or present, subsidiaries or agents thereof.*
- The applicant, not likely to fully understand what he or she is getting into, hammers a nail into his or her financial coffin: *I fully understand that any information I provide found to be false or fabricated will be grounds for denial of credit with Instant Cash Advance. I agree that I have fully read this statement.*

If an applicant borrows $100 from a payday lender by writing a check for $115 or $120 that the lender will hold until payday, the applicant is paying interest equivalent to taking out a loan at a 400% annual percentage rate (APR). When payday comes, a clerk asks the applicant if he or she would like to roll the loan over to the next pay period. Often the applicant agrees, perpetuating the cycle of revolving debt.

Recent legislation aims to curtail payday loan groups. In October 2002, The Office of the Comptroller of the Currency, the regulatory body that oversees federally chartered banks, ordered banks in Texas, Pennsylvania, California, and Virginia to stop subsidizing check cashers in certain localities.

Many more such efforts will be required to end the reign of the "ghetto banks." In the meantime, consumer advocates and lawmakers are urging low-income consumers to avoid payday loans. But for potential victims who are cash-strapped, have no cushion of wealth, and no access to low-interest credit, abstinence is easier said than done.

ban the selling of single-premium credit insurance and establish customer hotlines for complaints (e.g.,"Tell Citibank").

Despite Citigroup's and Household's mea culpa, the companies still differ in where they draw the line on abusive practice. And neither will concede that a good number of their predatory loans were issued based on race.

## The Fight for Predatory Lending Reform

"The fight needs to be taken to the seats of local, state and national governments," says ACORN spokesman David Swanson. And it has been. In the past year alone nearly a dozen state and local city government bodies have debated and passed anti-predatory lending legislation. By November of 2002 the New York, Los Angeles, and Oakland city councils had each passed such ordinances.

In New York, the ordinance bans the city from doing business with predatory lenders or companies that purchase predatory loans. ACORN members in Manhattan packed City Hall at each stage in this process and successfully promoted this bill over the fervent opposition of major lenders, including Citigroup. ACORN's New York branch estimates that the ordinance will save homeowners between $75 million and $100 million. The legislation is expected to take effect sometime this year. Los Angeles' proposed ordinance was even more comprehensive.

According to ACORN, there are several state-level bills on the table in New Jersey, Massachusetts, and New Mexico —where in November the group protested at a local branch of Wells Fargo, with victims talking about the damage caused by the predatory loans they received from the lender. Most of the bills would ban prepayment penalties, put caps on points, and establish Annual Percentage Rate (APR) thresholds.

Georgia and North Carolina already have strict predatory lending regulations. In North Carolina it is a violation to make a high-cost home loan if a lender believes the consumer will be unable to make the scheduled payments. North Carolina also makes it a violation to issue any loan that "does not have reasonable tangible net benefit to the borrower." Both states require all homeowners to seek loan counseling, a measure which consumer advocates support.

In the wake of the state bills, Sen. Paul Sarbanes (D-Maryland), the chair of the Senate Banking Committee in the 107th U.S. Congress, proposed a bill with provisions to ban certain practices characteristic in subprime lending, such as prepayment penalties, credit insurance bundling, financing of fees, and balloon payments (large, lump-sum payments scheduled at the end of a series of smaller payments).

But while ACORN's David Swanson praises these recent small victories, as well as the apparent move toward curbing or eradicating most forms of predatory lending, he is concerned about what might happen if a Republican-controlled Congress and White House decide to reverse the progress that has been made.

"I'd hate think that this will all go for naught. That's why we're urging people to get involved in whatever way they can. We can't let the work be in vain," Swanson adds.

Groups such as the Coalition for Responsible Lending, ACORN, and the Center for Community Change say predatory lenders are likely to push laws banning state and local restrictions on abusive lending.

Late last year, Rep. Bob Ney (R-Ohio) passed around a draft for a bill that ACORN claims bans states from passing laws to protect borrowers. ACORN also alleges that the bill was co-written by Wright Andrews of Butera and Andrews, the firm that represents a coalition of subprime lenders.

Time and filibusters will tell. There is uncertainty about which bills will or will not be passed by session's end. There is also uncertainty as to whether the financial settlements from Citigroup and Household will be enough to placate opponents of predatory lending. So, as the days go by, the lawmakers legislate, corporate mergers and acquisitions commence, and the seats of power shift, the interest accrues and the bills pile up—particularly in the black community.

And one thing does remain certain: Ms. J of Inglewood and those like her have bills to pay next month and the month after that.

*This story was produced under the George Washington Williams Fellowship for Journalists of Color, a project sponsored by the Independent Press Association.*

# FLAME BROILED SHARK

**BY DAVID SWANSON**
*July/August 2004*

If someone told you that a number of low-income people, most of them African-American or Latino, most of them women, most of them elderly, had been robbed of much of their equity or of their entire homes by a predatory mortgage lender, you might not be surprised. But if you heard that these women and men had brought the nation's largest high-cost lender to its knees, forced it to sell out to a foreign company, and won back a half a billion dollars that had been taken from them, you'd probably ask what country this had happened in. Surely it couldn't have been in the United States, land of unbridled corporate power.

And yet it was. In 2001, these families, all members of the Association of Community Organizations for Reform Now (ACORN), launched a campaign against the nation's largest and most notorious predatory lender, Household International (also known as Household Finance or Beneficial). The 2003 settlement included a ban on talking about the damage Household had inflicted on borrowers and neighborhoods. That's one reason many people haven't heard this story—the families who defeated Household are in effect barred from publicly criticizing the corporation and teaching others the lessons they learned. (I was ACORN's communications coordinator during much of the Household campaign but left before it ended. No one asked me not to tell this story.)

In low-income minority neighborhoods in the United States, the little wealth that exists lies in home equity (see "Home Equity as a Percent of Net Worth"). People of color have made gains in home ownership during the past few decades, thanks in part to efforts by community groups like ACORN and National People's Action to force banks to make loans in communities of color (see "Minority Homeownership Is Growing"). Overall, these gains have been good for the new homeowners and good for their neighborhoods.

But low-income home ownership is fragile. Half of all extremely low-income homeowners pay more than half of their income for housing, according to the National Low Income Housing Coalition. Because low-income homeownership is not protected by additional savings, a temporary loss of income or a sudden large expense, such as a medical bill, can mean the loss of the home.

High-cost lenders—including large national operations like Household, Wells Fargo, and Citigroup, as well as small-time local sharks—strip away, rather than build up, equity in poor neighborhoods. Predatory high-cost lenders turn the usual logic of lending upside down. They make their money by intentionally issuing loans that borrowers will be unable to repay. Their loans invariably leave borrowers worse off, not better off.

Most high-cost (also called "subprime") loans are home-mortgage refinance loans. They carry excessive, and sometimes variable, interest rates and exorbitant fees. The more abusive lenders bundle bogus products like credit insurance into their loans, which accrue more interest and fees. Some lenders quietly omit taxes and insurance costs from monthly mortgage statements, causing crises when the yearly tax and insurance bills arrive. Others encourage borrowers to consolidate credit card and other debt within the mortgage, which further decreases home equity and places the home at greater risk. Loans may even exceed the value of the home, trapping people in debt they cannot refinance with a responsible lender. Hidden balloon payments force repeated refinancing (with fees each time). When borrowers find themselves unable to meet payments, the predatory lender refinances them repeatedly and ultimately seizes the house. Borrowers often have little recourse, as mandatory arbitration clauses written into their loan contracts prevent them from taking lenders to court.

High-cost loans are not made only to people with poor credit. Fannie Mae estimates that as many as half of all subprime borrowers could have qualified for a lower-cost mortgage. After British financial corporation HSBC bought Household International in March 2003, it announced that 46% of Household's real estate-backed loans had been made to borrowers with 'A' credit. But Household had made no 'A' (standard low-cost) loans. In fact, Household was a leading cause of the rows of vacant houses appearing in ACORN neighborhoods in the 1990s.

### *MINORITY HOMEOWNERSHIP IS GROWING*

Over the past decade, homeownership rates among minority households have risen more quickly than among other groups. In 1993, 42.6% of African-American and 40.0% of Latino households owned homes. In 2002, 48.9% and 47.4% of those groups owned homes, respectively. This reflects a more rapid rate of increase than for whites, whose homeownership grew from an already high 70.4% to 74.7%. Minorities, as a share of all first-time homebuyers, rose from 19.1% in 1993 to 30% in 1999. Indeed, minorities accounted for 41% of net growth in homeowners during that same period, according to Harvard University's Joint Center for Housing Studies.

**HOME EQUITY AS A PERCENT OF NET WORTH, BY INCOME QUINTILE, 2000**

| | *Lowest* | *Next-Lowest* | *Middle* | *Next-to-Highest* | *Highest* |
|---|---|---|---|---|---|
| Non-Hispanic Whites | 85.6 | 77.7 | 70.8 | 62.9 | 44.4 |
| Hispanics | 90.0 | 73.5 | 76.3 | 70.9 | 64.9 |
| African Americans | NA | 78.7 | 70.9 | 73.5 | 67.8 |

*Source:* U.S. Census Bureau, May 2003.

## Fighting Back

ACORN members didn't take this abuse lying down. Their grassroots effort against Household relied on numerous strategies, including shareholder activism, political advocacy, and the old stand-by of direct action. It offers a model for low-income communities seeking to challenge exploitative corporations.

In 2001, ACORN members launched the campaign with simultaneous protests inside Household offices in cities around the country, and then began work to pass anti-predatory lending legislation at local, state, and federal levels.

Later that year, ACORN, together with the advocacy group Coalition for Responsible Wealth, introduced a shareholder resolution that proposed to tie Household executives' compensation to the termination of the company's predatory lending practices. When Household held its annual meeting in a suburb of Tampa, Fla., a crowd of ACORN members arrived at the event wearing shark suits and holding shark balloons. The resolution won 5% of the shareholders' vote. In 2002, Household held its meeting an hour and a half from the nearest airport in rural Kentucky. ACORN members weren't deterred by the remote location—they came from all over the country by car. The protest may have been the biggest thing the town of London, Ky., had ever seen. This time, 30% of the shareholders supported the resolution.

ACORN also helped borrowers file a number of class-action suits against Household for practices that were clearly illegal under existing law, and it let Wall Street analysts know what Household stood to lose from these lawsuits. ACORN urged state attorneys general and federal regulators to investigate the firm, and simultaneously put pressure on stores, including Best Buy, that issued Household credit cards. As a result of ACORN agitation, various local and state governments passed resolutions urging their pension funds to divest from the firm.

In the summer of 2002, ACORN members did something that really got the attention of Household executives and board members. On a beautiful day, thousands of Household borrowers poured out of buses onto the lawns of the company CEO and board members in the wealthy suburbs north of Chicago. They knocked on the officials' doors, speaking directly to the people whose policies had hurt them from a distance. When forced to leave, ACORN members plastered "Wanted" posters all over the neighborhood.

Through all of this, ACORN worked the media. It kept a database of borrowers' stories, and put reporters in touch with them, generating several hundred national print articles and television and radio spots. It also maintained an enormous website about Household (which has since been removed as part of the gag-order agreement).

Meanwhile, ACORN Housing Corporation, a nonprofit loan-counseling agency created by ACORN, helped many borrowers cancel rip-off services, such as credit insurance, that were built into their loans, and, when possible, refinance out of their Household loans altogether.

## Household's Concessions

For more than two years, a small handful of ACORN staff organized thousands of members in an unrelenting effort, until Household International could no longer sustain the negative attention, shareholder discontent, and legal and regulatory pressures. In early 2003, the lender agreed to pay $489 million in restitution to borrowers through the 50 state attorneys general. The company later agreed to pay millions more to ACORN to fund new financial literacy programs. This was one of the largest consumer settlements in history, but it amounted to only a fraction of what Household had taken from people, and it could not undo all the damage done to families who had lost their homes. In addition to the payments, the company will:

- Ensure that new loans actually provide a benefit to consumers prior to issuing the loans.
- Reform and improve disclosures to consumers.
- Reimburse states to cover the costs of the investigations into Household's practices.
- Limit prepayment penalties to the first two years of a loan.
- Limit points and origination fees, upfront charges built into the loan, to 5%. (A "point" is one percentage point of the loan amount.)
- Eliminate "piggyback" second mortgages. (When Household issued home loans, it would simultaneously issue a second, smaller, loan at an even higher rate. It often labeled these second loans "lines of credit" in order to avoid federal regulations that limit the rate that can be charged.)
- Implement a "Foreclosure Avoidance Program" to provide relief to borrowers who are at risk of losing their homes due to delinquent payments (for example,

reducing interest rates, waiving unpaid late charges, deferring interest, and reducing the principal).

ACORN-led efforts won legislative and corporate reforms as well. Several cities and states (including Arkansas, California, New Mexico, New Jersey, and New York) have banned abusive practices that were once routine. One practice ACORN targeted aggressively was "single-premium credit insurance," a nearly useless and overpriced insurance policy that predatory lenders added to many loans (often falsely describing it as a requirement or failing to tell borrowers it had been included). In 2002, Household and other major lenders announced they would drop the product. This was one of several corporate reforms ACORN won during the course of the campaign.

This campaign demonstrates that a well-organized grassroots effort can combat corporate exploitation and extract significant concessions. By pursuing different strategies at once, ACORN repeatedly hit Household with the unexpected, and put it on the defensive. The outcome is good news for low-income neighborhoods, and bad news for Wells Fargo, the predatory lender who is next on ACORN's list.

---

## AMERICA'S FRINGE ECONOMY

**BY HOWARD KARGER**

*November/December 2006*

Ron Cook is a department manager at a Wal-Mart store in Atlanta. Maria Guzman is an undocumented worker from Mexico; she lives in Houston with her three children and cleans office buildings at night. Marty Lawson works for a large Minneapolis corporation. (The names have been changed to protect the privacy of the individuals.) What do these three people have in common? They are all regular fringe economy customers.

The term "fringe economy" refers to a range of businesses that engage in financially predatory relationships with low-income or heavily indebted consumers by charging excessive interest rates, superhigh fees, or exorbitant prices for goods or services. Some examples of fringe economy businesses include payday lenders, pawnshops, check-cashers, tax refund lenders, rent-to-own stores, and "buy-here/pay-here" used car lots. The fringe economy also includes credit card companies that charge excessive late payment or over-the-credit-limit penalties; cell phone providers that force less creditworthy customers into expensive prepaid plans; and subprime mortgage lenders that gouge prospective homeowners.

### *CREDIT CARDS, COLLEGE STUDENTS, AND THE FRINGE ECONOMY*

Marty Lawson is one of the growing legions of the credit poor. Although he earns $65,000 a year, his $50,000 credit card debt means that he can buy little more than the essentials. This cycle of debt began when Marty received his first credit card in college.

Credit cards are the norm for today's college students. A 2005 Nellie Mae report found that 55% of college students get their first credit card during their freshman year; by senior year, 91% have a credit card and 56% carry four or more cards.

College students are highly prized credit card customers because of their high future earnings and lifetime credit potential. To ensnare them, credit card companies actively solicit on campus through young recruiters who staff tables outside university bookstores and student centers. Students are baited with free t-shirts, frisbees, candy, music downloads, and other come-ons. Credit card solicitations are stuffed into new textbooks and sent to dormitories, electronic mailboxes, and bulletin boards. According to Junior Achievement, the typical college freshman gets about eight credit card offers in the first week of the fall semester. The aggressiveness of credit card recruiters has led several hundred colleges to ban them from campus.

Excited by his newfound financial independence, Marty overlooked the fine print explaining that cash advances carried a 20% or more APR. He also didn't realize how easily he could reach the credit limit, and the stiff penalties incurred for late payments and over-the-credit-limit transactions. About one-third of credit card company profits come from these and other penalties.

Marty applied for a second credit card after maxing out his first one. The credit line on his second card was exhausted in only eight months. Facing $4,000 in high-interest credit card bills, Marty left college to pay off his debts. He never returned. Dropping out to repay credit card debt is all too common, and according to former Indiana University administrator John Simpson, "We lose more students to credit card debt than academic failure." Not coincidentally, by graduation the average credit card debt for college seniors is almost $3,000. Credit card debt worsens the longer a student stays in school. A 2004 Nellie Mae survey found the average credit card debt for graduate students was a whopping $7,831, a 59% increase over 1998. Fifteen percent of graduate students carry credit card balances of $15,000 or more.

The fringe economy is hardly new. Pawnshops and informal high-interest lenders have been around forever. What we see today, however, is a fringe-economy sector that is growing fast, taking advantage of the ever-larger part of the U.S. population whose economic lives are becoming less secure. Moreover, in an important sense the sector is no longer "fringe" at all: more and more, large mainstream financial corporations are behind the high-rate loans that anxious customers in rundown storefronts sign for on the dotted line.

## The Payday Lending Trap

Ron and Deanna Cook have two children and a combined family income of $48,000—more than twice the federal poverty line but still $10,000 below Georgia's median income. They are the working poor.

To make ends meet, the Cooks borrow from payday lenders. When Ron and Deanna borrow $300 for 14 days they pay $60 in interest—an annual interest rate of 520%! If they can't pay the full $360, they pay just the $60 interest fee and roll over the loan for another two weeks. The original $300 loan now costs $120 in interest for 30 days. If they roll over the loan for another two-week cycle, they pay $180 in interest on a $300 loan for 45 days. If the payday lender permits only four rollovers, the Cooks sometimes take out a payday loan from another lender to repay the original loan. This costly cycle can be devastating. The Center for Responsible Lending tells the tale of one borrower who entered into 35 back-to-back payday loans over 17 months, paying $1,254 in fees on a $300 loan.

The Cooks take out about ten payday loans a year, which is close to the national average for payday loan customers. Although the industry claims payday loans are intended only for emergencies, a 2003 study of Pima County, Ariz., by the Southwest Center for Economic Integrity found that 67% of borrowers used their loans for general non-emergency bills. The Center for Responsible Lending found that 66% of borrowers initiate five or more loans a year, and 31% take out twelve or more loans yearly. Over 90% of payday loans go to borrowers with five or more loans a year. Customers who take out 13 or more loans a year account for over half of payday lenders' total revenues.

## The Unbanked

Maria Guzman and her family are part of the 10% of U.S. households—more than 12 million—that have no relationship with a bank, savings institution, credit union, or other mainstream financial service provider. Being "unbanked," the Guzmans turn to the fringe economy for check cashing, bill payment, short-term pawn or payday loans, furniture and appliance rentals, and a host of other financial services. In each case, they face high user fees and exorbitant interest rates.

Without credit, the Guzmans must buy a car either for cash or through a "buy-here/pay-here" (BHPH) used car lot. At a BHPH lot they are saddled with a 28% annual percentage rate (APR) on a high-mileage and grossly overpriced vehicle. They also pay weekly, and one missed payment means a repossession. Since the Guzmans have no checking account, they use a check-casher who charges 2.7% for cashing their monthly $1,500 in payroll checks, which costs them $40.50 a month or $486 a year.

Like many immigrants, the Guzmans send money to relatives in their home country. (Money transfers from the United States to Latin America are expected to reach $25 billion by 2010.) If they sent $500 to Mexico on June 26, 2006, using Western Union's "Money in Minutes," they would have paid a $32 transfer fee. Moreover, Western Union's exchange rate for the transaction was 11.12 pesos for the U.S. dollar, while the official exchange rate that day was 11.44. The difference on $500 was almost $14, which raised the real costs of the transaction to $46, or almost 10% of the transfer amount.

Without a checking account, the Guzmans turn to money orders or direct bill pay, both of which add to their financial expenses. For example, ACE Cash Express charges 79 cents per money order and $1 or more for each direct bill payment. If the Guzmans use money orders to pay six bills a month, the fees total nearly $57 a year; using direct bill pay, they would pay a minimum of $72 in fees per year.

All told, the Guzmans spend more than 10% of their income on alternative financial services, which is average for unbanked households. To paraphrase James Baldwin, it is expensive to be poor and unbanked in America.

The Cooks and the Guzmans, along with people like Marty Lawson caught in a cycle of credit card debt (see sidebar on next page), may not fully appreciate the economic entity they are dealing with. Far from a mom-and-pop industry, America's fringe economy is largely dominated by a handful of large, well-financed multinational corporations with strong ties to mainstream financial institutions. It is a comprehensive and fully formed parallel economy that addresses the financial needs of the poor and credit-challenged in the same way as the mainstream economy meets the needs of the middle class. The main difference is the exorbitant interest rates, high fees, and onerous loan terms that mark fringe economy transactions.

## The Scope of the Fringe Economy

The unassuming and often shoddy storefronts of the fringe economy mask the true scope of this economic sector. Check-cashers, payday lenders, pawnshops, and rent-to-own stores alone engaged in at least 280 million transactions in 2001, according to Fannie Mae Foundation estimates, generating about $78 billion in gross revenues. By comparison, in 2003 combined state and federal spending on the core U.S. social welfare programs—Temporary Aid to Needy Families (AFDC's replacement), Supplemental Security Income, Food Stamps, the Women, Infants and Children (WIC) food program, school lunch programs, and the U.S. Department of Housing and Urban Development's (HUD) low-income housing programs—totaled less than $125 billion. Revenues in the combined sectors of the fringe economy—including subprime home mortgages and refinancing, and used car sales—would inflate the $78 billion several times over and eclipse federal and state spending on the poor.

There can be no doubt that the scope of the fringe economy is enormous. The Community Financial Services Association of America claims that 15,000 payday lenders extend more than $25 billion in short-term loans to millions of households each year. According to Financial Service Centers of America, 10,000 check-cashing stores process 180 million checks with a face value of $55 billion.

The sheer number of fringe economy storefronts is mind-boggling. For example, ACE Cash Express—only one of many such corporations—has 68 locations within 10 miles of my Houston zip code. Nationwide there are more than 33,000 check-cashing and payday loan stores, just two parts of the fringe economy. That's more than the all the McDonald's and Burger King restaurants and all the Target, J.C. Penney, and Wal-Mart retail stores in the United States combined.

ACE Cash Express is the nation's largest check-casher and exemplifies the growth and profitability of the fringe economy. In 1991 ACE had 181 stores; by 2005 it had 1,371 stores with 2,700 employees in 37 states and the District of Columbia. ACE's revenues totaled $141 million in 2000 and by 2005 rose to $268.6

million. In 2005 ACE:

- cashed 13.3 million checks worth approximately $5.3 billion (check cashing fees totaled $131.6 million);
- served more than 40 million customers (3.4 million a month or 11,000 an hour) and processed $10.3 billion in transactions;
- processed over 2 million loan transactions (worth $640 million) and generated interest income and fees of $91.8 million;
- added a total of 142 new locations (in 2006 the company anticipates adding 150 more);
- processed over $410 million in money transfers and 7.6 million money orders with a face value of $1.3 billion;
- processed over 7.8 million bill payment and debit card transactions, and sold approximately 172,000 prepaid debit cards.

Advance America is the nation's leading payday lender, with 2,640 stores in 36 states, more than 5,500 employees, and $630 million this year in revenues. Dollar Financial Corporation operates 1,106 stores in 17 states, Canada, and the United Kingdom. Their 2005 revenues were $321 million. Check-into-Cash has more than 700 stores; Check N' Go has 900 locations in 29 states. Almost all of these are publicly traded NASDAQ corporations.

There were 4,500 pawnshops in the United States in 1985; now there are almost 12,000, including outlets owned by five publicly traded chains. In 2005 the three big chains—Cash America International (a.k.a Cash America Pawn and SuperPawn), EZ Pawn, and First Cash—had combined annual revenues of nearly $1 billion. Cash America is the largest pawnshop chain, with 750 locations; the company also makes payday loans through its Cash America Payday Advance, Cashland, and Mr. Payroll stores. In 2005, Cash America's revenues totaled $594.3 million.

The Association of Progressive Rental Organizations claims that the $6.6 billion a year rent-to-own (RTO) industry serves 2.7 million households through 8,300 stores in 50 states. Many RTOs rent everything from furniture, electronics, major appliances, and computers to jewelry. Rent-A-Center is the largest RTO corporation in the world. In 2005 it employed 15,000 people; owned or operated 3,052 stores in the United States and Canada; and had revenues of $2.4 billion. Other leading RTO chains include Aaron Rents (with 1,255 stores across the United States and Canada and gross revenues of $1.1 billion in 2005) and RentWay (with 788 stores in 34 states and revenues of almost $516 million in 2005).

These corporations represent the tip of the iceberg. Low-income consumers spent $1.75 billion for tax refund loans in 2002. Many lost as much as 16% of their tax refunds because of expensive tax preparation fees and/or interest incurred in tax refund anticipation loans. The interest and fees on such loans can translate into triple-digit annualized interest rates, according to the Consumer Federation of America, which has also reported that 11 million tax filers received refund anticipation loans in 2000, almost half through H&R Block. According to a Brookings

Institution report, the nation's largest tax preparers earned about $357 million from fringe economy "fast cash" products in 2001, more than double their earnings in 1998. All for essentially lending people their own money!

The fringe economy plays a big role in the housing market, where subprime home mortgages rose from 35,000 in 1994 to 332,000 in 2003, a 25% a year growth rate and a tenfold increase in just nine years. (A subprime loan is a loan extended to less creditworthy customers at a rate that is higher than the prime rate.) According to Edward Gramlich, former member of the Board of Governors of the Federal Reserve System, subprime mortgages accounted for almost $300 billion or 9% of all mortgages in 2003.

While the fringe economy squeezes its customers, it is generous to its CEOs. According to Forbes, salaries in many fringe economy corporations rival those in much larger companies. In 2004 Sterling Brinkley, chairman of EZ Corp, earned $1.26 million; ACE's CEO Jay Shipowitz received $2.1 million on top of $2.38 million in stocks; Jeffrey Weiss, Dollar Financial Group's CEO, earned $1.83 million; Mark Speese, Rent-A-Center's CEO, made $820,000 with total stock options of $10 million; and Cash America's CEO Daniel Feehan was paid almost $2.2 million in 2003 plus the $9 million he had in stock options.

Fringe-economy corporations argue that the high interest rates and fees they charge reflect the heightened risks of doing business with an economically unstable population. While fringe businesses have never made their pricing criteria public, some risks are clearly overstated. For example, ACE assesses the risk of each check-cashing transaction and reports losses of less than 1%. Since tax preparers file a borrower's taxes, they are reasonably assured that refund anticipation loans will not exceed refunds. To further guarantee repayment, they often establish an escrow account into which the IRS directly deposits the tax refund check. Pawnshops lend only about 50% of a pawned item's value, which leaves them a large buffer if the pawn goes unclaimed (industry trade groups claim that 70% of customers do redeem their goods). The rent-to-own furniture and appliance industry charges well above the "street price" for furniture and appliances, which is more than enough to offset any losses. Payday lenders require a post-dated check or electronic debit to assure repayment. Payday loan losses are about 6% or less, according to the Center for Responsible Lending.

Much of the profit in the fringe economy comes from financing rather than the sale of a product. For example, if a used car lot buys a vehicle for $3,000 and sells it for $5,000 cash, their profit is $2,000. But if they finance that vehicle for two years at a 25% APR, the profit jumps to $3,242. This dynamic is true for virtually every sector of the fringe economy. A customer who pays off a loan or purchases a good or service outright is much less profitable for fringe economy businesses than customers who maintain an ongoing financial relationship with the business. In that sense, profit in the fringe economy lies with keeping customers continually enmeshed in an expensive web of debt.

## Funding and Exporting America's Fringe Economy

Fringe economy corporations require large amounts of capital to fund their phe-

## *A GLOSSARY OF THE FRINGE ECONOMY*

**Payday loans** are small, short-term loans, usually of no more than $1,500, to cover expenses until the borrower's next payday. These loans come with extremely high interests rates, commonly equivalent to 300% APR. The Center for Responsible Lending conservatively estimates that predatory payday lending practices cost American families $3.4 billion annually.

**Refund anticipation loans** (RALs), provided by outlets of such firms as H&R Block, Western Union, and Liberty Tax Service, are short-term loans, often with high interest rates or fees, secured by an expected tax refund. Interest rates can reach over 700% APR-equivalent.

**Check cashing stores** (ACE Cash Express is the biggest chain) provide services for people who don't have checking accounts. These stores are most often located in low-income neighborhoods and cash checks for a fee, which can vary greatly but is typically far higher than commercial banks charge for the same service. Check cashing fees have steadily increased over the past ten years.

**Money Transfer** companies (outlets of such companies as Western Union, Moneygram, and Xoom) allow people to make direct bill payments and send money either to a person or bank account for a fee, typically 10% of the amount being sent, not including the exchange rate loss for money sent internationally. the total cost can reach up to 25% of the amount sent.

**Pawnshops** give loans while holding objects of value as collateral. The pawnbroker returns the object when the loan is repaid, usually at a high interest rates. If the borrower doesn't repay the loan within a specified period, the pawnbroker sells the item. For example, the interest charge on a 30-day loan of $10 could be $2.20, equivalent to a 264% APR. Most pawnshops are individually owned but regional chains are now appearing.

**Rent-to-own** (RTO) stores—two leading chains are Rent-A-Center and Aaron Rents—rent furniture, electronics, and other consumer goods short-term or long-term. The consumer can eventually own the item after paying many times the standard retail price through weekly rental payments with an extremely high interest rate, commonly around 300% APR. If the consumer misses a payment, the item is repossessed.

**Buy here/pay here** (BHPH) car lots offer car loans on used cars on-site, with interest rates much higher than auto loans issued by commercial banks. Customers are often saddled with high-interest loans for high-mileage, overpriced vehicles. If a customer misses one payment, the car is repossessed. The largest BHPH company is the J.D. Byrider franchise, with 124 dealerships throughout the country.

—Barbara Sternal

nomenal growth, and mainstream financial institutions have stepped up to the plate. ACE Cash Express has a relationship with a group of banks including Wells Fargo, JP Morgan Chase Bank, and JP Morgan Securities to provide capital for acquisitions and other activities. Advance America has relationships with Morgan Stanley, Banc of America Securities LLC, Wachovia Capital Markets, and Wells Fargo Securities, to name a few. Similar banking relationships exist throughout the fringe economy.

The fringe economy is no longer solely a U.S. phenomenon. In 2003 the HSBC Group purchased Household International (and its subsidiary Beneficial Finance) for $13 billion. Headquartered in London, HSBC is the world's second largest bank and serves more than 90 million customers in 80 countries. Household International is a U.S.-based consumer finance company with 53 million customers and more than 1,300 branches in 45 states. It is also a predatory lender. In 2002, a $484 million settlement was reached between Household and all 50 states and the District of Columbia. In effect, Household acknowledged it had duped tens of thousands of low-income home buyers into loans with unnecessary hidden costs. In 2003, another $100 million settlement was reached based on Household's abusive mortgage lending practices.

HSBC plans to export Household's operations to Poland, China, Mexico, Britain, France, India, and Brazil, for starters. One shudders to think how the fringe economy will develop in nations with even fewer regulatory safeguards than the United States. Presumably, HSBC also believes that predatory lending will not tarnish the reputation of the seven British lords and one baroness who sit on its 20-member board of directors.

## What Can Be Done?

The fringe economy is one of the few venues that credit-challenged or low-income families can turn to for financial help. This is especially true for those facing a penurious welfare system with a lifetime benefit cap and few mechanisms for emergency assistance. In that sense, enforcing strident usury and banking laws to curb the fringe economy while providing no legal and accessible alternatives would hurt the very people such laws are intended to help by driving these transactions into a criminal underground. Instead of ending up in court, non-paying debtors would wind up in the hospital. Simply outlawing a demand-driven industry is rarely successful.

One strategy to limit the growth of the fringe economy is to develop more community-based lending institutions modeled on the Grameen Bank or on local cooperatives. Although community banks might charge a higher interest rate than commercial banks charge prime rate customers, the rates would still be significantly lower than in the existing fringe sector.

Another policy option is to make work pay, or at least make it pay better. In other words, we need to increase the minimum wage and the salaries of the lower middle class and working poor. One reason for the rapid growth of the fringe economy is the growing gap between low and stagnant wages and higher prices, especially for necessities like housing, health care, pharmaceuticals, and energy.

Stricter usury laws, better enforcement of existing banking regulations, and a more active federal regulatory system to protect low-income consumers can all play a role in taming the fringe economy. Concurrently, federal and state governments can promote the growth of non-predatory community banking institutions. In addition, commercial banks can provide low-income communities with accessible and inexpensive banking services. As the "DrillDown" studies conducted in recent years by the Washington, D.C., non-profit Social Compact suggest, low-income communities contain more income and resources than one might think. If fringe businesses can make billions in low-income neighborhoods, less predatory economic institutions should be able to profit there too. Lastly, low and stagnant wages make it difficult, if not impossible, for the working poor to make ends meet without resorting to debt. A significant increase in wages would likely result in a significant decline in the fringe economy. In the end, several concerted strategies will be required to restrain this growing and out-of-control economic beast.

*Resources:* "2003 Credit Card Usage Analysis" (2004) and "Undergraduate Students and Credit Cards in 2004" (2005) (Nellie Mae); Alan Berube, Anne Kim, Benjamin Forman, and Megan Burns, "The Price of Paying Taxes: How Tax Preparation and Refund Loan Fees Erode the Benefits of the EITC" (Brookings Institution and Progressive Policy Institute, May 2002); James H. Carr and Jenny Shuetz, "Financial Services in Distressed Communities: Framing the Issue, Finding Solutions," *Financial Services in Distressed Communities: Issues and Answers* (2001, Fannie Mae Foundation); "Making the Case for Financial Literacy: A Collection of Current Statistics Regarding Youth and Money" (Junior Achievement); Amanda Sapir and Karen Uhlich, "Pay Day Lending in Pima County Arizona" (Southwest Center for Economic Integrity, 2003); Keith Urnst, John Farris, and Uriah King, "Quantifying the Economic Cost of Predatory Payday Lending" (Center for Responsible Lending, 2004). Organizations working on these issues include U.S. Public Interest Research Group, www.uspirg.org; Association of Community Organizations for Reform Now (ACORN), www.acorn.org; Coalition for Responsible Credit Practices, www.responsible-credit.net; Community Financial Services Association of America, www.cfsa.net; Consumer Federation of America, www.consumerfed.org; Harvard University, Joint Center for Housing Studies, www.jchs.harvard.edu; National Consumer Law Center, www.consumerlaw.org.

# BUILD HOMES, NOT JAILS

## BY CHARLES E. KUBRIN & GREGORY D. SQUIRES

*September/October 2004*

Home mortgage lending has increased and crime has gone down in the nation's cities over the past 10 years. And these changes have been dramatic. Lending to low-income borrowers grew by 91%, compared to just over half that for wealthier borrowers. Lending to blacks increased by 80% and to Hispanics by 186%, compared to just a 30% increase for whites. Over the same period, violent and property crimes in the cities dropped by 23%.

Are these changes coincidental? Community development professionals and criminologists have long asserted a connection between investment and crime in city neighborhoods. More investment means more homeowners, a more stable population, and more committed eyes and ears in the community. In their book Comeback Cities, Paul Grogan, who now heads the policy group CEOs for Cities, and Tony Proscio concluded that "The pace and scale of urban rejuvenation of the 1990s is intimately connected to the rise in public safety."

The common-sense notion of a connection between investment and crime has now received empirical support in our study of Seattle, Washington. Our research offers evidence that greater investment in home mortgages, especially loans for low-income borrowers, is indeed linked to reductions in crime. These findings reinforce the wisdom of those states pursuing various investments as alternatives to increasingly unaffordable prison building and incarceration.

## The Evidence from Seattle

Seattle is a fairly representative city, with a population of just over 500,000 people, one-third nonwhite, and a crime rate just below the national average. The city has been the site of many neighborhood crime studies over the years. From publicly available reports on mortgage lending, we compared different census tracts across the city and found that as the amount of home mortgage lending increases, violent and property crime rates decrease. Even after controlling for many other variables that could explain this correlation—housing value, rates of home ownership, prevalence of female-headed households, household income, poverty, unemployment, racial composition, among others—we found a substantial and statistically significant relationship between mortgage lending and crime. A $10,000 increase in the average mortgage loan amount led to a reduction of 9.1 violent crimes per 1,000 residents. For a typical Seattle census tract, a community of around 5,000 residents, this translates into 45 fewer violent crimes each year.

Lower crime rates may, of course, attract mortgage money. But our statistical analysis found that more lending led to lower crime rates, even after taking into consideration the reverse impact of crime on lending. Furthermore, that the association held even when controlling for household income and racial composition offers some assurance that what we observed was not gentrification, but rather a drop in crime in neighborhoods that retained their original socioeconomic profile.

Perhaps more important, we found that the impact of lending on crime was greater when we examined just the loans made by financial institutions covered by the Community Reinvestment Act (CRA), a federal law that requires banks and savings institutions to serve the credit needs of low- and moderate-income neighborhoods in their service areas. Since it was enacted in 1977, the CRA has increased lending in low-income and minority neighborhoods throughout the United States, generating $1.7 trillion dollars in new loans for urban communities according to the

### *INVESTMENT, NOT IMPRISONMENT*

At a time when many states are confronting massive budget deficits, at least some are looking to alternatives to incarceration, particularly for offenders who committed technical violations but who pose no threat to public safety. Rather than spending $30,000 per year per inmate to incarcerate such offenders, some states are beginning to invest in training programs, drug rehabilitation, job-hunting assistance, and other initiatives to facilitate the successful re-entry of those who have served time. For example, legislation now being considered in Connecticut would free up as much as $50 million a year by diverting non-violent prisoners from jail. Texas averted $800 million in prison costs without jeopardizing public safety by simply adjusting its parole system. The state of Washington projects an annual savings of $45 million from new laws that shortened the sentences for selected drug crimes.

These efforts are being supported by the Open Society Institute of the Soros Foundation, other private foundations, and criminologists frustrated with the futility of many traditional approaches to law enforcement. As some criminologists have long argued, the race to incarcerate simply has not worked. In fact, recent research by John Jay College criminologist Todd Clear has shown that increasing incarceration rates above selected thresholds in attempts to reduce neighborhood crime actually increases crime rates in subsequent years. Clear and his associates suggest that this pattern reflects the further withdrawal of vital resources that make any neighborhood work. Many offenders are parents and spouses who are trying to raise their children and keep their families intact. Many are also workers who contribute to the neighborhood economy. As Clear observed, "The removal of offenders who pose no risk to society can deplete valued resources, a particularly costly outcome for already disadvantaged neighborhoods."

According to James Austin, director of the Institute on Crime, Justice and Corrections at George Washington University, "statewide initiatives are freeing up millions of dollars for a range of investments that can facilitate the re-entry of ex-offenders and increase the safety of our city streets." These savings, and the human capital investments they will permit, might well be complemented by more intensive community reinvestment activities.

National Community Reinvestment Coalition (NCRC). And the data from Seattle showed lending under the CRA rubric to have a particularly strong effect on crime rates: whereas a $10,000 increase in the average loan amount for all lenders led to a reduction of 9.1 violent crimes per 1,000 residents, for CRA-covered lenders the reduction was 12.1.

## Mortgage Money Matters

The benefits of access to capital and credit are clear to individuals seeking to buy a home. Without a mortgage loan, the vast majority of U.S. homeowners today would be renters. Homeownership, in addition to providing stable shelter, is also critical for wealth accumulation for most families. According to Harvard's Joint Center for Housing Studies, half of all homeowners in the United States hold 50% or more of their net wealth in home equity. As NCRC president John Taylor observed, "Lending is good for America. Access to credit and capital is the traditional method that allows any family to build equity and create wealth. CRA brings more wealth, more stakeholders, and more parity."

But more mortgage investment in a community also benefits neighborhood residents who did not apply for a loan in any given year and those who are not homeowners at all. Where injections of mortgage loans increase homeownership, property values tend to increase, including for homes owned by longstanding residents. Neighborhoods with relatively high levels of homeownership generally have superior public services including, most importantly, better public schools. And now we know that such neighborhoods have safer streets. An additional benefit of community reinvestment, therefore, is that it constitutes a crime-fighting tactic that can also be a money saver for taxpayers and state governments. (See "Investment, Not Imprisonment.")

The neighborhoods most likely to benefit from an increase in mortgage lending to low- and moderate-income urbanites are those which tend to be the most distressed, those least likely to be served by conventional financial institutions, and those to which former inmates generally return. A recent study of New Haven, Conn., by the Council of State Governments, for example, found that three such neighborhoods accounted for more than half the city's residents incarcerated in that state. Jeremy Travis and his colleagues at the Urban Institute found that more than 34% of ex-offenders returning to Chicago settled in just 6 of its 77 communities, all of which were economically disadvantaged. No doubt this is not unique to these two cities. And no doubt the impact of mortgage lending on crime is not unique to Seattle.

Investment matters. Policy counts. CRA and other fair lending rules have increased access to home mortgage loans and other types of credit in the nation's cities. And now there is evidence that such investment can and does reduce neighborhood crime rates.

But future progress cannot be guaranteed. And there is much to be done. While homeownership rates have reached record highs in recent years, critical racial disparities persist. According to the Joint Center's 2004 report "The State of the Nation's Housing," 75% of white households are homeowners, compared to less than 50% of black and Hispanic households. Yet at a time when CRA and related fair lending laws appear to be working, and when the need for them continues, they are under attack. Congress and the federal financial regulatory agencies have reduced the share of mortgage lenders covered by CRA and weakened the CRA examination process. NCRC's Taylor concluded that if steps are not taken to restore the authority of the CRA, "Americans' access to credit and capital will diminish dramatically." At a time when virtually all the available research demonstrates that CRA has been meeting its intended objectives and more, it is indeed time to strengthen, rather than weaken, the law.

Lower crime rates would be one result. "You can't incarcerate your way out of [the crime] problem," observed Dan Satterberg, chief of staff for the conservative Republican Norm Maleng, the King County (Seattle) prosecutor since 1979. Community reinvestment can be part of an effective alternative to incarceration.

# THE HOMEOWNERSHIP MYTH

## BY HOWARD KARGER

*May/June 2007*

Anyone who has given the headlines even a passing glance this winter knows the subprime mortgage industry is in deep trouble. Since 2006 more than 20 subprime lenders have quit the business or gone bankrupt. Many more are in serious trouble, including the nation's number two subprime lender, New Century Financial. The subprime crisis is also hitting Wall Street brokerages that invested in these loans, with reverberations from Tokyo to London. And the worst may be yet to come. At least $300 billion in subprime adjustable-rate mortgages will reset this year to higher interest rates. CNN reports that one in five subprime mortgages issued in 2005-2006 will end up in foreclosure. If these dire predictions come true, it will be the equivalent of a nuclear meltdown in the mortgage and housing industries.

What's conspicuously absent from the news reports is the effect of the subprime lending debacle on poor and working class families who bought into the dream of homeownership, regardless of the price. Sold a false bill of goods, many of these families now face foreclosure and the loss of the small savings they invested in their homes. It's critical to examine the housing crisis not only from the perspective of the banks and the stock market, but also from the perspective of the families whose homes are on the line. It is also critical to uncover the systemic reasons for the recent burst of housing-market insanity that saw thousands upon thousands of families getting signed up for mortgage loans that were highly likely to end in failure and foreclosure.

Like most Americans, I grew up believing that buying a home represents a rite of passage in U.S. society. Americans widely view homeownership as the best choice for everyone, everywhere and at all times. The more people who own their own homes, the common wisdom goes, the more robust the economy, the stronger the community, and the greater the collective and individual benefits. Homeownership is the ticket to the middle class through asset accumulation, stability, and civic participation.

For the most part, this is an accurate picture. Homeowners get a foothold in a housing market with an almost infinite price ceiling. They enjoy important tax benefits. Owning a home is often cheaper than renting. Most important, homeownership builds equity and accrues assets for the next generation, in part by promoting forced savings. These savings are reflected in the data showing that, according to the National Housing Institute's Winton Picoff, the median wealth of low-income homeowners is 12 times higher than that of renters with similar incomes. Plus, owning a home is a status symbol: homeowners are seen as winners compared to renters.

Homeownership may have positive effects on family life. Ohio University's Robert Dietz found that owning a home contributes to household stability, social involvement, environmental awareness, local political participation and activism, good health, low crime, and beneficial community characteristics. Homeowners are better citizens, are healthier both physically and mentally, and have children who achieve more and are better behaved than those of renters.

Johns Hopkins University researchers Joe Harkness and Sandra Newman looked at whether homeownership benefits kids even in distressed neighborhoods. Their study concluded that "[h]omeownership in almost any neighborhood is found to benefit children. ... Children of most low-income renters would be better served by programs that help their families become homeowners in their current neighborhoods instead of helping them move to better neighborhoods while remaining renters." (Harkness and Newman also found, however, that the positive effects of homeownership on children are weaker in unstable low-income neighborhoods.

### *THE NEW WORLD OF HOME LOANS*

The new home loan products, widely marketed in recent years but especially to low- and moderate-income families, are generally adjustable-rate mortgages (ARMs) with some kind of twist. Here are a few of these "creative" (read: confusing and risky) mortgage options.

**Option ARM:** *With this loan, borrowers choose each month which of three or four different—and fluctuating—payments to make:*

- full (principal + interest) payment based on a 30-year or 15-year repayment schedule.
- interest-only payment—does not reduce the loan principal or build homeowner equity. Borrowers who pay only interest for a period of time then face a big jump in the size of monthly payments or else are forced to refinance.
- minimum payment—may be lower than one month's interest; if so, the shortfall is added to the loan balance. The result is "negative amortization": over time, the principal goes up, not down. Eventually the borrower may have an "upside down" mortgage where the debt is greater than the market value of the home. According to the credit rating firm Fitch Ratings, up to 80% of all option ARM borrowers choose the minimum monthly payment option. So it's no surprise that in 2005, 20% of option ARMs were "upside down." When a negative amortization limit is reached, the minimum payment jumps up to fully amortize the loan for the remaining loan term. In other words, borrowers suddenly have to start paying the real bill.
- Even borrowers who pay more than the monthly minimums can face payment shocks. Option ARMs often start with a temporary super-low teaser rate (and correspondingly low monthly payments) that allows borrowers to qualify for "more house." The catch? Since the low initial monthly payment, based on interest rates as low as 1.25%, is not enough to cover the real interest rate, the borrower eventually faces a sudden increase in monthly payments.

Moreover, the study cannot distinguish whether homeownership leads to positive behaviors or whether owners were already predisposed to these behaviors.)

Faith in the benefits of homeownership—along with low interest rates and a range of governmental incentives—have produced a surge in the number of low-income homeowners. By 2003, 48% of black households owned their own homes, up from 34.5% in 1950. In 1994 Bill Clinton set—and ultimately surpassed—a goal to raise the nation's overall homeownership rate to 67.5% by 2000. There are now 71 million U.S. homeowners, representing close to 68% of all households. Much of this gain has been among low-income families.

Government efforts to increase homeownership for low-income families include

**Balloon Loan:** This loan is written for a short 5- to 7-year term during which the borrower pays either interest and principal each month or, in a more predatory form, interest only. At the end of the loan term, the borrower must pay off the entire loan in a lump sum—the "balloon payment." At that point, buyers must either refinance or lose their homes. Balloon loans are known to real estate pros as "bullet loans," since if the loan comes due during a period of high interest rates, it's like getting a bullet in the heart. According to the national organizing and advocacy group ACORN, about 10% of all subprime loans are balloons.

Balloon loans are sometimes structured with monthly payments that fail to cover the interest, much less pay down the principal. Although the borrower makes regular payments, her loan balance increases each month: negative amortization. Many borrowers are unaware that they have a negative amortization loan until they have to refinance.

**Shared Appreciation Mortgages (SAM):** These are fixed-rate loans for up to 30 years that have easier credit qualifications and lower monthly payments than conventional mortgages. In exchange for a lower interest rate, the borrower relinquishes part of the future value of the home to the lender. Interest rate reductions are based on how much appreciation the borrower is willing to give up. SAMs discourage "sweat equity" since the homeowner receives only some fraction of the appreciation resulting from any remodeling. Not surprisingly, these loans have been likened to sharecropping.

**Stated-Income Loan:** Aimed at borrowers who do not draw regular wages from an employer but live on tips, casual jobs that pay under-the-table, commissions, or investments, this loan does not require W-2 forms or other standard wage documentation. The trade-off: higher-interest rates.

**No-Ratio Loan:** The debt-income ratio (the borrower's monthly payments on debt, including the planned mortgage, divided by her monthly income) is a standard benchmark that lenders use to determine how large a mortgage they will write. In return for a higher interest rate, the no-ratio loan abandons this benchmark; it is aimed at borrowers with complex financial lives or those who are experiencing divorce, the death of a spouse, or a career change.

*—Amy Gluckman*

both demand-side (e.g., homeowner tax credits, housing cost assistance programs) and supply-side (e.g., developer incentives) strategies. Federal housing programs insure more than a million loans a year to help low-income homebuyers. Fannie Mae and Freddie Mac—the large, federally chartered but privately held corporations that buy mortgages from lenders, guarantee the notes, and then resell them to investors—have increasingly turned their attention to low-income homebuyers as the upper-income housing market becomes more saturated. Banking industry regulations such as the Community Reinvestment Act and the Home Mortgage Disclosure Act encourage homeownership by reducing lending discrimination in underserved markets.

The Housing and Urban Development department (HUD) has adapted some of its programs originally designed to help renters to focus on homeownership. For instance, cities and towns can now use the federal dollars they receive through HOME (the Home Investment Partnerships Act) and Community Development Block Grants to provide housing grants, down payment loans, and closing cost assistance. The American Dream Downpayment Initiative, passed by Congress in 2003, authorized up to $200 million a year for down payment assistance to low-income families. Private foundations have followed suit. The Ford Foundation is currently focusing its housing-related grants on homeownership rather than rental housing; the foundation views homeownership as an important form of asset-building and the best option for low-income people.

While homeownership has undeniable benefits, that doesn't mean it is the best option for everyone. For many low-income families, buying a home imposes burdens that end up outweighing the benefits. It is time to re-assess the policy emphasis on homeownership, which has been driven by an honest belief in the advantages of homeownership, but also by a wide range of business interests who stand to gain when a new cohort of buyers is brought into the housing market.

## The Downsides of Homeownership

Low-income families can run into a range of pitfalls when they buy homes. These pitfalls may stem from the kinds of houses they can afford to buy (often in poor condition, with high maintenance costs); the neighborhoods they can afford to buy in (often economically distressed); the financing they can get (often carrying high interest rates, high fees, and risky gimmicks); and the jobs they work at (often unstable). Taken together, these factors can make buying a home a far riskier proposition for low-income families than it is for middle- and upper-income households.

Most low-income families only have the financial resources to buy rundown houses in distressed neighborhoods marked by few jobs, high crime rates, a dearth of services, and poor schools. Few middle-class homebuyers would hitch themselves to 30-year mortgages in these kinds of communities; poor families, too, have an interest in making the home-buying commitment in safe neighborhoods with good schools.

Homeownership is no automatic hedge against rising housing costs. On the contrary: lower-end affordable housing stock is typically old, in need of repair, and expensive to maintain. Low-income families often end up paying inflated prices for homes that are beset with major structural or mechanical problems masked by cosmetic repairs. A University of North Carolina study sponsored by the national nonprofit organization NeighborWorks found that almost half of low-income homebuyers experienced major unexpected costs due to the age and condition of their homes. If you rent, you can call the landlord; but a homeowner can't take herself to court because the roof leaks, the plumbing is bad, or the furnace or hot water heater quits working.

Besides maintenance and repairs, the expenses of homeownership also include property taxes and homeowners insurance, both of which have skyrocketed in cost in the last decade. Between 1997 and 2002 property tax rates rose nationally by more than 19%. Ten states (including giants Texas and California) saw their property tax rates rise by 30% or more during that period. In the suburbs of New York City, property tax rates grew two to three times faster than personal income from 2000 to 2004.

Nationally, the average homeowner's annual insurance premiums rose a whopping 62% from 1995 to 2005—twice as fast as inflation. Low-income homeowners in distressed neighborhoods are hit especially hard by high insurance costs. According to a Conning and Co. study, 92% of large insurance companies run credit checks on potential customers. These credit checks translate into insurance scores that are used to determine whether the carrier will insure an applicant at all, and if so, what they will cover and how much they will charge. Those with poor or no credit are denied coverage, while those with limited credit pay high premiums. Needless to say, many low-income homeowners do not have stellar credit scores. Credit scoring may also partly explain why, according to HUD, "Recent studies have shown that, compared to homeowners in predominantly white-occupied neighborhoods, homeowners in minority neighborhoods are less likely to have private home insurance, more likely to have policies that provide less coverage in case of a loss, and are likely to pay more for similar policies."

With few cash reserves, low-income families are a heartbeat away from financial disaster if their wages decline, property taxes or home insurance rates rise, or expensive repairs are needed. With most—or all—of their savings in their homes, these families have no cushion for emergencies. HUD data show that between 1999 and 2001, the only group whose housing conditions worsened—by HUD's definition, the only group which saw a larger share of households paying over 30% of gross household income for housing in 2001 than in 1999) were low- and moderate-income homeowners. The National Housing Conference reports that 51% of working families with critical housing needs (i.e., those paying more than 50% of gross household income for housing) are owners.

Most people who buy a home imagine they will live there for a long time, benefiting from a secure and stable housing situation. For many low-income families this is not what happens. Nationwide data from 1976 to 1993 reveal that 36% of low-income homeowners gave up or lost their homes within two years and 53% exited within five years, according to a 2005 study by Carolina Katz Reid of the University of Washington. Reid found that very few low-income families ever bought another house after returning to renting. A 2004 HUD research study by Donald Haurin and Stuart Rosenthal reached similar conclusions. Following a national sample of African Americans from youth (ages 14 to 21) in 1979 to middle age in 2000, the researchers found that 63% of the sample owned a home at some point, but only

34% still did in 2000.

Low-income homeowners, often employed in unstable jobs with stagnant incomes, few health care benefits, limited or no sick days, and little vacation time, may find it almost impossible to keep their homes if they experience a temporary job loss or a change in family circumstances, such as the loss of a wage earner. Homeownership can also limit financial opportunities. A 1999 study by economists Richard Green (University of Wisconsin) and Patric Hendershott (Ohio State University) found that states with the highest homeownership rates also had the highest unemployment rates. Their report concluded that homeownership may constrain labor mobility since the high costs of selling a house make unemployed homeowners reluctant to relocate to find work.

Special tax breaks have been a key selling point of homeownership. If mortgage interest and other qualifying expenses come to less than the standard deduction ($10,300 for joint filers in 2006), however, there is zero tax advantage to owning. That is one reason why only 34% of taxpayers itemize their mortgage interest, local property taxes, and other deductions. Even for families who do itemize, the effective tax saving is usually only 10 to 35 cents for every dollar paid in mortgage interest. In other words, the mortgage deduction benefits primarily those in high income brackets who have a need to shelter their income; it means little to low-income homeowners.

Finally, homeownership promises growing wealth as home prices rise. But the homes of low-income, especially minority, homeowners generally do not appreciate as much as middle-class housing. Low-income households typically purchase homes in distressed neighborhoods where significant appreciation is unlikely. Among other reasons, if financially-stressed property owners on the block can't afford to maintain their homes, nearby property values fall. For instance, Reid's longitudinal study surveyed low-income minority homeowners from 1976 to 1994 and found that they realized a 30% increase in the value of their homes after owning for 10 years, while middle- and upper-income white homeowners enjoyed a 60% jump.

## "Funny Money" Mortgages And Other Travesties

Buying a home and taking on a mortgage are scary, and people often leave the closing in a stupor, unsure of what they signed or why. My partner and I bought a house a few years ago, and like many buyers, we didn't retain an attorney. The title company had set aside one hour for the closing. During that time more than 125 single-spaced pages (much of it in small print) were put in front of us. More than 60 required our signature or initials. It would have been difficult for us to digest these documents in 24 hours, much less one. When we asked to slow down the process, we were met with impatience. After the closing, Anna asked, "What did we sign?" I was clueless.

Yet buying a home is the largest purchase most families will make in their lifetimes, the largest expenditure in a family budget, and the single largest asset for two-thirds of homeowners. It's also the most fraught with danger.

For low-income families in particular, homeownership can turn out to be more a crushing debt than an asset-building opportunity. The primary reason for this is the growing chasm between ever-higher home prices and the stagnant incomes of millions of working-class Americans. The last decade has seen an unprecedented surge in home prices, which have risen 35% nationally. While the housing bubble is largely confined to specific metropolitan areas in the South, the Southwest, and the two coasts (home prices rose 50% in the Pacific states and 60% in New England), there are also bubbles in Midwestern cities like Chicago and Minneapolis. And although the housing bubble is most pronounced in high-end properties, the prices of low-end homes have also spiked in many markets.

Current incomes simply do not support these inflated home prices. For example, only 18% of Californians can afford the median house in the state using traditional loan-affordability calculations. Even the fall in mortgage interest rates in the 1990s and early 2000s was largely neutralized by higher property taxes, higher insurance premiums, and rising utility costs.

This disparity might have put a dent in the mortgage finance business. But no: in 2005, Americans owed $5.7 trillion in mortgages, a 50% increase in just four years. Over the past decade the mortgage finance industry has developed creative schemes designed to squeeze potential homebuyers, albeit often temporarily, into houses they cannot afford. It is a sleight of hand that requires imaginative and risky financing for both buyers and financial institutions.

Most of the "creative" new mortgage products fall into the category of subprime mortgages—those offered to people whose problematic credit drops them into a lower lending category. Subprime mortgages carry interest rates ranging from a few points to ten points or more above the prime or market rate, plus onerous loan terms. The subprime mortgage industry is growing: lenders originated $173 billion in subprime loans in 2005, up from only $25 billion in 1993. By 2006 the subprime market was valued at $600 billion, one-fifth of the $3 trillion U.S. mortgage market.

Subprime lending can be risky. In the 37 years since the Mortgage Bankers Association (MBA) began conducting its annual national mortgage delinquency survey, 2006 saw the highest share of home loans entering foreclosure. According to the MBA, in early 2007 13.5% of subprime mortgages were delinquent (compared to 4.95% of prime-rate mortgages) and 4.5% were in foreclosure. By all accounts, this is just the tip of the iceberg. However, before the current collapse the rate of return for subprime lenders was spectacular. Forbes claimed that subprime lenders could realize returns up to six times greater than the best-run banks.

In the past there were two main kinds of home mortgages: fixed-rate loans and adjustable-rate loans (ARMs). In a fixed-rate mortgage, the interest rate stays the same throughout the 15- to 30-year loan term. In a typical ARM the interest rate varies over the course of the loan, although there is usually a cap. Both kinds of loans traditionally required borrowers to provide thorough documentation of their finances and a downpayment of at least 10% of the purchase price, and often 20%.

Adjustable-rate loans can be complicated, and a Federal Reserve study found that fully 25% of homeowners with ARMs were confused about their loan terms. Nonetheless, ARMs are attractive because in the short run they promise a home with an artificially low interest rate and affordable payments.

Even so, traditional ARMs proved inadequate to the tasks of ushering low-income families into the housing market and generally keeping home sales up in the face of skyrocketing home prices. So in recent years the mortgage industry created a whole range of "affordability" products with names like "no-ratio loans," "option ARMS," and "balloon loans" that it doled out like candy to people who were never fully apprised of the intricacies of these complicated loans. (See sidebar for a glossary of the new mortgage products.) These new mortgage options have opened the door for almost anyone to secure a mortgage, whether or not their circumstances auger well for repayment. They also raise both the costs and risks of buying a home—sometimes steeply—for the low- and moderate-income families to whom they're largely marketed.

Beyond the higher interest rates (at some point in the loan term if not at the start) that characterize the new "affordability" mortgages, low-income homebuyers face other costs as well. For instance, predatory and subprime lenders often require credit life insurance, which pays off a mortgage if the homeowner dies, to be added to the loan. This insurance is frequently sold either by the lender's subsidiary or else by a company that pays the lender a commission. Despite low pay-outs, lenders frequently charge high premiums for credit life insurance.

As many as 80% of subprime loans include prepayment penalties if the borrower pays off or refinances the loan early, a scam that costs low-income borrowers about $2.3 billion a year and increases the risk of foreclosure by 20%. Prepayment penalties lock borrowers into a loan by making it difficult to sell the home or refinance with a different lender. And while some borrowers face penalties for paying off their loans ahead of schedule, others discover that their mortgages have so-called "call provisions" that permit the lender to accelerate the loan term even if payments are current.

And then there are all of the costs outside of the mortgage itself. Newfangled mortgage products are often sold not by banks directly, but by a rapidly growing crew of mortgage brokers who act as finders or "bird dogs" for lenders. There are approximately 53,000 mortgage brokerage companies in the United States employing an estimated 418,700 people, according to the National Association of Mortgage Brokers; BusinessWeek notes that brokers now originate up to 80% of all new mortgages.

Largely unregulated, mortgage brokers live off loan fees. Their transactions are primed for conflicts of interest or even downright corruption. For example, borrowers pay brokers a fee to help them secure a loan. Brokers may also receive kickbacks from lenders for referring a borrower, and many brokers steer clients to the lenders that pay them the highest kickbacks rather than those offering the lowest interest rates. Closing documents use arcane language ("yield spread premiums," "service release fees") to hide these kickbacks. And some hungry brokers find less-than-kosher ways to make the sale, including fudging paperwork, arranging for inflated appraisals, or helping buyers find co-signers who have no intention of guaranteeing the loan.

Whether or not a broker is involved, lenders can inflate closing costs in a variety of ways: charging outrageous document preparation fees; billing for recording fees in excess of the law; "unbundling," whereby closing costs are padded by duplicating charges already included in other categories.

All in all, housing is highly susceptible to the predations of the fringe economy. Unscrupulous brokers and lenders have considerable latitude to ply their trade, especially with vulnerable low-income borrowers.

Time to Change Course

Despite the hype, homeownership is not a cure-all for low-income families who earn less than a living wage and have poor prospects for future income growth. In fact, for some low-income families homeownership only leads to more debt and financial misery. With mortgage delinquencies and foreclosures at record levels, especially among low-income households, millions of people would be better off today if they had remained renters. Surprisingly, rents are generally more stable than housing prices. From 1995 to 2001 rents rose slightly faster than inflation, but not as rapidly as home prices. Beginning in 2004 rent increases began to slow—even in hot markets like San Francisco and Seattle—and fell below the rate of inflation.

In the mid-1980s, low- and no-downpayment mortgages led to increased foreclosures when the economy tanked. Today, these mortgages are back, along with a concerted effort to drive economically marginal households into homeownership and high levels of unsustainable debt. To achieve this goal, the federal government spends $100 billion a year for homeownership programs (including the $70+ billion the mortgage interest deduction costs the Treasury).

Instead of focusing exclusively on homeownership, a more progressive and balanced housing policy would address the diverse needs of communities for both homes and rental units, and would facilitate new forms of ownership such as community land trusts and cooperatives. A balanced policy would certainly aim to expand the stock of affordable rental units. Unfortunately, just the opposite is occurring: rental housing assistance is being starved to feed low-income homeownership programs. From 2004 to 2006, President Bush and the Congress cut federal funding for public housing alone by 11%. Over the same period, more than 150,000 rental housing vouchers were cut. And, of course, policymakers must act to protect those consumers who do opt to buy homes: for instance, by requiring mortgage lenders to make certain not only that a borrower is eligible for a particular loan product, but that the loan is suitable for the borrower.

The reason the United States lacks a sound housing policy is obvious if we follow the money. Overheated housing markets and rising home prices produce lots of winners. Real estate agents reap bigger commissions. Mortgage brokers, appraisers, real estate attorneys, title companies, lenders, builders, home remodelers, and everyone else with a hand in the housing pie does well. Cities raise more in property taxes, and insurance companies enroll more clients at higher premiums. Although housing accounts for only 5% of GDP, it has been responsible for up to 75% of all U.S. job growth in the last four years, according to the consulting firm Oxford Analytica. Housing has buffered the economy, and herding more low-income families into homes, regardless of the consequences, helps keep the industry ticking. The only losers? Renters squeezed by higher rents and accelerating conversion of rental units into condos. Young middle-income families trying to buy their first house. And, especially, the thousands of low-income families for whom buying a home turns into a financial nightmare.

*Resources:* Carolina Katz Reid, "Studies in Demography and Ecology: Achieving the American

Dream? A Longitudinal Analysis of the Homeownership Experiences of Low-Income Households." Univ. of Washington, CSDE Working Paper No. 04-04; Dean Baker, "The Housing Bubble: A Time Bomb in Low-Income Communities?" *Shelterforce Online*, Issue #135, May/June 2004, http://www.nhi.org/online/issues/135/bubble.html; Howard Karger, Shortchanged: Life and Debt in the Fringe Economy (Berrett-Koehler, 2005); National Multi Housing Council (www.nmhc.org).

# THREE MILLION AMERICANS ARE DEBT POOR

**BY STEVEN PRESSMAN AND ROBERT SCOTT**

*July/August 2007*

Signs of the debt crisis facing a growing number of U.S. households are not hard to find. The subprime lending debacle, with its mushrooming rates of mortgage default and foreclosure, has been front-page news for months—perhaps because it has made victims of Wall Street firms as well as Main Street homeowners. Although less of a focus in the media, consumer debt—that is, household debt excluding mortgages and home-equity loans—is rising as well. Consumer indebtedness has reached record levels in the United States, currently averaging more than $21,000 per household, according to Federal Reserve data.

Rising consumer indebtedness can put families from across the income spectrum into precarious financial straits. However, it is poor and low- to middle-income families for whom the combination of stagnating incomes and rising debt creates the greatest risks. Yet the standard approach to calculating a poverty level of income and estimating the number of Americans who are poor fails to account for rising debt and the interest payments on that debt. If it did, about three million more Americans, including over half a million children, would be recognized as living below the poverty line.

## Weighing Debt, Measuring Poverty

Consumer debt comes in many shapes and sizes (see sidebar). To measure the burden of household debt, economists generally look at the consumer debt-to-income ratio. Households with high incomes generally have lower debt-to-income ratios (see "Household Debt-to-Income Ratios"). Poor and near-poor households, on the other hand, are heavily in debt. The average amount of consumer debt per poor household is over $7,300, with debt-to-income ratios exceeding 60%.

Such high levels of consumer debt are new. For the median U.S. household, consumer debt has increased nearly tenfold in real terms (i.e., adjusted for inflation) since the early 1960s and is now growing at over 5% a year. Debt levels and debt-to-income ratios for low-income households have risen even faster than for more prosperous households. And predictably, interest payments (relative to income) have now reached their highest level ever. In 2005, the average household spent over 4% of its income servicing consumer debt, compared to just 0.8% in 1959 (see "Servicing Consumer Debt").

Rising debt and interest payments distort much economic data; most noteworthy is how they affect estimates of poverty. In 2005 (the most recent year for which data are available), 12.6% of Americans were poor according to the official U.S. Census Bureau tabulation. The poverty rate stood at 11.7% in 2001, when the Bush administration took office; it rose each year, hitting 12.6% in 2004 and again in 2005. But even these disheartening figures are too optimistic. Policymakers assume that when income (adjusted for inflation) goes up, households' living standards rise as well. But this assumption ignores the problem of rising debt. When more income must go to pay down debt or even just to cover interest charges, households have less money to meet day-to-day expenses and their living standards stagnate or fall.

The U.S. government's official definition of poverty was developed in the early 1960s by economist Mollie Orshansky of the Social Security Administration. In Orshansky's model, still used by the federal government today, the poverty-level income is equal to a basic food budget for a family of a given size multiplied by three. The model assumes, in other words, that food represents about one-third of a family's budget. Every year, the poverty threshold is adjusted based on the annual rise in consumer prices.

For a single person under age 65, the poverty threshold was $10,488 in 2006; for a single mother with two children, it was $16,242. For a family of four, the 2006

**SERVICING CONSUMER DEBT**

Share of income required to service consumer debt for the average U.S. household

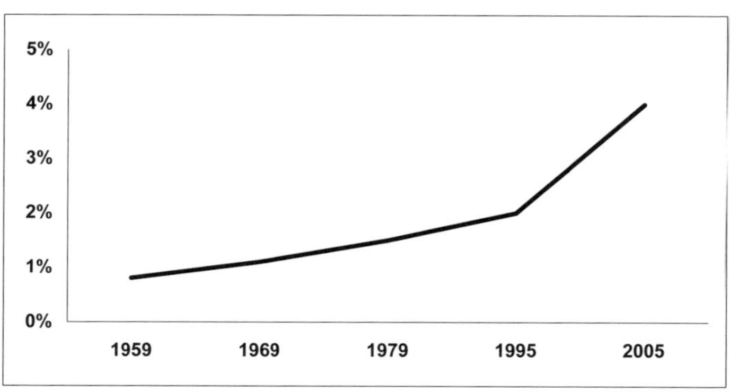


*Source:* Authors' calculations based on data from Federal Reserve Board, Release G.19; and U.S. Department of Commerce, Bureau of Economic Analysis.

### *TYPES OF CONSUMER DEBT*

Families take on consumer debt for many reasons and in many ways. Here are the most significant forms of consumer debt:

**Installment debt**— The largest category of consumer debt for the average household, amounting to more than $8,000 per household (2004). These loans are used for large purchases (computers, televisions, furniture, home appliances) and typically have long repayment periods and low interest rates.

**Vehicle debt**— Averaging more than $5,000 per household, the second largest category of consumer debt. With increasing sprawl, people rely on their cars more and more to get to work and school; U.S. households now have on average 1.9 vehicles—for 1.8 drivers. But vehicles are expensive; few people can afford to buy one (let alone two or three) outright. Those with strong credit histories may qualify for optimal terms on car loans, including very low interest rates, but others can borrow only in the subprime market, at far higher rates.

**Education debt**— A relatively new phenomenon, but one that has been rising rapidly. College tuitions have risen far faster than inflation over the past two decades, in part because the government has reduced aid to colleges and universities. At the same time, financial aid for students has increasingly come in the form of loans rather than grants. These factors, in combination, account for the fact four-year college students today graduate with a median debt of about $16,000.

**Revolving credit card debt**— Different from installment debt in that monthly payments and interest rates can both vary over time. Unless a credit card bill is paid in full each month, interest charges are applied to the remaining balance. Interest rates on credit card debt range from 0% to over 30%, with a national average of 14%; the average U.S. household owes about $3,000 in credit card debt.

figure was $20,444—equal in real dollars, i.e., in purchasing power, to the 1962 poverty line of $3,100 for a family of four.

The current poverty thresholds are widely seen as unrealistic at best. So how to measure poverty has become a contentious issue, and Orshansky's methodology has for some time been criticized on a number of grounds by academics and policymakers. Some have pointed out that the food budgets Orshansky used were meant for emergency purposes only and could not sustain people for an extended period of time. Indeed, the food budgets she used were set at 80% of a permanent nutritionally adequate diet. Others have complained that her estimates fail to account for taxes paid by the poor and the near-poor, who may pay little or no income tax but are still subject to payroll taxes. Still others criticize the model for overlooking government benefits that low-income families receive, such as Food Stamps, Medicaid, and housing vouchers, arguing that the value of these benefits should be added to household income.

In all these debates, Americans' rising indebtedness has gone unnoticed. Many

Americans have incomes above the poverty line, but because they must use a portion of their income to service their debt, they cannot buy the goods and services needed to escape poverty. These people are debt poor, and they should be recognized as poor by the government.

Using the Federal Reserve's *Survey of Consumer Finances*, we calculated that indebtedness of households with incomes up to 50% above the poverty line increased from $150 (the equivalent of around $1,000 today) in the early 1960s to over $4,000 in 2005. At the going interest rate, a typical low-income household in 2005 spent more than $400 servicing its past debt, compared to interest payments of just $10 to $20 (around $100 today) in the early 1960s. In the late 1950s, when poverty was first measured, both consumer debt and interest were negligible for poor households—mostly because the poor had limited access to formal credit markets.

Taking account of higher interest payments by American households, we calculate that the poverty rate for 2005 should have been around 13.6%, nearly 8% higher than the official rate. Put into concrete terms, this means that three million additional Americans should be counted as poor due to their high consumer debt and interest payments.

The effect of consumer debt on child poverty rates is particularly worrisome. Ayana Douglas-Hall and Heather Koball of the National Center for Children in Poverty already refer to children as the United States' "new poor" because 18% of children (13.4 million, in 2005) live in households with incomes below the poverty level. This marks an increase of 12% over the past five years. But again, this figure is too low. When interest on consumer debt is factored in, child poverty rises to 19%. Over half a million children in the United States are debt poor today, none of whom are included in official government poverty estimates.

## Lifting the Burden

There are several reasons for the growing phenomenon of debt poverty. The federal minimum wage has been set at $5.15 an hour since 1997 and, until the increase Congress enacted this year takes effect, is at its lowest level in real terms (i.e., in purchasing power) in the past 50 years. At the same time, globalization, the skill requirements of a global economy, and an administration hostile to U.S. workers have all been forces restraining real income gains for low- and middle-income households.

A number of policy changes would help to remedy the problem. In addition to the minimum-wage increase, Congress should raise the child care tax credit

**HOUSEHOLD DEBT-TO-INCOME RATIOS, BY INCOME (2004)**

| *Income Range* | $35,000 to $40,000 | $40,000 to $45,000 | $45,000 to $50,000 | $50,000 to $55,000 | $55,000 and more |
|---|---|---|---|---|---|
| *D-I Ratio* | 61% | 44% | 48% | 39% | 29% |

Source : Federal Reserve Board, Survey of Consumer Finances, 2004.

and enact limits on credit-card interest rates. We also need to educate low-— and middle-income people about the potential dangers of consumer credit. Finally, the government must provide more money to colleges and universities, especially those that cater to middle- and low-income students, so that they can keep their tuition and fee increases under the rate of inflation. Doing so would both reduce families' debt and increase college attendance and future earnings.

Unless the problem of fast-rising consumer indebtedness is recognized and addressed in short order with steps such as these, George W. Bush is likely to become one of the very few presidents since the Great Depression to preside over rising poverty rates. And if we take rising consumer debt into account, he is likely to preside over the largest increase in poverty since the government began to measure it.

*Resources:* Jeffrey J. Williams, "Debt Education: Bad for America, Bad for the Young," *Dissent,* Summer 2006; Leslie Miller, "Cars, Trucks Now Outnumber People," *Salon,* Aug. 29, 2003; Federal Reserve Board, *Survey of Consumer Finances,* 2004.

Chapter 6

# THE INTERNATIONAL FINANCIAL SYSTEM

## LEARNING FROM THE SOUTHEAST ASIAN CRISIS

**BY JOHN MILLER**

*November/December 1998*

***Summer 1997: By August, bullishness on Asia's miracle economies disappears. The Thai economy suffers a financial meltdown. The Thai currency, the baht, loses 40% of its value vis-a-vis the dollar. The Thai stock market crashes, off 70% from its peak in 1994.***

The miracle economies of Southeast Asia are in depression. Conditions vary from country to country. Recession prevails in Malaysia, and in Thailand the steep downturn will cost over two million workers their jobs by the end of 1998. In Indonesia, crippling stagflation threatens to double prices at the same time that it pushes nearly one half the population into poverty.

These once high-flying Southeast Asian economies are tending to the wounds from their sudden fall to earth. Thailand and Indonesia are in receivership, undergoing austerity measures administered by the International Monetary Fund (IMF) in return for emergency loans to help repay foreign lenders. Meanwhile Malaysia independently administers similar austerity measures. The $63 billion bailout crafted by the IMF and the U.S. Treasury exceeds the U.S. financed bailout of Mexico in 1995. With South Korea added in, the East Asian bailout package is over $100 billion.

The IMF continues to say that the leading economies in the region — Indonesia, Malaysia, the Philippines, and Thailand — will recover in 1999, if only modestly. But the Thai and Indonesian economies may not have hit bottom yet.

More pessimistic observers fear that the Southeast Asian financial crisis has triggered a deflationary spiral likely to suck all of East Asia, and perhaps the world, into a depression. The threat of economic collapse is real enough, especially if conditions worsen in Japan, the region's most important economy and already suffering a decade-long recession. During most of the 1990s, East Asia accounted for nearly one-half of the expansion of the world economy. In addition, the region's financial crisis has rattled financial markets around the globe in a way the Mexican peso crisis of 1995 never did. Latin American, European, and Russian currencies all have come under attack. Even the booming U.S. economy slowed this summer under the weight of a ballooning trade deficit caused by fewer exports to East Asia.

For those not blinded by free market faith, the Southeast Asian crisis is a shocking reminder of the failures of markets. Capitalism remains much as Marx and Engels described it one hundred and fifty years ago in the Communist Manifesto — dynamic but unstable and destructive. We need to look more closely at what lessons we can learn from the economic sufferings and financial miseries of Southeast Asia.

## A Story of Market Failure

The financial crisis in Southeast Asia differs in important ways from previous crises in the developing world. Unlike the Latin American debt crisis of the 1980s, the roots of the current turmoil are in private sector, not public sector, borrowing. Most of the afflicted countries have run budget surpluses or minimal budget deficits in recent years. At the same time, private sector borrowing increased heavily, especially from abroad and especially short-term. For instance, loans to Thai corporations from international banks doubled from 1988 to 1994. By 1997, Thai foreign debt stood at $89 billion — four-fifths of which was owed by private corporations. But most disturbingly, one-half of the debt was short-term, falling due inside a year.

The Southeast Asian miracle economies got into trouble when their export boom came to a halt as these short-term loans were due. For instance, stymied by a decline in First World demand, especially from recession-ridden Japan, Thai exports grew not at all in 1996. Also, opening domestic markets to outside money (under an early round of pressure from the IMF) brought a deluge of short term foreign investment and spurred heavy short-term borrowing from abroad, fueling a building boom. By the mid '90s, a speculative binge in everything from high-rise office towers to condos to golf courses accounted for nearly 40% of growth in Thailand.

Now that the bubble has burst, the region endures a horrendous drying out process. Southeast Asian exports from autos to computer chips to steel to textiles now glut international markets, all made worse by intensifying competition from Chinese exports. Foreign financial capital has fled. Domestic spending is collapsing. Banks fail at unprecedented rates. Unemployment mounts, and as more and more people across the region fall into poverty, the Southeast Asian financial crisis has become a story of tremendous human suffering.

In the language of economists, the crisis is also a story of market failure. Southeast Asian capital markets failed in three critical ways. First, too much capital rushed in. Lured by the prospect of continued double digit growth and searching for new places to invest its overflowing coffers, financial capital continued to flow into the real estate sectors of these economies even when financial instability was widespread and obvious to all. Second, the capital markets and the banking system could not channel these funds into productive uses. Too much money went into real estate and too little went into productive investments likely to sustain the export boom. Third, too much capital rushed out, too quickly. The excessive inflow of capital reversed itself and fled with little regard for the actual strength of a particular economy.

In their more candid moments, leaders of the financial community have owned up to these market failures. For instance, late in 1997, just a few months into the crisis, Stanley Fischer, economic director of the IMF, confessed at a regional meeting in Hong Kong that: "Markets are not always right. Sometimes inflows are excessive and sometimes they may be sustained too long. Markets tend to react late; by then they tend to overreact."

## Where the Right went Wrong

Despite the doubts of their high priests, most financial conservatives continue to believe that international markets are stable, if subject to periodic excesses, and that whatever their excesses in the East Asian crisis might be, they can be traced back to a misguided interference into those markets. The culprit varies — industrial policy, crony capitalism, fixed exchange rates or some other shibboleth. But in each case, these conservatives would have it that the economies of Southeast Asia ran into trouble because nonmarket forces had a hand in allocating credit and economic resources better left entirely up to the financiers.

The conservative solution to the crisis? That is easy, if painful: Put an end to these nonmarket allocations of resources. Alan Greenspan, the chair of the U.S. Federal Reserve, believes that the current crisis will root out "the last vestiges" of this sort of thing and ultimately will be regarded as a milestone in the triumph of market capitalism.

But none of the leading economies of the region relies on government-managed industrial policies to direct economic growth. One World Bank study placed Malaysian and Thai trade policies as among the most open in developing economies. Since the 1970s, another study reports, the Thai government tended to "allow free markets rather than to intervene with them."

Nor was the crony capitalism which the right derides the cause of the current crisis. This widespread practice — of political connections guiding private sector investment decisions — was a constant, not a new element in the Southeast Asian economic mix, just as present in the boom as in the crisis.

"Transparency" refers to the dislosure publicly traded companies are required to make about their operations to their investors. But signs galore of financial instability and overcapacity were there for anyone to see, even first-time visitors to the region. Bangkok alone had over $20 billion of vacant residential and commercial units by 1997. Despite plunging returns, foreign investors pumped more loans into Thailand betting that double-digit growth would continue and make these risks pay off.

In addition, we should remember that this crisis hit first and hardest in Thailand and then Indonesia, the two Asian economies with private domestic banking systems recently deregulated and opened to foreigners. The shortfall of Japanese investment in the early 1990s left Thailand desperate for foreign funds. Under pressure from the IMF and the WTO, Thai authorities moved to further open their economy to foreign investors, allowing foreigners to own stock, real estate and banking operations as well. On top of this, government policies lifted Thai interest rates above those in the West, making Thailand a place where westerners could turn a quick buck.

Tying the value of their currencies to the dollar didn't cause the crisis either. Having stable exchange rates was an important building block for the region's trade relations. It allowed manufacturers to import components from Japan and Korea for assembly in Thailand and elsewhere in Southeast Asia, before being sold in the United States and Europe. And pegging the value of their currency to that of the dollar allowed the Thais, for example, to lure capital into their country, fueling investments. But the Thai authorities did not take the next step of regulating the foreign capital that it attracted into its economy this way.

What seems clear now is that the cause of the economic crisis of Southeast Asia was not misaligned exchange rates, or mistaken domestic policy, or even a lack of transparency in the banking sector, although that surely didn't help. Rather the root cause of the crisis now threatening the world with depression is the abrupt reversal of the excessively rapid rise of capital inflows and the falling global demand for the exports from the region that arose from a global economy increasingly turned over to the rule of markets.

By the end of 1997, the Southeast Asian economies suffered "the equivalent of a massive bank run on the region without any lender of last resort," says economist Jan Kregel. In 1996, a net $78 billion flowed into the region from foreign bank loans and short-term portfolio investments like stocks. In 1997, that turned into a $38 billion outflow from the countries most hit by the crisis — Indonesia, Malaysia, South Korea, Thailand and the Phillippines. The biggest drop came in short-term portfolio investment, such as stocks, and bank lending.

The IMF, the prime candidate to act as lender of last resort, turned down the role — instead putting in place policies that imposed more austerity and yet tighter credit conditions. Steadfastly insisting that the cause of crisis was "home grown" as Stanley Fischer of the IMF put it, the IMF tightened credit for these countries already suffering from the disappearance of capital.

Even by the IMF's standard, these austerity measures were applied in an arbitrary and disproportionate manner. First world economies facing financial crises came in for far different treatment. The leading industrialized economies (and the IMF) are urging Japan to increase government spending, cut taxes, and keep interest rates low to counteract its continued economic stagnation — just the opposite of the IMF prescription for the rest of East Asia.

In the Southeast Asian crisis, some reckless behavior was punished, while other reckless behavior was forgiven. Surely international investors are just as much or more responsible for the instability of the region as its local capitalist, bankers, governments, and workers. Yet foreign investors are being bailed out by the IMF, not punished. That is, foreign lenders will have their loans repaid. The IMF has not deemed the foreign shareholders ravaged by plummeting stock prices and collapsing currencies worthy of a bailout. Go figure.

## Lessons For The Left

Left analyses of the crisis need to guard against two excesses: concluding with too much confidence that the Southeast Asian economies have collapsed with rapid growth never to return, and taking the current depression as proof that the growth that preceded the crisis was artificial.

Depressions happen. Or depressions happen again, as Hyman Minsky, the left-leaning economic theorist of financial fragility, would have put it. Financial crises and economic downturns are the flipside of periods of unbridled capitalist growth. For these rapidly expanding, high debt, and now even less regulated Southeast Asian economies to have fallen into crisis is hardly surprising.

But has the current crisis brought the Asian miracle to an end or unleashed the forces that will bring down the world economy? I am not sure. Whether or not the current crisis is the death knell for rapid growth in the region, or the world economy for that matter, I do know that the growth preceding the crisis was dynamic and unstable — much like the capitalist growth that Marx and Engels observed transforming Europe in the middle of the last century. That the growth was based on brutal super-exploitation and relied more often on capital from the outside does not make it artificial or "ersatz," ready to disappear for that reason, as some might claim. After all, the region sustained growth over a long time, not just for the last decade when Japanese investment was heaviest.

The enhanced mobility of capital — domestic and foreign — during the 1990s adds to the instability of these economies and reduces the bargaining power of labor. This is a very real concern, especially in economies such as Indonesia and Thailand where a numbing absence of social accountability has left the investors and corporations to operate unchecked. A profoundly flawed economic development has taken hold, both in their earlier period of rapid growth and in the current crisis.

## Limited Capital Mobility, Sound Economic Development

The proposal most favored in the region to limit capital mobility is a transaction tax on all cross-border flows of capital, designed by Nobel prize winning economist James Tobin. Although on its own it could not cool out a speculative fever or capital panic, the Tobin tax would discourage speculation. As a bonus, the tax revenues collected would more than adequately fund an IMF-style agency, freed from the dictates of the United States, that would bail out bankers and capital investors only when they invest long term, pay living wages, and respect international labor standards.

In September, Malaysia took the more immediate action of imposing capital controls — banning the trading of the Malaysian Ringgit outside of the country. Malaysia's prime minister Mahathir called the plan, "the only way to isolate the economy from the currency speculators and traders" whom he blames for causing the country's economic crisis. Banning the trading of the ringgit in overseas markets in effect decouples the Malaysian economy from the international currency markets. While Malaysian stock prices plummeted in response, the value of the ringgit remained steady, and Mahathir's move found support from some surprising sources.

Maverick mainstream economist, M.I.T.'s Paul Krugman, endorsed the concept of capital controls, for they allowed Malaysian authorities to lower interest rates to counteract Malaysia's recession without causing the ringgit to collapse.

In addition to controlling international capital, whether internationally or domestically, public policy must also compel domestic capital and local elites to accept greater social accountability. Elites seldom pay taxes in these countries. Taxing elites will add to sources of domestic savings and at the same time make more equal the distribution of income. Also giving these governments more money could add to domestic demand — providing a buffer against the shortfall in global demand that had a hand in this crisis. This social accountability must extend to conditions of work as well — notoriously dangerous in Southeast Asia — recognizing the rights of workers to organize, to work in safe conditions, and to earn a living wage.

These forms of social accountability would foster a more sustainable and equitable economic development, and perhaps lay the groundwork for a Southeast Asian economy that does more to relieve human suffering and less to add to it.

# UNFETTERED CAPITAL WREAKS HAVOC

**BY ELLEN FRANK**

*September/October 1998*

Once upon a time, and not so very long ago, most countries restricted the flow of money across their borders. National sovereignty in economic affairs depended upon this. In order to manage their economies, in order to prevent mass unemployment and social upheaval, governments needed the ability to invest, borrow, spend, hire people. To pay for their spending, they needed the ability to print money and control interest rates. But the power to print money and control interest rates is meaningless if the wealthy, who own most of the money, can simply trade their money for a foreign currency and abscond with the wealth. Thus, after World War II, virtually every nation (the U.S. being a very rare exception) placed restrictions on how, when, and how much of its currency businesses and speculators could take out of the country. These restrictions were known as short-term capital controls.

As businesses went global in the 1980s, they pressured governments to eliminate capital controls. An American company producing appliances in Italy for the European market didn't want to be stuck holding its earnings forever in the form of lira in Italian banks. The home office wanted dollars in New York. Multinational businesses and banks wanted the freedom to cash in lira for dollars or francs for yen, as they wished. As global companies spread their operations over the world, capital controls dissolved in their wake. And as controls dissolved, first in Europe, then South America, finally in Asia, speculators — bankers, currency traders, mutual fund managers — moved in. In country after country, financial operators poured money in, eagerly trading dollars or yen for pesos, cruzieros, rupiahs, and rubles, then using the proceeds to lend (at high interest rates) to new, fast-growing businesses or to play the local stock market. Fortunes were made in the receiving countries. In Russia, Mexico, Brazil, Indonesia — the list goes on and on — savvy businessmen and corrupt government officials, touting their open markets, sold off parts of the local economy and pocketed the proceeds.

Today, the concerns that drove countries in the past to restrict this sort of money-trading have, as they say, come home to roost. In Mexico, in Russia, in Korea and Thailand, the bankers and fund managers who lent and bought so eagerly proved just as quick to turn heel and flee. When foreign money pulled out of these countries, their stock markets crashed, banks failed, businesses defaulted on loans and closed for lack of credit. The value of the local currencies plummeted, rendering essential imports unaffordable. While the international banks run to the International Monetary Fund (IMF), clamoring for repayment, the victims of these financial hit-and-runs remain in critical condition. Mexico, for example, with its corrosive unemployment, still has not recovered from its encounter with global banks in 1994 (remember the peso crisis?). The countries of East Asia, whose "crisis" began one year ago, are still reeling, the bottom not yet in sight. Russia, virtually comatose since the ruble crisis of 1991, is now devastated by a new round of capital flight.

Boosters of unfettered money — the global finance industry and its mouthpiece, the IMF — predictably, blame the victims. "Crony capitalism!" "Inefficiency!" "Poor fiscal management!" they crow. They, the public is assured, knew it all along. They, we are told, do the world a service, forcing backwards countries to modernize. What the free-market folks fail to explain is this: If these markets were so inefficient, these economies so badly managed, why were the global banks and fund managers so hot to lend them money in the first place?

Market-boosters have another argument. If the public (via the IMF) doesn't pay off the banks' bad loans and restore their shaken confidence, who will provide new loans to these, now desperate and depressed, economies? How will Mexicans buy corn, Indonesians buy rice, Russians buy grain for their hungry? Are they to starve? Furthermore, if the crisis countries can't buy American-made stuff, Americans will lose jobs. The banks appear to have the world economy in a choke-hold. Countries that can't attract money from the global financial markets can't buy goods on world markets. But the global finance companies won't lend countries money — particularly little countries whose currencies aren't of much use internationally — unless the public underwrites the debt. And here's the kicker. If the banks and mutual funds lend lots of money to a country, then get spooked and start pulling out, thereby setting off a financial panic and causing their own losses — they still want to be repaid.

It is by now obvious that the IMF's response to these "crises" — forcing countries to raise interest rates, the better to attract foreign money to pay their debts to foreign money-lenders — while a boon to financial institutions, is disastrous for the world economy. The crisis in Asia has made it abundantly clear that the prospects for world economic cooperation and development can no longer rest on the whims and dictates of the global financial establishment. It is time to reinstate controls on short-term capital movements. Simple restrictions like imposing taxes, waiting periods, or quotas on cross-border money flows are workable, enforceable and demonstrably effective. The power and mobility of global finance must be curbed.

---

# BYE BYE IMF? A NEW BLUEPRINT FOR THE GLOBAL ECONOMY

**BY ELLEN FRANK**
*July/August 1999*

Just two years ago, the juggernaut of globalization seemed unstoppable. Advocates of labor rights and ecological stability, busy battling the latest corporate-sponsored drives to deregulate global markets, didn't dream of devising their own agenda for global reform. But the catastrophic economic events in East Asia, Russia, and Brazil have altered the policy landscape.

Suddenly, even respectable members of officialdom, like financier George Soros and World Bank vice-president Joseph Stiglitz, speak of the "chaos of global markets" and call for renewed global regulations. Canada's parliament is considering a tax on currency trading, the so-called Tobin tax; the Vatican and the National Conference of Catholic Bishops endorsed Jubilee 2000, a plan to cancel the debts of poor developing countries. Even the G-24, an organization of 24 developing countries, called for thorough reform of the international financial system.

With criticism of deregulated global markets mounting, officials of the International Monetary Fund (IMF), a quasi-public lending institution, and representatives from the seven largest economies began laying the groundwork for a new "global financial architecture" at the IMF's annual meeting in April. In their discussions of international banking laws and currency trading, however, the well-being of humanity and the future of the planet received scarcely a mention.

If global reform is to address such pressing issues as world poverty and climate change, the job can not be left to the architects of the current fiasco. Recognizing this, U.S. progressives have developed their own global architecture emphasizing workers rights, expanded democracy, and ecological sustainability. The details can be found in the Global Sustainable Development Resolution, which was scheduled to be filed in June by Congressman Bernie Sanders (I-Vt.) with Sherrod Brown (D-Ohio), Cynthia McKinney (D-Ga.) and Dennis Kusinich (D-Ohio) signed on as cosponsors.

Given the conservative climate in Washington, the act is more a wish list than a realistic piece of legislation — but what a wish list it is. For those seeking alternative solutions to global economic ills, the resolution presents state-of-the-art thinking about the prospects for sustainable and democratic economic reform and is evidence that reasonable alternatives to the IMF's vision exist.

The danger with any blueprint for international finance and trade policy — and there have been dozens recently, from the left and the right — is that international institutions are easily hijacked by powerful countries and, with the complicity of authoritarian client states, transformed into instruments of corporate and imperial control. Many would be surprised to learn, for example, that the IMF, as economist John Maynard Keynes had originally conceived it in the 1940s, was to be a lender of first resort to countries needing to borrow foreign currencies to purchase goods abroad. Had the IMF developed as Keynes intended, poorer countries would have more control of the terms under which they borrow. Rich countries would have been stripped of the economic power to force poorer nations into debt.

In practice, of course, the U.S. government demanded the lion's share of the votes, and the IMF was itself stripped of power and transformed into an enforcement agent for international corporate interests. The IMF, like other international economic institutions, is intensely secretive and top-heavy with U.S. and European representatives whose allegiance to corporate interests is generally unquestioned. No plan for economic reform, no matter how pleasing or sensible on paper, can promote democratic development when the institutions of the global economy are themselves profoundly undemocratic and fully controlled by the large global corporations.

For this reason, the progressive resolution begins by calling for "democratic control over the global economy." Attention to democratic process and participation is evident throughout the act's 20 pages. Drafted with input from dozens of nongovernmental organizations, labor unions, and intellectuals, the bill addresses virtually every aspect of the global economy, from trade, to international debt, to environmental destruction. Among numerous suggestions, the resolution would:

- Cancel debts of poorer countries to alleviate world poverty.
- Regulate international money flows to prevent currency crises and reduce financial instability.
- Develop binding codes of corporate conduct and mandate that international trade agreements raise labor standards to protect the rights of workers.
- Make environmental sustainability a priority in all trade, lending, and corporate conduct negotiations.
- Support green development projects by establishing new public lending facilities.

In each of the many proposals, drafters paid careful attention to the political composition of the international bodies that would implement changes and set standards. The resolution may not be the answer to all the ills that trouble the global economy, but it correctly locates the source of those ills in the degradation of democracy and popular accountability.

In the past, sterile debates — over jobs versus the environment or free trade versus isolationism — have stymied political discussion of globalization and environmental sustainability. The plan's creators strove to transcend these roadblocks by proposing institutions which, in their mandate and structure, would be forced to address the human and ecological failings of unfettered markets. In proposing reforms of international lending institutions like the IMF, for example, the resolution insists not only that the IMF consider workers' rights in loan negotiations, but mandates that "a representative from the International Labor Organization [will] take the lead in negotiating labor issues [and] local labor unions shall participate in these negotiations."

The resolution repeatedly emphasizes the political, rather than the strictly economic, nature of global economic reform. With this emphasis, the drafters clearly perceived the essential failing of official reform proposals. Technical matters of money, exchange rates, tariffs and trade, while important, are not at the heart of the what is wrong with the global economy. At the recent IMF meetings, for example, officials were at least as preoccupied with who would participate in reforming the global financial architecture as they were with the reform itself. Despite appeals from other governments, the G-7 rejected "a task force with participation from a broad, representative group of countries" to discuss financial reform, according to Nancy Alexander of the Globalization Challenge Initiative, a progressive nonprofit. There was widespread resentment of U.S. efforts to "handpick" countries to participate in the reform process.

Reasonable people may disagree on the precise details of global economic reform, but it is not only the details that policy elites worry about. Ensuring that decisions are made outside of public view and with input from only a few powerful nations and institutions is the hallmark of official economic policymaking.

Drafters of the resolution therefore paid careful attention to the political composition of international bodies. They propose, not only that votes in trade and lending institutions be proportionate to population, but that membership in these institutions be extended to groups representing workers, consumers and other constituents who can keep officials' feet to the fire. "Economic decision making," the resolution states, "should be exercised as close to the locus of the actual activity being decided as possible."

Nor would local democratic input be hampered by corporate and official secrecy or misinformation. The proposal mandates a national Commission on the Global Economy to hold hearings and town meetings and report back to Congress, a United Nations Commission on the Global Economy to initiate global discussion of reform, and a Global Economy Truth Commission, to monitor, investigate and publicize the abuses of international institutions.

While the resolution advances numerous reforms of international labor law, financial regulation, and trade laws, it is less a detailed blueprint than a broad outline of how a decent and democratic world economy might be structured. Specifics are left sketchy, as they should be. Detailed legislation for the global economy, if it is to conform truly to democratic principles, would need wider input and discussion than was solicited in drafting this resolution. What the proposal does well is spell out the goals reforms should strive to achieve: to create an economic system operated for the benefit of all humanity, not for the profit of corporations.

Give humanity a voice in creating such a system, the drafters believe, and it can work out the details itself.

## THE IMF VERSUS THE WORLD BANK

**BY ARTHUR MACEWAN**
*July/August 1999*

Dear Dr. Dollar:

Who are the people really running the IMF and World Bank? How do they get their money? And what's the difference between the two institutions?

— *Charlie Tesch, Somerville, Mass.*

The International Monetary Fund (IMF) and World Bank are run by their member governments, but not on the basis of one-country-one-vote. Instead, governments have votes based on the amount of money they pay in to the organizations. In this sense, they operate much like private corporations, except that the owners of shares are governments instead of individuals.

The U.S. government has by far the largest share of votes in both the IMF and World Bank and, along with its closest allies, effectively controls their operations. In 1998, the U.S. held 18% of the votes in the IMF and 15% in the World Bank. Together, the United States, Germany, Japan, the U.K. and France control about 40% of the shares in both institutions. With the rest of the shares spread among 175 other member governments, some holding a tiny number of votes, the United States is effectively in charge.

So the people running the IMF and the World Bank are the same folks who run the U.S. government and the governments of its closest allies. Since the institutions were founded at the end of World War II, the president of the World Bank has always been a U.S. citizen, and the head of the IMF has always been a European. These are all men, generally coming from the top of the financial industry.

While the IMF and the Bank operate as extensions of the U.S. government's foreign policy, they are well insulated from democratic accountability. Congress, to say nothing of the populace in general, has no role overseeing their operations, and they operate largely outside the public eye (though Congressional ire sometimes appears in response to a request for more funds).

What the IMF and the World Bank do is lend money to governments. Because many governments, especially governments of poor countries, are often in dire need of loans and cannot readily obtain funds through financial markets, they turn to these institutions. And if the IMF and World Bank will not loan to a country, international banks certainly won't. As a result, the IMF and the World Bank have great power, and are able to insist that governments adopt certain policies as a condition for receiving funds.

The IMF and the Bank make sure that U.S. allies get the financial support they need to stay in power, abuses of human rights, labor, and the environment notwithstanding; that big banks get paid back, no matter how irresponsible their loans may have been; and that other governments continually reduce barriers to the operations of U.S. business in their countries, whether or not this conflicts with the economic needs of their own people.

In the division of functions between the IMF and the World Bank, the IMF provides funds to governments in immediate financial emergencies and the Bank provides funds for long-term development projects. For example, when the financial crisis that developed in 1997 spread through several Asian countries, capital fled to safer havens. The values of local currencies fell drastically relative to the dollar. Governments (and private firms) whose revenues were in their own local currencies could not meet their dollar obligations to international bankers. This forced governments to turn to the IMF for funds to maintain the values of their currencies and meet their obligations to international banks. Along with the loans, however, came conditions: the IMF's program for economic stability.

The World Bank may receive fewer headlines, not being on the spot in crises, but over the long run it shapes the economies of countries where it makes loans. Its loans cover a wide spectrum of projects, from large hydro-electric dams to local business training programs. Many of the Bank's programs appear desirable in themselves — who would object to clean water facilities, education in animal husbandry, or better roads? Yet the particular projects promote a development strategy that minimizes the role of the public sector, and demands the privatization of communal lands and other public property.

As to the source of their funds, the IMF gets most of its money as subscriptions from member governments — the amount determining the number of votes each government has in running the operation. When, in extreme circumstances, the IMF needs an especially large amount of funds, it can activate a line of credit it has established with governments and large banks.

The World Bank raises its money by taking loans from the private sector, operating through financial markets as would private firms or governments. Because the Bank is backed by funds from member governments, it can obtain private funds at relatively low interest rates. It then turns around and loans this money to the governments of poor countries to support development projects. In effect, the Bank allows governments of poor countries to borrow, through it, on the international capital markets and at lower rates than they could borrow were they to seek funds on their own.

# EXPORT CREDIT AGENCIES: INTERNATIONAL CORPORATE WELFARE

**BY DANIELLE KNIGHT**
*November/December 1999*

Dubbed by some of its critics as the "Chernobyl of hydro power," China's Three Gorges dam may prove one of the most destructive dam projects on earth. Experts predict that the dam, to be built on a section of China's Yangtze River underlaid by several seismic faults, will flood thousands of acres of farmland and part of the city of Chongqing. It's also expected to displace as many as 2 million people living in the region, triggering violent social unrest.

Opponents of Three Gorges include scientists and parliamentarians within China, as well as environmental and human rights groups around the world. Even the U.S. Bureau of Reclamation, probably the world's top dam-building agency, pulled out of the project in 1993, announcing that it was "not environmentally or economically feasible."

As plans for Three Gorges go forward, however, little is reported of how this wonder of concrete topography is being funded. In fact, the dam — like other potentially destructive projects worldwide — has been made possible partly by foreign financing, in the form of taxpayer-subsidized loan guarantees and other assistance.

Corporations hoping to cash in on projects like Three Gorges — in this case, by providing turbines and other engineering equipment — are becoming increasingly reliant on public subsidies from their home countries to do so. And many of these subsidies, designed to help a nation's firms compete for business abroad, are coming through government-sponsored organizations known as export lending credit agencies and investment insurance agencies.

Indeed, in recent years much of the funding that used to flow to developing countries in the form of aid has been diverted into subsidizing for-profit investments, through export credit agencies.

Bruce Rich, a senior attorney with the Environmental Defense Fund, says that through such agencies, "leading governments like the U.S. have been pushing the idea of subsidizing the private sector to replace certain forms of aid, rather than continuing with the traditional big loans to governments for things like power infrastructure." But though the switch is being touted as unleashing the "free market," Rich and others point out that corporate investors typically won't get involved in a risky venture like Three Gorges without guarantees from a government-backed agency that if the project loses money, taxpayers will help foot the bill.

"Usually, if multinational corporations are to attract loans by the huge international private banks, they must have some public taxpayer money guaranteeing risk insurance or directly financing the projects," says Rich. He adds, "In the brave new era of the free flow of capital, we're discovering that the private sector isn't as private as it seems. It's really been a privatization of profits and the public assumption of risk, not only financial risk but also environmental and social risk."

Export credit agencies, of which the U.S.-based Export-Import Bank and Overseas Private Investment Corporation (OPIC) are examples, are bilateral finance agencies, whose deals involve two nations or parties. They provide publicly backed loans, guarantees and insurance to corporations from their countries that are seeking to do business in developing countries and emerging markets. The United States, Japan and most Western European countries each sponsor at least one such agency.

At a recent meeting in Washington, D.C., more than 40 non-governmental organizations (NGOs) from about 23 countries kicked off an international campaign to reform these agencies and push them to adopt common human rights and environmental standards. While multilateral international development banks like the World Bank have been successfully pressured to adopt minimal environmental and social guidelines for their projects, most export credit and public insurance agencies still have few or no such standards.

In the case of Three Gorges, Hermes, a German export-credit agency, provided loan guarantees of up to $833 million to the German engineering giant Siemens AG and the turbine manufacturer Voith Hydro. A Swiss lending agency known as Exportrisikogarantie/ERG provided almost $300 million to the Swedish-Swiss company Asea Brown Boveri and the Swiss Sulzer Escher- Wyss, to provide equipment. Canada's Export Development Corporation (EDC) provided a $12.5 million taxpayer-backed loan, enabling the Calgary-based company, Agra Inc. to secure its first contract on the project. Since then, EDC has extended a further $153 million in support of a turbine contract awarded to General Electric Canada.

Between 1988 and 1996, according to a report issued last March, governments around the world pumped enough new money into their export credit and investment insurance agencies to allow them to quadruple their financial commitments, from about $26 billion to $105 billion (this figure includes agencies in the 26 rich nations represented in the Organization for Economic Cooperation and Development, as well as some developing countries). This increase came during a time when lending by other multilateral financial institutions, such as the World Bank, stayed relatively flat.

The report, titled "Race to the Bottom," was put out by the Environmental Defense Fund, the Center for International Environmental Law, an Indonesia-based coalition called Bioforum, India's Narmada Bachao Andolan, and other groups. It warns that even as export credit agencies take an expanding role in financing projects around the globe, they remain the least transparent of all international financial institutions, not even sharing key information on their operations with other agencies and the World Bank.

Because they seldom apply even minimal human rights and environmental standards (though that's changing somewhat for the Export-Import Bank and OPIC), most export credit agencies are able to fund projects like Three Gorges, which institutions like the World Bank avoid. According to the industry publication Canada Business, World Bank officials advised China not to approach them for loans after it became clear that if the bankers funded it, "they would become lightning rods for criticism of the project."

Having succeeded in getting minimal environmental standards adopted at many development banks, activist groups are now turning their attention to the export credit agencies, though many argue that the multilateral institutions have made only token progress in adhering to such guidelines.

"These agencies are often financing projects — many riddled with corruption — that other taxpayer-supported agencies like the World Bank reject as environmentally and economically unsustainable," says Rich.

In this way, taxpayers' funds — which go to both the World Bank and the export credit agencies — are working at cross purposes, he adds. "Of what use is it," Rich wonders, "for the World Bank to implement environmental policies, when projects for which they would require environmental mitigation measures will be financed by publicly supported ECAs without such measures?"

## EX-IM Bank and OPIC

Situated directly across Lafayette Park from the White House stands the Export Import Bank. Known as Ex-Im, this independent government agency was created in the 1930s. Its stated purpose is to promote U.S. jobs through the support of exports, by providing guarantees of working capital loans for U.S. exporters. Ex-Im guarantees the repayment of loans, finances loans to foreign purchasers of U.S. goods and services, and also provides credit insurance against non-payment by foreign buyers for political or commercial risk.

Ex-Im claims that during fiscal year 1998, it supported nearly 13 billion dollars in US exports by 2,060 U.S. exporters, by authorizing some $10.5 billion in loans, guarantees and export credit insurance for US companies. Though the bank had an income of $390 million in 1997, it recorded a net loss on operations of about $1.7 billion last year.

By its own estimates, Ex-Im directly supports and maintains approximately 200,000 jobs annually, while indirectly supporting nearly another million jobs. These numbers are based on Department of Commerce calculations, which add up the claimed financial value of a project, then divide that figure by the amount of money the department believes is needed to create one job. A staff member at the Ex-Im, however, who did not want to be identified, acknowledged that it is "somewhat impossible to calculate the amount of jobs Ex-Im supports."

In fact, many of Ex-Im's clients are actually downsizing their U.S. workforces. General Electric, for example, one of Ex-Im's largest clients, reportedly cut its domestic workforce from 243,000 to 150,000 between 1985 and 1995, while it modestly expanded offshore. In another instance in 1994, Boeing borrowed $1 billion from the bank to export planes to China. Part of the construction was performed in Xian, China; two years later this factory signed a major contract that displaced Boeing workers in Wichita, Kansas.

OPIC, a wholly owned government corporation, has a slightly differently focus. Founded in 1971, its stated mission is "to mobilize and facilitate the participation of United States private capital and skills in the economic and social development of less developed countries and areas, and countries in transition from nonmarket to market economies, thereby complementing the development assistance objectives of the United States."

Specifically, the agency insures investments overseas against a broad range of political risks, such as losing income due to war, insurrection, terrorism or sabotage, or having an investment nationalized by the host country's government. It also finances U.S. corporations overseas through loans and loan guarantees, and finances private investment funds that provide equity to businesses overseas.

OPIC has only been funding this last type of venture since the mid-1980s, when it began setting up private funds to buy part ownership in overseas companies. By 1998, it had set up nearly 30 such funds. OPIC chooses the managers of the funds, and provides loans and loan guarantees to back up their privately raised capital. In 1998, the agency's portfolio was $18.3 billion.

OPIC claims to pay for itself by selling loans and insurance. Actually, in 1998, according to the Interhemispheric Resource Center and Institute for Policy Studies, more than half its revenues came from interest on its U.S. Treasury securities. Also, Congress will on occasion provide funds for particular projects out of the foreign aid budget. On its web page, OPIC claims that during its existence it has made $3 billion in profits. But Doug Norlen, policy director for the Pacific Environment and Resources Center, an environmental group that has been tracking investment in environmentally harmful projects, argues that this supposed "profit" may be largely a result of the way OPIC keeps its books.

"If OPIC is profitable, then somebody needs to tell us why they need to go and ask Congress for money every year," says Norlen. And of course, if any loans or guarantees go bad, the public picks up the tab. As of last year, OPIC estimated that it was carrying $7 million in non-collectable loans, and was exposed via guarantees and insurance claims to the tune of more than $13 billion.

One example of a credit agency-financed project that went south is provided by the Ok Tedi copper and gold Mine in Papua New Guinea, majority-owned and -operated by the Australian company, Broken Hill Proprietary (BHP). Australia's Export Finance and Insurance Corporation provided a $243.8 million line of credit, while the U.S. Ex-Im approved a loan of $81.2 million to an undisclosed U.S. company involved in the project.

The mine devastated 500 square miles of once fertile land when BHP began daily dumping of tens of thousands of tons of mining waste — containing lead, cadmium and other toxic heavy metals — into the nearby Fly and Ok Tedi rivers. In 1996, the company agreed to a $100 million out-of court settlement to compensate about 15,000 parties who claimed fish stocks and crops were destroyed by the pollution. A key component of that agreement is a binding commitment that BHP and their subsidiary, Ok Tedi Mining Ltd., construct tailings containment facilities, expected to cost approximately $300 million.

## Global Loan Sharks

As export credit agencies' funding has increased, their share of developing-country debt has also shot up. The IMF estimates that in 1996, loans made or guaranteed by these agencies accounted for 24 percent of developing countries' total indebtedness — more than what's owed to the World Bank and IMF combined.

Often it is national governments, not corporations, that end up in debt to export credit agencies. Pam Foster with the Halifax Initiative, a Canadian organization that works to reform financial institutions, says this occurs because even though the guarantees and loans are granted to companies, in many cases the nation hosting the project is asked to share the risk or loan.

Indonesia offers a prime example of how a country can fall into the clutches of the credit agencies. About 24 percent of its total external debt — approximately $28 billion — is held by such agencies. Titi Soentoro, coordinator of Bioforum, a coalition of 70 Indonesian environmental and human rights organizations, says this funding long helped prop up the family of President Suharto, who was forced from office last year after three decades of autocratic rule.

"ECAs played a key role in assisting many foreign investors in supporting the Suharto regime's system of economic and political monopolies," she says. "Foreign investors, often supported by ECA finance, competed to align themselves with the powerful business interests close to the Suharto Family."

## Lack of Common Standards

Some credit agencies notably the two based in the United States, have begun to accept some restrictions on the kind of projects they'll fund. Their analogous agencies in other industrialized countries, however, remain ready and eager to take on deals rejected by OPIC and the Ex-Im Bank.

After years of pressure from U.S. environmental groups, in 1992 the Export-Import Bank did adopt some basic environmental and social standards. Then in February 1998, the Clinton administration updated OPIC's 1985 environmental guidelines.

By law, OPIC is supposed to promote the economic development of the countries in which the investments it insures are located. Therefore, according to Rich of the Environmental Defense Fund, its environmental standards are stricter than Ex-Im's. Since last year, for example, OPIC is not supposed to provide financial backing for large dams or projects that go through primary forests.

Because of its new standards, Ex-Im joined the World Bank in refusing to support Three Gorges, citing a lack of substantive information on mitigating environmental and social impacts. But even while Ex-Im steered clear of the project, German, Swiss and Canadian ECAs stepped into the gap.

"When the Americans pulled back, Canada very smartly stepped in," observed Peter Mayers, vice- president of Agra Inc., one of the Canadian firms involved with the dam.

The Environment Defense Fund and other groups say the lack of common environmental and social standards for export credit and investment insurance agencies allows this kind of ready substitution among funders. Those who monitor the agencies worry that competition among them may actually pressure Ex-Im into weakening the standards it has. Following the Hermes decision to support Three Gorges, U.S. Rep. Donald Manzullo, R-Illinois, the chairman of the House Sub-Committee on Exports, threatened to strip the Export-Import Bank of its environmental mandate. Manzullo represents a district where Caterpillar, Inc. — which was counting on the support of Ex-Im to secure contracts for Three Gorges — has large factories.

Using the example of Three Gorges and loss of contracts for Caterpillar, Sen. Frank Murkowski, R-Alaska, has proposed legislation that would prohibit the Ex-Im from withholding financing from a project based on its failure to satisfy environmental policies, if any other government is providing funds to its domestic companies.

## Campaign for Common Standards

Many of the nations that have approved human rights and social standards for the World Bank, including France and Germany, have repeatedly thwarted efforts to adopt common guidelines for export credit agencies, as urged by the Clinton Administration through the OECD.

Such resistance, says Rich, one of the organizers of the NGO conference in March, shows the "hypocrisy" of the French and German governments "who present themselves as green at international environmental gatherings."

One might expect the new "Red-Green" coalition that has come to power in Germany to be more receptive to reforming Hermes, the German export credit lending agency. The reality, however, is that in Germany, a powerful industial lobby is able to resist such reform. Heffa Shucking of the Urgewald, a coalition of German church, development and environmental groups, says that "Schroder doesn't seem to have a clue" about ECAs, and that the new government "hasn't prioritized the issue."

NGOs that have traditionally worked to reform World Bank policies are just beginning to follow the money and pay attention to export credit and investment insurance agencies, according to Norlen of the Pacific Environment and Resources Center. He and others have been pressing for the OECD to adopt common standards for these agencies, since most member nations have at least one.

Such standards should "at the very least be equal to World Bank guidelines," Norlen maintains. Under pressure from organizations like Urgewald and Environmental Defense Fund, the "Group of Seven" wealthy industrialized nations said earlier this year it hoped to develop common environmental guidelines for export finance agencies by 2001.

"The public wants to know what their agencies are funding," says Norlen. "Once these projects are held up to the light of day, people will demand reforms for these agencies, just as they have for the World Bank. Transparency is key."

*Resources:* "A Race to the Bottom," the report by Environmental Defense Fund and other NGOs, is available on the Internet at www.eca-watch.org/eca/race_bottom.pdf

# CAFTA'S DEBT TRAP

## BY ALDO CALIARI

*July/August 2005*

*The Central American Free Trade Agreement (CAFTA) is designed to create a trade and investment block that includes the United States, Costa Rica, El Salvador, Guatemala, Honduras, Nicaragua, and the Dominican Republic. Modeled on the failed 11-year-old North American Free Trade Agreement (NAFTA), the deal aims to liberalize trade among the signatory countries by removing barriers to the flow of goods, services, and capital. CAFTA is widely viewed as a stepping stone to the creation of a larger Free Trade Area of the Americas. President Bush signed the legislation into law in August 2005.*
*—Eds.*

Critics of the Central American Free Trade Agreement have focused on concerns that the treaty will devastate Central American farmers by forcing them to compete with heavily subsidized U.S. agribusiness. Others point out that the deal will perpetuate low-road development based on poverty wages and lax environmental enforcement, while undermining governments' authority to ensure basic services. These are all valid concerns, but CAFTA poses yet another danger that deserves equal attention.

Rules buried in the technical language of the investment chapter of the agreement would make it more difficult for the six Central American nations to escape their heavy debt burdens or recover from debt crises should they, for example, find themselves unable to meet their obligations to holders of government bonds and other creditors. The investment provisions of CAFTA—like the 1994 North American Free Trade Agreement between the United States, Canada, and Mexico—are based on the argument that strong investment protections encourage foreign private investment. CAFTA subscribes to this same precept, and, like NAFTA, it would require governments to comply with a long list of investor protections and even grant foreign private investors the right to sue governments for damages if those obligations are violated.

Both treaties require governments to treat foreign investors at least as favorably as domestic investors, a principle known as "national treatment." Governments must also ensure "most favored nation" treatment for other treaty members, meaning they cannot give special preferences to, or discriminate against, the investors of any one country that is a party to the agreement. As a result, member governments can no longer favor domestic interests or investors even to support social goals or other national interests.

But whereas NAFTA's investor protections explicitly exclude "sovereign debt" (the bonds, loans, and other securities issued from or guaranteed by national governments) from investor protection rules, CAFTA specifically includes these forms of public liabilities.

As the U.S. House deliberates on CAFTA, it's important for the public to recognize that in subjecting government bonds and other forms of sovereign debt to stringent investment protections, the deal would place huge constraints on indebted countries' ability to prevent or survive debt crises —and to protect the basic needs of their citizens.

## National Treatment and Most Favored Nation Status

The "national treatment" and "most favored nation" principles were originally born in agreements dealing with trade in goods, only later extending to investment. Their application to sovereign debt introduces a number of serious problems.

### *1. CAFTA dismantles essential tools governments need to recover from crisis.*

Requiring that foreign creditors be offered favorable treatment equal to domestic creditors is dangerous for the developing-country members of CAFTA, since they all, with the exception of Honduras, owe a significant share of public debt to domestic creditors. In some countries, including Costa Rica, domestic debt is actually higher than external debt.

When undergoing a debt restructuring, a government makes an "offer" to all creditors, typically reducing the value of outstanding bonds and loans substantially. Once the offer is agreed to, the country can regain its footing and restart the flow of investment.

There are a variety of reasons why a country might want to offer domestic creditors preferential conditions in restructuring its sovereign debt. In a financial crisis, domestic creditors often take a double hit. They're forced to accept a reduction in the value of their loans, and they face high interest rates and other costs. Yet domestic capital markets are critical in a recovery. By addressing the needs of domestic investors first, a country will be better able to return to domestic capital markets quickly during what is likely to be a sustained interruption in access to foreign capital. This can feed a resumption of growth, which, in turn, can facilitate repayment of other obligations and reverse the precipitous fall in a country's standard of living that typically accompanies a debt crisis. Even the International Monetary Fund (IMF), a staunch defender of the rights of foreign private investors, acknowledges that "the restructuring of certain types of domestic debt may have major implications for economic performance, as a result of its impact on the financial system and the operation of domestic capital markets."

Prioritizing domestic debt may also be necessary to protect a country's banking system. Argentinean economist José Luis Machinea has pointed out that sovereign debt restructuring has a double impact on domestic holders of debt: On the one hand, the value of their bonds is reduced. On the other, they suffer the general impact of the crisis on the real economy and on their access to finance. The IMF has stated that in crises, affording special treatment to domestic debt might help protect "a core of the banking system by ensuring the availability of assets required for banks to manage capital, liquidity, and exposure to market risks."

More generally, countries may need to provide special treatment to domestic debtors as part of their national development strategy—that is, for the same legitimate reasons that can lead them to accord special treatment to domestic industries.

### *2. CAFTA prevents states from paying salaries and pensions.*

Under CAFTA, member governments would no longer be able to prioritize domestic debts consisting of, among other things, wages, salaries, and pensions. This could have dire ramifications for state workers. According to the national treatment principle, governments are bound to treat these obligations the same way they treat foreign debts held by transnational banks and foreign investors. If the state has only enough resources to cover a portion of its debts, it will be prohibited from choosing to direct those funds first to wages and salaries. In this way, too, CAFTA would deal a setback to national governments' ability to prioritize their obligations to the basic human rights of their citizens and put their own economic development above the claims of foreign creditors.

Unlike a private corporation in bankruptcy, an indebted nation has human rights obligations and social responsibilities toward its people. That's why civil society groups have called for developing new debt-crisis protocols that take into account the broader mission of the state and its role in society. Models already exist—for example, Chapter 9 of the U.S. bankruptcy code which applies to municipalities. Even the IMF's proposed rules for restructuring sovereign debt excluded "wages, salaries and pensions" from their application.

### *3. It reduces the leverage of domestic debtors.*

A government's debt restructuring offer can take on added clout if it has first cut a deal with supportive domestic creditors. Giving these domestic creditors preferential terms is a way for the state to win back their support. If the principles of national treatment are applied to sovereign debt, however, any incentive offered to domestic creditors would have to be offered to the foreign creditors as well, effectively foreclosing this avenue of recovery.

Argentina's offer of preferential conditions to domestic creditors was a crucial element in enhancing the government's leverage in negotiating with its foreign private creditors after it suffered the largest sovereign default in history in December 2001. In September 2003, the government released its initial proposed debt restructuring conditions, which included a 75% cut in the value of its bonds. Some groups of bondholders quickly rejected this offer, claiming that it was woefully insufficient and, in light of the country's latest growth figures, below what the country could repay. The creditors also strongly lobbied the G7 group of industrialized countries, which, both directly and through the IMF, put more pressure on Argentina to sweeten its offer. With pressure mounting from the G7 and the IMF, Argentina turned to its domestic pension funds. By granting domestic pension funds preferential conditions, Argentina was able to reach an agreement with them. The funds held more than 17% of the country's total debt and their coming on board was a critical first step in Argentina's eventually garnering the support of a full 76% of its creditors.

The government's ability to treat domestic bondholders differently from foreign ones was crucial to reaching an agreement with the majority of creditors. This option would have been out of the question if the government had been bound by CAFTA's national treatment principle.

## Investor-State Lawsuits

Under CAFTA, governments that violate these investor protections can face expensive lawsuits. As under NAFTA and numerous bilateral investment treaties, CAFTA grants private foreign investors the right to bypass domestic courts and sue governments in international tribunals.

Such "investor-state lawsuits" are highly controversial for a number of reasons. First, many arbitration tribunals operate with an absolute lack of transparency, having no obligation to disclose relevant documents or allow any form of public participation. The system for choosing arbitrators has also drawn criticism, as the arbitrators can be chosen from the ranks of practicing investment lawyers, with no obligation to appoint people who will be independent, that is, who have no stake in the treaty interpretation. These unelected tribunals may well rule on difficult questions with far-reaching social and economic implications that rightfully belong under the domestic jurisdiction of states.

* * * * *

CAFTA's application of investor protections to sovereign debt would suppress the few options available to countries trying to prevent or exit from debt crises. History shows that the inability to exit a crisis situation causes economic losses far outweighing any commercial gains achieved through a free trade agreement.

Central American activists are already calling on their governments to reject CAFTA. In the United States, activists must also urge Congress to reject CAFTA because in addition to all the concerns that have been voiced already, it will tightly tie the hands of member countries in dealing with their large stocks of external debt.

An earlier version of this article appeared in *Foreign Policy In Focus* <www.fpif.org>, June 2005.

# THE DECLINE OF THE DOLLAR SYSTEM

**BY JAMES K. GALBRAITH**
*May/June 2003*

Today, the U.S. dollar is the world's reserve currency. Nations around the world invest most of their foreign exchange reserves in dollar assets. The international economic position of the United States depends on this.

So long as foreign central banks and international investors are willing to take and hold U.S. assets (including stocks, bonds, and cash) this system works—and shamefully to the interest of Americans. Their demand keeps the value of the dollar high. This means that we have been able to consume comfortably, and in exchange for very little effort, the products of hard labor by poor people. (As the supplier of liquidity to the world system, our situation is akin to that of, say, Australia in the late 19th century when gold fields were discovered, except that, in our case, no actual effort is required to extract the gold.) And meanwhile (thanks to ample cheap imports), we are not obliged to invest unduly in maintaining our own industrial base, which has substantially eroded since the 1970s. We could afford to splurge on new technologies and telecommunications systems whose benefits were, to a very great extent, figments of the imagination. And even when the bubble burst in those sectors, life went on, for most Americans, substantially undisturbed—at least for now.

But for how long can this system endure? There can be no definitive answer; the few economists who have worried about this issue are far from being in agreement. On one side, it is argued that the dominant currency holds a "lock-in advantage"; that is, there are economies (reduced transaction costs and reduced risk) associated with keeping all reserves in one basket. The United States in particular is in a strong position to pressure foreign central banks—notably Japan's—to absorb the dollars that private parties may not wish to hold, at least within limits.

Furthermore, oil is bought and sold in dollars. As a result, oil importers must buy dollars in order to buy oil, and oil exporters accumulate dollars as they sell oil. To some extent this arrangement further strengthens the dollar—though it is not obvious why it requires anyone to hold dollars for very long, once they start falling in value.

Against this, the question remains: As the U.S. trade position continues to erode, will foreigners be willing to add to their holdings of dollar assets by enough to allow the United States to return to full employment? The amount to be absorbed at present—the trade deficit at full employment—is in the range of half a trillion dollars per year. This was easily handled when dollar asset prices were rising. But now that these prices are falling, they are not as attractive as they once were. If foreigners are not willing to absorb all the dollars we need to place, and if asset prices do not quickly fall to the point where U.S. stocks appear cheap to investors, dollar dumping is, sooner or later, inevitable.

To keep the dollar's fall from getting out of hand, the United States will be strongly tempted to slow the rate at which new U.S. assets reach the world system, by restricting its imports. Having renounced the traditional tools of trade protectionism, it can only do this by raising interest rates, holding down economic growth, and keeping incomes, and therefore imports, well below the full-employment level. In that situation—which may actually already have arrived—the United States joins Brazil and other developing nations as a country effectively constrained by its debts. Indeed, the world prognosis from that point forward becomes grim, since high levels of American demand have been just about the only motor of growth and development (outside, perhaps, of China and India) in recent years.

## The United States as a Debtor Nation

There are economists who advocate dollar devaluation, believing that the richer countries of the world would quickly rally to purchase increasing quantities of made-in-America exports, thus reversing the manufacturing decline of the past 20 years. But this is very unlikely. Exports to the rich regions may not be very price-sensitive.

And exports to the developing regions are very sensitive to income and credit conditions, which would get worse. At least in the short and medium term, there is no foolproof adjustment process to be had by these means. Where a high dollar provides U.S. consumers with cheap imports and capital inflows to finance domestic activity, a falling dollar would have opposite effects. A falling dollar would raise the price of imports into the United States, especially from the richer countries. Meanwhile, a declining dollar would hit at the value of developing countries' reserves and their access to credit, and so it would diminish their demand for our exports. (It would help, in some cases, on their debts.) The most likely outcome from dollar devaluation is a general deepening of the world slump, combined with pressure on American banks and markets as global investors seek safer havens in Europe.

This specter of financial vulnerability means that for the United States, the combination of falling internal demand, falling asset prices, and a falling dollar represents a threat that can best be described as millennial. (My colleague Randall Wray has called it the "perfect fiscal storm.") The consequences at home would include deepening unemployment. There would be little recovery of privately financed investment, amid a continued unraveling of plans—both corporate and personal—that had been based on the delirious stock market valuations of the late 1990s. The center of the world banking industry would move, presumably to continental Europe. Over time, the United States could lose both its position as the principal beneficiary of the world financial order and its margin of maneuver on the domestic scene. This would be not unlike what happened to the United Kingdom from 1914 to 1950.

It is not obvious that senior financial policymakers in the United States have yet grasped this threat, or that there is any serious planning under way to cope with it—apart from a simpleminded view among certain strategic thinkers about the financial advantages of the control of oil. Instead it appears that the responsible officials are confining themselves to a very narrow range of Third-World debt management proposals, whose premises minimize the gravity of the issue and whose purpose is to keep the existing bonds of debt peonage in place as long as possible.

The alternative? It would involve rebuilding a multilateral monetary system, demolished for the benefit of the private commercial banks in 1973. The way forward would probably entail new regional systems of financial stabilization and capital control, such as the Asian Monetary Fund proposed by Japan in 1997. Such a course would be unpalatable to current American leadership. But we may find, down the road, that for the sake of our own prosperity, let alone that of the rest of the world, there is no other way.

Adapted from "The Brazilian Swindle and The Larger International Monetary Problem," published by the Levy Economics Institute in 2002. The full article is available at <www.levy.org>.

# DOLLAR ANXIETY: REAL REASONS TO WORRY

**BY JOHN MILLER**

*January/February 2005*

The value of the dollar is falling. Does that mean that our economic sky is falling as well? Not to sound like Chicken Little, but the answer may well be yes. If an economic collapse is not in our future, then at least economic storm clouds are gathering on the horizon.

It's what lies behind the slide of the dollar that has even many mainstream economists spooked: an unprecedented current account deficit—the difference between the country's income and its consumption and investment spending. The current account deficit, which primarily reflects the huge gap between the amount the United States imports and the amount it exports, is the best indicator of where the country stands in its financial relationship with the rest of the world.

At an estimated $670 billion, or 5.7% of gross domestic product (GDP), the 2004 current account deficit is the largest ever. An already huge trade deficit (the amount exports fall short of imports) made worse by high oil prices, along with rock bottom private savings and a gaping federal budget deficit, have helped push the U.S. current account deficit into uncharted territory. The last time it was above 4% of GDP was in 1816, and no other country has ever run a current account deficit that equals nearly 1% of the world's GDP. If current trends continue, the gap could reach 7.8% of U.S. GDP by 2008, according to Nouriel Roubini of New York University and Brad Setser of University College, Oxford, two well-known finance economists.

Most of the current account deficit stems from the U.S. trade deficit (about $610 billion). The rest reflects the remittances immigrants send home to their families plus U.S. foreign aid (together another $80 billion) less net investment income (a positive $20 billion because the United States still earns more from investments abroad than it pays out in interest on its borrowing from abroad).

The current account deficit represents the amount of money the United States must attract from abroad each year. Money comes from overseas in two ways: foreign investors can buy stock in U.S. corporations, or they can lend money to corporations or to the government by buying bonds. Currently, almost all of the money must come from loans because European and Japanese investors are no longer buying U.S. stocks. U.S. equity returns have been trivial since 2000 in dollar terms and actually negative in euro terms since the dollar has lost ground against the euro.

In essence, the U.S. economy racks up record current account deficits by spending more than its national income to feed its appetite for imports that are now half again exports. That increases the supply of dollars in foreign hands.

At the same time, the demand for dollars has diminished. Foreign investors are less interested in purchasing dollar-dominated assets as they hold more of them (and as the self-fulfilling expectation that the value of the dollar is likely to fall sets in). In October 2004 (the most recent data available), net foreign purchases of U.S. securities—stocks and bonds—dipped to their lowest level in a year and below what was necessary to offset the current account deficit. In addition, global investors' stock and bond portfolios are now overloaded with dollar-denominated assets, up to 50% from 30% in the early '90s.

Under the weight of the massive current account deficit, the dollar has already begun to give way. Since January 2002, the value of the dollar has fallen more than 20%, with much of that dropoff happening since August 2004. The greenback now stands at multiyear lows against the euro, the yen, and an index of major currencies.

Should foreign investors stop buying U.S. securities, then the dollar will crash, stock values plummet, and an economic downturn surely follow. But even if foreigners continue to purchase U.S. bonds—and they already hold 47% of U.S Treasury bonds—a current account deficit of this magnitude will be a costly drag on the economy. The Fed will have to boost interest rates, which determine the rate of return on U.S. bonds, to compensate for their lost value as the dollar slips in value and to keep foreigners coming back for more. In addition, a falling dollar makes imports cost more, pushing up U.S inflation rates. The Fed will either tolerate the uptick in inflation or attempt to counteract it by raising interest rates yet higher. Even in this more orderly scenario of decline, the current expansion will slow or perhaps come to a halt.

## Imperial Finance

You can still find those who claim none of this is a problem. Recently, for example, the editors of the *Wall Street Journal* offered worried readers the following relaxation technique—a version of what former Treasury Secretary Larry Summers says is the sharpest argument you typically hear from a finance minister whose country is saddled with a large current account deficit.

First, recall that a large trade deficit requires a large surplus of capital flowing into your country to cover it. Then ask yourself, would you rather live in a country that continues to attract investment, or one that capital is trying to get out of? Finally, remind yourself that the monetary authorities control the value of currencies and are fully capable of halting the decline.

Feel better? You shouldn't. Arguments like these are unconvincing, a bravado borne not of postmodern cool so much as the old-fashioned, unilateral financial imperialism that underlies the muscular U.S. foreign policy we see today.

True, so far foreigners have been happy to purchase the gobs of debt issued by the U.S. Treasury and corporate America to cover the current account deficit. And that has kept U.S. interest rates low. If not for the flood of foreign money, Morgan Stanley economist Stephen Roach figures, U.S. long-term interest rates would be between one and 1.5 percentage points higher today.

The ability to borrow without pushing up interest rates has paid off handsomely for the Bush administration. Now when the government spends more than it takes in to prosecute the war in Iraq and bestow tax cuts on the rich, savers from foreign shores finance those deficits at reduced rates. And cash-strapped U.S. consumers are more ready to swallow an upside-down economic recovery that has pushed up profit but neither created jobs nor lifted wages when they can borrow at low interest rates.

How can the United States get away with running up debt at low rates? Are other countries' central banks and private savers really the co-dependent "global enablers" Roach and others call them, who happily hold loads of low-yielding U.S. assets? The truth is, the United States has taken advantage of the status of the dollar as the currency of the global economy to make others adjust to its spending patterns. Foreign central banks hold their reserves in dollars, and countries are billed in dollars for their oil imports, which requires them to buy dollars. That sustains the demand for the dollar and protects its value even as the current account imbalance widens.

The U.S. strong dollar policy in the face of its yawning current account deficit imposes a "shadow tax" on the rest of the world, at least in part to pay for its cost of empire. "But payment," as Robert Skidelsky, the British biographer of Keynes, reminds us, "is voluntary and depends at minimum on acquiescence in U.S. foreign policy." The geopolitical reason for the rest of the capitalist world to accept the "seignorage of the dollar"—in other words, the advantage the United States enjoys by virtue of minting the reserve currency of the international economy—became less compelling when the United States substituted a "puny war on terrorism" for the Cold War, Skidelsky adds.

The tax does not fall only on other industrialized countries. The U.S. economy has not just become a giant vacuum cleaner that sucks up "all the world's spare investible cash," in the words of University of California, Berkeley economist Brad DeLong, but about one-third of that money comes from the developing world. To put this contribution in perspective: DeLong calculates that $90 billion a year, or one-third of the average U.S. current account deficit over the last two decades, is equal to the income of the poorest 500 million people in India.

The rest of the world ought not to complain about these global imbalances, insist the strong dollar types. That the United States racks up debt while other countries rack up savings is not profligacy but a virtue. The United States, they argue, is the global economy's "consumer of last resort." Others, especially in Europe, according to U.S. policymakers, are guilty of "insufficient consumption": they hold back their economies and dampen the demand for U.S. exports, exacerbating the U.S. current account deficit. Last year U.S. consumers increased their spending three times as quickly as European consumers (excluding Britain), and the U.S. economy grew about two and half times as quickly.

## Global Uprising

Not surprisingly, old Europe and newly industrializing Asia don't see it that way. They have grown weary from all their heavy lifting of U.S. securities. And while they have yet to throw them overboard, a revolt is brewing.

Those cranky French are especially indignant about the unfairness of it all. The editors of *Le Monde*, the French daily, complain that "The United States considers itself innocent: it refuses to admit that it lives beyond its means through weak savings and excessive consumption." On top of that, the drop of the dollar has led to a brutal rise in the value of the euro that is wiping out the demand for euro-zone exports and slowing their already sluggish economic recoveries.

Even in Blair's Britain *the Economist*, the newsweekly, ran an unusually tough-minded editorial warning: "The dollar's role as the leading international currency can no longer be taken for granted. ... Imagine if you could write checks that were accepted as payment but never cashed. That is what [the privileged position of the dollar] amounts to. If you had been granted that ability, you might take care to hang to it. America is taking no such care. And may come to regret it."

But the real threat comes from Asia, especially Japan and China, the two largest holders of U.S. Treasury bonds. Asian central banks already hold most of their reserves in dollar-denominated assets, an enormous financial risk given that the value of the dollar will likely continue to fall at current low interest rates.

In late November, just the rumor that China's Central Bank threatened to reduce its purchases of U.S. Treasury bonds was enough to send the dollar tumbling.

No less than Alan Greenspan, chair of the Fed, seems to have come down with a case of dollar anxiety. In his November remarks to the European Banking Community, Greenspan warned of a "diminished appetite for adding to dollar balances" even if the current account deficit stops increasing. Greenspan believes that foreign investors are likely to realize they have put too many of their eggs in the dollar basket and will either unload their dollar-denominated investments or demand higher interest rates. After Greenspan spoke, the dollar fell to its lowest level against the Japanese yen in more than four years.

## A Rough Ride From Here

The question that divides economists at this point is not whether the dollar will decline more, but whether the descent will be slow and orderly or quick and panicky. Either way, there is real reason to believe it will be a rough ride.

First, a controlled devaluation of the dollar won't be easy to accomplish. Several major Asian currencies are formally or informally pegged to the dollar, including

### *IF THE UNITED STATES WERE AN EMERGING MARKET*

If the United States was a small or less-developed country, financial alarm bells would already be ringing. The U.S. current account deficit is well above the 5%-of-GDP standard the IMF and others use to pronounce economies in the developing world vulnerable to financial crisis.

Just how crisis-prone depends on how the current account deficit affects the economy's spending. If the foreign funds flowing into the country are being invested in export-producing sectors of the economy, or the tradable goods sectors, such as manufacturing and some services, they are likely over time to generate revenues necessary to pay back the rest of the world. In that case, the shortfall is less of a problem. If those monies go to consumption or speculative investment in non-tradable (i.e., non-export producing) sectors such as a real estate, then they surely will be a problem.

By that standard, the U.S. current account deficit is highly problematic. Economists assess the impact of a current account deficit by comparing it to the difference between net national investment and net national savings. (Net here means less the money set aside to cover depreciation.) In the U.S. case, that difference has widened because saving has plummeted, not because investment has picked up. Last year, the United States registered its lowest net national savings rate ever, 1.5%, due to the return of large federal budget deficits and anemic personal savings. In addition, U.S. investment has shifted substantially away from tradable goods as manufacturing has come under heavy foreign competition toward the non-traded goods sector, such as residential real estate whose prices have soared in and around most major American cities.

Capital inflows that cover a decline in savings instead of a surge in investment are not a sign of economic health nor cause to stop worrying about the current account deficit.

the Chinese yuan. The United States faces a $160 billion trade deficit with China alone. U.S. financial authorities have exerted tremendous pressure on the Chinese to raise the value of their currency, in the hope of slowing the tide of Chinese imports into the United States and making U.S. exports more competitive. But the Chinese have yet to budge.

Beyond that, a fall in the dollar sufficient to close the current account deficit will slaughter large amounts of capital. *The Economist* warns that "[i]f the dollar falls by another 30%, as some predict, it would amount to the biggest default in history: not a conventional default on debt service, but default by stealth, wiping trillions off the value of foreigners' dollar assets."

Even a gradual decline in the value of dollar will bring tough economic consequences. Inflation will pick up, as imports cost more in this bid to make U.S. exports cheaper. The Fed will surely raise interest rates to counteract that inflationary pressure, slowing consumer borrowing and investment. Also, closing the current account deficit would require smaller government deficits. (Although not politically likely, repealing Bush's pro-rich tax cuts would help.)

What will happen is anyone's guess given the unprecedented size of the U.S. current account deficit. But there is a real possibility that the dollar's slide will be anything but slow or orderly. Should Asian central banks stop intervening on the scale needed to finance the U.S. deficit, then a crisis surely would follow. The dollar would drop through the floor; U.S. interest rates would skyrocket (on everything from Treasury bonds to mortgages to credit cards); the stock market and home values would collapse; consumer and investment spending would plunge; and a sharp recession would take hold here and abroad.

The Bush administration seems determined to make things worse. Should the Bush crew push through their plan to privatize Social Security and pay the trillion-dollar transition cost with massive borrowing, the consequences could be disastrous. The example of Argentina is instructive. Privatizing the country's retirement program, as economist Paul Krugman has pointed out, was a major source of the debt that brought on Argentina's crisis in 2001. Dismantling the U.S. welfare state's most successful program just might push the dollar-based financial system over the edge.

The U.S. economy is in a precarious situation held together so far by imperial privilege. Its prospects appear to fall into one of three categories: a dollar crisis; a long, slow, excruciating decline in value of the dollar; or a dollar propped up through repeated interest rates hikes. That's real reason to worry.

*Resources:* "Dollar Anxiety," editorial, *Wall Street Journal*, 11/11/04; D. Wessel, "Behind Big Drop in Currency: U.S. Soaks Up Asia's Output," *WSJ*, 12/2/04; J. B. DeLong, "Should We Still Support Untrammeled International Capital Mobility? Or are Capital Controls Less Evil than We Once Believed," *Economists' Voice*, 2004; R. Skidelsky, "U.S. Current Account Deficit and Future of the World Monetary System" and N. Roubini and B. Setser "The U.S. as A Net Debtor: The Sustainability of the U.S. External Imbalances," 11/04, Nouriel Roubini's Global Macroeconomic and Financial Policy site <www.stern.nyu.edu/globalmacro>; Rich Miller, "Why the Dollar is Giving Way," *Business Week*, 12/6/04; Robert Barro, "Mysteries of the Gaping Current-Account Gap," *Business Week*, 12/13/04; D. Streitford and J. Fleishman, "Greenspan Issues Warning on Dollar," *L.A. Times*, 11/20/04; S. Roach, "Global: What Happens If the Dollar Does Not Fall?" Global Economic Forum, Morgan Stanley, 11/22/04; L. Summers, "The U.S. Current Account Deficit and the Global Economy," The 2004 Per Jacobsson Lecture, 10/3/04; "The Dollar," editorial, *The Economist*, 12/3/04; "Mr. Gaymard and the Dollar," editorial, *Le Monde*, 11/30/04.

# GEORGE BUSH'S FAVORITE VULTURES

**BY GREG PALAST**
*Spring 2007*

It's quite a heartwarming story. Rock stars in designer glasses, lefty clergymen, blond-bearded anti-poverty campaigners all joining hands with George Bush and the International Monetary Fund to cut the debts of Africa's poorest nations. The money the African nations save would buy AIDS medicine. Bush did the photo-op thing in the Oval Office with Bono, and the president even popped debt relief into his State of the Union address: "the best hope for lifting lives and eliminating poverty."

However, Bush lies.

And Africans die.

Here's the reality, off camera. Billions of dollars in debt owed by African nations to the U.S. Treasury, the IMF and several European nations were, indeed, written off. But these acts of taxpayer generosity did not buy medicine. Almost all of the savings meant for Africans has been picked off by a crew of speculators known as "vultures."

Zambia, for example, won debt relief last year which was supposed to provide $40 million to improve health care in a nation where 17% of adults suffer from HIV or AIDS.

Forget the medicine. Zambia won't get it. Half the money has been snatched away by a vulture named Donegal International, an affiliate of a Washington, D.C.-based investment group, Debt Advisory International.

"Vulture" is not a name I made up. It's the label used in government circles for investors who, for a small payment, take over the debts owed by one nation to another, then use political muscle, lawsuits, forgery, or bribery to push the debtor nations to cough up payments five, ten, or twenty times the amount of the vultures' original investment.

Consider Zambia. In 1998, Romania offered to let Zambia pay only $4 million to completely write off a $30 million debt. Strangely, the African nation turned down the generous offer. Instead, one Michael Francis Sheehan, using inside information, grabbed the deal for a fund he operates, paying less than $4 million for the right to collect $30 million from Zambia. In January 1999, just weeks after Zambia rejected Romania's offer to pay only $4 million to terminate this debt, its finance ministry agreed, in writing, to pay Sheehan $15 million on that same debt.

Why would Zambia turn down an excellent deal from Romania and, instead, promise a multimillion-dollar windfall to this "vulture"? This mystery was solved when my producer at BBC Television Newsnight obtained the text of an email by Sheehan. The undated note states boldly, "The deal is going to get done for political reasons." Zambia would give Sheehan's firm the higher sum in return for a private $2 million payment to "the [Zambian] President's favorite charity."

A few weeks ago, I greeted Mr. Sheehan as he approached his customized Cadillac. It's quite a car, by the way. Sheehan, who calls himself "Goldfinger" on a Caddy owners' website, has pimped out his ride with magnesium rims and racing tires.

"It was a charitable initiative which did end up building several thousand houses," said Goldfinger. Perhaps.

Goldfinger is a small pecker compared to Paul Singer, the billionaire who controls the biggest vulture fund, Elliott Associates. Singer's group paid just $10 million for Congolese bonds on which he's already won the right to collect $127 million in a U.S. courtroom. He's now suing to parlay that into $400 million, money he may be able to collect only because the sums that Congo owed to U.S. taxpayers have been forgiven.

And Bush could put a halt to it with the stroke of a pen. Under the doctrine of "comity," the president has the constitutional power to halt the speculator's seizure of Congo's cash. U.S. courts won't let concerned citizens overturn the foreign policy established by the president via lawsuit. Instead they are awaiting Bush's note to halt the collection actions. Bush has sent nothing.

Why? Did I mention that since Ken Lay's checkbook was laid to rest, Singer is now the big sugar-daddy for the Republican Party? He put $1.3 million into the Republican campaigns in 2004 (including funding the "Swift Boat" smear of John Kerry). Singer has committed $10 million to Rudy Giuliani's presidential campaign.

Does Bush know that the debt relief for the Congo is getting eaten by Singer the Vulture? Until February 15, Bush could pretend he knew nothing. But on that day, Congressman John Conyers confronted Bush, nose to nose, in the Oval Office, wanting to know why the president had failed use his powers to stop Singer from ripping off the Congo's money—in effect, money donated in the form of debt forgiveness by U.S. taxpayers.

Conyers also wanted the president to explain why the Justice Department stalled an investigation of "Goldfinger" for the $2 million payment to the former president of Zambia. Conyers pointed out, as if the president didn't know, that pay-outs for profit violate anti-bribery laws, including the Foreign Corrupt Practices Act.

Bush promised to "take care of it all in a week." That was three months ago.

# WOLFOWITZ AND THE WORLD BANK

**BY LARRY PETERSON**
*July/August 2007*

For many on the left, the departure of Paul Wolfowitz from his position as head of the World Bank was cause for celebration. To see one of the architects of a vicious, illegal war brought down by a conflict-of-interest scandal that would embarrass any ordinary personnel director made for a good laugh. And this despite the fact that the scandal, over Wolfowitz's reassignment of his companion to the State Department (under nepotism rules, she couldn't retain her job at the World Bank) at a salary higher than Secretary Rice's, didn't begin to approach the spectacular levels of conspicuous corruption we've come to expect from Bush & Co. But the Wolfowitz episode, however gossip-worthy, is a distraction from the complex trends that have recently been reshaping the World Bank's role in the global economic development game and that will determine the contours of its role well into the future.

In recent years, the World Bank and its sister organization, the International Monetary Fund (IMF), have adopted a lower profile. Today one rarely reads about the banks imposing structural adjustment programs on countries which have no choice but to comply or risk their continued access to capital (though coerced structural adjustment programs still exist: Naomi Klein notes that Sri Lanka was forced to privatize its water system as a condition of receiving aid in the wake of the 2004 tsunami).

But it was only a decade ago, following the Asian financial meltdown, that such conditions were forced on numerous economies, including ones that the World Bank and IMF themselves had acclaimed as star performers not long before: South Korea, Thailand, and Argentina, to name a few. To qualify for desperately needed loans to repay foreign creditors, with the aim of restoring their currencies to health and staunching capital flight, several of these countries were directed by the World Bank and the IMF to impose the usual austerity measures—cuts in health and education spending, for instance—*and* to privatize state assets. The austerity measures hastened the bankruptcies of many domestic companies, some of which had been quite profitable; and many of these assets were then scooped up by Western firms at fire-sale prices.

Policymakers in these countries not only witnessed the damage that bank-mandated policies did to their economies. They also saw China and Malaysia emerge from the Asian crisis not only intact, but invigorated, thanks to the use of strategies such as capital controls to limit the damage done by global currency speculators—strategies the World Bank prohibited to its protégés. These experiences convinced finance ministries throughout Asia and Latin America that they might be better off accumulating their own reserves than relying on international institutions like the

World Bank and the IMF, with their sadistic lending practices.

And lo, as a post-9/11 Federal Reserve pumped money into the staggering U.S. economy, American businesses and consumers bought imported goods by the boatload with those dollars, thus piping them into the coffers of major exporters to the United States. This accumulation of U.S. dollars, in turn, gave many of these economies the means to protect themselves from future financial panics. Moreover, super-low global interest rates and financial liberalization ensured that cheap capital would remain available in global markets, so recourse to the IMF and the World Bank for loans just wouldn't be as necessary as it once was. The global boom in commodities (oil, copper, tin, etc.) has only reinforced this trend, expanding the cash reserves of a number of poor countries unable to export much in the way of manufactured goods but whose minerals or other natural resources are suddenly garnering greater demand and higher prices. In addition, some developing countries, especially China and Venezuela, flush with cash, have become alternative sources of loans and grants to poorer countries.

These developments, taken together, have increased the financial wiggle room of many poor countries considerably; this has allowed them to keep the international financial institutions at bay, at least for now.

Even before Wolfowitz's appointment, but especially under his tenure, the catchwords at the World Bank have been "good governance" and "anti-corruption measures" rather than those old mainstays of fiscal prudence and monetary austerity. This shift reflects the fact that the bank's purview is increasingly limited to some of the most benighted economies on the planet: Congo, Angola, and—God help us (or them)—Iraq. In countries like these, the bank continues to fund infrastructure projects employing expensive foreign consultants from multinational corporations even though these countries can finance such projects only by exposing themselves to dangerous levels of debt. As Mark Weisbrot, economist and co-director of the Washington, D.C.-based Center for Economic and Policy Research, has written, the bank is still active primarily in places where it can do the most harm.

To be fair, the bank will also still be tapped if important but fragile economies like Turkey find themselves in the midst of a panic. The bank also remains, as attorney and global justice activist Terra Lawson-Remer has noted, a crucial—if not at all adequate—source of funding for things like malaria eradication, subsistence agriculture, and education for young girls. Another possible role for the bank has been mentioned by former U.S. Treasury Secretary Lawrence Summers: as a kind of clearinghouse for climate-change reduction subsidies for the developing world.

So given the complex mixture of trends currently shaping the World Bank's role, how should progressives view the bank today?

First of all, we should be extremely cautious about the anticorruption push. For one thing, the campaign reeks of double standards. As I write, news has emerged from the UK that the attorney general there not only halted an anticorruption investigation into payments of more than one *billion* pounds (about $1.97 billion) to Saudi Arabia's Prince Bandar for his role in setting up Britain's largest-ever arms deal, but misled the Organization for Economic Cooperation and Development's anticorruption watchdog as well. When corruption in some countries is treated as no big deal, other countries can be forgiven for questioning the motivations behind the bank's high-profile focus on *their* corruption.

Here's one step that might begin to reassure the developing world. The United States should relinquish the right to appoint the head of the bank—especially as U.S. contributions to the bank's coffers have lagged behind its agreed-upon obligations. The demand for broader participation in the selection of the bank's head looks all the more salient given that Bush's choice for a successor to Wolfowitz, former U.S. Trade Representative Robert Zoellick, has shown himself to be an economic nationalist of the first order, cajoling desperate economies like Nicaragua into lopsided bilateral trade agreements worse (for them) than even the draft regional or WTO agreements would have been. Even economist Jagdish Bhagwati, an outspoken advocate of free trade and corporate globalization, has characterized Zoellick's appointment as nothing less than "a dagger drawn at the developing countries."

It's ironic: The World Bank and IMF were created to allow countries experiencing difficulties balancing their international books the opportunity to retain access to credit in a manner compatible with steady economic development—and so avoid the downward spiral of capital flight, monetary gyrations, and protectionism that led to the Depression and World War II. Instead, they have ended up prompting their clients to liberate themselves by building up humungous reserves, at some cost to development and with no small distorting effects on the global economy. Far from being aided by the multilateral banks, middle- and even low-income developing economies now go out of their way to amass reserves while skimping on crucial expenditures in such arenas as education and health care for their own people. This is a huge price to pay to keep the World Bank and the IMF at bay, but it's one that many developing countries (or their elites, anyway) consider worth paying.

*Resources:* Naomi Klein, "The World Bank Has the Perfect Standard Bearer," *Guardian*, 4/27/07; Tessa Lawson-Remer, "Neocons in the Wings," TomPaine.com, 5/23/07; David Leigh & Rob Evans, "Attorney General Knew of BAE and the One Billion Pounds. Then Concealed It," *Guardian*, 6/8/07; Bradford Plumer, "Is Bob Zoellick the Next Paul Wolfowitz?" *New Republic*, 6/8/07; Lawrence Summers, "Practical Steps to Climate Control," *Financial Times*, 5/28/07; Mark Weisbrot, "Wolfowitz and the Bank," *The Nation*, 6/11/07; James Crotty & Gary Dymski, "Can the Global Neoliberal Regime Survive Victory in Asia? The Political Economy of the Asian Crisis," *Int'l Papers in Political Economy* 5(2), 1998.

# MICROCREDIT AND WOMEN'S POVERTY

## BY SUSAN F. FEINER & DRUCILLA K. BARKER

*November/December 2006*

The key to understanding why Grameen Bank founder and CEO Muhammad Yunus won the Nobel Peace Prize lies in the current fascination with individualistic myths of wealth and poverty. Many policy-makers believe that poverty is "simply" a problem of individual behavior. By rejecting the notion that poverty has structural causes, they deny the need for collective responses. In fact, according to this tough-love view, broad-based civic commitments to increase employment or provide income supports only make matters worse: helping the poor is pernicious because such aid undermines the incentive for hard work. This ideology is part and parcel of neoliberalism.

For neoliberals the solution to poverty is getting the poor to work harder, get educated, have fewer children, and act more responsibly. Markets reward those who help themselves, and women, who comprise the vast majority of microcredit borrowers, are no exception. Neoliberals champion the Grameen Bank and similar efforts precisely because microcredit programs do not change the structural conditions of globalization—such as loss of land rights, privatization of essential public services, or cutbacks in health and education spending—that reproduce poverty among women in developing nations.

What exactly is microcredit? Yunus, a Bangladeshi banker and economist, pioneered the idea of setting up a bank to make loans to the "poorest of the poor." The term "microcredit" reflects the very small size of the loans, often less than $100. Recognizing that the lack of collateral was often a barrier to borrowing by the poor, Yunus founded the Grameen Bank in the 1970s to make loans in areas of severe rural poverty where there were often no alternatives to what we would call loan sharks.

His solution to these problems was twofold. First, Grameen Bank would hire agents to travel the countryside on a regular schedule, making loans and collecting loan repayments. Second, only women belonging to Grameen's "loan circles" would be eligible for loans. If one woman in a loan circle did not meet her obligations, the others in the circle would either be ineligible for future loans or be held responsible for repayment of her loan. In this way the collective liability of the group served as collateral.

The Grameen Bank toasts its successes: not only do loan repayment rates approach 95%, the poor, empowered by their investments, are not dependent on "handouts." Microcredit advocates see these programs as a solution to poverty because poor women can generate income by using the borrowed funds to start small-scale enterprises, often home-based handicraft production. But these enterprises are almost all in the informal sector, which is fiercely competitive and typically unregulated, in other words, outside the range of any laws that protect workers or ensure their rights. Not surprisingly, women comprise the majority of workers in the informal economy and are heavily represented at the bottom of its already-low income scale.

Women and men have different experiences with work and entrepreneurship because a gender division of labor in most cultures assigns men to paid work outside the home and women to unpaid labor in the home. Consequently, women's paid work is constrained by domestic responsibilities. They either work part time, or they combine paid and unpaid work by working at home. Microcredit encourages women to work at home doing piecework: sewing garments, weaving rugs, assembling toys and electronic components. Home workers—mostly women and children—often work long hours for very poor pay in hazardous conditions, with no legal protections. As progressive journalist Gina Neff has noted, encouraging the growth of the informal sector sounds like advice from one of Dickens' more objectionable characters.

Why then do national governments and international organizations promote microcredit, thereby encouraging women's work in the informal sector? As an antipoverty program, microcredit fits nicely with the prevailing ideology that defines poverty as an individual problem and that shifts responsibility for addressing it away from government policy-makers and multilateral bank managers onto the backs of poor women.

Microcredit programs do nothing to change the structural conditions that create poverty. But microcredit *has* been a success for the many banks that have adopted it. Of course, lending to the poor has long been a lucrative enterprise. Pawnshops, finance companies, payday loan operations, and loan sharks charge high interest rates precisely because poor people are often desperate for cash and lack access to formal credit networks. According to Sheryl Nance-Nash, a correspondent for Women's eNews, "the interest rates on microfinance vary between 25% to 50%." She notes that these rates "are much lower than informal money lenders, where rates may exceed 10% per month." It is important for the poor to have access to credit on relatively reasonable terms. Still, microcredit lenders are reaping the rewards of extraordinarily high repayment rates on loans that are still at somewhat above-market interest rates.

Anecdotal accounts can easily overstate the concrete gains to borrowers from microcredit. For example, widely cited research by the Canadian International Development Agency (CIDA) reports that "Women in particular face significant barriers to achieving sustained increases in income and improving their status, and require complementary support in other areas, such as training, marketing, literacy, social mobilization, and other financial services (e.g., consumption loans, savings)." The report goes on to conclude that most borrowers realize only very small gains, and that the poorest borrowers benefit the least. CIDA also found little relationship between loan repayment and business success.

However large or small their income gains, poor women are widely believed to find empowerment in access to microcredit loans. According to the World Bank, for instance, microcredit empowers women by giving them more control over household assets and resources, more autonomy and decision-making power, and greater access to participation in public life. This defense of microcredit stands or falls with individual success stories featuring women using their loans to start some sort of small-scale enterprise, perhaps renting a stall in the local market or buying a sewing machine to assemble piece goods. There is no doubt that when they succeed, women and their families are better off than they were before they became micro-debtors.

But the evidence on microcredit and women's empowerment is ambiguous. Access to credit is not the sole determinant of women's power and autonomy. Credit may, for example, increase women's dual burden of market and household labor. It may also increase conflict within the household if men, rather than women, control how loan moneys are used. Moreover, the group pressure over repayment in Grameen's loan circles can just as easily create conflict among women as build solidarity.

Grameen Bank founder Muhammad Yunus won the Nobel Peace Prize because his approach to banking reinforces the neoliberal view that individual behavior is the source of poverty and the neoliberal agenda of restricting state aid to the most vulnerable when and where the need for government assistance is most acute. Progressives working in poor communities around the world disagree. They argue that poverty is structural, so the solutions to poverty must focus not on adjusting the conditions of individuals but on building structures of inclusion. Expanding the state sector to provide the rudiments of a working social infrastructure is, therefore, a far more effective way to help women escape or avoid poverty.

Do the activities of the Grameen Bank and other micro-lenders romanticize individual struggles to escape poverty? Yes. Do these programs help some women "pull themselves up by the bootstraps"? Yes. Will micro-enterprises in the informal sector contribute to ending world poverty? Not a chance.

*Resources:* Grameen Bank, grameen-info.org; "Informal Economy: Formalizing the Hidden Potential and Raising Standards," ILO Global Employment Forum (Nov. 2001), www-ilo-mirror.cornell.edu/public/english/employment/geforum/informal.htm; Jean L. Pyle, "Sex, Maids, and Export Processing," World Bank, *Engendering Development*; *Engendering Development Through Gender Equality in Rights, Resources, and Voice* (Oxford University Press, 2001); Naila Kabeer, "Conflicts Over Credit: Re-Evaluating the Empowerment Potential of Loans to Women in Rural Bangladesh," *World Development* 29 (2001); Norman MacIsaac, "The Role of Microcredit in Poverty Reduction and Promoting Gender Equity," South Asia Partnership Canada, Strategic Policy and Planning Division, Asia Branch Canada International Development Agency (June, 1997), www.acdi-cida.gc.ca/index-e.htm.

# CONTRIBUTORS

**Sylvia Allegretto** is an economist at the Institute for Research and Labor and Employment at the University of California, Berkeley.

**Dean Baker** is co-director of the Center for Economic and Policy Research.

**Drucilla K. Barker** is professor of economics and women's studies at Hollins University.

**William K. Black** is executive director of the Institute for Fraud Prevention and teaches economics and law at the University of Missouri at Kansas City.

**Aldo Caliari** is coordinator of the Rethinking Bretton Woods Project at the Center of Concern.

**Jim Campen** teaches economics at University of Massachusetts Boston and is a *Dollars & Sense* associate.

**Richard B. DuBoff** is professor emeritus of economic history at Bryn Mawr College.

**Steve Fahrer** is a partner at Progresive Asset Management, Inc.

**Susan F. Feiner** is professor of economics and women's studies at the University of Southern Maine.

**Ellen Frank** is senior economic analyst at the Poverty Institute at Rhode Island College and a member of the *Dollars & Sense* collective.

**James K. Galbraith** is professor at the Lyndon B. Johnson School of Public Affairs, University of Texas at Austin, and Senior Scholar of the Levy Economics Institute.

**Teresa Ghilarducci** is a professor of economics at the University of Notre Dame and director of the Higgins Labor Research Center at the University.

**William Greider** has been a political journalist for more than 35 years. He is currently the national affairs correspondent for *The Nation* magazine.

**Dorene Isenberg** is a professor of economics at the University of the Redlands.

**Howard Karger** is professor of social policy at the University of Houston.

**Danielle Knight** is a reporter for *U.S. News & World Report*, assigned to its investigations team.

**Charis E. Kubrin** is associate professor of sociology at George Washington University.

**Jabulani Leffall** is an award-winning journalist and former editor for both *The London Financial Times* and *Variety.*

**Mark Maier** teaches economics at Glendale Community College in Glendale, Ca.

**Arthur MacEwan,** a *Dollars & Sense* associate, teaches economics at the University of Massachusetts Boston

**John Miller** is a member of the *Dollars & Sense* collective and teaches economics at Wheaton College.

**Doug Orr** teaches economics at Eastern Washington University.

**Greg Palast** is an investigative reporter for the BBC.

**James Petras** is an activist-scholar working with socio-political movements in Latin America, Europe, and Asia.

**Larry Peterson** is a member of the *Dollars & Sense* collective and also of the Union for Radical Political Economics.

**Joseph Pluta** is professor and chair of the economics department at St. Edward's University in Austin, Texas.

**Robert Pollin** teaches economics and is co-director of the Political Economy Research Institute at University of Massachusetts Amherst. He is also a *Dollars & Sense* associate.

**Stephen Pressman** is a professor at Monmouth University and a co-editor of the *Review of Political Economy.*

**Nomi Prins** is a former investment banker turned journalist and senior fellow at Demos.

**James Ridgeway** is *Mother Jones'* Washington senior correspondent and former Washington correspondent for the *Village Voice.*

**Adria Scharf** is director of the Richmond Peace Education Center in Richmond, Va. and a former co-editor of *Dollars & Sense.*

**Robert Scott** teaches in the Department of Economics and Finance at Monmouth University.

**Abby Scher** is senior editor of *Public Eye* and a former co-editor of *Dollars & Sense.*

**William E. Spriggs** is a senior fellow with the Economic Policy Institute and was the former executive director of the National Urban League Institute for Opportunity and Equality.

**Gregory D. Squires** is a professor of sociology and public policy and public administration at George Washington University.

**Joseph Stiglitz** is a professor of economics at Columbia University and former chief economist of the World Bank.

**David Swanson** is a board member of the Progressive Democrats of America and is the Washington director of democrats.com.

**Vince Valvano** is a Principal Analyst at Berkeley Policy Associates.

**Stephen Zarlenga** is the director of the American Monetary Institute and creator of the AMI Monetary Reform Conferences held annually in Chicago.